Abraham Joshua Heschel

EDWARD K. KAPLAN &
SAMUEL H. DRESNER

Yale University Press / New Haven & London

Abraham Joshua Heschel

Prophetic Witness

Printed in the United States of America.

The Library of Congress has cataloged the hardcover edition as follows:

Kaplan, Edward K., 1942–
Abraham Joshua Heschel : prophetic witness /
Edward K. Kaplan, Samuel H. Dresner.
p. cm.
Includes bibliographical references and index.
ISBN 0–300–07186–8
1. Heschel, Abraham Joshua, 1907–1972—Homes
and haunts—Poland. 2. Heschel, Abraham Joshua,
1907–1972—Homes and haunts—Germany.
I. Dresner, Samuel H. II. Title.
BM755.H34K37 1998 296.3′092
[B]—DC21 97-36810

A catalogue record for this book is available from
the British Library.

The paper in this book meets the guidelines for
permanence and durability of the Committee on
Production Guidelines for Book Longevity of
the Council on Library Resources.

ISBN 978-0-300-12464-4 (pbk. : alk. paper)

Contents

Introduction

Abraham Joshua Heschel: Prophetic Witness is the history of a man of prayer, compassion, and moral courage confronting an increasingly horrifying world. Born in Warsaw, Poland, in 1907, Abraham Joshua Heschel came of age in his family's Hasidic community and reached maturity in secular Jewish Vilna and cosmopolitan Berlin, speaking out as a religious philosopher during the advent of Nazism. He became a teacher in Berlin, later in Martin Buber's education program in Frankfurt, again in Warsaw and in London, while the several Jewish cultures he had absorbed were being destroyed. Within Heschel's complex identity lies an archaeology of these worlds, secular and religious.

This biography traces Heschel's life in Europe up to the point of his immigration to the United States in 1940, by which time he had already matured intellectually and spiritually. When he arrived in New York City, he was a poet, theologian, biblical scholar, interpreter of Jewish tradition, and voice for a social conscience, fully prepared for his role as a witness to the living God and to the urgent relevance of the Hebrew Bible. In 1951 Reinhold Niebuhr correctly predicted that Heschel "will become a commanding and authoritative voice not only in the Jewish community but in the religious life of America."[1]

Abraham Joshua Heschel: Prophetic Witness allows us to understand in depth the charisma—and the shortcomings—of this Eastern European Jewish refugee who became an activist in the 1960s. Heschel devoted his American mission (from 1940 to his death in 1972) to awakening modern Jewry to a life compatible with its destiny, threatened as it was by the destruction of its European foundation. As a writer in the United States, he fulfilled his ambition to write a systematic exposition of Jewish faith, prayer, and ethics. A second volume will trace how Heschel's works of religious thought and interpretation can explain his public life, his commitment to civil rights, Israel and the diaspora, and interfaith dialogue and Vatican II, his view of the Holocaust, and his opposition to American intervention in Vietnam.

Within two years of his emigration, Heschel became a master of English prose, publishing sensitive works on religious experience, Jewish theology, and the Hebrew prophets. In the 1960s he was widely known for marching with the Rev. Martin Luther King, Jr., in Selma, Alabama, and for his vehement opposition to the Vietnam War. Some of his critics distrusted what appeared to be arrogance as he judged harshly certain religious and political institutions, and some of his Jewish colleagues felt that he overvalued the admiration of Christians. The majority, Jewish or Christian, considered him to be saintly.

An account of Heschel's life in Europe elucidates his complex, contradictory personality. As a thinker and an activist, he achieved a synthesis of Jewish tradition and modernity. He firmly believed in the reality of God, and his judgment of events was reminiscent of a Hebrew prophet. From childhood he mastered the classic Jewish texts: liturgy, Bible, Talmud, Midrash, legal codes, medieval and modern philosophy, mystical tradition, and his ancestral Hasidic sources, written and oral. His eloquent American books—including *Man Is Not Alone, God in Search of Man,* and *The Prophets*—attempt to communicate his unique blend, that of a university-educated East European Jew inspired by God.

Heschel's deepest identity was formed by Hasidism, the eighteenth-century pietistic movement initiated by Rabbi Israel ben Eliezer, the Baal Shem Tov (1690–1760), "Master of the Good Name." This Jewish mystical consciousness, according to Heschel, assumed a spontaneous feeling for God's presence: "Miracles no longer startled anyone, and it was no surprise to discover among one's contemporaries men who had attained the holy spirit, men whose ear perceived the voice of heaven."[2] All of Heschel's ancestors can be traced to the Hasidic founders, and he was expected to inherit the position of rebbe—a spiritual and community leader—held by his father and uncles. Throughout his several metamorphoses, Heschel's loyalty to the living God remained constant as he became a rebbe for the world at large.

Heschel also absorbed the Jewish Enlightenment, the Haskalah, an eighteenth-century movement for secularization that provided Hebrew translations of European philosophy and literature. Even as a theologian, he celebrated the powers of Jewish humanism: "There arose the Enlightenment movement (Haskalah), Zionism, the Halutzim movement [pioneer settling in Palestine], Jewish socialism." Yet Heschel insisted upon its religious essence: "Their belief in new ideals was infused with age-old piety."

As a twentieth-century Jew, however, Heschel identified most fully with the Hebrew prophets. He did not deny or compromise his earliest influences but expanded the sacred vision of his Hasidic childhood and youth to face history's perplexing realities. His sensibility experienced the ancient biblical prophets' passion for justice as "a form of living, a crossing point of God and man."[3] Responding realistically to the insecurities of this century, he translated into contemporary terms his sense of holiness, finding a new idiom to express his essential identity.

We conclude the present book with Heschel's emigration—albeit with an epilogue—because we did not want to subordinate the story of his childhood and maturity to what we know about him as an American. More important, we did not want the positive energy and cultural richness of pre-Holocaust Jewish Europe to be contaminated by an inappropriate nostalgia or a retrospective teleology of the Destruction. The story of Heschel's life *before* the Second World War reveals the fullness of Europe's pluralistic Jewish cultures, today fragmented almost beyond recognition.

Heschel's world is no more, but the diverse Jewish cultures which shaped his thought and motivated his actions—Hasidic, Yiddishist, German Jewish, and ethical—continue to provide answers to our fragile faith, our anguish of meaninglessness, as they strengthen our commitment to righteousness and truth.

Both authors knew Abraham Joshua Heschel personally and spoke with him over a period of many years. Samuel Dresner, who initiated this biography, first met Heschel in 1942 at Hebrew Union College in Cincinnati, where Heschel (then a recent refugee) was a faculty member and Dresner was a rabbinical student. Dresner recognized his teacher's genius, studied with him, and in 1945 went with Heschel to New York, to the Jewish Theological Seminary, continuing to be his disciple. Dresner wrote his dissertation on the zaddik under Heschel's direction, published several essays on him, and edited both a spiritual anthology and a volume of Heschel's Hasidic studies. I first met Heschel in 1966 while earning a Ph.D. in French literature at Columbia University. I participated with Heschel in the anti-Vietnam war movement, had long, earnest discussions, shared with him family and religious events, and also published extensively on Heschel's works.

The idea for this biography was formed when Samuel Dresner, as Heschel's student, took notes of his conversations, classes, and seminars with his revered teacher. Dresner's "Diary," an invaluable resource for the present work, gathers the notes he took over many years. Later, urged by Heschel's widow, Sylvia Straus Heschel, to write a biography and supported by a generous grant from the National Endowment for the Humanities, Dresner assembled a Heschel Archive consisting of bibliographical data, personal documents, and numerous interviews with Heschel's relatives and people who knew him in Europe and the United States, many of them since deceased. Without this foundation this biography would not have been feasible.

In 1988, Samuel Dresner asked me to write the biography that his fragile health did not allow him to venture. I did extensive research in archives, visited Israel and the sites of Heschel's European life, conducted numerous interviews, and wrote this book. Although I am solely responsible for the conception and the writing of *Abraham Joshua Heschel: Prophetic Witness,* Rabbi Dresner's personal encouragement, his help in obtaining further interviews, and his reviewing the manuscript at various stages of composition have been precious and a source of mutual pleasure.

My hope is that readers, having gained an understanding of Heschel's European past, will penetrate the sources of his ethical and spiritual courage. His loyalty to God and to the sanctity of every human being challenges the persistent evidence of barbarism as he insists upon our moral responsibility. In exploring Heschel's coming to maturity before the Holocaust, we enter a passionate Jewish open-mindedness which both explains and challenges our wary era. His uncanny mixture of holiness with compassion and fierce demand for justice speak to us still.

Edward K. Kaplan

For transliterations from the Hebrew we generally follow the *Encyclopaedia Judaica* and the YIVO system for Yiddish, but without diacritical marks. No attempt has been made to duplicate regional pronunciations, and the spelling of many words in common usage has been simplified.

The Heschel Dynasty

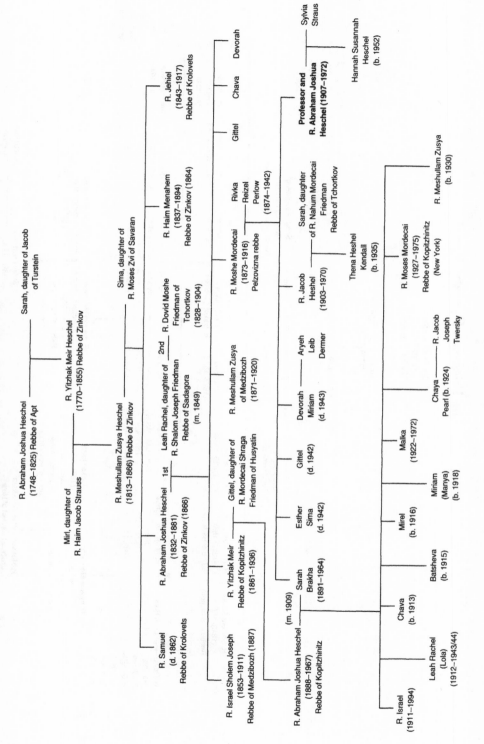

The Friedman Dynasty

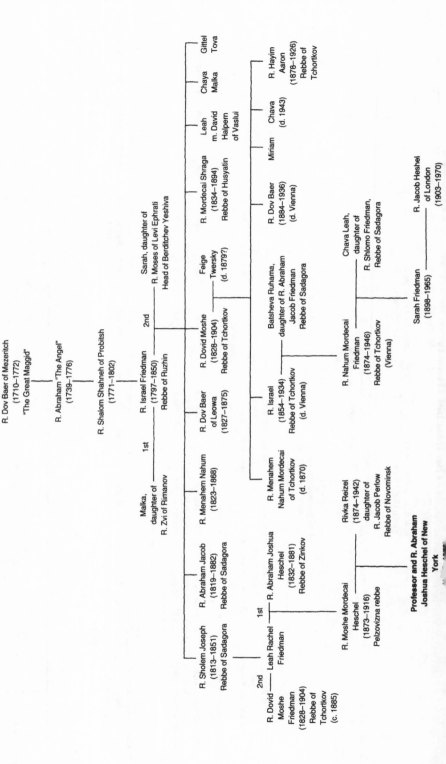

The Perlow Dynasty

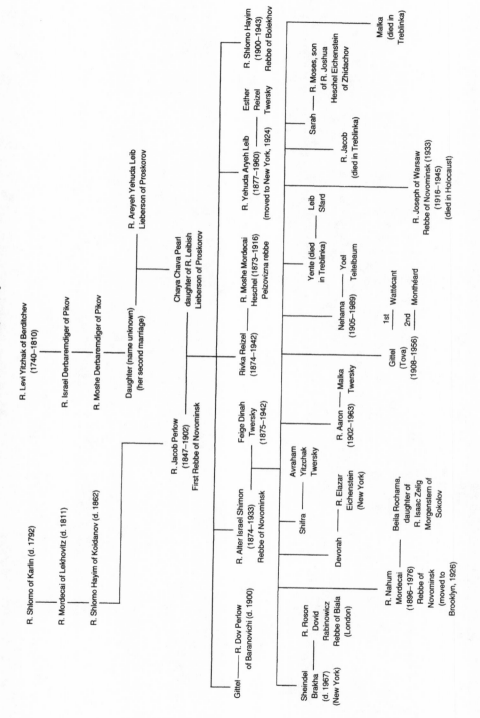

Part One
Warsaw: Childhood and Adolescence

In my childhood and in my youth I was the recipient of many blessings.
I lived in the presence of quite a number of extraordinary persons I could
revere. And just as I lived as a child in their presence, their presence
continues to live in me as an adult.

Heschel, "In Search of Exaltation" (1971)

HESCHEL WAS BORN IN WARSAW, POLAND, A METROPOLIS WHERE JEWISHNESS flourished in many forms. Warsaw was the center of Congress Poland, which from 1815 to 1915 belonged to the Russian Empire, though it enjoyed the fullest autonomy of any province controlled by the Tsarist regime. Its Jewish community steadily increased to become the largest and most significant in Europe. By 1917, when Heschel was ten years old, the Jews comprised 41 percent of Warsaw's population, fostering a vigorous diversity of religious and secular groupings. Heschel's Hasidic family was among the most traditional.

Over the years, thousands of Jewish refugees had entered Warsaw, some maintaining their religious way of life, others bringing worldly trends and radical fervor. In Warsaw, Hasidism made up the largest grouping among observant Jews. In 1880 they composed two-thirds of the three hundred officially sanctioned synagogues, and many small *shtiebls* (houses of prayer and study); a short time later *mitnagdim* (opponents—traditional Jews suspicious of what they considered to be Hasidic overemphasis on prayer and ecstasy) arrived in droves from various parts of Eastern Europe. Jewish political life was equally sundry. There were numerous Zionist organizations (some of them religious) and other youth and student circles. Several Jewish workers' movements soon established the socialist Bund.

A cosmopolitan literary and cultural life—which attracted Heschel during his adolescence—flourished in the city. The lives of these modern Jews were enriched by Yiddish theater, poetry, fiction, and journalism. There were important Hebrew publishing efforts as well, and a remarkable array of newspapers and periodicals in both Hebrew and Yiddish. A legacy of the Haskalah, this secular Jewish creativity was effecting a shift from religious conservatism to modernity.

Heschel's childhood was protected and illumined by sacred study and ancestral legends. Yet even before he was born, traditional Jewish life in the Pale of Settlement, the area of western and southern Russia within which Jews had been required to live since the time of Catherine II, was disintegrating. Then, when he was seven years old, Europe became engulfed in World War I, a massive conflict of unprecedented brutality. Remaining within his Hasidic community, he reached adolescence during this international crisis.

The way of life of Heschel's relatives was severely threatened by the turmoil, which began long before the world war. His grandparents and parents were all Hasidim, the élite of their dynasties. Eastern European Jews were especially devastated by the First World War. They were forced by the harsh realities to join the huge migrations following local pogroms, the Russian Revolution, and the ensuing civil wars—as well as the world war. Thousands of Jewish soldiers in the opposing camps were drafted to the slaughter. Jews from cities and shtetls of Tsarist Russia, Poland, and Austria-Hungary were caught in the crossfire of national and regional interests over which they had no control. Ancestral towns were decimated. Thousands chose to flee. Cities such as Warsaw and Vienna provided havens for the survivors.

This was the unstable world Heschel inherited. The religious Judaism in which he was raised was directly undermined. In Poland, many yeshivas (academies of higher Torah and Talmud learning) were closed. Sacred learning was declining as young Russian and Lithuanian Jews were captivated by socialism, communism, Zionism, and other movements. Believers feared that such freedom would threaten faith, increase skepticism, and destroy their communities. The enticements of modernity, which penetrated the cities, reached even the small towns of Hasidic Poland. Heschel had just turned ten when the February 1917 revolution abolished the Russian monarchy. In Warsaw, and later in Vilna, he established ties with many utopian militants while remaining essentially a Hasidic Jew.

1

Heschel's First Home (1907–1914)

I was named after my grandfather, Reb Abraham Joshua Heschel—
"the Apter Rav," and last great rebbe of Medzibozh. He was marvelous
in all his ways, and it was as if the Baal Shem Tov had come to life
in him. . . . The Apter Rav claimed that his soul had lived in several
incarnations, and for his descendants it was as if he had never died.

Heschel, *A Passion for Truth* (1973)

HESCHEL'S GENEALOGY SUMMARIZES HIS CULTURAL INFLUENCES AND MAPS OUT the path he was expected to continue. This prehistory, a realm where eternal creeds and legends faced the harshness of current events, formed his family's expectations. His intricate family tree, in fact, shaped his primal identity. Children of distinguished Jewish dynasties often memorized their genealogy and recited it fluently, and, as an adult, he proudly traced his pedigree (in Yiddish, *yikhus*) back to the fifteenth century, telling an interviewer, "For seven generations, all my ancestors have been Hasidic rabbis."[1] Ancestry was the foundation of his personality.

Heschel recognized that his personal gifts and prophetic mission were defined by his family's locations, names, and legends. As a child or youth, he consecrated his ideals privately by drawing up, probably from memory, a list of 250 ancestors, starting with his father's lineage, then his mother's, following them back several centuries.[2] In his Riverside Drive apartment hung a lithograph called the Baal Shem Tov's "Tree of Life," a genealogy of the movement printed in Warsaw in the 1920s and found in Hasidic prayer rooms and the homes of rebbes. To continue this "golden chain," as the holy tradition was called, meaningful names were repeated and passed from generation to generation.

Legends and Legacies

Heschel's dynastic prototype was Rabbi Abraham Joshua Heschel (1748–1825), the rebbe of Apt (in Polish, Opatow). Five generations separated the boy from his namesake, known by the title of his book, *Ohev Israel* (Lover of the Jewish people). This "grandfather" (as Hasidim refer even to distant ancestors) was also called "the Apter Rav" because he exercised the legal authority of a community rabbi or Rav.[3] Venerated for his diplomatic as well as spiritual skills, Rabbi Heschel of Apt mediated disputes among Hasidic leaders during a period of extreme factionalism. After the death of the founder, the Baal Shem Tov, Rabbi Heschel of Apt became a spokesman for the third Hasidic generation.

Here was one mythic model for Heschel's personality, for the child was imbued with his ancestor's exalted conception of himself—not unusual in a *zaddik* (spiritual leader, literally, "righteous one") whose followers expected him to perform miracles. The Apter rebbe was said to possess supernatural qualities. Known for his ecstatic prayer, even to the point of speaking in tongues, he believed in reincarnation and claimed to remember standing at Mount Sinai as Moses received the Torah from God, even noticing the person standing next to him! Although he was not a *kohen* (of the priestly tribe), he felt that he possessed the soul of a high priest at the First Temple in Jerusalem. While leading his congregation in prayer on the Day of Atonement, he changed the text of the *Avodah,* which describes the Temple service, from "Thus did he (i.e., the High Priest) say" to "And thus did I say."[4]

Heschel himself claimed continuity with such models. Even his ancestor's name, following custom, sustained a spiritual continuum: the rebbe of Apt was said to be as kindhearted as Abraham, father of the Jewish people; as great a teacher as Joshua, the successor of Moses; and as learned as Rabbi Joshua Heschel of Kraków (d. 1664), the earliest namesake.[5]

R. Abraham Joshua Heschel of Apt (1748–1825)
|
R. Yitzhak Meir Heschel of Zinkov (1770–1855)
|
R. Meshullam Zusya Heschel of Zinkov (1813–1866)
|
R. Abraham Joshua Heschel of Medzibozh (1832–1881)
|
R. Moshe Mordecai Heschel of Pelzovizna (1873–1916)
|
Rabbi and Professor Abraham Joshua Heschel of New York (1907–1972)

Heschel's family came from Medzibozh (in Polish, Miedzyborz), where the Apter Rav was buried next to the Baal Shem Tov. As Heschel wrote: "I was born in Warsaw, Poland, but my cradle stood in Medzibozh (a small town in the province of Podolia, Ukraine), where the Baal Shem Tov, founder of the Hasidic movement, lived during the last twenty years of his life. That is where my father came from, and he continued to regard it as his home."[6]

According to Heschel, his earliest sense of identity formed from fantasies of this setting: "That little town so distant from Warsaw and yet so near was the place to which my childish imagination went on many journeys. Every step taken on the way was an answer to a prayer, and every stone was a memory of a marvel. For most of the wondrous deeds my father told about either happened in Medzibozh or were inspired by those mysterious men who lived there."[7]

Closer to actual memory, Heschel's grandfather—also named Abraham Joshua Heschel (1832–1881)—sustained the dynasty. He established his family in Medzibozh, where he became rebbe. Heschel's father, Moshe Mordecai (1873–1916), was born there, as were his uncles and aunts. Marriages with scions of other Hasidic clans and subsequent intermarriages within the same families comprise the vista of this Hasidic prince, expected to became a rebbe and forge more links in the golden chain.

A Regal Heritage

In the paternal tree, Heschel's father received his outlook from the noble Hasidic dynasty of Rabbi Israel Friedman (1797–1850), rebbe of Ruzhin (in Polish, Radzyn). Rabbi Israel, Heschel's father's great-grandfather, traced *his* ancestry back to the biblical King David, and some devotees even considered him to be a reincarnation of the Baal Shem Tov.[8] It was said that the Apter Rav honored the young Israel Friedman by picking up his *gartel* (ritual belt) which had dropped, saying that it was precious as a wrapping for the Torah. Some Gentiles respected him as "King of the Jews."

Stories also circulated about how the Ruzhiner rebbe was honored by Rabbi Levi Yitzhak of Berditchev (1740–1810), another Hasidic master, a close disciple of Dov Baer, known as the Maggid (preacher) of Mezeritch (1710–1772), the successor of the Baal Shem Tov. In fact, on his mother's side, Heschel was related to Levi Yitzhak, a learned, compassionate man known for his love of all Jews.[9]

Yet Israel of Ruzhin was a controversial figure because of his wealth and luxurious style of living. After all, the little towns in the Jewish Pale of Settlement were invariably poor. Adversaries were disgusted at the opulence of the Ruzhiner rebbe's court, whereas believers revered his hidden piety and compassion: "On the outside wonderful decorations of gold and silver, carriages hitched to powerful horses, and inside a broken heart and tortured body, which relished nothing of this world."[10] Five of his sons married daughters of other Hasidic dynasties and established their own courts in Sadagora, Tchortkov, and Husyatin.

Among these spiritual alliances were the Heschels. Abraham Joshua Heschel of Medzibozh (Heschel's grandfather), married Leah Rachel Friedman, a daughter of the Ruzhiner rebbe's oldest son, Sholem Joseph, rebbe of Sadagora. The bridegroom remained in Sadagora with his in-laws for about fifteen years of board and lodging (in Yiddish, *kest*), a widespread custom allowing sons-in-law to continue their studies and to incorporate the bride's traditions. The old Ruzhiner rebbe often visited them, and so Heschel's grandfather enjoyed the privilege, as the saying goes, of "eating at the Ruzhiner's table."[11]

Later, Heschel's grandfather, after replacing his own father as rebbe of Zinkov, established his court in Medzibozh. His seven children were born there—Heschel's uncles and aunts, and his father, Moshe Mordecai Heschel.[12]

After the death of Heschel's grandfather, the story becomes more complicated. His widow, Leah Rachel Friedman, returned to her family in Sadagora.

Palace of Dovid Moshe Friedman, rebbe of Tchortkov. Postcard, courtesy of YIVO Institute for Jewish Research, New York.

Following custom, she married Rabbi Dovid Moshe Friedman (1828–1904), one of her father's younger brothers, himself recently widowed. Dovid Moshe Friedman was the rebbe of Tchortkov (in Polish, Czortkow), whose court was established in a castle previously owned by the counts of Borkowski.[13] Heschel's father was about eight years old at the time.

R. Israel Friedman of Ruzhin (1797–1850)
|
R. Sholem Joseph Friedman of Sadagora (1813–1851)
|
Leah Rachel Friedman m.(1) R. Abraham Joshua Heschel of Medzibozh (1832–1881)
|
m.(2) R. Dovid Moshe Friedman of Tchortkov (1828–1904)
|
R. Moshe Mordecai Heschel of Pelzovizna (1873–1916)
|
Rabbi and Professor Abraham Joshua Heschel of New York (1907–1972)

In Tchortkov, the Heschel children grew up in a community accustomed to miracles. Dovid Moshe, who nurtured and guided them, was a saintly man. His Hasidic court was sumptuous, but he led an ascetic life of prayer and study. It was said that at his birth the Ruzhiner rebbe exclaimed: "I have brought you a soul which will lead Jewish souls to their heavenly father."[14] Stories circulated about uncanny happenings. On the Sabbath, "Awe and admiration prevailed in the prayerhouse when [Dovid Moshe] said *kiddush* [the blessing over the wine at the beginning of the Sabbath], and the wine in his goblet bubbled in a wondrous manner. He was always closed up in his room, separated even from his family. He slept only two hours at night."

During his youth in Tchortkov, Moshe Mordecai memorized anecdotes and legends meticulously preserved from the beginning of the Hasidic movement; years later he taught them to his young son, Abraham Joshua, who was encouraged to emulate a regal attitude.[15] People who knew the ways of Ruzhin, and its descendants, observed that Heschel, even after he left Warsaw at age eighteen, had the bearing of a rebbe.[16] Ruzhin was one cultural source of this demeanor.

Torah Study and Piety

Heschel also absorbed the Lithuanian Hasidic tradition of his mother, Rivka Reizel Perlow (1874–1942). Her father, Rabbi Jacob Perlow (1847–1902), al-

Dovid Moshe Friedman, rebbe of Tchortkov.
Courtesy of Yitzhak Meir Twersky.

though born in Poland, was brought up in the home of his maternal grandfather, Shlomo Hayim of Koidanov (1797–1862), a great Lithuanian rebbe.[17] At age fifteen, Heschel's grandfather married a descendant of Rabbi Levi Yitzhak of Berditchev, a mystic, Talmudic scholar, and lover of humanity who upheld compassion for suffering Jews even against God's strict judgment.[18] Heschel was especially attached to this ancestor who interceded directly to pardon a sinner, calling the Creator to judgment in the Yiddish vernacular, rather than in Hebrew, the sacred tongue. The first time Heschel put on *tefillin* (phylacteries), for his bar mitzvah, he used those of Levi Yitzhak for the occasion.

It was said that Heschel's mother and her twin brother were born of a miracle. Heschel's grandparents Jacob and Chaya Perlow had a daughter, but they yearned for a son to continue the dynasty. A relative advised them to leave Russia for Poland, where they would have sons. They eventually settled in Minsk-Mazowiecki (known by Jews as Novominsk), an industrial town located about nineteen miles from Warsaw. After a silver ruble, which had been blessed, was placed in the foundation of the *bes-medresh* (house of prayer and study), Chaya Perlow gave birth to twins, a boy and a girl, Alter Israel Shimon and Rivka Reizel—Heschel's uncle and mother.[19]

Heschel's parents—Moshe Mordecai Heschel and Rivka Reizel Perlow—were married in about 1890 in Novominsk, where they lived for ten years at the Hasidic court of the bride's father. It was a vital Jewish environment. Rabbi Perlow had built a large yeshiva, the first such Hasidic school of higher Torah learning in Poland, where hundreds of students came to live. (Hasidim usually preferred to send their boys to local schools while they continued to live at home.) Novominsk became such a popular pilgrimage that the authorities organized special trains to accommodate the large numbers of Hasidim who made the journey. The rebbe of Novominsk combined devotion to Torah study, Talmudic learning, and inner piety. He was reputed to inspire *teshuvah* ("turning" or repentance) by the very sound of his voice.

Novominsk also fostered modern movements. Heschel's sisters and brother were born in this town, which included several Jewish cultures. By the 1890s considerable Zionist and social-democratic activity developed there, in addition to the eminent rabbinic presence. In 1902, after Jacob Perlow died, Rivka's twin brother, Alter Israel Shimon, at age twenty-eight, became rebbe of Novominsk. By then the "old Tchortkover rebbe" (as Dovid Moshe Friedman was known) advised his stepson Moshe Mordecai to relocate closer to Warsaw. An entirely different future became possible for their next child, Abraham Joshua Heschel.

Heschel's parents, Rivka Reizel Perlow Heschel and Moshe Mordecai Heschel, the Pelzovizna rebbe. Courtesy of Yitzhak Meir Twersky.

A Family Mystery

Heschel was a private person who spoke about his past only to make a point, and his attachment to ancestry produced a touching revelation. For his father concealed another prehistory, this one less idealized, though also enigmatic. Moshe Mordecai Heschel had previously been married and divorced and confided this fact to his son, Abraham Joshua, then eight years old.

Decades later, in New York City during the fall of 1968—more than twenty-five years after he emigrated—Heschel spoke about his father's youth to William Sloane Coffin, Jr., the Protestant chaplain at Yale University with whom he was opposing the Vietnam War. Coffin had been arrested for draft resistance and he was anguished by his impending divorce. After a board meeting of Clergy and Laymen Concerned About Vietnam, their protest organization, they walked back to Heschel's apartment for their customary nightcap. "Father Abraham," as Coffin enjoyed calling him, slipped his hand under his arm and gently observed,

"I understand, my friend, that you have been through much suffering."
"That's right, Father Abraham, it's been hell. It still is."

"You should have called me," he said.

"You were in Los Angeles all summer."

"You still could have called me."

"Well, I didn't want to bother you. Besides, I had other friends I could talk to and I don't like talking about such things over the phone."

"That was a mistake. I could have helped you."

Irked by his self-assurance I stopped and faced him. "All right, how could you have helped me?"

As I had seen him do so often he raised his shoulders and his hands, palms up. "I would have told you about my father, the great Hasidic rabbi, blessed be his memory, who too was divorced. You see, you Christians are so vexed by your perfectionism. It is always your undoing."

He continued to talk in this vein, and I felt the tears running down my cheeks. He was so right. And it was nice that a Jew was reminding a Christian that his salvation lay not in being sinless, but in accepting [God's] forgiveness. Without pausing, he wiped my face with his handkerchief. Then after again assuring me that God still loved me—"even as I do, and maybe more"—he said, "Now we shall continue to my apartment. I have just been given some excellent cognac."[20]

Heschel remained curious about his father's first, unfruitful marriage, for its details might further clarify his ancestry. His friend F. E. Rottenberg, a modern Orthodox rabbi also from distinguished Hasidic stock, speculated that Moshe Mordecai's first wife might have come from the Zhidachov dynasty, one of the most learned and kabbalistically expert lines.[21]

Heschel did not resolve these conjectures. But he never forgot his father telling him "how beautiful" and without conflict the separation had been. Over fifty years after the event, compassion for his anguished American friend revived this scene of Heschel's Warsaw childhood.

Family and Father

Abraham Joshua Heschel's parents, four sisters—Sarah Brakha, Esther Sima, Gittel, and Devorah Miriam—and brother, Jacob—were born in Novominsk. Around 1904, they moved to Warsaw's Pelzovizna district, a rather poor, predominantly Jewish area on the right bank of the Vistula River. There Heschel's father, Moshe Mordecai, established himself as a *vinkl rebbe* (a neighborhood or "corner rebbe"). His following was modest—until the world prepared for battle.

Their next move decided Heschel's future. His father established his Hasidic court at 40 Muranowska Street, in the thriving center of Warsaw's Jewish district. Still known as "the Pelzovizna rebbe," Moshe Mordecai worked, studied, and prayed in the large, new apartment building of gray stone blocks where the family also lived. That urban area became a threshold to Warsaw's many religious and secular Jewish worlds.

On 11 January 1907, Abraham Joshua Heschel, their second son, was born. His ancestral name reinforced the dynasty's continuity and shaped his predetermined identity. His brother, Jacob, the first son, was born in 1903, the year after their grandfather Jacob Perlow, the Novominsker rebbe, died. Jacob was given the name of his mother's deceased father.[22] (To this day, Jacob is a revered name among the Perlows.)

The new son's complete name—Abraham Joshua Heschel Heschel—consolidated his father's line. (Hasidim often place a full name before the family name.) That designation paid homage to their distant ancestor, Abraham Joshua Heschel, known as the rebbe of Apt; the name of his grandfather Rabbi Abraham Joshua Heschel Heschel of Medzibozh also honored the primal ancestor. As the youngest, "Avrumele" (little Abraham, as they called him in Yiddish, their native tongue) soon became the family's most favored member.

Heschel learned the role of rebbe in the family apartment, also his father's Hasidic center. The "dearest friend of Heschel's youth," Yehiel Hofer, describes the place, the activities, and the atmosphere.[23] At the front were the prayerhouse (the *bes medresh*, a room for study and religious services) and the rebbe's private study. Family quarters were separated by a single door, guarded by an assistant (*gabai*), an old man known as Reb Yankev Yeshue. (In Yiddish, Reb is an honorific term like Mister.) The rebbe's other gabai, Reb Yosl, collected petitions from those who came to consult the master.

Moshe Mordecai Heschel received people in his study. Hofer writes that "the right wall was entirely taken up by a large bookcase which reached the ceiling. The left wall was empty. At the very end of the room, near the window which opened onto the courtyard, stood a table, near which the rebbe sat in an armchair." Petitioners entered to adjudicate personal or business problems, to determine questions of ritual law, seek solace and advice—all of which would be sealed by blessings.

Reflecting Hasidic protocol, domestic relationships were governed by rules that were formal but loving. When the rebbe entered a room, everyone stood up. Jacob remembered that he rarely sat down in his father's presence. Conversation followed similar strictures, for even privately the children never addressed him directly. Instead of asking, "Father, do you want something?" they addressed him in the third person, saying, "What does Father want?" (in Yiddish, *Vos vil der Tate?*).[24] Yet Avrumele enjoyed special status. His father recognized him as a prodigy and often spoke with him, sometimes confiding his personal thoughts, as he had regarding his divorce.

From the very first, Heschel internalized his family's Hasidic ideals by observing his father. Correct external behavior was crucial, for a zaddik must embody Torah, the sacred Jewish teachings. Names, legends, and family history comprise the essence of a Hasidic child's nascent identity, but a father's actions—and his entire physical bearing—can shape a perceptive child's inward self.

Reb Moyshele, as he was called with affection, was thirty-four years old when Avrumele was born. He was fairly tall and carried himself with a noble and gentle demeanor. Hofer depicts him as "above average in height, narrow and straight as a *lulav* [a palm branch used in the holiday of Sukkot]." His face was pale and long, his dark beard had already begun to turn gray, and "his earlocks (*pey'ot*), thick and straight, reached only as far as his earlobes." Even that detail carried ancestral meaning, for Moshe Mordecai, instead of displaying his sidecurls, rolled them up behind his ears, as was characteristic of descendants of his maternal ancestors, the dynasty of Ruzhin.[25]

Heschel's father's aristocratic manner of dressing emphasized his Ruzhin upbringing. "He wore a silk *kaftan* [a long black coat] with velvet button loops. The collar of his shirt was stiffly pressed and tied with a long, colorful cravat. On his white collar was visible a black silk string, on which hung a pair of spectacles in thin horn rims." And his gestures were as exquisite as his apparel. "The rebbe often held his glasses in his right hand, and when he wanted to read something, he brought them to his nose in a graceful semicircle. The rebbe wore long pants and slippers. On his head a plush hat over a tall velvet *yarmulke* [skullcap]. He always stuck a white handkerchief into the left sleeve of his silk *kaftan*." Since every Jew is a "prince," so as not to demean himself, while eating he would not bend to reach his food, but lifted it to his mouth. Throughout his life, Heschel emulated his father's erect posture, his deliberate motions, and other vestiges of Ruzhin elegance, adjusting them, as best he could, to secular society.

Yet these cherished customs alienated Heschel's father from some rabbis native to Warsaw. The meticulousness with which observant Jews obeyed sacred law also applied to certain habits distinguishing one dynasty from another. Uprooted from their towns and villages and crammed together in a metropolis, some Hasidim criticized Moshe Mordecai as an outsider. He came from Galicia, the Austrian side of the Pale of Settlement, and his dignified style of dressing was typical of Galician rabbis; he wore pressed pants, a collar, and a tie.[26] Polish Hasidim, on the contrary, preferred the style of Russian peasant clothing. One day a Polish rebbe criticized Moshe Mordecai's fastidious attire: "My friend! You should change your clothing to the Polish style because pride must not overpower the leaders of our generation." Rabbi Heschel answered, "As for pride, whom would the Evil One first attack, the man who carefully places the knot of his necktie to one side, or the man who doesn't care?"[27] Dress code was a religious issue, since careful appearance was one way to honor the Torah, which a rebbe should embody.

Moshe Mordecai's loyalty to his ancestral culture required courage, for his family lived in bitter privation. He was not a practical man and he had very little money, for several reasons. His small and mostly humble following provided modest fees for his advice and blessings. Moreover, like others from his clan, he never kept money in his house overnight. At the end of each day, he distributed any remaining cash to the needy. His children remembered that, even for Sabbath dinner, all too often, instead of the customary carp or pike (the more savory river fish) or even salt herring, the family had to be satisfied with sardines.[28] It was an insecure but noble existence, as Hofer remembers: "A descendant of the rabbi of Apt, known as the Lover of Jews, the rebbe Reb Moyshele loved a poor person to the bottom of his soul, and he was ready to sacrifice for each and every pauper. But poverty itself tormented him terribly, pained him deeply."

Yet at home, Moshe Mordecai personified the majesty of his Ruzhin forebears. Heschel remembers that, even lacking adequate food, his father always had a flower placed on his desk. "The rebbe smoked cigars in a holder made of black amber. On the High Holy Days he took snuff from a golden snuffbox, which Napoleon himself had presented to the Kozhinitzer Maggid."[29] It was said that at the home of Moshe Mordecai's ancestor the Ruzhiner rebbe's home there were "golden knobs on the doors, the food was brought to the table on golden vessels, and the family rode in coaches drawn by three horses. Here in Warsaw he became acquainted with Jewish poverty."

While facing his flock's suffering, Moshe Mordecai found some consolation in remnants of the dynasty's luxury. After saying the morning prayers, the rebbe, still wearing his *tallit* and *tefillin* (prayer shawl and phylacteries), neglected breakfast and drank only one large glass of tea. Later his assistant refreshed the master in genteel style: "Around one o'clock in the afternoon no one else was allowed to go in to see the rebbe, and his secretary Yankev Yeshue brought him lunch. A plate of chicken broth was served in a silver serving dish on a stand resembling a hoop skirt and with a silver cover. In a similar closed silver dish was placed a plate of chicken. All this carried on a silver platter, and next to it was a white roll, covered with a napkin."

Most important, the rebbe used ancestral relics to heal others, for they were believed to be instruments of inherited powers: "He used to let poor people borrow the Apter rebbe's cane with its golden ferrule, so that they could place it as an amulet by the head of a sick child. . . . He granted the poor his finest blessings, calling his grandfathers and great-grandparents and relatives to their aid, the great men of Hasidism and of the people Israel, whose blood and heritage were his—for Reb Moyshele's family tree reached back to King David." Heschel's father carefully preserved his charisma.

Spiritual Exile and Moral Delicacy

He is not insensitive. On the contrary he is keenly sensitive to pain and suffering, to adversity and evil in his own life and in that of others; but he has the inner strength to rise above grief, and, with his understanding of what these sorrows actually are, grief seems to him a sort of arrogance.
Heschel, "An Analysis of Piety" (1942)

The family's poverty and dislocations, however, had theological meaning that deeply affected the younger son. Heschel wrote that Moshe Mordecai in cosmopolitan Warsaw considered himself to be in exile from Medzibozh, the town of his holy ancestors: "He confided in me, 'For I was indeed stolen out of the land of the Hebrews' (Genesis 40:15)."[30] This image of spiritual exile echoes a family tradition as it recalls a commentary by Moshe Mordecai's own father, Rabbi Heschel of Medzibozh. The original Torah passage reads: "Then Israel said unto Joseph, 'I am about to die; but God will be (*ve-hayah*) with you and bring you back to the land of your fathers'" (Genesis 48:21). The interpretation of Heschel's grandfather was preserved:

Now Jacob's promise was that even after his death, while they were still exiled in Egypt, God would still be with them and return them to the land of their fathers. The meaning is difficult to clarify since the Torah refers to the time of exile with the word *ve-hayah* which can mean 'joy' (*simkha*) (see the Prologue to Midrash Esther). It is well known that the Holy One blessed be He is grieved and participates in the sufferings of Israel, as it is written

(Psalm 91:15), 'I will be with them in distress,' and (Isaiah 63:9), 'In all their troubles He was troubled.' Therefore we see that when Israel is in exile the Divine Presence is in exile with them. This brings them 'joy' since they are certain that God [has not abandoned them but] will hasten to redeem them.

Heschel formed his theology by applying these sacred insights to current conditions—and also through textual interpretation and philosophical analysis. His grandfather had adapted an idea found in Talmud and Kabbalah, that the *Shekhinah* (God's Indwelling Presence) is exiled in the world and that God suffers with humankind. Later, Heschel's doctoral dissertation at the University of Berlin identified the biblical source: the Hebrew prophets who vibrated with "God's pathos" (divine "feelings," as it were). Heschel's own "religion of sympathy" with God in exile became his beacon.

Heschel's most profound emulation of his father, however, drew from Moshe Mordecai's ethical sensitivity, his intense compassion. Years later he retold one of his father's stories about their ancestor, the Apter Rav. "He was asked by many other rebbes, 'Why are your prayers always accepted and not ours?' He gave the following answer: 'You see, whenever a Jew comes to me and pours out his heart and tells me of his misery and suffering, I have such compassion that a little hole is created in my heart. Since I have heard and listened to a great many Jews with their problems and anguish, there are a great many holes in my heart. I'm an old Jew and when I start to pray I take my heart and place it before God. He sees this broken heart, so many holes, so many splits, so He has compassion for my heart and that is why He listens to me. God listens to my prayers.'"[31]

His father's actions were Heschel's most concrete instruction. As his friend Yehiel Hofer remembered, "The rebbe would take the 18-groshn donations from the poor in the same way as he took the golden imperials of the rich, but more delicately. With the long fingers of his white, noble hands, he unwrapped the paper in which the few coins were gathered, and lay them in his pocket so that the poor person would see that he was taking them, that he welcomed them." Heschel's father demonstrated in subtle ways reverence for each and every person.

Compassion was also an affliction for Heschel's father: "The rebbe trembled uncontrollably when poor women burst into the prayerhouse, would fall in front of the Holy Ark, pull the curtain aside, open the doors and, weeping and wailing, grab the Torah scrolls, begging mercy for a desperately ill husband or sick child, or sometimes for a mother of children who was on the verge of leaving this world. He could find no rest. Quietly he slipped out of his private room, discreetly entered the living room, sat down on the ottoman under the large photograph of the old Tchortkover rebbe hanging there, and slowly recovered his composure." Before they were nine years old, Avrumele and Yehiel Hofer must have seen and discussed many such scenes. Hofer goes on to describe Reb Moyshele at the brink of despair at such commotion: "He would cover his eyes with his hands as if in shame and utterly withdraw into himself when he heard the women shouting in their distress: 'Help, holy Zaddik!'" Such empathy was a double-edged sword.

Heschel's father was his first model of piety, for he actualized within himself the spirit of the prayerbook. On the Sabbath, he shut his eyes and became one with his *neshama yetera,* the "additional soul" one is said to receive with the arrival of the holy Seventh Day. On Passover, he became a *ben horin,* as if "newly liberated by God" from Egypt; on Shavuot, the holiday commemorating God's revealing the Torah on Mount Sinai, he himself received the Law.[32] Ritual was inseparable from reality in Heschel's childhood, as he later wrote: "In every event there is something sacred at stake, and it is for this reason that the approach of the pious man to reality is in reverence. This explains his solemnity and his conscientiousness in dealing with things both great and small."[33]

On a more familiar level, Hofer recounts an incident involving his own father, Itchi (a nickname for Yitzhak or Isaac) Meir, who accompanied Moshe Mordecai to morning prayers every day.[34] One time Heschel's mother, sleeping late, was awakened by screams of "Water, water!" It appears that Itchi Meir, who liked to regale the rabbi with bits of gossip, had seen the local druggist, a notorious skeptic, eating ham. When Moshe Mordecai heard that a Jew had eaten forbidden meat, he began to gasp and vomit, as if he, himself, had violated God's law. Such was the father's gift of sympathy.

Warsaw Walks

Mundane realities entered Heschel's home by reason of the rebbe's community responsibilities. But the family participated in the wider world because of its urban location. The apartment building was itself a multifarious society, with poor and wealthy people living in close proximity. Prosperous people enjoyed the large apartments while entire families might inhabit one room, the indigent living in cellars, risking tuberculosis; active workshops were maintained on the ground floor. The neediest neighbors were probably the most visible. One boy was sent regularly to guard the family laundry as it dried on an upper landing.[35]

The courtyard was public ground with narrow and wide alleys to explore, even a small garden, where children played buttons or other games.[36] Religious rituals such as *shlogen kaporos* (sacrifice of a chicken as vicarious atonement for sins the day before Yom Kippur) were communal activities, and Avrumele and his family would get up at three o'clock in the morning to participate.[37] Hard work normally reigned, for artisans worked at home, helped by their spouses, children, and apprentices—shoemakers, tailors, lacemakers, makers of mirrors, box- and buttonmakers.[38]

Recent political conflicts were summoned up by the songs of workers in the tin button factory, amidst the din of stamping machines. Some of the tenants, wealthy Hasidim who lived at the front of the building, shut their windows. "They didn't do this only because girls and boys were singing together—which they considered to be indecent—but mostly because the songs reminded them of the restless years of strikes, of the Revolution of 1905, when Jewish youngsters and girls spoke openly about overthrowing the Russian Tsar."

Heschel and his friend Yehiel explored Muranowska Street, a wide and relatively short passage, which led to a busy commercial center, the lively market of Muranow Square. Hofer describes this area as "surrounded by high, solid brick houses, looking more like a large courtyard. . . . It was square, flat as a platter, and paved with stones gray as steel." The seasons created gracious contrasts: "Summer provided the most cheerful days at the market. With nimble motions and wide-open eyes, young girls in the booths spread out the assorted dyed cretonnes, which dazzled the eyes of the Christian servants, village girls who served in the Jewish homes in the Muranow neighborhood. . . . In the winter evenings the booths were illuminated by lanterns, in which a single tallow candle burned. The poor little bit of red light, fine and slender, drew thick wide shadows toward itself, like a heavy burden. . . . The place of the fresh vegetables had been captured by pickled herring and whitefish."

A few blocks away was the society that gripped a more skeptical temperament, that of Isaac Bashevis Singer, who relished Jewish Warsaw's contradictions: "Here, a bearded Jew with earlocks walked by in a fur-lined hat and satin gabardine—probably one of the Hasidim late after services—and soon a dandy came by in modern clothes, yellow shoes, a straw hat, clean-shaven and with a cigarette between his lips. He smoked openly on the Sabbath demonstrating his lack of faith in the Torah. Now came a pious young matron with a bonnet on her shaven head, to be closely followed by a girl with rouged cheeks, a kind of blue eye shadow, and a short-sleeved blouse that revealed her bare arms. She stopped to talk to the street loafers and even exchanged kisses with them."[39]

Heschel's own neighborhood was noisy and exciting enough. Peddlers went about hawking cheap candies and toys, and those without the required permits were chased by the market watchman. An electric tram turned from Nalewki Street, the main shopping thoroughfare, into Muranow Square, ringing the bell to warn people to get out of the way. Thursday evenings were the busiest, for Jewish women crowded the square to buy the customary fish and other necessities for the Sabbath. Yet books remained for some time Heschel's main adventure.

2

Early Studies and Catastrophes (1914–1917)

When taken for the first time to the heder *[elementary Hebrew school], the child was wrapped in a prayer shawl, like a scroll. Schoolboys were referred to as "the holy flock," and a mother's tenderest pet name for a boy was "my little* zaddik," *my little saint.*

Heschel, *The Earth Is the Lord's* (1951)

AVRUMELE'S CHILDHOOD REMAINED INSULATED FROM WARSAW'S PLURALISTIC society. By age three he entered the male universe of Torah study. It was a serious life, but a happy one: prayer, learning, debate on sacred texts, seeking holiness everywhere. Born of spiritual royalty, an offshoot of seven generations of Hasidic leaders, he was one of whom much was expected. His future was almost predestined.

He was a prodigy (in Hebrew, *illui*), displaying a remarkable memory but also precocious charm and wit. Religious Jews take special care to cultivate a prodigy, and such children are eagerly trained. From an early age, he began to learn Bible, the Mishnah and the codes of law, before entering the "sea of Talmud."[1] The family had a recent model, Heschel's maternal uncle, Rabbi Shlomo Hayim Perlow (1900–1943), rebbe of Bolekhov, who wrote brilliant commentaries on *halakhah* (Jewish law) by age twelve and by sixteen completed a study on rarely discussed tractates of the Talmud.[2] Avrumele might follow that path. In any case, as a future dynastic leader he received exemplary training.

Quite simply, however, Heschel enjoyed special attention because he was the youngest among four sisters and a brother. At home, the cute and lively Avrumele became a star performer. When hardly more than a toddler, family members enjoyed placing him on a chair or table to recite the *kiddush* "and they all rejoiced." (Heschel remembered that around age three he frolicked among the adults at the wedding of his sister Sarah and their first cousin, Rabbi Abraham Joshua Heschel of Medzibozh.)[3] He recited the family's extensive genealogy, and at age four or five, people admired his clever answers about religious texts. Avrumele was truly a "little zaddik" who amused everyone.[4]

Nothing is left to chance in grooming a Hasidic rebbe. As a child of an aristocratic line, Heschel was not sent to school. He began formal studies with tutors by age three or four, when most other boys enter *heder*.[5] (The girls also had tutors.) A private teacher directed his study of texts, accompanied him on walks and visits, and might even sleep in his room. Above all, the little rebbe's character was cultivated so that his very presence announced his inner piety. Heschel repeated a tale which illustrates the ideal of embodying Torah guiding his childhood: " 'Why do you go to see the rebbe?' someone asked an eminent rabbi who, although his time was precious, would trudge for days to visit his master on the Sabbath. 'To stand near him and watch him lace his shoes,' he answered. When Hasidim were gathered together, they told each other how the rebbe opened the door, how he tasted his food at the table—simple deeds, yet full of wonder."[6]

Sanctification of Learning

Heschel's boyhood education followed the common pattern, inaugurated by a picturesque ceremony. When an ordinary boy enters school for the first time, the father wraps him in a prayer-shawl and deposits the living bundle at the classroom or at the teacher's house. In Heschel's Hasidic tradition, this ceremony takes place at home and in the presence of distinguished witnesses; there the child is enticed with candies or coins placed on an open prayerbook, since learning is sweet, a delight.[7] Study and worship are inseparable.

The pedagogical method was ancient—at first, the child memorized the basic texts: the prayerbook (*siddur*) and the Torah (the Five Books of Moses). Following the injunction, "Let the holy flock come and study holy things," Torah study began with the Book of Leviticus: "Be ye holy for I the Lord am Holy." Assuming the divine origin of the *mitzvot* (commandments, legal and ritual obligations), the devout made the regimen of observant life second nature. Laws governing kosher foods, celebration of the Sabbath, festivals, and holy days, and for men (and some women) prayer three times daily, were kept zealously by the community.

The schoolboy's entire day was devoted to rigorous study. The boys began by reciting the weekly selection of the Torah and translating it into Yiddish, the native idiom of Eastern European Jews known as *mame-loshn* (mother tongue). Teacher and pupil discussed the text's meaning and applied it to key human situations and spiritual issues. Translation without insight was the norm. But Heschel's family was surprised at how much he understood early on. In addition to his exceptional memory, retaining practically everything he read or heard, he seemed to display precocious wisdom.

During the next stage of learning, special attention is given to *Humash mit Rashi*, the Pentateuch with the classic interpretations of Rashi (acronym of Rabbi Shlomo Itzhaki, 1040–1105), which Heschel came to know by heart. Along with Bible come elements of the *Shulhan Arukh*, the standard code of Jewish law compiled by Joseph Caro. A rabbi was expected to know codes in order to justify legal decisions and proffer advice to people; a Hasidic rebbe must possess as well the lore of his clan, oral and written, in order to inspire listeners.

By age eight Heschel probably began the study of Talmud, the foundation of Jewish life, communal, spiritual, and personal—and, soon after, Midrash and Hasidic texts. Text study was a physical and social process. The boys "learned" with a partner, a *haver* (in Hebrew, comrade). One of them read the text out loud, swaying and chanting the words to a *nigun* (a special study melody). Pondering a sacred text was a form of prayer, and the boys, with their hats, earlocks, and fringed garments, imitating their fathers and teachers, rocked back and forth (called *shukl*ing), while their high sing-song voices rose and fell. Targeting the text with his index finger, every boy rested his head on one hand—while with the other he swept his thumb up and down a page. They did not simply recite the text with their mouths and lungs; they absorbed it into their bodies, chanting and rocking rhythmically.

Yet, Heschel was not simply a prodigy who excelled in one—albeit vast—field, religious books. He applied his mental energy in other ways. For the sheer challenge, he catalogued and learned by heart all the products in the millinery store of Yehiel Hofer's father. Early on he relished the intricacies of chess, one of the few amusements favored by Hasidim. He was serious but lively, bursting with enthusiasm. When Avrumele and Yehiel met each other on the street, they laughed with pleasure at being together.[8] Yet Heschel's independent curiosity eventually drove him beyond his family's world.

Hasidic Schools in Warsaw

After preparation by tutors, Heschel entered the larger Hasidic community of Warsaw. He proceeded with his studies at a *shtiebl* (literally, a small hall) associated with the dynasty of Ger, one of which was located on his street, at 17 Muranowska.[9] Shtiebls, a uniquely Hasidic institution found throughout the city, were abundant in Heschel's neighborhood. Two of them thrived on Dzika Street, two on Twarda, and also on nearby Nalewki and Franciszkanska Streets. For Hasidim, the shtiebl was a place for prayer and study, as well as conversation.

In Warsaw's many shtiebls, it was possible to approximate the Hasidic customs of the ancestral villages. More loosely organized than yeshivas, shtiebls had no charter, no professional management, nor did they follow the tightly organized curriculum of the network of non-Hasidic yeshivas in Poland. Pupils were not governed in the style of a *rosh yeshiva* (the principal of a Talmudic academy), for they were required to develop a pattern of self-discipline, inspired by the opening of the *Shulhan Arukh:* "Be swift as a deer, light as an eagle and strong as a lion to serve the Lord." Nor would the sharp scholar, the intellectual prodigy, receive the most praise; the greatest accomplishment was "Torah learning with good deeds."

The shtiebl's rigorous daily schedule typifies the regimen of Heschel's childhood and early adolescence. The boys lived at home and woke at five A.M., walked to the shtiebl, where they sat at long wooden benches and tables, and began to recite the text to each other as preparation for the morning prayers. From seven to eight they prayed the *Shaharit* (morning) service with fervor, for study at daybreak was considered to be excellent preparation for worship; Rabbi Simha Bunam, the "Holy Jew" from Przysucha, was often quoted: "One page from Talmud with commentaries purifies the brain the way a *mikveh* [ritual bath] purifies the body." After prayers the boys returned to their families for breakfast. They came back punctually by ten, studying at their tables until noon.

Learning was a cooperative venture. Two or three boys worked with an older student; the younger ones began by repeating what they learned the previous day. In the afternoon, the older students left the beginners and studied together at a higher level. In contrast to yeshivas, students in shtiebls used the time between their sessions to study non-Talmudic subjects, such as the Torah portion of the week with commentaries, Midrash, and Hasidic books recommended by their rebbes. (Non-Hasidic education tends to concentrate on law and ritual.) Each day ended with *Minha*, the afternoon service, although often the boys returned after dinner to study well into the evening.

Like that of all religious children, Heschel's text education was reinforced by daily worship. Together study and prayer embodied tradition, which he later rhapsodized as "the austere music of the Talmud's groping for truth or the sweet melodies of exemplified piety of ancient sages."[10] The theory of language that Heschel developed in his American books of religious philosophy attempts to explain the profound participation in words during this period of the "study songs" and frequent prayers.[11]

Heschel's lifelong abhorrence to "killing time" (in Hebrew, *bitul z'man*, nullification of time) originated during this period.[12] Jewish students were expected to spend most of their waking hours studying or praying, and this strict principle was widely respected by Jews in all walks of life. Losing just one precious moment in frivolity or laziness was a sin.[13] Study was worship and must not be compromised.

Jewish spirituality was the foundation, engraved in the boys' consciousness by the liturgical calendar that governed their lives. A continuous process of meditation and thought was nurtured every Sabbath as another section of the Torah and the prophets was read and examined, at the same seasons, year after year. Heschel was accustomed to the presence of distinguished rabbis. Discussions of holiness with tutors and family began in early childhood, as he wrote, "The atmosphere in which I grew up was full of theology. Day and night, I heard them speak only about 'prayer' and *kavanah* (undivided attention, especially in prayer), and about '*Ha-Kadosh Borukh Hu*' (The Holy One, Blessed Be He) and about '*mesiras nefesh*' (extreme devotion, lit. giving over of one's soul)."[14]

In an attempt to convey this atmosphere to English-speaking readers, Heschel emphasized his family's fervent preparations for the ceremonial Friday evening meal. The Holy Day, although it occurred weekly, was a major opportunity. As he wrote in *The Sabbath* (1951), one of his first American books: "Then comes the sixth day. Anxiety and tension give place to the excitement that precedes a great event. The Sabbath is still away but the thought of its imminent arrival stirs in the heart a passionate eagerness to be ready and worthy to receive it."[15] The Sabbath became Heschel's key to transforming the values of modern readers, teaching us to "strive for spiritual integrity . . . [a daily life of] inwardness, compassion, justice and holiness."[16]

Yet, some Hasidic leaders raised bold ethical questions about the isolation required by sacred study. Characteristic of his modern approach to Jewish law was a tale Heschel told about "killing time." Imagine a rabbi, immersed in reflection, he said, who is interrupted by a simple man in despair who needs support.[17] After conversing with him, the rabbi dies. Some might regret that the scholar died while neglecting the Torah (*bitul Torah*) and not while studying, a more holy death. The Baal Shem Tov replied, "No. It may be that his entire life and studies were directed toward the few moments the rabbi spent with the unfortunate man. When the rabbi's task on earth was accomplished, he died." For Heschel, compassion could take precedence over Torah study.

But Heschel especially valued the boldness of Hasidic thought. When may ethical action become neglect of Torah? Where do we draw the line? To explain, Heschel repeated a parable attributed to his ancestor the rebbe of Ruzhin. Two Jews were condemned to death by a wicked king. But, to amuse himself, the king devised a condition: if they could walk across a wire, they would be saved. Anything but athletes, they nevertheless accepted. The first Jew crossed safely. The second one called back, "How did you do it?" The first replied, "Just remember one thing. When you feel yourself falling to one side, move to the other." Hasidic wisdom supplies no simple answers. We must decide by doing; insight may arise from the practice.

Grooming a Hasidic Prince

The training of Heschel's inner integrity, of his personality as zaddik, was as deliberate as mastering texts.[18] His legacy provided many examples of spiritual ideals: the Baal Shem Tov's love for every Jew, ignorant or learned; the compassion of Levi Yitzhak of Berditchev, champion of ordinary people to the point of challenging God's rigorous justice; the Apter Rav's mediation of rabbis in conflict and his belief in reincarnation; and the Ruzhiner's regal opulence that masked his compassion and piety. Heschel's father retained some of his Ruzhin aristocratic manners while practicing generosity and humility. How would Heschel define his own path?

Intellectual skill seemed to be his dominant quality. Like other gifted, traditionally trained Jewish boys, around age seven Heschel could read books quickly, cover to cover, remembering their contents. Driven by a desire for knowledge—or perhaps a nascent ambitiousness—Heschel at nine or ten began to consume the books in his father's library. He was treated like a rebbe, with deference, and questioned with the expectation of receiving wise answers. People rose to greet him when he entered a room.[19] People even brought him *kvitlakh* (petitions), teasingly predicting that if he became a rebbe all the others would lose their Hasidim. He was groomed to further his dynasty's mission.

Around age eight or nine, Heschel began to master Talmud, the true test of his mind, and he excelled in Talmud learning at an early age. These massive folio tomes contain debates that span the centuries. Each page of Talmud is a composite of several texts: the central document, the *Mishnah* (the original oral law written in Hebrew), is followed by the *Gemara* (a discussion of it written in an Aramaic-Hebrew idiom), surrounded by several medieval commentaries. Talmud contains a record of oral explications where *halakhah* (principles of Jewish law) is supplemented by *aggadah* (lore, parable, history, ethics, philosophy—what we now call theology). Rabbis and sages from ancient to medieval times engage in intricate debates, analyses, dialectics, fantasy—raising all sorts of questions, both practical and mysterious. The subjects, which are nearly limitless, include the holiday ritual in the Temple of Solomon, the ethics of person-to-person dealings, the laws of divorce, the rules governing connubial behavior during menstruation, and so on.

Many religiously educated Jewish boys have an extraordinary mental aptitude in secular endeavors, due in large part to Talmud study and its archaic methods. Deliberation on Talmud and dialectical reasoning—called "*pilpul*, the characteristic method of study developed in the East European period"—teach students how to think: "Its goal was not only to acquire information about the Law, but rather to examine its implications and presuppositions."[20] In addition to developing analytical skills, Talmud study can increase the ability to scan a page and read quickly; an effective eidetic (or visual) memory may also develop. This religious education advanced Heschel's unusual ability to retain large amounts of reading matter.

Talmudic investigation was a crossroads. Heschel recognized that meandering Talmud study can become exaggerated or it can lead to spiritual insight and self-discipline. (The term *pilpul*, in fact, took on negative connotations for the practical-minded.) The intellect may remain involved with its own dialectics, enter the daily world, or seek the divine: "Tension of the soul found an outlet in contriving sagacious, almost insoluble riddles. They invented new logical devices in explaining the Word of God, thrilled with yearning after the Holy." His mind was launched on a path to deeper spirituality.

Heschel fulfilled the expectations of an *illui*, an intellectual and religious prodigy. Prepared for greatness, he spent his days in an exacting routine: worship, scrupulous study of holy texts, ethical self-discipline. He learned to review complete Talmud pages; he could read books of all sorts quite rapidly, retaining their contents. His analytical skills played with passages recalled easily from myriad sources. Heschel cherished the more imaginative world of Midrash, compendia of interpretation, lore, and wisdom based upon the Torah and the five scrolls (the *Megillot*).[21] To this he added Hasidic sources which supplemented these freer—more "theological" than strictly legal—ways of thinking.

During this period, the family noticed an early sign of Heschel's independence: pride. Of course, a scion of generations of Hasidic rebbes who were believed to possess supernatural qualities cannot help but feel a sense of entitlement. But the boy was reprimanded for his excessive self-regard—an event of which his sisters reminded him several times. He claimed to have read most of— if not all—his father's books by age ten or twelve. Once, finishing one book, he shocked his brother, Jacob, by saying that he could write a better one himself.[22] Already, it seems, Heschel let slip a personal voice seeking expression.

In his Hasidic tradition, however, some forms of self-confidence were acceptable. As a true prodigy and heir to a noble pedigree, could he avoid feeling that he deserved such praise? His pride, in any case, was less extreme than that of the Ruzhiner rebbe, who is reported to have claimed: "I was an orphan. No one taught me but God. Even before the Messiah I shall not bend, but insist that my teaching is true."[23] In spite of that aspect of the Ruzhin inheritance, Heschel's family insisted upon modesty and discretion.

Father's Court in 1914

When Heschel was seven, his intense but relatively secure existence was disrupted by the signs of impending war. Its liturgical "palaces in time" (the title of one of Heschel's Yiddish poems)[24] did not insulate his family from the terrors and sorrows of his people—quite the contrary. Heschel's father—the Pelzovizna rebbe—embraced his daunting responsibilities as the Russian and Austro-Hungarian empires prepared for war.

Involvement with the events of the larger world was to be expected, for a Hasidic rebbe is a spiritual guide available to all people, not a cloistered scholar. Yehiel Hofer describes how Moshe Mordecai's "court on Muranowska Street was filled with Jews drafted for the Russian army and about to be sent to the front. Their pleas and those of their families that he should pray for them and free them from their troubles gave him no rest. He could not eat anything, and when his wife tried to induce him to eat, he replied that any food nauseated his soul."[25]

All sorts of Jews arrived, waited in line, writing petitions for the rebbe to bless. Heschel's home now welcomed Warsaw's diverse population: "Tall, broad-shouldered Jews with thick black and brown beards and sunburned faces, Jews who sold cheap merchandise, peddlars and travelers to distant fairs, clerks in great manufacturing warehouses on Gensza and Nalewki Streets, employees of shipping departments in the *zayazdn* of Muranowska and Bonifraterska Streets, Jews with large hands and feet and wide, tall boots, now sat in the prayerhouse quietly, fearfully, like children in a home where someone was seriously ill. Next to them sat their wives—small, shriveled Jewish women with flushed faces and sharp noses."

The rebbe's assistant, the *gabai* Reb Yosl, sat at a wood table, writing the names of the petitioners and, according to Hasidic custom, their mother's name. They placed a coin into a tin platter and waited their turn to see the rebbe. Many of the men now mustered from the reserves were veterans who had served in remote areas of the Russian Empire, even in the war with Japan.

Yehiel Hofer noticed how Moshe Mordecai's supplicants tested his own faith, for violent civil forces had invaded his sanctuary. The rebbe's anguish was especially acute since these troubles were no longer just "Jewish troubles, involving the Jewish God, Psalms, amulets and charms, all of the Jewish and Hasidic things which he knew so well. For although these Jewish troubles pained him so, it was purely Jewish pain." His gift for empathy with others' woes made him ill with grief. "For the past several days, the rebbe had been utterly broken."

For a pious Jew, the moral dilemma was irremediable. The rebbe believed that "the Russian Tsar himself, who has a powerful agent in Heaven, had personally called the Jews to wage war for him." But as a consequence, he was forced to support an evil State "which harrassed Jews, organized pogroms against them, murdered and robbed, and passed various cruel decrees against the Jews." These tensions undermined his health. The "Talmudic principle that 'the law of the State is law for the Jews' weakened the rebbe, took away his rebbe's powers, bound him, made him helpless against the suffering of the Jews, who so often stood before him now. The rebbe knew that he could in no way measure up to their naïve faith in his saintly merit, and in the merit of his great ancestors."

Responsible for giving strength to others, Moshe Mordecai could not indulge in doubts. He was expected to buttress hope: "The rebbe swayed over the petition as if he were studying a difficult passage. Then he removed his glasses, which remained attached to the black silk string, leaned his left arm against the table and covered his eyes with his palm. He rocked back and forth, right and left several times. The rebbe took his hand away, raised his head and turned it toward the Jews who stood in front of him, looked at them with his kind, warm eyes and said out loud: 'May the Almighty help you!'"

Heschel's father was especially anguished when men asked if they should go into hiding or injure themselves to avoid conscription. "In those cases the rebbe fell to trembling, his teeth clattered. He clasped his noble hands and shaking them as if they were a *lulav,* he repeated over and over again, 'May the Almighty help you.' When one of those Jews left the room, the rebbe sat mournfully, filled with sadness and depression." Heschel's father harbored as few illusions about his own powers as he did about the surrounding world.

Moshe Mordecai questioned his strength but not his duty, even as he despaired that the Jews might be fated to wander forever. "The rebbe Reb Moyshele shrank from the thought, and filled with sorrow and pain he almost shouted, 'Master of the Universe, when will you free your people Israel from this bitter exile!' On days like that, the rebbe didn't even taste the lunch that was brought him." Acknowledging that even God could neither deny nor abolish historical forces, he continued to bless his people. The Hasidic chronicles report that Moshe Mordecai Heschel not only inspired followers; he had saved them: "*Everyone* he blessed remained uninjured in the War."[26] Would young Abraham inherit father's sacred powers?

Avrumele Heschel was around eight years of age when the world order was shattered. One of his future teachers in Berlin, the historian Ismar Elbogen, graphically summarized its epoch-making significance: "On August 1, 1914, the First World War broke out, bringing with it black catastrophe and shaking Europe and its civilization to their very foundations. Ten million dead, fifty million maimed and crippled, the progress of the century destroyed, every moral standard erased, every animal instinct aroused—such were the consequences of the war."[27] After the experience of two world wars, Heschel acknowledged the perplexing, frightful reality: "Militarism is whoredom, voluptuous and vicious, first disliked and then relished."[28]

WARSAW

Family Emigrations

Heschel's far-flung clan, as well, was uprooted. For six years, from August 1914 to October 1920, the ancestral towns of Jews in Galicia and the Russian Pale of Settlement were battered by military actions. Two of his father's brothers—Rabbis Meshullam Zusya Heschel and Israel Sholem Joseph Heschel— were Hasidic leaders in the Ukrainian town of Medzibozh. The other brother, Yitzhak Meir Heschel, presided over his court in Kopitzhinitz (in Polish, Kopyczynce, located between Tchortkov and Husyatin), a Galician shtetl in Austria-Hungary. Each rabbi had to bless Jewish soldiers compelled by their oppressive governments to slaughter each other on the battlefield.

These calamities eventually brought the Heschel generations closer geographically. While the Russian military was expelling Jews from villages near the front, Rabbi Yitzhak Meir Heschel fled by way of Vizhnitz to Vienna, arriving in September 1914 with his family, including his son, also named Abraham Joshua Heschel, and Abraham's wife, Sarah (Avrumele's eldest sister). They and several of the town's high officials had escaped just in time. When the Russians

Heschel's uncles, Israel Sholem Joseph Heschel, rebbe of Zinkov, and Yitzhak Meir Heschel, rebbe of Kopitzhinitz. Courtesy of Yitzhak Meir Twersky.

Heschel's first cousin Abraham Joshua Heschel as a
child. Son of Yitzhak Meir Heschel of Kopitzhinitz.
Courtesy of Yitzhak Meir Twersky.

entered Kopitzhinitz, they took as hostages the head of his Hasidic court and the
town's wealthiest merchants. They were exiled to marshlands on the Russian-
Chinese border—not to return until 1916.

Leaders and their communities were violently transplanted. Cities such as
Berlin, Vienna, and Warsaw—where the largest Jewish populations were already concentrated—provided protection and a chance for continuity. Along
with tens of thousands of others, the Heschels and the Friedmans—the rebbes
of Tchortkov, Husyatin, Sadagora, and Boyan—also emigrated to Vienna. They
maintained regular contact with the Warsaw branch of the family and participated in all significant decisions.

Vienna became the vital center of Heschel's paternal branch. The Kopitzhinitzer rebbe established his court at 9 Ruepp Gasse, in the Austrian capital's predominantly Jewish Second District. His thriving community became the

Warsaw relatives' second home. (An express train might cover the 433 miles between the cities in sixteen hours.) Eventually Heschel's sister Devorah Miriam married and moved to Vienna, and his sister Gittel went there for a short time, then returned to her mother in Warsaw. His brother, Jacob, eventually married Sarah Friedman, a cousin in Vienna.

The Vienna clan exerted a strong conservative influence on Heschel. The Heschels and the Friedmans of Vienna, connected by marriage with the Ruzhin dynasty, were prominent leaders of the Agudat Israel, the Jewish Orthodox organization established to combat the increasing assimilation and secularization of European Jews.[29] In 1912, their uncle, Rabbi Israel Friedman of Tchortkov, son of Dovid Moshe Friedman, helped convene the historic Chernovitz Conference (Kattowitz in Upper Silesia), which joined devout Jews from Germany and Poland, Hasidic and otherwise, to bolster traditional Jewish education and create the political party which became the Agudat Israel. This coalition of Orthodox Jews became an authoritative force during the 1915 German occupation of Poland, joining representatives from the academic, political, and religious

Heschel's sister, Sarah Brakha Heschel, and her husband, Abraham Joshua Heschel, of Kopitzhinitz, Vienna. Courtesy of Yitzhak Meir Twersky and Thena Heshel Kendall.

worlds. The Agudah consolidated as a Jewish political force at the two "Great Assemblies" held in Vienna in 1923 and 1929.

Heschel's mother's twin brother, Alter Israel Shimon Perlow (1874–1933), was also brought closer by the war. Although the German invasion of 1914 endangered his Hasidic court in Novominsk, the rebbe refused to flee, so as not to abandon his followers. His son, Nahum Mordecai, remembered that "most Polish Jews were happy to be freed from the Russian authorities and the terrible decrees and pogroms wrought upon the Jewish population. The Jews wanted to be liberated from their 'Russian exile' and anxiously awaited the Germans to occupy Poland. But [the Novominsker rebbe], his name be blessed, was not of this opinion."[30] Even after the Russians were defeated, Rabbi Perlow angrily reproached anyone who sympathized with the Germans.

By Hanukah 1915, the rebbe finally left Novominsk secretly when an official—a German-born Russian—told him that "an order had been issued to arrest him and bring him to Russia."[31] By then most of his community had already reached Warsaw. With his wife and eight children (there would eventually be twelve), Rabbi Perlow became the Heschels' neighbor, establishing his Hasidic court at 10 Franciszkanska Street, one long block away. Heschel was eight years old when his maternal uncle, who made Talmud study and contemplative prayer the focus of his existence, arrived, reinforcing his father's example of holiness. In later years Heschel described his uncle as "the ideal y'rei shamayim" (pious man, in Hebrew; literally, fearer of Heaven).[32] Rabbi Perlow's daily schedule was widely admired. He would rise at four A.M. and at sunrise purify himself in the mikveh. Then he studied Talmud and concluded by reciting from memory twenty-three chapters of Mishnah (the foundational text of the Talmud). (He also studied Midrash, the Zohar, principal source book of Jewish mysticism, and Hasidic writings.) To guarantee that the rebbe did not miss a word of Mishnah, Avigdor, his old attendant, stood next to him checking the text. Every month the Novominsker rebbe finished reciting all six books of Mishnah. "Only after completing these studies did he eat something and then turn to his work of receiving the people who came to him from near and far for advice and comfort."[33]

As a boy, Heschel observed his uncle's piety almost every day. This spiritual source was a comfortable walk away: first the short distance to Muranow Square, then a right at Nalewki Street, and then the first left onto Franciszkanska. Accompanied by a tutor, he visited his uncle to study and talk. There he might also hear conversations among Warsaw's leading rabbis. By that time, immersed in Torah wisdom, Heschel was absorbed by their ideals of utmost purity.

Grief and Inner Crisis

In 1916, however, the family experienced a cruel loss. Warsaw was by then occupied by the German army, and a typhus epidemic spread throughout the city, aggravated by the British blockade. Moshe Mordecai Heschel was one of its victims.[34] On 16 November, six weeks before Avrumele's tenth birthday, Heschel's father died suddenly at forty-three years of age.

After the time of death, traditional Jews gather at the bereaved home and sit *shiva* for a week, reciting prayers and receiving visitors. Following custom, Heschel's father was buried within a day in the Jewish cemetery whose entrance on Okopowa Street stood about three blocks away from his Hasidic court. A tombstone was erected later, with a summary of his *yikhus* and his life, engraved in Hebrew script.[35]

Tombstone of Heschel's father, Moshe Mordecai Heschel, Warsaw Cemetery. Photograph by Maciej Mierzejewski. Courtesy of "Our Roots," Warsaw. The marker reads: "Zaddik, Moshe Mordecai / Blessed be his memory / from Peltzovizna, son of Zaddik / Abraham Joshua Heschel from Medzibozh, / grandson of the holy man, author of Ohev Israel / from Opatow and grandson of the holy man / from Ruzhin, and the son-in-law of the holy man, / the Rebbe from Novominsk. / Let his good deeds always protect us. / departed 27 Heshvan 5678."

Heschel did not write about his father's early death. His shock and private sorrow, mixed with the effects of military occupation, poverty, and disease, cannot be gauged.[36] But it ended his childhood in unexpected ways.

As an adult, Heschel interpreted death religiously as both a supreme loss and an opportunity to renew trust in God. In 1969, speaking at an international conference on sudden death, he recognized bereavement as an opportunity: "Death is grim, harsh, cruel, a source of infinite grief. Our first reaction is consternation. We are stunned and distraught. Slowly, our sense of dismay is followed by a sense of mystery. Suddenly, a whole life has veiled itself in secrecy. Our speech stops, our understanding fails. In the presence of death there is only silence, and a sense of awe."[37]

These thoughts might echo his childhood trauma and the gradual working through of his father's lethal illness. Heschel concluded his speech by repeating the final sentences of his first essay in English, "An Analysis of Piety," published more than twenty-five years earlier: "This is the meaning of death: the ultimate dedication to the divine. Death so understood will not be distorted by the craving for immortality, for this act of giving away is reciprocity on man's part for God's gift of life. For the pious man it is a privilege to die."[38] According to this mature statement, faith can assimilate the loss, but not without struggle and reflection.

Yet his father's passing was not reassuring to the child. Soon after Heschel turned ten on 11 January 1917, he experienced an internal crisis of vast consequence, both psychological and cultural. His uncle Alter Israel Shimon Perlow, the Novominsker rebbe, took over his education and, indirectly but decisively, introduced him to the Hasidic manner of Kotzk, a radical perspective that clashed with the optimistic traditions that had shaped his identity until then. The result, as Heschel described it, sundered his personality between opposite poles, "the joy of Medzibozh [the home of the Baal Shem Tov] and the anxiety of Kotzk."[39] Heschel's mature personality—and his modern temperament—emerged from that inner tension.

3

"The Blessings of Humiliation" and Triumphal Adolescence (1917–1924)

It was in my ninth year that the presence of Reb Menahem Mendl
of Kotzk, known as the Kotzker, entered my life. Since then he has
remained a steady companion and a haunting challenge. Although he
often stunted me, he also urged me to confront perplexities that I might
have preferred to evade.
Heschel, *A Passion for Truth* (1973)

HESCHEL WROTE NOTHING ABOUT THIS PERIOD OF HIS DEVELOPMENT UNTIL after a near-fatal heart attack in 1969. (Until then, Heschel's writings tended to emphasize God's presence and the potentials of ethical conscience and holiness.) During the last years of his life, he appears to have been possessed, despite failing health, to publish two books of exceptional personal consequence, one in English, the other in Yiddish: *A Passion for Truth* and *Kotsk: A gerangl far emesdikeyt* (Kotsk: Struggle for integrity). These books expressed his forthright anger at mediocre institutionalized religion and timid morality. And both trace to his "ninth year" the author's encounter with the uncompromising demands of Kotzk Hasidism.[1]

Heschel finally acknowledged the conflict within his personality that both tore him apart and gave him energy in "Why I Had to Write This Book," the introduction to his final work in English, *A Passion for Truth*. He worked feverishly to finish the typescript, despite his anguish during a period of extreme American violence against North Vietnam. About three weeks after submitting the manuscript, he died peacefully in his sleep on the Sabbath night of 23 December 1972, at age sixty-five. Perhaps the emotional time bomb of his childhood trauma finally detonated.

A Passion for Integrity

In 1917, as the Germans continued to occupy Warsaw, the Heschel household on Muranowska Street now consisted of his mother, his brother, Jacob, and sisters Esther, Gittel, and Devorah.[2] Rivka Reizel maintained her husband's shtiebl after his death, dogged by poverty. She received financial support from her brother in Warsaw and the Heschels in Vienna, although they also lacked resources for their large families. (The Kopitzhinitzer rebbe practiced the custom of giving away all cash at the end of each day, and the Novominsker rebbe had twelve children to support.) Heschel's mother was sometimes forced to send her two boys into the street to sell matches or other small items.[3]

The Novominsker rebbe supervised Heschel's education, directing him toward the influential Hasidism of Ger, headed by Rabbi Abraham Mordecai Alter (1866–1948), Poland's most prominent Jewish religious leader. The Gerer rebbe considered Rabbi Perlow to be his close friend and a model of piety; when he made his first visit to Palestine, he told many of his followers, if they had problems, "Go to the rebbe from Novominsk."[4] Known to some as "the King of Polish Hasidism," the Gerer rebbe could decide a community election, and his arrival in town was as ceremonious as a state visit.[5] Young Heschel found superior guidance in the Ger network of teachers and scholars.

What Heschel's uncle may not have anticipated was the radical influence of Rabbi Menahem Mendl Morgenstern of Kotzk (1787–1859), founder of the original tradition. Many Ger Hasidim followed the path of Kotzk, for there was a direct historical connection. The first Gerer rebbe, Yitzhak Meir Rothenberg (1789–1866) (the surname was later changed to Alter), presided over the community of Kotzk (in Polish, Kock), after Reb Mendl's death. Yitzhak Meir then went to Warsaw and established his dynasty in Gora Kalwaria (in Yiddish, Ger; in Hebrew, Gur), a town located about twenty miles southeast of Warsaw.[6] There the Kotzk tradition was transformed, accommodating society and becoming politically effective.

Nevertheless, Ger Hasidism preserved the iconoclasm of Kotzk. The enigmatic Kotzker rebbe battled for personal and spiritual authenticity; unlike the generous Baal Shem Tov, who taught compassion and respected human limits, the Kotzker rebbe was dismayed at human mediocrity and militantly defended absolute standards. But it was suspected that his severe judgments were pathological. Many believed that the Kotzker rebbe was victim of a depression for the last twenty years of his life, isolating himself from his followers and from the world; rumors circulated that he even made blasphemous remarks.[7] The Kotzker rebbe's "passion for truth" (as Heschel defined it) could be destructive—to the community and to himself.

Heschel entered this world of strife with a new tutor, Bezalel Levy, a Gerer Hasid who followed the way of Kotzk. Reb Bezalel, as the family called him, lived in their apartment building on Muranowska Street. A short man with fierce eyes and unusually long *pey'ot* (earlocks),[8] he accompanied Avrumele everywhere, teaching and interrogating him. His influence was decisive, psychologically damaging in some ways, but strengthening the boy's drive for spiritual integrity.

Ten-year-old Avrumele and Bezalel began in ordinary fashion, studying Talmud and other texts together. On long walks, the tutor expounded esoteric teachings of Jewish mysticism. Even for an older child, it was unusual to begin such complex speculations. Men are advised to marry or reach the age of forty before pondering the lush symbolism of the Zohar. Several times, unduly challenged, the boy implored, "I don't understand." The tutor replied, both hopeful and unconsoling, "Some day you will." (Heschel recounted this anecdote to American rabbinical students. Spiritual leaders, he felt, should not talk down to their congregants but should elevate them.)[9]

But the boy's real battle was with himself. Reb Bezalel assaulted Heschel's already ripened pride. After all, he was handsome, blessed with a remarkable memory, and secure in his sense of entitlement. Bezalel understood that the adulation the youth received might induce complacency or even arrogance. Heschel described his tutor's harsh questioning of his self-worth as a "bolt of lightning."

Nothing less than radical humility was the goal; only absolute honesty could burn away self-satisfaction and make true piety possible. Systematically and relentlessly, Reb Bezalel undermined the boy's self-esteem. Speaking carefully and distinctly, every word pronounced like the striking of a hammer, the tutor instilled the rigorous standards of Kotzk, the futility of human efforts, the foolishness of pride. As Heschel recalled: "His one aim was to plant in my heart the feeling of contrition, of repentance, the danger of being a rebbe's son. He would constantly break down my ego, my self-confidence. To such an extent that whatever inferiority complexes I have . . ."[10] He did not complete the sentence, and his candid self-analysis went no further.

There was a bitter contrast between his earlier education and the outlook that marked his study with Bezalel. Before his father's death, he absorbed the manner of the Baal Shem, the Apter Rav, Levi Yitzhak, and the rebbe of Ruzhin. Now he was confronted by a contrary, but equally powerful, Hasidic view—that of the skeptical rebbe of Kotzk. With hindsight of a lifetime, he summarized the opposition: "The Baal Shem dwelled in my life like a lamp, while the Kotzker struck like lightning." Heschel was now seized by a discordant, negative thrust—but one, according to his own images, no less illuminating.

Henceforth, as Heschel admitted in retrospect, he was a person divided, plagued by contradictory perceptions of self. In the preface to *A Passion for Truth,* he summarized its ambivalent effects: "The Baal Shem gave me wings; the Kotzker encircled me with chains. I never had the courage to break the chains and entered into joys with my shortcomings in mind. I owe intoxication to the Baal Shem, to the Kotzker the blessings of humiliation."

Battling the Ego

Heschel emulated Reb Bezalel by embracing religious extremism, normal for some adolescents, but disturbing to his family. He let his earlocks grow almost to his waist, like his tutor. (Moshe Mordecai, his father, on the contrary, following the restraint of Ruzhin, tucked his shorter earlocks out of sight.)

Heschel also exaggerated common customs preserving purity. Jewish modesty expresses reverence for persons, and pious men are not supposed to look at women directly, and even children avoid direct contact with the opposite sex. Heschel remembered, at age five, being sent to borrow something from a female neighbor and asking her to place it on a table to avoid receiving it "from a woman's hand" (which ultra-Orthodox custom forbids).[11] But, influenced by Bezalel, Heschel even removed himself from his aunts and female cousins. On a family vacation at Otwock, a resort village near Warsaw that was popular among devout Jews, he immediately jumped off a bench when some girls sat on the other side. They laughed, for the boy's fastidiousness surprised even this religious family.[12] When Heschel was about eleven years old, he shocked a Perlow cousin who visited his home and found him studying with great fervor. The cousin greeted him but did not interrupt and left to visit Heschel's mother and sisters in another room. They were engaged in conversation for about ten minutes when Heschel walked in and said, "Don't waste your time talking to the women. Come in here and learn."

Heschel was attracted to Ger Hasidism, for it was a flourishing movement. Around age twelve, he wanted to visit Gora Kalwaria, where tens of thousands of followers approached the rebbe. His mother was alarmed that Avrumele might yield to the Ger charisma and remain there to study, joining the multitudes. She did not want to lose her son, who was still expected to lead his father's small following. She wrote to her family in Vienna, asking them to pray for Avrumele. For whatever reasons, Heschel did not go.

But Bezalel's challenges in the end strengthened Heschel's ego, helping him achieve an appropriate self-assertion. Heschel began to take charge of his own discipline, seeking books that could transform him, some of which his family judged to be dangerous, including works by Rabbi Nahman of Bratslav (1772–1810), the Baal Shem Tov's great-grandson. None of Rabbi Nahman's works appeared on his father's shelves, and his uncle Rabbi Perlow disapproved of this reading. Perhaps "the tormented master" (as Rabbi Nahman has been called) was too radical?[13] Nahman's alternation between a grandiose view of himself and depression or self-abhorrence was well known. In his family's view, it was better for Avrumele to master Talmud than ponder Nahman's often pessimistic writings, many of which voice anguish at God's remoteness.

But Heschel reached a cooperative neighbor, a Hasid named Moshe, who lent him a copy of Nahman's principal work of spiritual discipline and theology, *Likutei Moharan* (Collected teachings of the sage Rabbi Nahman). For six months Heschel scrutinized this powerful but difficult work, attempting to live by its rigorous precepts. He stopped chewing his food, since that would release its flavor; he swallowed it whole. Eat in order to live was the rule, but avoid pleasure. Heschel later reported that, after several weeks of similar afflictions, "I almost died!"[14]

Like most adolescents, Heschel was contending with distressing emotions. Perhaps he felt the pull of melancholy flowing under Rabbi Nahman's repeated insistence on joy and practical Jewish living. Perhaps Nahman's struggle with identity aggravated his own. In a footnote to *A Passion for Truth*, Heschel referred sympathetically to withdrawal from the world, a well-known teaching of Nahman: "I recall that in the prayer rooms of Rabbi Nahman's followers in Warsaw, there were narrow cells in which individuals could retire for an hour or more, since their homes were overcrowded and the surrounding fields offered no seclusion."[15]

Perhaps Heschel glimpsed his most intimate desire. "Solitude was a common practice among mystically inclined Jews." On the same page of *A Passion for Truth* Heschel probed the burdens which gave him creative drive: "For a soul can create only when alone, and some are chosen for the flowering that takes place in the dark avenues of the night. They may live on the brink of despair, alternating between a longing for fellowship and privacy."[16] Only in his Yiddish poetry, written about ten years later, did Heschel confess directly his inner alienation and essential loneliness as a man of God.

Heschel's wounded personality survived a fundamental breach, and he remained inhibited—yet in some ways energized—by his own unrealistic standards. He admitted that his confident spirit was irremediably compromised: "I never had the courage to break the chains and entered into joys with my shortcomings in mind."[17] An excessive, almost self-defeating conscience lacerated his pleasures. Such were "the blessings of humiliation," as he wrote many years later. At the time, however, Heschel's insights probably remained unconscious. His exaggerated modesty was the most obvious symptom of self-questioning. But the slash to his ego never healed.

Even after achieving fame in the United States, Heschel, long after he left his Hasidic environment, still craved the support and sometimes adulation he received as a child and youth in Warsaw. He remained personally insecure; sometimes, almost childishly, he showed a colleague, or even a student, an unfinished manuscript to solicit approval—in addition asking for practical advice on improving its content.[18] Jokingly he confided that Bezalel had been the instrument of his "inferiority complex."[19] Heschel's facetious confession was that of a vulnerable prince deprived of his kingdom before touching the throne.

Heschel's inner conflict became above all a source of energy, and piety became for him inseparable from ethics. His adolescent scourging of pride became a spiritual discipline as he sought to surrender his robust ego to God and to acts of goodness. Later he insisted, "The 'I' becomes the central problem in the Kotzker's thinking; it is the primary counterpart to God in the world. The sin of presumptuous selfhood is the challenge and defiance that God faces in the world."[20] God's very presence was at stake in Heschel's ongoing battle with self-regard.

A Paragon of Authentic Piety

All the while, Heschel continued to be fortified by his community. His family yearned for him to become a rebbe and admired him. In Hasidic terms, he was seen as a *baal nefesh* (master of rare spiritual power) and a *baal hitragshut* (an exquisitely sensitive person).[21] Regular communication with his uncle the Novominsker rebbe reinforced his ideal of piety.

At the time, Rabbi Alter Israel Shimon Perlow was around forty-four years old and, like his twin sister, Heschel's mother, was quite small in stature—about five feet tall—and frail of health, as were several other relatives.[22] Their home was lively, for the Perlows had eight daughters and four sons. Their nine rooms on Franciszkanska Street consisted of two adjoining apartments with a separate entrance for the rebbe. The family lived in the rear unit, while the prayerhouse was in the front.[23] Food for the family and dozens of guests was prepared in a huge kitchen on the ground floor.

Unlike the Gerer rebbe, who was active in politics and a multitude of practical decisions, the Novominsker rebbe was "a rabbi's rabbi" who devoted most of his waking hours to study and prayer. Continuing his lifelong practice, he recited the Mishnah by heart almost constantly, using his prodigious memory to maintain a state of *devekut,* attachment to God. (Playing on the Hebrew letters M-SH-N-A, Rabbi Perlow considered the Mishnah to be the "soul"—or *neshama*—of Jewishness.) Because of a delicate constitution and a demanding schedule (he ate very little—twice a day, at two in the afternoon, after receiving many people, and at midnight), the rebbe was often ill.

The Novominsker rebbe was a paragon of Jewish spirituality. As devout Jews strive to transform themselves on the Sabbath, Heschel's uncle became "completely immersed in its holiness." His prayers, "full of soulfulness and longing for the Creator," lasted for hours, and when eating he would say before each bite, "In honor of the holy Sabbath." On the Seventh Day the family spoke only Hebrew, the sacred tongue.[24]

The rebbe's reputation of sanctity was reflected in some amusing stories about his physician, a Dr. Soloveitchik, scion of great Lithuanian Talmudists.[25] One time the rebbe, accompanied by a son, went for a checkup. The doctor usually examined rabbis immediately, but he kept Rabbi Perlow waiting. When the son protested, the doctor explained, "You don't understand. I take the other rabbis

Heschel's uncle, Alter Israel Shimon Perlow, rebbe of Novominsk, and his son-in-law Rabbi Elazar Eichenstein, Carlsbad. Courtesy of Harry Rabinowicz.

quickly, so that there should be as little *bitul Torah* [time wasted from the study of Torah] as possible. But there is no such danger with the Novominsker rebbe. Since he is constantly reciting the Mishnah by heart, there is no waste of time."[26] Another story recalled a surgery on Rabbi Perlow to save his legs. The operation was done at home, and even while under ether he recited Mishnah. After the procedure was completed, the devout doctor left the rebbe's room walking backward, as one does when leaving the Holy Ark which holds the Torah.

The entire community participated in the rebbe's Sabbath. Every Saturday toward evening, when the afternoon prayer (the Minhah service) was complete, the men assembled for a ceremonial meal called *Shalosh Seudos* (literally, "three meals").[27] In this dramatic Hasidic ritual, everyone gathered around a large table, called the rebbe's *Tish*. To begin, the rebbe said blessings for washing hands and blessings over bread and wine. The Hasidim and other visitors watched the master taste bits of food, the remnants of which (called *shirayim*) he then distributed. Heschel often took the privileged place at his uncle's right side.[28] He remembered being especially transfixed by the rebbe's face during his awe-inspiring communion with the ritual.

Heschel imbibed the ancestral charisma at the Novominsker rebbe's Tish. Prayers were recited and songs were sung, some lines antiphonally, some by the rebbe alone, some softly, some in a whisper. The words came from the Bible, the prayerbook, the Zohar, the Ari, the famed Kabbalist of Safed, and others. The rebbe ate a small bit of fish. More singing of *nigunim* (melodies without words), and the after-meal grace was chanted.[29] By now darkness had fallen and those present could barely see one another, the Hasidim swayed, chanting the nigunim of the ancestors of Karlin, Stolin, and Koidanov, evoking a sense of mystery.

The rebbe's discourse was the culmination, bringing intimate emotion to the Jewish knowledge shared by both traditional and modern listeners. There was silence, and the rebbe, with closed eyes, began by quoting a passage from the week's Torah portion. He raised questions, citing by memory passages from Talmud, Midrash, the prophets, and teachings of his dynastic fathers. He spoke for at least an hour and a half, often longer. After the speech, the impassioned Hasidim sang more nigunim and then prayed *Ma'ariv* (the evening service). To extend the sanctified Sabbath, they remained long after sunset, for it is said that on the Seventh Day each person receives an additional soul. At the end, they recited *havdalah*, the ceremony separating holy time from the week.

Heschel's adolescence was thus guided by this great zaddik whose entire life conveyed holiness. Years later in the United States, in his first article in English (1942), Heschel celebrated the "piety" summarized by his uncle's presence: "Awareness of God is as close to him as the throbbing of his own heart, often deep and calm, but at times overwhelming, intoxicating, setting the soul afire. The momentous reality of God stands there as peace, power, and endless tranquility, as an inexhaustible source of help, as boundless compassion, as an open gate awaiting prayer."[30]

Bar Mitzvah and Ordination

Adjusting inwardly to his father's death, his family's poverty, and Reb Bezalel's ruthless supervision, Heschel reached religious maturity under the guidance of Warsaw's distinguished Torah and Talmud scholars. The Novominsker rebbe gave substance to his nephew's piety by placing him within his network.

Study was the way. Heschel entered a period of higher sacred learning, while his wounded sense of self gained strength and independence. Yet, without knowing it at first, he was preparing to look beyond.

Heschel was mastering the textual foundations of Jewish life—Bible, Talmud, Midrash, codes, and commentaries. He was reading widely in Hasidic, kabbalistic, and aggadic literature. He took special interest in Hasidic classics such as the *Me'or Einayim* (Light of the eyes) by Menahem Nahum of Chernobyl, *Kedushat Levi* (The holiness of Levi) by his ancestor, Levi Yitzhak of Berditchev, and the powerful writings of Yaakov Yosef of Polnnoye, especially *Toldot Yaakov Yosef* (The generations of Jacob Joseph, major teachings of the Baal Shem Tov). Yaakov Yosef was a man of fierce temperament who denounced the rabbis of the time as "Jewish devils" (*shedim yehudayim*) and whose book was put to the flames.

Further, Heschel began to examine other works that fascinated him for the rest of his life: *Shnei Luhot Habrit* (Two tablets of the covenant) by Isaiah Horowitz, the vast compendia of the *MaHaRal* (Judah Loew of Prague, 1609), as well as the *MaHarSHa* (Rabbi Shmuel Edels, c. 1631). Heschel later extolled Rabbi Edels's commentary on the aggadic portions of the Talmud as being written by one of the supreme intellectual figures of Judaism whose genius had been passed by. Heschel's spiritual education was proceeding rapidly.

On 11 January 1920 he turned thirteen, the age of becoming a *bar mitzvah* (literally, son of the commandments), an adult with full religious responsibilities. For observant Jews, the public act of accepting the yoke of the *mitzvot* is not exceptional, as by that age boys possess the necessary knowledge. The event takes place during Monday or Thursday services when the Torah is read in the synagogue. For Hasidic Jews, the special ceremony of *hanahat tefillin* (literally, putting on phylacteries) is part of the daily morning prayer.

Heschel's bar mitzvah, three years after his father's death, was a significant dynastic event in which he consecrated his duties as a mature Jew.[31] It was a special honor that his grand-uncle Rabbi Yitzhak Meir Heschel, the old Kopitzhinitzer rebbe of Vienna, risked his fragile health to attend.[32] Other rabbinic scholars, known as "leaders of the generation," were also present. Heschel had the extraordinary distinction of putting on the tefillin of Rabbi Levi Yitzhak of Berditchev, his maternal ancestor. A festive meal with invited guests was held after the morning service.

The highlight of a bar mitzvah was the boy's *drasha,* a homiletic interpretation of the week's Torah portion. Heschel was nervous, for he knew that his talk, delivered from memory, should include rabbinic sources from Talmud and

Midrash, and perhaps references from the Zohar and Hasidic masters, especially sayings or writings by ancestors. As he was known to have already studied the entire Talmud, he felt the pressure of high expectations. Years later, consoling some rabbinical students, Heschel mentioned how he couldn't sleep the night before. But, he reported, his discourse was appreciated by everyone there.

Rabbinical ordination (*smikha*) was the next stage. By age thirteen, Heschel mastered the texts qualifying him to become a practicing rabbi: the relevant sections of Talmud and all four parts of the *Shulhan Arukh,* the code of Jewish law pertaining to every aspect of social, personal, and ritual life. Although Hasidic rebbes were not required to, the family felt that Heschel should be ordained. But he was advised to wait and advance his competence in Talmud more profoundly.

Heschel's new mentor was the prominent Talmud scholar Rabbi Menahem Zemba (1883–1943), a member of the Warsaw Rabbinical Council who was also active in the Agudat Israel political party and a follower of the Gerer rebbe.[33] Zemba was an unusual person and teacher, combining simplicity, extraordinary learning, and intelligence. The Novominsker rebbe's influence was palpable in this choice of a teacher for the gifted young man.

Heschel might have appreciated Zemba's background. He was born in the Praga suburb of Warsaw to a family of very poor Hasidic Jews, and his father had died when he was nine years old. He was raised by his grandfather Abraham Zemba, a follower of Kotzk and Ger.[34] When he was eighteen the family married him to the daughter of a wealthy iron merchant who promised twenty years of *kest* (board and lodging) so he could, as the expression goes, devote "twenty hours a day" to Torah.

Heschel was about sixteen years old when he was ordained by Rabbi Zemba. Studying with Zemba alone or with small groups of young men, he gained a high level of competence in Talmud, demonstrating his intellectual autonomy. The next year, his mentor Reb Bezalel asked Heschel to officiate at his marriage, recognizing the young rabbi's sturdy sense of self.

By this time Heschel had studied at the Mesivta Yeshiva—the foremost Hasidic institution of traditional learning—which his brother, Jacob, was already attending.[35] Zemba was one of its leading teachers. Founded in 1919 by rabbinic authorities and the Agudat Israel community, it conceived learning differently from the Lithuanian-style yeshivas, adding spiritual enthusiasm and Hasidic customs to intellectual rigor. The rebbe of Ger, as president of the Agudah, became the honorary head of the institute.

Paradoxically, this urban Hasidic academy may have kindled Heschel's drive for secular knowledge. The Mesivta Yeshiva's curriculum did not just allow, it

*Menachem Zemba in Montreux, Switzerland.
Agudath Israel Archives, New York. Courtesy of
Shaul Shimon Deutsch.*

required its students to supplement Jewish studies (with its mystical world-view)
with some acquaintance with contemporary civilization. The Polish Ministry of
Education required all schools, even religious seminaries, to introduce secular
subjects, so the Mesivta established a separate program with its own principal
and teachers to offer courses on Polish language, mathematics, history, and other
literary or scientific topics. This minimal (two hours a day) modern curriculum
gave rabbinical candidates rights that were similar to those of students in public institutions.[36] Orthodox young men could thus prepare to enter a *Gymnasium*
(a secular government high school), which was the prerequisite for university
matriculation.

First Publications

By age fourteen Heschel was a qualified Talmud scholar, well versed in the
early commentators from the eleventh century to recent times, and the later
codes, especially the code of Maimonides (1135–1204), the greatest medieval
philosopher and legal authority. In 1922 his first commentaries on Talmud and
later rabbinic works began to appear in the Hebrew-language Warsaw monthly,
Sha'arey Torah: Kovetz rabbani hodshi (Gates of Torah: Monthly rabbinic jour-

nal), whose editorial office was located at 4 Muranowska Street, near Heschel's home.[37] His first essay appeared in the fall in the special student supplement, *Bet Midrash*, followed by two more in winter and spring 1923.[38] It was likely that Rabbi Zemba and other teachers at the Mesivta Yeshiva urged him to display his Talmudic deftness and learning. With these publications Heschel now emerged as a member of the community of Talmud scholars. Contributors included rabbis from Poland and Russia, Hasidic and non-Hasidic. His commentaries are called *hidushei torah* ("novellae" on points of rabbinic law); these short, elliptical pieces, written in concise rabbinic Hebrew, some not more than ten lines long, clarify difficult passages and detect minute distinctions.[39]

Heschel's early Talmudic discussions suggest where his traditional education might lead him. He could teach Talmud, develop into an original interpreter, a halakhic judge, in addition to becoming a Hasidic rebbe responsible to a community. His meticulously argued essays follow ancient procedure by quoting a problem from the Talmud, then assessing commentaries from various classic Jewish sources, followed by a tentative conclusion.[40] They demonstrate Heschel's mastery of Jewish legal method.

We find little or nothing of the mature thinker's fervor and spiritual depth in these purely judicial analyses. His third piece, for example, published in the January–March 1923 issue, examines how sales are legitimized and how Talmudic law deals with property ownership transferred by means of a sale or gift. He compares approaches of biblical law with those of later rabbinic law, citing authorities from many sources. For example, a thirteenth-century sage, Rabbi Aaron Halevi, judged that those "acquisitions derived from the Bible take place irrespective of one's interest in its ownership." Another authority objected to that opinion by citing the Talmud (*B Bava Kama* 66a): "Rabbah said in the name of the Rabbis that [after a period of time] giving up hope of recovering a lost item is sufficient reason to transfer ownership of it [to the finder]. However, we do not know whether this rule is derived from Scriptures or is purely rabbinic." Heschel then cites several other authorities from different centuries, summarizes their arguments, and draws his own conclusions. Most significant, the byline on these first scholarly efforts defines this stage of his identity: "Avraham Yehoshua Heschel, son of my teacher Moshe Mordecai, May His Memory Be Blessed." With the full name of the Apter rebbe as his own, he thus dedicated his first published words to his deceased father.[41]

Heschel's Talmudic labors placed him at a crossroads. In later years, he acknowledged how these exercises might either become "hairsplitting dialectics," "intellectual phantoms," or nourish the imagination. Yet for Heschel, Talmudic study "stimulated ingenuity and independence of mind, encouraging the students to create new out of old ideas. Over and above that, the storm of the soul that was held in check by rigorous discipline, the inner restlessness, found a vent in flight of intellect. Thinking became full of vigor, charged with passion."[42]

Heschel found another voice within a year. His medium became Yiddish literary prose and poetry—and it was indeed "charged with passion."

A Mother's Foresight

Another milestone required by custom helped redirect Heschel's future. When he was fifteen years of age, his uncle the Novominsker rebbe wanted him to be betrothed, as were most Hasidic boys of his station. His uncle proposed a *shiddukh* (a match) with one of his eight daughters, Gittel (1908–1956), considered to be the brightest and the most beautiful.[43] Were Avrumele to marry Gittel Perlow, he would receive kest from her family and reside with them for several years before establishing his own Hasidic court. Warsaw's leading rebbes, as well as venerated elders of the family, supported this excellent prospect.

Although Heschel's mother revered their way of life, she did not want to place her gifted son prematurely under her brother's total authority. Rivka Reizel made a momentous choice. Her strict piety did not prevent her from recognizing Avrumele's need for independence, and she felt compelled to safeguard his opportunities. A complicated drama ensued as both families tried to maintain the best interests of all.

Heschel was asked to visit the Perlow family for a longer period than he usually did. Still excessively observant and perhaps shy, he refused to remain in the same room as his female cousins, whose apartment he visited almost daily. He did not look even once at his prospective partner, which was considered unusual even within sober Hasidic protocol. Was his aloofness calculated? Or was he attracted to the brilliant, vivacious Gittel Perlow, but timid and frightened? Perhaps he was indifferent to the situation?

Eventually his mother rejected the match, explaining that her son was too young to marry. But that was not the end of it. Her brother did not relent and exerted pressure. He enlisted the Tchortkover rebbe, now in Vienna—the son of Dovid Moshe Friedman—to write, urging his sister to reconsider. Avrumele needed to continue religious studies for several years; how could she refuse her brother's protection?

At last Rivka Reizel Heschel ventured a clever, though harsh, solution. She requested an exorbitant dowry in Polish zlotys that amounted to about $10,000

Gittel (Tova) Perlow, Heschel's first cousin. Courtesy of Thena Heshel Kendall.

then (about $250,000 in today's currency). The Novominsker rebbe was shocked. In the meantime, Heschel finally learned about these negotiations. Jokingly he alluded to the betrothal of Rebekkah to Isaac, pointing out that Scripture only says, "Let us ask her" (Genesis 24:57)—and not, "Let us ask him." Nevertheless, Heschel thought, if the engagement were completed he must deliver a worthy Torah lesson for the noble assembly to be convened. He deliberated for weeks and constructed a discourse of two to three hours. "Whatever the outcome," he recalled with a smile, "I was prepared!"[44]

Heschel was not betrothed at age fifteen.[45] Although he gratified his family's hopes with his halakhic articles in *Sha'arey Torah*, his mother understood and loved him as an individual—not only as a Talmud prodigy. His mother demonstrated unusual foresight. Perhaps she already knew that, certified for rabbinic ordination, but living in cosmopolitan Warsaw, Heschel was attracted to other Jewish cultures. As restrictive as his community was, it was not impermeable, and many Hasidim read modern books and periodicals which carried their minds beyond the past. His mother trusted him to open the doors.

A Spiritual Diagnosis

Around this time, Heschel met the energetic and versatile Fishl Schneersohn (1887–1958), a regular visitor to the Novominsker rebbe's Sabbath discourses. Schneersohn was a physician, psychiatrist, writer, acclaimed public speaker, and descendant of the founders of Lubavitch (or Habad) Hasidism. They met around 1923, while Schneersohn was director of a "psychological-hygiene clinic" in Warsaw. Although Heschel performed brilliantly, he remained in conflict within himself, and Schneersohn noticed that he was driven by yearnings that could not be fulfilled by religious study alone. Heschel soon understood that his Hasidic world was too narrow.

The Professor, as the family called Schneersohn, helped the young man discover his direction. It was said that when Jewish mothers brought their boys to Fishl Schneersohn, he usually attributed their emotional difficulties to excessive study. "He should be allowed to play outside more often" was often his advice.[46] Rivka Reizel Heschel probably did not deliver her adolescent rebbe to Schneersohn's clinic. Rather, the "clinic" came to Avrumele.[47] Schneersohn visited his home and helped wean Heschel from the tyrannical Reb Bezalel and from his family's authority.[48] Schneersohn's greatest achievement, as it turned out, was to rescue Heschel from their parochial expectations without alienating him from their love and spiritual ideals.

Fishl Schneersohn, 26 August 1927, Berliner
Bleter, *p. 1.*

Schneersohn ushered Heschel across the threshold, and soon became a model of the writer, modern scholar, religious thinker, and social activist Heschel would become. Schneersohn persuaded Rivka Reizel Heschel to let her son more deliberately add secular studies to religious learning. Her love for Avrumele allowed her to realize that his intellectual needs surpassed the traditional boundaries. And she could trust Professor Doctor Fishl Schneersohn (as his stationery announced), a scientist who kept the *mitzvot* (the regimen of Jewish law). Schneersohn embodied Warsaw's several Jewish cultures, secular as well as religious. Habad (or Lubavitch) Hasidim still recognized him as one of their own, as did other religious groups. Among non-religious Jews, socialists appreciated his support of the Bund-sponsored Yiddish school system in Poland. Zionists admired the lectures he gave in Warsaw in flawless Hebrew.[49]

Fishl Schneersohn was Heschel's first modern mentor, having completed the journey from shtetl to university on which Heschel was embarked. Born into a Hasidic family in Kamenetz-Podolsk (in Polish, Kamieniec Podolski), Schneersohn was raised by his grandfather, the Retshitzer rebbe, learning Talmud and Kabbalah in the manner of Shneour Zalman of Liadi, the first rebbe of Lubavitch.[50] Ordained a rabbi by age sixteen, Schneersohn went on to earn a medical degree from the University of Berlin. In 1920 Schneersohn became professor of "curative-pedagogy" at the University of Kiev. The medical psychiatrist, who specialized in the education of children, was developing a "science of mankind" meant to integrate the physical, intellectual, and religious dimensions of human experience—including mystical insight.

It was probably Fishl Schneersohn who directed Heschel to study in Berlin, where two of his mentor's friends later influenced him significantly. During his student years in Berlin, Schneersohn met Martin Buber, and at the University of Kiev, he began a close collaboration with David Koigen, another evolved child of Lubavitch Hasidic parents and a social philosopher who later settled in Berlin. Schneersohn established himself professionally while traveling, in Warsaw, Berlin, Vilna, and New York.

Schneersohn's writings during this postwar period elucidate Heschel's adolescent struggles. His Yiddish-language novel, *Hayim Gravitzer* (two volumes published in Berlin, 1922–26), depicts a Lubavitcher Hasid caught between a strictly regulated existence and spontaneous creativity. Schneersohn's scientific manifesto (also written in Yiddish), entitled *Der weg tsum mentsh* (The path to humanity, Vilna, 1928), synthesizes psychology, the nascent field of psychoanalysis, art, philosophy, and Hasidic piety.[51]

Heschel at age fourteen or fifteen was afflicted by his era's anxieties, in addition to his personal dramas. Schneersohn may have understood that Heschel's "spheres" of interest were unfulfilled and certainly not integrated. The doctor called such unresolved conflicts "psychical scurvy" (analogous to the somatic disease of vitamin deficiency); this was a "state of neurosis, or disturbance of psychical equilibrium, bought about by a [one-sided] style of life."[52] The young rebbe-to-be was ripe for Schneersohn's integrative therapy (he called it "psycho-expedition"), adapted from Hasidic practice.

They developed a friendship, for Schneersohn's synthesis of psychoanalysis, mysticism, art, and social science could help Heschel direct his religious and intellectual yearnings. Schneersohn conceived of the psychotherapist as a spiritual guide who helped the patient, through systematic self-discipline, to reach the equivalent of what he called "Hasidic ecstasy (*devekut*), an intimate ecstatic concentration."[53] He expected this liberation of consciousness to produce "an immense healing soul-force, from the point of view of both individual and social psychology." In an age when religion lacked authority, artistic creation provided opportunities that the spiritual traditions—such as Hasidism—had in previous eras methodically fostered.

Schneersohn wanted contemporaries to integrate these diverse needs and energies. His description of a psychological breakthrough anticipates Heschel's notion of "radical amazement" as leading to religious insight.[54] Schneersohn wrote: "A man, in such moments, is overwhelmed with a still-glowing shudder, akin to an emotion aroused in artists by spells of inspiration, and one which may descend upon any person in the rare revelatory moments of ecstatic and tragic experiences. At all times, men, in such states, have immediately, in themselves and from themselves, visualized the Absolute, have merged with God, without losing sight of His impenetrability."[55] The mature Heschel did not conflate art and spirit so nimbly, but his early poems evoke a similar "shudder" of God's presence. Heschel's American writings evoke awe before sublime nature and the mysteries of the human mind, leading to divine inspiration.

At least within himself, Heschel realized his freedom. Only a strong initiative by Schneersohn could compete with Reb Bezalel—and with the Novominsker rebbe. Only a firm, independent personality, like Heschel's, could take the leap. Still, Heschel's restlessness—noticed by Fishl Schneersohn, who responded vigorously—remained relatively unexpressed. Heschel was not rebellious in his behavior, although his mind reached far beyond the world of his upbringing.

Something was stirring within him that reached symbolic expression. Decades later, Heschel confided to an American rabbinical student, Marshall Meyer, his youthful fascination with cathedral bells. One night he imagined that he climbed to the top of the highest church in Warsaw to ring the knell.[56] Heschel's vivid image expresses his condition as a Jew in Poland. He could not help but associate Catholicism with anti-Semitism. In the 1960s, during his work as advocate for the Jews at the Second Vatican Council, he reminded a priest that he had "been stoned and beaten up many times by young boys who had just come out of church."[57] Did his attraction to church bells represent his drive to emancipate his people from generations of persecution? Perhaps he was drawn to the sacred architecture, forbidden to him? The Hasidic prayerhouses which sheltered his studies and devotions were plain and unadorned.

Whatever their precise meaning, bells declared Heschel's longing for new instruments. This music, as he suggested years later, orchestrated a fervent dissatisfaction: "For faith is not the clinging to a shrine but an endless pilgrimage of the heart. Audacious longing, burning songs, daring thoughts, an impulse overwhelming the heart, usurping the mind—these are all a drive towards serving Him who rings our hearts like a bell."[58]

4

Expanding the Self Through Literature (1924–1926)

---

*Our flesh is not evil but material for applying the spirit. The carnal
is something to be surpassed rather than annihilated. Heaven and earth
are equally His creation.*

Heschel, *Man Is Not Alone* (1951)

HESCHEL ACHIEVED A SENSE OF CERTAINTY DURING THIS PERIOD—SELF-confidence, but also confidence in the living God. As some of his later writings suggest, the adolescent might even have felt that his talents were a form of divine inspiration (in Hebrew, *ruah ha-kodesh*, Holy Spirit), for spiritual and mental gifts might be considered as originating from God's mind. Although Heschel never admitted it directly, his doctoral dissertation on prophetic consciousness, his biography of Maimonides, and his monographs on the Holy Spirit and revelation imply a personal identification with his subjects.[1]

In lyric Yiddish poetry—Heschel's first truly autobiographical writings—he gradually declared himself to the secular world. Geographically, as well, he began to separate from his ancestral pattern, venturing beyond the house of prayer. He added current periodicals, newspapers, and secular books to his voluminous religious inquiries. His independence was noticed by some acquaintances who saw him reading at a café table for several hours. This apparently profane pursuit upset them, but Heschel claimed to be pondering sacred volumes. To his mind, they were part of the same reality.

In addition to neighborly coercion, Heschel's intellectual curiosity met legislative obstacles. The Warsaw Public Library was off-limits to people who were not dressed in modern European style. This regulation was aimed particularly at Hasidic men garbed in long dark coats and hats in defiance of Polish government standards. The authorities and some emancipated Jews believed that these religious customs demonstrated reactionary or anti-patriotic intentions. To support his pursuit of knowledge, Heschel entered one of Warsaw's literary communities.

Jews Confronting Modernity

Heschel's passage beyond the fence of Torah learning took place during unstable years, the decade following World War I and the Bolshevik revolution. Europe was in crisis, and competition was fierce for his generation's minds and souls. Zionist and socialist organizations possessed effective vehicles of education and propaganda: newspapers, clubs, public gatherings, and schools trained children according to their ideology. Religious leaders feared that these militant groups threatened their very existence. Particularly in Poland, young Jews from traditional families were stirred by the free-thinking brought by refugees from Russia and Lithuania.

Heschel was enflamed, as the title of his final book suggests, with a "passion for truth." His painful dialogues with Reb Bezalel, after all, were strivings toward integrity—religious, ethical, but also intellectual. Would he reject his background? The number of devout youth who abandoned the way of *halakhah*, the rules of religious behavior, was increasing. Even people from Poland's Hasidic communities were beginning to question the strict boundaries between Torah Judaism and the wider world. Many people who remained faithful to rabbinic authority became worldly in their outward appearance. Photographs of Heschel and his brother, Jacob, around sixteen to eighteen years of age show them without beards and earlocks, and his unmarried sisters dressed stylishly.

Social and political instability affected the Heschel and Perlow clans, for they knew the dangers that forced minority peoples to seek their futures elsewhere. Jews were particularly oppressed by miserable economic conditions, and earning a livelihood was made more difficult by anti-Semitic regulations. Although Heschel's uncle Alter Israel Perlow, the Novominsker rebbe, opposed modernity, he also lived pragmatically within his strict boundaries. Emulating the Agudat Israel party's tactics of compromise in the Polish Parliament, he eschewed the confrontational attitude favored by the Bund and Zionists.[2]

Most of Heschel's relatives remained within the fold while becoming aware of other forms of Jewish expression. The Novominsker rebbe's support of the anti-modern, anti-Zionist Agudah did not prevent his children from exploring worldly thought and taking intense interest in events in Palestine. They received secular as well as religious education, reading newspapers and periodicals such as *ha-Tekufa*, the modern Hebrew literary journal. In Warsaw and especially in Vienna, some wives of rebbes attended concerts and visited museums, while some of the daughters—of the Novominsker rebbe as well—attended Gymnasium after being tutored by religious scholars. The Novominsker rebbe's wife even engaged a known Zionist, Yakov Kaufmann, to teach her daughters Hebrew,[3] while all the sons, more narrowly supervised, prepared for rabbinical ordination.[4]

To escape grim conditions, some Perlow family members emigrated. The first to leave was Heschel's uncle, Rabbi Yehuda Aryeh Leib Perlow, one of his mother's brothers.[5] Around 1924 he and his family arrived in the United States and settled in the Williamsburg section of Brooklyn.[6] Some two years later, Heschel's first cousin Rabbi Nahum Mordecai Perlow (1896–1976), a son of Alter Israel, the Novominsker rebbe, settled in the Borough Park section of Brooklyn.[7] (Heschel's uncle and cousin were both, in turn, known as the Novominsker rebbe of New York.) These traditional communities overseas could receive Heschel and other relatives, should they wish to leave Poland.

Heschel's brother, Jacob, four years older, dreamed of becoming a religious *halutz* (pioneer) in Palestine.[8] He was a practical man who enjoyed working

Abraham Joshua Heschel, Warsaw, about the age of seventeen. Courtesy of Yitzhak Meir Twersky and Thena Heshel Kendall.

Jacob Heshel, Warsaw, about the age of eighteen. Courtesy of Thena Heshel Kendall.

with his hands, and he yearned to be close to the land. Around 1923 he received rabbinic ordination from the Mesivta Yeshiva and taught in a Talmud Torah (Jewish school) in Warsaw. By 1926, he moved to Vienna, joining his sister Sarah's community, the Kopitzhinitzer rebbe and the Friedmans from Sadagora and Tchortkov.[9] (Jacob reinforced family ties in 1931 by marrying Sarah, a daughter of Rabbi Nahum Mordecai Friedman, their cousin the Tchortkover rebbe; they remained in Vienna until their emigration to London in 1939.)

Only one child apparently rebelled, at least from the family's perspective— Gittel Perlow, Heschel's first cousin and almost fiancée. Around 1925 she left Warsaw for Palestine and became involved with the socialist labor Zionist movement. Soon after, she went to Belgium around 1926 to study, and a year later she settled in Paris.

In 1924, at age seventeen, Heschel was in no position to emigrate, nor were there pressing reasons to do so. By now he was reading much that was available

Top left: *Heschel's sister Devorah Miriam, who married Aryeh Leib Dermer, of Vienna. Courtesy of Yitzhak Meir Twersky and Thena Heshel Kendall.*
Top right: *Heschel's sister Gittel, Warsaw. Courtesy of Yitzhak Meir Twersky and Thena Heshel Kendall.*
Heschel's sister Esther Sima. Courtesy of Thena Heshel Kendall.

in Yiddish and modern Hebrew—which was practically everything, as newspapers published serialized novels, critical essays, and translations, as well as discussions of national and world events. Two authors, in particular, exemplified Jews who transformed the strict Hasidism of their childhood and youth into cosmopolitan, critical creativity.

The works of the writer, philosopher, and mystic Hillel Zeitlin bridged Hasidic spirituality and the search for contemporary meaning. Heschel may have known Zeitlin, the most conspicuous visitor to his uncle's Sabbath discourses.[10] Zeitlin arrived at twilight, almost surreptitiously, with his flowing black hair and reddish beard, wearing a cape and wide-brimmed hat. The Perlow children noticed that he took particular interest in the rebbe's comments on Kabbalah and the Zohar, cherishing the distinctive *nigunim,* wordless melodies giving tone to the devotions. After listening intently to the speech, Zeitlin slipped out of the room and disappeared.

Hillel Zeitlin's transformation was a prototype for Heschel's own journey. Born in the Belorussian town of Korma, Zeitlin was educated in Habad Hasidism (like Fishl Schneersohn), combining fervor, Talmudic rationalism, and Kabbalah. Zeitlin was another child prodigy who mastered the classic Jewish texts, particularly works by Maimonides and Judah Halevi as well as the Zohar and teachings of Hasidic masters. He assimilated world culture by means of Hebrew translations of Western literature and philosophy, fostered by the Haskalah. He learned Russian and German, discovered Hegel, Schopenhauer, Nietzsche, among others—and left the traditional Jewish way.

But Zeitlin, considered to be a mystic kindled by ecstatic experiences of the Godhead, returned to his roots after the devastating 1903 pogroms in Kishinev, which were described in Bialik's famous poem "City of Slaughter." To teach the Jewish spirit to outsiders, Zeitlin published essays in Yiddish newspapers, featuring Hasidic ideas and thinkers such as Rabbi Nahman of Bratslav. His Yiddish-language introduction, *Der alef-beys funem yudentum* (ABC of Judaism, 1922), bolstered resistance to assimilation and religious indifference.

At the time Heschel probably met him, Zeitlin was translating the Zohar from the original Aramaic dialect into Hebrew. (Later, Heschel, who was highly critical of modern studies of Kabbalah and Hasidism, recommended Zeitlin's introduction to the Zohar.) Everyone in Warsaw recognized Hillel Zeitlin, who since 1908 presided over his own Tish at 60 Shliska Street. Heschel knew Zeitlin's son Aaron, himself a poet and writer, and they renewed their friendship after World War II.[11]

Young Heschel would have found Hillel Zeitlin's many articles in the Warsaw Yiddish daily, *Haynt,* and *Der Moment* compatible with his values, for Zeitlin developed an approach to mystical faith that respected contemporary perplexities. He opposed Haim Nahman Bialik, the major Hebrew poet of the day (who wrote in Yiddish as well), by defending the importance of metaphysical questions. Zeitlin's intuitions were congruent with Fishl Schneersohn's writings on art and mystical insight. According to Zeitlin, the modern person needs to seek "a revealed and hidden secret which, if we gain even the slightest awareness of its existence, fills us with awe and amazement, with an unendurable shudder."[12] Heschel's "depth theology" of wonder refines this universal religiosity.

Of immediate importance, Zeitlin deplored what he viewed as the decadence of present-day Hasidism. True religion must nurture inwardness, deep spiritual emotion, he believed: "The love of God, Torah and Israel no longer prevail. Hasidism has become, for some, merely an external phenomenon; they study without fervor, pray without pathos, pursue honor and wealth in no less measure, and in some instances, in a far greater degree, than other Jews . . . ; they confine Hasidism to superficialities of dress and posture; they confuse fanaticism and piety."[13] Decades later, Heschel's *Passion for Truth* echoed Zeitlin's demands: "The Kotzker, a soul living in dissent, was all protest against the trivialization and externalization of Judaism. Rejecting half-truths, mediocrity, compromise, he challenged even the Lord."[14]

Another of Heschel's modern Jewish authors was Micha Josef Berdyczewski, who had also been energized by the conflict between secular thought and his ancestral faith.[15] Berdyczewski, a descendant of Hasidic rabbis, was born in Medzibozh, like Heschel's father and grandfather. His early education was traditional, but he combined religion and a wide knowledge of Western culture. Berdyczewski collected hundreds of popular tales and wrote stories in Hebrew, Yiddish, and German.[16] He applied Nietzsche's critical task of "transvaluing" European intellectual history to Judaism, making the ancient tradition relevant to doubters and the anguished.

Heschel may have been stirred by the controversial novel of Joseph Opatoshu, *In Poilishe velder* (In Polish woods), published in 1921.[17] This immensely popular novel castigated the decadence of Hasidism. It depicted the Kotzker rebbe as depressed and enraged, a man who encouraged secular learning and even denied the existence of God. The book was banned by the Hasidim, and the author was excommunicated.

Heschel's eclectic adolescent reading must have been as inspiring—and unsystematic—as the paths followed by Zeitlin, Berdyczewski, and a multitude of other Eastern European shtetl Jews impassioned with world culture. While Heschel was outwardly loyal to his family's expectations, his mind was seething with contradictions.

Crossing the Threshold

A need for self-expression drew Heschel to the secular Yiddish-speaking community embraced by emancipated but still observant Jews like Fishl Schneersohn and Hillel Zeitlin. The center of modern Jewish culture was within walking distance. Leaving his home on Muranowska Street, instead of turning left off Nalewki Street to reach his uncle's court on Franciszkanska, he continued down Nalewki to the headquarters of the Yiddish Writers and Journalists Association (later to become the PEN club) at 13 Tlomackie Street. This cosmopolitan meeting place enlarged his circle of acquaintances and his knowledge of the world.

Heschel already possessed the language of the people who congregated there. These men and women used Yiddish—the daily idiom of the majority of Jews in Poland, Lithuania, and Russia—to create a new literature and integrate *Yiddishkayt* (Jewishness) with European civilization. In 1923, the year of Heschel's final Talmudic publications, Warsaw's Yiddish Writers and Journalists Association had published the first major anthology of Yiddish literature since the war, entitled *Varshaver Almanach*.[18]

Two years later, Heschel took a decisive step. A recently established Yiddish weekly, *Literarishe Bleter* (Literary pages: Illustrated weekly of literature, theater, and art), announced that Melekh Ravitch (1893–1976), its literary editor, was preparing another collection. Ravitch, who was also secretary of the Yiddish Writers Association, welcomed manuscripts at their Tlomackie Street headquarters.[19]

Ravitch's memoirs provide the earliest portrait—verbal or otherwise—of Abraham Joshua Heschel standing, literally, at the threshold of modernity. Dressed in his Hasidic garb of Ruzhin, Heschel crossed town to present several manuscripts to the editor, himself an experimental poet and writer.

The room was calm and quiet, and Ravitch could hear the muffled voices of the people behind the wall. The well-organized administrator was absorbed in the association's budget when he sensed a strange presence.

> Suddenly I begin to think that someone has entered the room and is looking at me. I pay no attention. Five minutes pass. There is still someone in the room. I raise my eyes and for a moment I am startled. In a corner by the green door stands a tall and slender young lad, in Warsaw Hasidic attire. A long, black garment, almost to the ground, scarcely showing his boots, a round hat on his head with a small, pinched peak. A severe face, though he looks at me very gently and guiltily, he also looks gruff. His eyes are black, deep, large; his skin brownish, with the first, young sprouts of a dark beard. His lips are

*Melekh Ravitch, 1922, Warsaw. Courtesy of YIVO
Institute for Jewish Research, New York.*

full, passionate, deep red. Somewhat of a twitch and a thin grimace around
the mouth, something like a whimsical reproach. His face is not too strongly
Jewish, not so classically Semitic—but the twitch immediately makes him
a Jew, a Hasid, even like a rabbi. The young man knows that I am preparing
a literary almanac—he has brought some "songs."

I remember. In an instant, it flashed through my mind: a new Sholem
Asch.[20]

Heschel's emotional turmoil—his gentleness, reticence, anger—revived in
Melekh Ravitch's memory several well-known personal and cultural struggles.
Other young Hasidic men had embarked upon a literary career. Heschel called
to mind Sholem Asch, the Yiddish novelist and playwright who had been inspired by I. L. Peretz, and who, it was also said, appeared in Hasidic garb in an
editorial office. Another liberated scion of Lubavitch, Zalman Schneour, became
a poet and novelist.

Heschel's uneasy look both revealed and concealed his inner conflicts. The
worldly editor and writer was especially struck by the neophyte's tenseness. After all, Heschel was at the mercy of this tall, heavy—and influential—man in

his neatly arranged office. Perhaps Ravitch's memory of the young Hasid's "full, passionate" lips, contrasting with his archaic attire, was a retrospective justification of the first poem of Heschel's he selected for publication.

Ravitch was favorably impressed and took some prose and several poems. Heschel's first poem was published late in 1926 in Ravitch's new anthology, entitled *Varshaver Shriftn* (Warsaw writings), which was distributed in installments. Three years after his début in *Sha'arey Torah,* Heschel decided to enter the modern world for good. His 1922 Talmudic analysis dedicated to his deceased father, "My Teacher," became his farewell to his family's expectations.

Heschel's Written Unconscious

The undisguised individual emerged in Heschel's literary works. Heschel's first known original writing soon appeared, a short prose piece in Yiddish entitled *Der zaddik fun freyd* (The zaddik of joy). Probably selected from the manuscripts submitted to Ravitch, it was published in the 21 May 1925 issue of the Warsaw weekly *Illustrirte Vokh.*[21] The author, now calling himself Avruhum Heschel, described an unnamed man, an ailing "zaddik" who conducts an unusual Tish.

This strange story of an anonymous sage may reflect Heschel's enthrallment with the Tish of his uncle, the Novominsker rebbe, in Warsaw, as he sat by his side. Or it might express his intense feelings about his father's death late in 1916. Here is the story: The zaddik lay in bed dying; instead of elaborating a *dvar Torah* (a homily on a biblical text), he spoke only a word or two, "enflamed, all his limbs shook, frightening everyone, and his words fell like spears into their hearts." Heschel noted, especially, that the man's face threw fear into everyone. He ordered his young disciples to dance joyously around his bed. He died and was buried on Friday before the Sabbath. As the young men danced around his grave, singing nigunim, a fiery beam emerged. In both instances, their wretched dancing ironically highlights the dying master's unspoken depression and their own unendurable mourning.

Heschel's first story is rich in ambiguities. Its paradoxical "joy" is sophisticated and deceptive, countering the story's title, which suggests a more conventional Hasidic celebration. Heschel confronts the death of a beloved sage with holy fear and horror, celebrating life in the face of sadness and loss. These contradictions are in fact intrinsic to Hasidic spirituality. Rabbi Nahman of Bratslav, the rebbe of Kotzk, and other Hasidic masters were known to have experienced severe depression or melancholy.[22] Toward the end of his life, in *A Passion for Truth,* Heschel insisted that his own spirit included both "fervor and horror, awe and consternation."[23]

Another dimension of Heschel's sensibility was unveiled about a year later, in a poem that expresses yearning for sensual love. (It was among the manuscripts submitted to Melekh Ravitch in 1925, when he was seventeen years old.) The issue of *Varshaver Shriftn* containing Heschel's piece repeats the author's modern name in Yiddish script: Avruhum Heschel. Heschel's untitled *lid* (in Yiddish, song or poem) is completely secular. As the author distances himself from ascetic piety, its three stanzas play the full range from delicate longing to intense desire to shyness and inhibition.

The poem is a bit stiff, constructed like a syllogism—a thesis and antithesis (and perhaps synthesis) of fervor and restraint. He begins by evoking a woman's "silken skin," an almost chaste, delicate image soon challenged surprisingly by the eroticism of stanza two: the woman's teeth "plow" the man's aroused ("moist") lips. Her dark "voluptuous face" in that passage also reinforces the contrast with her silvery brightness in the first stanza, which suggests Sabbath purity. Now she becomes aggressive. In the third and final stanza, however, the poet's own reticence takes over, as he concludes:

> So eyes can no longer kiss
> With alert glances,
> Hearts can only tremble, tremble
> And not be joyful.[24]

This poem was Heschel's passport to the world of modern men and modern women, effectively communicating his (unrealized) passions as much as his modesty. At the end, the repeated words emphasize inhibition, and the poem concludes by attempting to reconcile enjoyment (*freyen*) and fright: "So eyes can no longer kiss"—"Hearts can only tremble, tremble."

Yet this is a healthy poem celebrating the ambiguous energies of secular love. Even more significant than his "erotic" subject matter (surprising or not in an aristocratic Hasid drawn to asceticism) is the fact that Heschel expressed intimate yearnings without coyness. Restrained but artistically honest, his poem expresses a free sensibility struggling toward fulfillment.

The poet's instinctive anxiety in the face of a woman's otherness also symbolizes Heschel's ambivalence about new ideas and his thirst for experience. Its somewhat rigid form suggests self-discipline: new wine—and potentially volcanic passion—in an old bottle. Discontent and ardent craving churned beneath the decorum of his symmetrical verse.

Leaving Warsaw

*Religion becomes sinful when it begins to advocate the segregation of
God, to forget that the true sanctuary has no walls. . . . It has often done
more . . . to petrify the sacred than to sanctify the secular.*
Heschel, *God in Search of Man* (1955)

Heschel's initiative in publishing his poetry uncovered his personal ambitions, and literature became his vehicle of self-expression. Within two years the Yiddish Writers Association on Tlomackie Street began to provide financial as well as emotional and professional support. Heschel now envisaged a university education, probably urged upon him by Fishl Schneersohn, who also belonged to that international community. This shift was massive, for all of Heschel's proficiency in Torah, Talmud, Midrash, Zohar, and Hasidic texts still did not qualify him for admission to a university in Poland or Germany.

Candidates were required to earn a diploma from a government-certified Gymnasium, capped if possible by the *Abitur* examination, which included Latin and modern languages (especially Polish and German), history, literature, and mathematics. The limited nonreligious program at the Mesivta Yeshiva would not suffice. Heschel had to find a secular school and apply his formidable learning skills and memory in order to acquire this basic humanistic and scientific knowledge.

In Warsaw, there were Hebrew-language Zionist Tarbut schools that trained students for emigration to Palestine. More appropriate for Heschel were the Yiddish-language schools unified under the Central Yiddish School Organization (CYSHO), a non-Zionist movement promoting Yiddish-language culture around the world. But Heschel did not want to make this decisive transition under the eyes of his family; it would embarrass them. And also to avoid the labyrinth of Jewish ideologies in Warsaw, he left the city of his birth, childhood, and adolescence—and his Hasidic community—for Vilna.

At first, it was difficult to obtain the family's support. With the help of Fishl Schneersohn and other Yiddish writers, Heschel hired tutors to teach him Polish and Latin. (Jews living in villages or self-sufficient neighborhoods often disregarded the language and culture of the majority population.) He trained for higher education at home, at first secretly.[25] To disguise his subject matter from

68

his mother, Heschel chanted his Polish declensions and other books in a distant room, as if he were studying Talmud. Later he was tutored in German, which he did not know at all.

Hasidic Warsaw was not as restrictive as many ultra-Orthodox communities today. His family feared for his purity but did not oppose his craving for knowledge. After all, his mother, admiring his unusual gifts, insulated him from Ger Hasidism. She rejected her brother's offer of his daughter Gittel as a bride for Avrumele, and she let Fishl Schneersohn influence her son's worldly education.

Yet, when Heschel first told his mother of his plans to leave for Vilna, another thriving center of secular Jewish political and literary movements, Rivka Reizel panicked. She appreciated the imperatives of his mind, but feared the influences of assimilation and disbelief. She alerted her brother the Novominsker rebbe in Warsaw and relatives in Vienna. The elders took action. It is said that the Tchortkover rebbe, Rabbi Israel Friedman, summoned Heschel to Vienna for a meeting.[26] A Hasidic prince should not enter a purely secular institution such as he was planning to attend. They tried to convince him to extend his religious studies in Warsaw, but he would not be persuaded.

Heschel's aspirations were respected, with some misgivings. The family proudly remembered how he once dropped a history book on the floor, gently picked it up, and touched it with his lips, as an observant Jew kisses a prayerbook or another sacred text which fell. His mother had little money to support his lessons, but she allowed others—even his married sister in Vienna, Devorah Miriam Dermer—to contribute.

Perhaps Heschel assured his family that he would study Talmud with Vilna rabbinic authorities. After all, Vilna was famed for sacred learning and for its renowned standard editions of classical religious texts. There were almost countless houses of study and several famous yeshivas where he could advance his knowledge of Torah.

Hasidic Radicalism

One incident during his incipient secular studies brought Heschel an extraordinary insight into Hasidic spirituality.[27] Heschel, who remained always a meticulously observant Jew, concealed this story for years, speaking of it confidentially, to our knowledge, only with Samuel Dresner, in the late 1940s a student at the Jewish Theological Seminary in New York. "Consider the paradox," Heschel told him. "This event represents the true greatness of Hasidism, yet I cannot tell it. People would not understand."

In Warsaw, Heschel ran out of money, forcing him to stop Latin and Polish language lessons. His friend Yitzhak Meir Levin, a merchant who prayed every Sabbath at his father's shtiebl and a follower of Kotzk Hasidism, noticed that Heschel was despondent. One late Friday afternoon, Levin arrived before the Minha (afternoon) service to greet the Sabbath. Heschel wanted to talk with him. But Levin was preoccupied, fortifying his emotions for the holy day's arrival. He told the young man, "Der gehenem brennt in mir" (hellfire is burning within me), meaning that he was in the throes of suppressing his inner demons to welcome the bliss of Heaven. Conversation was not possible.

They did speak after the evening service, but Heschel refused to explain why he was upset. "*Atzvut* (sadness) on Shabbes?" asked Levin. Knowing him well, Levin guessed that lack of money had compelled Heschel to cancel his lessons and had made him depressed. So Levin told him about a book sure to interest him, a new edition of sayings by Rabbi Pinhas of Koretz, Heschel's ancestor and a friend of the Baal Shem Tov. The young man was delighted.

The next morning Heschel was sitting in his father's chair before the Shaharit (morning) service and in came Levin with the holy book. (There was an *eruv* in Warsaw, an artificial enclosure allowing observant Jews to carry objects on the Sabbath.) Levin handed it to Heschel, who opened it with anticipation. To his horror, he saw that it contained money, forbidden to touch on the Sabbath. He dropped the book at once. Levin then explained, countering the boy's astonishment with a story from Kotzk showing that one may violate a lesser rule pertaining to the Sabbath to remove depression—the most perilous sin according to Hasidism.

This was a shocking but precarious lesson, profoundly helpful to Heschel in his struggle for spiritual integrity. Heschel knew many Hasidic sources for Levin's bold attempt to remove his sadness on the Sabbath. A positive passion— even one that violates a moral taboo—can be redirected by an act of will. The Baal Shem Tov recognized that even improper thoughts can be sublimated heavenward. Thinking of a woman's beauty during prayer, for example, can be transformed into an affirmation of divine beauty—but this was not possible for *atzvut*. Sadness contained no holy spark.[28] The young Hasid's Sabbath melancholy put him at great spiritual risk.

Heschel revealed this story years later for a sacred purpose: his fervent midnight conversation with an American rabbinical student illustrated the competition, within Judaism, between devotion to God and the externals of Jewish law. Those who concentrated only on rules, ignoring inwardness, he later called "religious behaviorists."[29] Yitzhak Levin's act of generosity taught Heschel the necessity, in certain crises, of spiritual audacity, without which, Heschel asserted, Judaism could not survive in the modern world. This story suggests that Heschel was distressed with the rigidity of Jewish Orthodoxy during his adolescence. Yitzhak Levin's Kotzk radicalism helped Heschel to remain observant.[30] It may also explain his choice of a secular school in Vilna and a Liberal Jewish academy in Berlin; both institutions respected his loyalty to Jewish law, but on his terms.

Heschel acknowledged Yitzhak Levin's personal importance from the beginning to the end. In 1933, after settling in Berlin, Heschel dedicated to him a Yiddish poem, "Help!" written some years before. In 1972, Heschel included Levin's name in the dedication to his final book, on the Kotzker rebbe, also written in Yiddish.[31] Kotzk Hasidism saved Judaism for Heschel, preserving his Sabbath joy, reminding him that rules are made in order to hallow the person and God.[32]

Paradoxes of Jewish Modernity

Still, Heschel's departure for Vilna required a family decision. An edifying story is told about the departure of their Hasidic prince.[33] After much discussion, the Novominsker rebbe released him: "You can go, but *only* you." Following the custom that one should bless a departing person with a word of Torah, an old Hasid was said to have quoted the Mishnah (Avot 5:8), which cites as "one of the ten miracles of the Temple in Jerusalem" that, no matter what the provocation, "the holy flesh [of the sacrifice] did not ever become polluted." Then he told Heschel how his ancestor Barukh of Medzibozh interpreted the passage: "One of the most wondrous miracles was, indeed, *Lo hisriah besar kodesh mei-olam*, that is, 'the holy flesh'—the people Israel—'did not become polluted, *mei-olam*, from the world.'"

"Avrumele," the old man concluded, taking him by the shoulders, "remember the word of Rabbi Barukh, *Lo hisriah besar kodesh mei-olam*. You, you are holy flesh, do not become polluted from the world!" Whatever path he chose to pursue, Abraham Joshua Heschel guarded the "holy flesh" of his dynasty.

Heschel left Warsaw on a Saturday night after the close of Sabbath. Fishl Schneersohn gave the young man his coat, for he possessed practically nothing. Heschel exchanged his velvet Sabbath cap for an ordinary weekday cap and, accompanied by his cousin Aaron Perlow, a son of the Novominsker rebbe, he boarded the train to Vilna.

This tale has a ring of truth—and an aura of wishful thinking. Perhaps the Novominsker rebbe's insistent "only you" expressed anxiety that their future Levi Yitzhak might not return from the secular city, as they still hoped, to save

Hasidism for their generation.[34] His rebellious daughter Gittel had just left for Palestine. In reminding Heschel of his spiritual responsibility, his family could not anticipate his new manner of understanding Jewishness. Nor could he.

Each cousin formed a vastly different modern Jewish life without relinquishing the spirit of their childhood. Heschel's cousin and almost fiancée Gittel Perlow (who now took the Hebrew form of her name, Tova) achieved her synthesis in the secular world. By 1926, Gittel went from Palestine, where she had been involved with the socialist labor Zionist movement, to Belgium, where she studied pedagogy at the University of Brussels. Reaching Paris in 1927, she completed a doctoral dissertation at the Sorbonne in 1930. Her subject: Jewish education in the Talmudic period, documented with historical analyses of original texts.[35] Paradoxically, this Hasidic daughter had been tutored to become a Jewish historian. When she published her thesis as a book, Gittel dedicated it to her father and mother. From her perspective, she remained loyal.

Yet, according to some reports, Tova Perlow broke with Judaism. She married a Gentile, who became a secretary to Maurice Thorez, head of the French Communist Party. Her first marriage ended in divorce, and her second husband, Paul Gaston Monthéard, a wealthy industrialist, may have been converted to Judaism by her brother-in-law, Rabbi Noson Dovid Rabinowicz, the Biala rebbe of London, husband of Tova's eldest sister.[36] (Others deny that he ever converted.) Her son married a Gentile woman, but her daughter married a Moroccan Jewish *shohet* (ritual slaughterer) and lived in an Orthodox community in Israel.

Heschel also left home but stayed in touch with his family, regularly making the eight-hour train ride between Vilna and the city of his birth. Upon arrival in Warsaw he immediately visited the Novominsker rebbe; they embraced and sat for hours in intense conversation. Heschel remained loyal to both worlds. To use Fishl Schneersohn's image, Heschel absorbed another sphere of life—this time, Yiddish culture—into his already complex identity. Avrum Yehoshua, as his companions knew him, effected his transition into the modern world on a round-trip ticket.[37]

Part Two

Vilna: The Jerusalem of Lithuania

Other Jewish communities too were rich in creative personalities—rabbis,
heads of yeshivas, scholars, authors, artists, cantors, preachers—and in
philanthropic, political and cultural institutions, yeshivas and modern
schools. But all of these combined—such color, such diversity of colors,
such scope—in this respect Vilna ranks above all other communities.
Heschel, *Jerusalem of Lithuania* (1974)

HESCHEL MADE A QUANTUM LEAP FROM HASIDIC WARSAW TO COSMOPOLITAN Europe as he entered the seven-year-old Mathematics-Natural Science Gymnasium (in Polish, Matematyczno-Przyrodnicze Gymnazjum; diplomas were printed in both Yiddish and Polish), known as the Real-Gymnasium of Vilna. Founded in 1918 by the Vilna Jewish Central Education Committee (TsBK), the Real-Gymnasium offered the entire Polish curriculum. Although the sciences were emphasized (hence the German term *Real*, concrete reality), its humanities classes were extraordinary. It was especially distinguished by the literature courses given by Yiddish poets and university-trained professors.

In Vilna, Heschel observed Europe's political turmoil, its history still in the making. Located over eight hundred miles northeast of Warsaw, Vilna was the five-hundred-year-old capital of Lithuania, known in Lithuanian as Vilnius, in Polish as Wilno, and in Yiddish as Vilne. After the First World War, Bolsheviks dominated the city; then for a short time the Lithuanians ruled. The Poles regained authority in October 1920. In May 1922 Vilna was incorporated into Poland, when, under Jozef Pilsudski, Poland became a republic.

But Vilna remained a Jewish city; according to the 1921 census, its 46,559 Jews comprised 36.1 percent of the total population. It was said that Vilna, transformed by so many invasions, had been Russian, then German, then Lithuanian, and then Polish. But it always remained Jewish. Known as the "Jerusalem of Lithuania," Vilna was the most Jewish city in the new Republic of Poland.

All aspects of Jewishness coexisted in that small space. By the seventeenth century, Vilna consolidated its reputation for sacred learning, particularly Talmudic studies. During the eighteenth century, the city was dominated by the genius and personality of Elijah ben Solomon Zalman, the "Vilna Gaon." His extraordinary mind embraced scientific subjects in addition to all holy texts; he was the century's leading authority on Talmud and knew the mystical books of Kabbalah. Yet he and his followers, the *mitnagdim* (opponents), clashed fiercely with the Hasidic movement then emerging in Poland and the Ukraine.

Jewish secularism also flourished there. Vilna was the birthplace of the Jewish socialist labor movement (the Bund) in 1897. In 1925, the year of Heschel's arrival, the Yidisher Visnshaftlekher Institut (Jewish scientific institute; YIVO) was founded and began to document Yiddish-speaking Eastern European Jewry. Young Zionists were active in Vilna, and Heschel relished, as well, the Hebrew-speaking modern intellectuals known as *maskilim*, "caustic" spirits, as he wrote, so different from the devout scholars of his childhood and youth.

Above all, he shared the mother tongue of these pioneers, for the Vilna Real-Gymnasium was the first school of its kind to teach all subjects in Yiddish. It was a thoroughly progressive institution in its pedagogy and coeducational, academically rigorous, and politically to the left. Students were well prepared to enter universities in Poland, Germany, France, or Belgium—Heschel's larger goal.

5

A Rebbe Among Revolutionaries (1925–1927)

The zeal of the pious Jews was transferred to their emancipated sons and grandsons. The fervor and yearning of the Hasidim, the ascetic obstinacy of the Kabbalists, the inexorable logic of the Talmudists, were reincarnated in the supporters of modern Jewish movements.

Heschel, *The Earth Is the Lord's* (1950)

BY THE TIME HESCHEL REACHED VILNA AT AGE EIGHTEEN, HE LOOKED LIKE A European student. He was clean shaven, without earlocks. His facial hair was sparse, so he did not have to eliminate a beard. In Vilna, he continued writing poetry while preparing himself for the university. All the while, people could sense the Hasidic dignity of his childhood and youth in his decorous, somewhat reserved demeanor. Heschel's educational transition did not break with the past. His ability to communicate with others, not his own identity, was the trouble.

The mails sustained Heschel's contact with his family, and periodically he returned to Warsaw and Vienna. While visiting his sister Sarah in Vienna, Heschel shared a room with her son, Israel Heschel (1911–1994), who told his young uncle about some difficulties with his Talmud studies.[1] Israel was worried, because, as the Kopitzhinitzer rebbe's eldest son, he was expected to lead the clan after his father's death. Israel was overly sensitive, withdrawn, and not quickly at ease with people—nor was he an exceptional student. Israel thought that the right study partner (*haver*) would solve his problem.

Heschel recognized his nephew's distress to be a crisis of self-confidence. "Don't worry," he told Israel. "Even if you don't have a *haver*, you can still learn Talmud. For a *haver* can give as much trouble as help. Your true *haver* is God, the *Rebono shel olam* (Master of the Universe), and He is constantly at your side. If you really trust Him and study Talmud night and day with all your energy, you will receive *siyata dishmaya* (heavenly assistance), and learning will follow. Above all, don't waste time. Stop going to meetings, to weddings, and other such events which Hasidim enjoy. Just devote yourself to study."

Self-discipline was the answer, and Heschel did what he could to reinforce Israel's efforts. After returning to Vilna, Heschel mailed Israel a postcard every week. In each one he asked how much Talmud he had learned that week and whether he had studied the Torah portion of the week with Rashi, the classic medieval commentator. Each note closed with the admonition: "Don't waste time." This support, according to Israel, deeply influenced his life and enabled him to persevere with his education.

Portrait of Heschel in Vilna

Heschel rented a cheap room on Poplawes Street at the home of a simple, very devout old Jewish man. (Students of the Real-Gymnasium either lived at home or boarded in town.) Far from the city center, this area was sparsely populated by poverty-stricken Jews.[2] Heschel's room contained only a drab iron bed. Acquaintances could not understand why he did not locate a better space or even

Abraham Joshua Heschel, Warsaw, about the age of seventeen. Courtesy of Yitzhak Meir Twersky and Thena Heshel Kendall.

a small apartment, for modest lodgings could easily be found in Vilna for about 20–25 zlotys. Living in the midst of Jewish indigence—and almost destitute himself—Heschel identified with the suffering and hopes of the dispossessed.

In Vilna, Heschel, who had known poverty in Warsaw, lived among secular Jews who supported revolution. His street led into town toward the west; toward the east, beyond the Poplawes district, was the Belmont Forest, a favorite recreation and walking spot. Parallel to Poplawes Street was Subocz, where poor Jews also lived. That road led directly to the Real-Gymnasium. Heschel repeatedly walked through this large expanse of subsidized housing, the center of Bund activity. In that area, socialists, some communists, and other leftist groups had celebrations and meetings.

Heschel's reading opportunities were now practically limitless. In town, next to the Great Synagogue, Jewish students frequented the Strashun Library, under the benevolent care of the modest but learned librarian, Heykhel Lunsky. There Heschel could find all the Jewish classic texts, rare editions, and manuscripts— as well as current Yiddish literature, Hebrew and Yiddish translations of European masterpieces, and Jewish newspapers and periodicals from Europe and around the world.[3] The public library of Vilna was also well stocked with German books.

Religious observance was, of course, no problem. For group services, near the Strashun Library, there were about thirty small places of worship in and around the synagogue courtyard, each belonging to a different trade, including a Hasidic shtiebl.

A Secular Jewish Utopia

The Vilna Real-Gymnasium, where Heschel was acquiring western European knowledge and becoming acquainted with avant-garde politics and literature, was a vibrant community whose humanistic values were compatible with his sacred commitments.[4] The school itself was located in a large, attractive building in the Jewish district of Vilna, at 6 Rudnitski Street, at the end of a row of houses and a trading market. Student activities were divided between the academic curriculum and extracurricular clubs. The coeducational school provided a completely nonreligious Jewish environment, rich in social and intellectual opportunities.

It was probably Fishl Schneersohn, himself active in pedagogical reform, who judged that a secular, Yiddish-language Gymnasium would best prepare Heschel for the University of Berlin. Schools within the progressive Central Yiddish

School Organization system—inspired by the principles of Johann Heinrich Pestalozzi and Maria Montessori, among others—were the most compatible with Heschel's skills and values. CYSHO had been established in 1921 in Warsaw as an umbrella for several Yiddish-language groups, and its ideals were reform-minded and democratic. Instead of learning from professorial-style lectures, students and teachers worked together, developing cooperative relationships both inside and outside the classroom. A Yiddish-speaking school was Heschel's best choice for deeper reasons as well. He knew Yiddish and biblical and rabbinic Hebrew thoroughly and was proficient in modern Hebrew literature. Yet Yiddish remained the idiom of home, friendships, and his inner life. Yiddish was his language of cultural emancipation and his bridge to modernity.

Yiddish was the exclusive medium of communication, even on restroom door signs. All classes of its eight grades geared to university preparation, which covered the complete Polish curriculum, were given in Yiddish: courses on mathematics, biology, chemistry, physics, geography, Polish and Jewish history, world history, Yiddish, German, Polish, Hebrew, Bible, and other subjects. High quality in both secular and Judaic subjects was maintained, and classes at all levels were taught by specialists.

In Vilna, Heschel probably specialized in language and literature rather than in the sciences. Classes on political economy, Jewish history, philosophy, or pedagogical theory would also be useful to him. Before leaving Warsaw he had been tutored in Polish and in German; in Vilna he probably concentrated on Yiddish and German literature, as he needed to perfect his knowledge of German culture—while Yiddish was his true love. His transition from Hasidic Warsaw to modern Europe was complete.

Yet, despite its standard of excellence (and because of it), the Real-Gymnasium suffered under the Polish government's anti-Semitism. Although the Treaty of Versailles protected national minority rights and Poland supported Jewish educational systems among others, graduates were not allowed to enter Polish universities. Even those who passed the Abitur examination were excluded because the courses were given in Yiddish, not Polish.[5]

As in Israel today, students attended classes from Sunday to Friday. In the morning, they could borrow books for the day from the school library, as most students could not afford to buy their own. The library was modest, but it contained volumes in Yiddish and Hebrew literature, science, and philosophy, as well as a good representation of German and Polish classics. During the lunch break students could buy a large glass of tea in the cafeteria for five groshn, and a roll for one more groshn. Classes were dismissed at three o'clock in the afternoon.[6]

In this urban setting, its narrow streets traversed by arches preserved in old photographs, the students relaxed in the large, grassy yard between classes and afterward. But at the school itself, they had a complete life. At four o'clock, hundreds of students eagerly returned, filling the rooms where they discussed literature, learned skills in craft workshops, among many other offerings. These extracurricular or club activities truly bound the community together.

Friendships and Activities

Students recall Heschel as shy and quiet, a loner who had few friends. There were reasons for him to remain somewhat apart. He grew up with limited school experience, having studied alone or under Hasidic tutors; infrequent and formalized social contact with girls or women in Hasidic Warsaw would have ill-prepared him for coeducation. Lacking basic cultural background, he had to exert tremendous efforts to master subjects that other students had been preparing for years. In addition, he spent time with writers and artists, most of them not associated with his classes.

Heschel's immediate goals were pragmatic: gain knowledge and earn academic certification. At the Real-Gymnasium, Heschel probably limited himself to study and to many serious conversations.[7] He remained on the periphery of a group of classmates consisting of Nahum (Nakhte) Faynshtayn, Benjamin Wojczyk, and Abram (Abrashke) Lewin, whose parents lived in Vilna and were Bundists. These three young men (all born in 1909) spent considerable time at Lewin's home. Wojczyk remembers Heschel as a somewhat withdrawn person with perhaps only one true confidant.

Heschel spoke most often with Nakhte Faynshtayn, a dynamic leftist who later emigrated to Paris and edited a Yiddish-language Communist newspaper, the *Naye Presse* (New press).[8] But their relative closeness was probably a personal, not a political, alliance, as most students (and teachers) were radicals. Everyone was outraged at the poverty and injustice in Poland and Russia. Heschel shared with Faynshtayn his aspirations as a poet.

At the school, Heschel participated in the uplifting atmosphere of Jewish secularism. Academic excellence and enthusiasm for Jewishness comprised the essence of the Real-Gymnasium. This academy was much more than a school; in fact, it was a community—almost a family network—which is probably why Fishl Schneersohn directed Heschel there in the first place. Teachers and students shared an intimate, imponderable love of being Jewish, an idealistic sense of self and peoplehood encompassed in the term *Yiddishkayt*. Students revered their teachers as nurturing parents who instilled pride and inward strength.[9] They were the vanguard of a humanistic but Jewish utopia.

An essential part of student life, the clubs, run by a democratically elected student administration, were the training ground. Its faculty supervisor, the acclaimed author Josef Giligitsh, considered the Real-Gymnasium to be "a true children's republic, in which each person knew his or her rights, but also felt their obligations."[10]

At the reading club, which subscribed to Yiddish periodicals from North and South America and Europe, students discussed selections from European or Jewish literature. There was a Radio Club, a novelty in the 1920s. Workshops taught skills like dressmaking, sewing, and embroidery. There was a book bindery, which was urgently needed. Students could buy used books cheaply and, under the supervision of Mr. Zametchek, a well-known Vilna art-book professional, prepare them for their own use. The same energy was found in the carpentry shop where students, directed by Mr. Shneyderman, made small pieces of furniture and other items. The famous drama club, supervised by the poet, playwright, and novelist Moyshe Kulbak, brought the Real-Gymnasium to wide public attention.

Personalities and Teachers

The school community made up a microcosm of postrevolutionary Eastern Europe. One example was Ivan, the non-Jewish janitor who combined Russian and Polish Vilna.[11] Ivan had arrived when the building was still a private school for wealthy girls, named after the Russian Empress Maria Fyodorovna. He was a short, broad-shouldered Russian, usually wore swashbuckling boots, and never learned to speak Yiddish properly, though he understood everything. He and his wife cleaned the large classrooms, laboratories, offices, corridors, gymnastics and game rooms, and workshops. In winter, they fired up the porcelain coal ovens that heated the school.

Another strong nonfaculty presence was Mr. Shenkman, who supervised the physical plant. He was also responsible for collecting late tuition payments.[12] One former student remembered his compassion: "He had so much love for 'his children' that when he had to enter a classroom and send a child home whose parents had failed to pay the tuition for too long, he literally stood with tears in his eyes." During the long examinations required for graduation, "the same warmhearted Shenkman" served tea with buttered bread and sometimes placed "a special little note inside it with several historical dates or a mathematical equation."

In 1924, shortly before Heschel's arrival, Yosef Yashunsky became the director, replacing the German-born Dr. Berliner, a strict overseer.[13] Yashunsky, who was more flexible and had a warmer personality, was a mathematician from St. Petersburg with a broad humanistic education. In order to foster personal responsibility, his classroom method was Socratic, and his advanced classes on cosmography and mathematics demonstrated how theory related directly to everyday life.[14]

Yashunsky soon earned the name of "Tate" (in Yiddish, father) because of his kindness and the trust he inspired in students and teachers. Once Yashunsky made a special effort to rescue a friend and classmate of Heschel's, Benjamin Wojczyk, who came from a needy Vilna family. When the director learned that Wojczyk had been compelled to leave the school for three weeks for failing to pay tuition, he called him back and personally tutored him to help recover the instruction he had missed.[15]

Heschel may have appreciated the Real-Gymnasium's excellent science programs, and for university admissions he needed the courses on German language, history, philosophy, Latin, and mathematics. But he was especially devoted to Yiddish literature. Although most graduates became mathematicians, engineers, or technicians of one sort or another, they all loved the Yiddish classics. During 1925–27, the years of Heschel's matriculation, the two most outstanding literature teachers were Max Erik and Moyshe Kulbak.

Left to right: *Max Erik, Joseph Opatashu, and Moyshe Kulbak. Courtesy of YIVO Institute for Jewish Research, New York.*

The erudite Max Erik (pseudonym of Zalman Merkin) taught Yiddish and Polish literature. He came to Vilna in 1922, after graduating from Polish officers' school. He had already earned a scholarly reputation and was preparing a historical survey of Yiddish literature from its inception through the eighteenth century. His teaching style was formal, and he lectured from a thick notebook filled with small print. "He was an organized scholar who weighed every word and measured his time. Planning and system were part and parcel of his personality."[16] Max Erik successfully conveyed the attitudes and methods of serious academic research.

But the teacher who dominated all memories and who impressed Heschel most profoundly was Moyshe Kulbak, poet, playwright, novelist, and political idealist. He was a modern writer, left-wing and artistically avant-garde, a child of the Jewish countryside, born in the town of Smorgon, near Vilna.[17] He knew this earthy life intimately, for his father was a forest ranger and wood merchant and his mother came from a Jewish agricultural colony. Kulbak's early education was both secular and traditional, in a Folk-school and *heder*. He studied Talmud with a private teacher, going on to yeshiva in Swencian and Volozhyn. Kulbak learned Hebrew, Russian, and of course Yiddish, and first began to write in Hebrew. He then became a convinced Yiddishist.

When Kulbak's first collection of Yiddish poetry, *Shirim* (Songs or poems), appeared in Vilna in 1920, the critic Shmuel Niger announced "a new dawn" in Yiddish literature.[18] Between 1920 and 1923, Kulbak joined a dynamic group of Yiddish writers in Berlin, at that time a haven for Jewish thinkers from towns in the Pale of Settlement seeking to enter the modern world.[19] Also in Berlin, Kulbak worked as a prompter in the militant theater of Erwin Piscator.

Moyshe Kulbak then returned to Vilna and became the city's most charismatic teacher. In addition to his classes at the Real-Gymnasium, he gave courses at the two other Yiddish-language schools, the Sophia Markovna Gurevitsh Gymnasium and the Yiddish Teachers Institute (*Lehrer Seminar*). At the Real-Gymnasium he taught Yiddish literature to the two highest classes. While teaching he also published prose narratives in 1924 and 1925.

Kulbak's unique method inspired commitment—a personal involvement with the text which Heschel in later years expected of his own students and readers. Kulbak, a marvelous communicator, was able to provoke spontaneous reflection. Other instructors usually read and analyzed a text in class, assigning passages for students to memorize and recite the next day, without discussion; then the sequence would be repeated. Kulbak defined a theme or idea from the work under consideration and assigned a student to explore that theme the next day. Kulbak then listened carefully to the student's report and expanded upon his or her observations. The students and teacher discussed the issues over the next few days. Kulbak's classes were masterpieces of collaborative learning.[20]

Students retained vivid memories of Kulbak's emotional and spiritual intimacy with Yiddish authors: "He might ask a student to retell a folktale in her or his own words. Then he would walk slowly and quietly around the room—you could almost hear a fly buzz—and he listened with such intensity, as if he were hearing the voice of the master himself in the student's retelling who in her youthful enthusiasm identified completely with the original. I remember another episode when Kulbak, worried about a student's ignorance, said to us with a strange look in his eyes that no one could consider himself a Jewish intellectual (the ideal to which everyone should be striving) if he did not know 'by heart' the names of all eighteen volumes of Peretz's works in Kletskin's edition!"[21]

Kulbak's students were unanimous in their reverence for the master. One enthralled but rational student—Dina Abramowicz—testifies to his charisma: "To say that we loved Kulbak is too pale. We were bound to him like limbs of the same body. Every flutter of his aroused a response within us. When he but moved his brow, we would already open our eyes wide. When a light smile quietly touched his lips, warmth would pour into our hearts. Like a fish in water, Kulbak moved in the stream of world literature; he wanted, as also we did, to bathe in its beauty."

Kulbak's sensitivity to words seems to anticipate Heschel's own theory of "prayer as expression and empathy."[22] For Kulbak, "literature was a marriage between the writer's texts and the reader's feelings. Kulbak did not conceive of the text as printed pages, but as read, recited or 'sung out' interpretations. The voice, the intonation, a wrinkle of the forehead, when bringing forth the written word, had as much meaning for him as the text itself."[23] Heschel, writing years later of the cantor's vocation, insisted that "a word has a soul, and we must learn how to attain insight into its life. Words are commitments, not only the subject matter for esthetic reflection."[24]

Students were also touched by Kulbak's poverty. He was forced to supplement the small salary from his three teaching jobs by working as a tailor.[25] A "conspiracy" of students collected money from their jobs in the bindery or carpentry shops or tutoring younger pupils. They bought snacks and a bottle, inviting Kulbak to Ivan's private quarters. "With this spare little glass of liquor, Kulbak used to speak about Yiddish and European literature and, sometimes, he read his latest songs and poems, to which even Ivan listened with perked ears, so musically beautiful were the recitations."[26]

Heschel shared his classmates' admiration for the master, and probably participated in similar gatherings: "And, as the liquor reached the bottom of the bottle, we hoped that this Jewish Pushkin, this poet of rich and deep vision, would not toss back the few zlotys which the group used to place into his pocket by force, or furtively. Afterwards, they would accompany him home with tears in their eyes."

Moyshe Kulbak's triumphal production of the third act of Shakespeare's *Julius Caesar* (in the Yiddish translation by Y. Y. Schwartz) provides an emblem of modern Jewish culture in Vilna. In 1926, Kulbak mobilized the school for the performance.[27] Almost every member of the two highest classes participated as actors, chorus, extras in the crowd scenes, or technical help. Although Heschel apparently did not participate, two of his classmates took leading roles: Benjamin Wojczyk played Brutus, and Mordecai Eydelzon played Marc Antony.[28]

It was a genuine avant-garde production, inspired by Kulbak's experience in Berlin at the theater of Piscator. Audience and actors worked together—all in Yiddish. "Costumed boys were placed in various corners of the hall, making the audience forget the theatrical representation. From the lower flight of stairs, fittingly dressed heralds shouted, '*Vi geht Caesar!*' (There goes Caesar!) And on their long trumpets, they played a greeting for the ruler of Rome. Both young and old became drawn in and were excited by the performance."[29]

After the production was presented three times in Vilna, it went to Warsaw, where CYSHO was campaigning to open a similar Yiddish gymnasium. Josef Giligitsh, who was in charge of supervising the students, describes the boisterous night-long train ride from Vilna: "There was singing and joke telling; Shimshon Kahan, [later a] poet of the 'Young Vilna' group, then a student in the class [of 1926], recited poems in imitation of Kulbak, and his impersonation was so clever that people were twisted with laughter. Kulbak himself laughed more than anyone."

After a sleepless night, they made the required pilgrimage to the Gensher cemetery in Warsaw. In a formal ceremony, they placed flowers on the tombs of the three founding fathers of Yiddish literature, I. L. Peretz, Saul Anski, the author of *The Dybbuk*, and Jacob Dinezon, author of children's books and novels.[30]

Later, the audience at the Kaminski Theatre was overwhelmed by this Yiddish Shakespeare presented by young people. Warsaw's Yiddish newspapers raved about the occasion. This Shakespeare performance in Yiddish took place just a few blocks from the Heschel apartment on Muranowska Street. An English masterpiece had been translated into the daily idiom of Eastern European Jews, who previously had been isolated from the world. Their mother tongue communicated the universal struggle for freedom—and the heights and depths of heroism and betrayal.

Piety and Poetry

*The writer of these lines, who lived for a while in Vilna and was
a co-founder of "Young Vilna," was privileged to absorb the spirit
of the city, where even the poorest were bearers of refinement and
spiritual exaltation.*
Heschel, *Jerusalem of Lithuania* (1974)

Heschel advanced his literary career during his two years in Vilna. In addition to his academic work at the Real-Gymnasium, Heschel joined a group of innovative Yiddish-speaking writers and artists, probably encouraged by acquaintances in Warsaw. These men with left-wing ideals—who later became known collectively as Young Vilna (in Yiddish, Yung Vilne)—provided a context for his personal writing. Heschel continued to develop the poetry he began in Warsaw, expanding his subject matter and furthering his ambitions for publishing.

Avrum Yehoshua, as he was known, was a strong presence among these intellectuals, a figure who was both appealing and out of place. It was difficult for politically militant Jews—most of them socialists and communists—to fathom Heschel's essential identity. Shlomo Beilis, a poet and journalist who was born in Vilna (and after the war remained in communist Warsaw), astutely discerned Heschel's Hasidic spirit, describing him as "a good-looking young man, with the deep eyes of a scholar. A person of an entirely different type than we. Pious. Very solid, and not loose in any way."[31] Heschel stood out among these skeptics as a *ben-toyre* (literally, son of the Torah), a thinker steeped in religious learning.

Beilis and his comrades, as most progressive Jews of the time, were familiar with the religious culture they had rejected. They easily recognized piety, and Beilis recalled that "Heschel always wore a black hat. He looked like a rabbi, a genuine rabbi. Medium height, broad shoulders, thick-set, with very deep-set, beautiful eyes. And he looked like a scholar." Heschel had gained weight. More important, the artists vaguely perceived his inner solitude, suggested by his enigmatic quietness. Some understood his reserve as pensiveness, yet to others he appeared aloof.

An unusual formality marked their different mental worlds. Beilis continued, "Our relations with him were correct, but distant, as though there were a barrier between us." They never addressed Heschel directly with the familiar *du* (thou), but with the formal *ihr*—just as Heschel's father, the Pelzovizna rebbe, was spoken to in the third person. Their cultural disparity made it hard to communicate spontaneously: "With him we couldn't make jokes, and he wasn't, as they say, *anshei shloymaynu*, not one of our crowd. He was from another world. We respected him."

Heschel's lifelong cultural alienation had begun. In Warsaw, he had been a budding modern among Hasidic Jews. In Vilna, he and his fellow writers could not relax together. What was the source of their discomfort, perhaps mutual? Was Heschel tense? Haughty? Reserved? Modest? Or simply shy? Did Heschel represent a form of spirituality they had repudiated? Their uneasiness in his presence may also have reflected Heschel's internal struggle with his identity, despite their shared commitment to literature, art, and (as Heschel's poems soon demonstrated) social justice.

Such dissonance did not prevent Beilis and Heschel from enjoying walks together and having long conversations. Beilis collected him at his dismal room on Poplawes Street and they strolled to the Belmont Forest. Or they might reach the other side of town, the wealthier western district near the Zakreta Forest, on the banks of the Vileyke river. There they observed "the *tsop*, as it was called, where the Vileyke would fall noisily into the water from above, because there was a mill." Their exchanges, however, were not personal: "We used to walk together and talk, but we never asked each other about our *yikhus*, our ancestors and so forth."

For the secularist Beilis, Heschel's family tree, revered by Hasidim everywhere, had little authority. But Heschel did not disguise his sense of closeness to God. One day, after a meeting at the home of the poet Zalman Halpern on Pohulanke Street, they walked to the Zakreta Forest located a little over two miles beyond town. As soon as they entered the woods, Heschel put on his hat. It was a hot day and the forest was cooler—but Beilis was still surprised. "'Heschel,' I asked him—we never addressed him informally or by his first name, 'What does this mean? How do you explain it? the whole time you were carrying the hat in your hand, but just as we entered the forest, you put it on. Why?' Avrum Yehoshua replied graciously, 'It would be hard for you to understand. For me a forest is a holy place (a *makom kodesh*). And a Jew, when he walks into a holy place, covers his head.'" Heschel then developed his idea poetically, explaining that the stately trees seemed to be "standing *shimen esre*" (Yiddish for *shemone esre*, the

Eighteen Benedictions recited during the Amidah standing prayer). As Heschel later wrote of Eastern Europe, "even the landscape became Jewish."[32]

Poetry of Restraint and Aspiration

The poems Heschel shared with his artist companions revealed his complex personality struggling to communicate. Form seemed to inhibit his self-disclosure. When he read some pieces at meetings, the group appreciated his poems but found them somewhat outdated. "They were very fine, intelligently written poems. In the old style, in a very old style. They didn't possess a drop of irony; they were dead serious. As a person he was 'dead pious' so to speak, as were his poems," wrote Beilis.

Yiddish poetry liberated Heschel, but as an artist he was not revolutionary. His poems, still somewhat immature stylistically, were too cerebral. Although listeners were attracted by his engagement with intimate emotions, the poems "seemed to be a bit stiff. But they possessed density, mass. Every feeling was enveloped in an idea." His verse was more deliberately constructed than any inspired by the avant-garde movements they admired—Dada, Surrealism, Expressionism—which were flourishing then in Paris, Zurich, and Berlin.

Yet, if one considers the poems as biographical documents, Heschel's experience (the *content*) surpassed the restrained *form* of his verse, for he was consolidating his own voice. Some poems evoked a surprising sensuality, which intrigued Beilis and the group: "We marveled at how such a zaddik came to write such erotic poems. It was a wonder, the erotic—modest, with Jewish discretion—but still erotic, in his religious poems." Heschel evidently shared pieces similar to the one Melekh Ravitch chose for his 1926 anthology. Listeners were almost shocked that this "Torah scholar"—as they perceived him—was equally comfortable with religious and sexual themes. But for Heschel there need be no contradiction.

Heschel's Yiddish verse, with its shortcomings, was indeed his authentic voice. His "love" poems bespeak anxiety, but not avoidance or neurosis, for they assert his basic trust of the flesh. Beilis perceptively noted that "daring" was absent from the poems, by which he meant that Heschel as poet was not "bold," defying censure. For Heschel, human nature spoke of its many impulses without shame.

Beilis called Heschel's refinement his "Jewish discretion." Heschel's love poems reminded him of Sholem Aleichem's familiar story "Stempenyu," in which a man so reveres the modesty of his beloved that he is afraid to look at her, afraid even to fall in love. This was the time, late in 1926, when Heschel's first published poem ("The womanly skin/ Silvers so purely . . . ") appeared in the fifteenth installment of *Varshaver Shriftn*. Heschel's short "erotic" piece was printed in the second poetry issue—prominently displayed on the last page.[33]

Heschel had entered the Yiddish literary establishment, for this anthology marks an era. Pieces were selected to promote new writers and to circulate the works of established ones. Heschel took his place among Sholem Asch, Yitzhak Bashevis (pen name of I. B. Singer), Max Weinreich, Peretz Markish, Aaron Zeitlin, Moyshe Kulbak, and Melekh Ravitch. After the installments were finished, a book of over a thousand pages, dated 1926–27, was circulated internationally with Heschel's poem on page 32.

Heschel was a modern Jew seeking an idiom for his piety, which included a solid but delicate sensuality. In that he followed a tradition from Biblical times through Jehuda Halevi, who associated physical impulses with a passionate attraction to God. Heschel was familiar with the sanctified passion of Hasidism, as he wrote later: "One can serve God with the body, with his passions, even with 'the evil impulse' (Sifre Deuteronomy #32). . . . The road to the sacred leads through the secular."[34] Years later, Heschel used the term "embarrassment" to convey his tender humility before God.

This passion for God was the deeper source of Heschel's energy and may explain the discomfort of his secular companions. These realists could not fathom the holy dimension. Yet Heschel's demeanor, despite their estrangement, impressed them: "He spoke beautifully; his words were spare and considered. His very bearing inspired respect." Beilis described Heschel's charisma, reflecting Ruzhin delicacy, as "subtlety, the silk and satin he possessed in his soul." Among these socialists, communists, and avant-garde artists, he was a rebbe—but without a community. Or rather, Heschel belonged to a community on paper alone, a virtual fellowship which formed all too slowly.

Toward the end of his stay in Vilna, around the time of his graduation, Heschel's second poem was published. On 3 June 1927, an untitled piece appeared in Warsaw's *Literarishe Bleter* (Literary pages), a recently established Yiddish weekly whose literary editor was Melekh Ravitch.[35] Heschel's contribution was printed on a page with poems by eight other "young Warsaw poets," including Mordecai Olyt, Moshe Taytelboym, Shmuel Zarumb, and Sh. L. Shneyderman. Heschel had known some of them before leaving home, and later in Berlin he remained in touch.[36]

Heschel's second poem is more philosophical (or almost religious) than his contribution to *Varshaver Shriftn*. Like the previous "love" poem, it contains three stanzas—but here the poet's voice progresses from personal desire to a broader, more abstract openness. He plunges first into his body, and then into his inner life, to recover spiritual meaning:

> I can no longer carry my heart
> Pressed in cramped fingers.
> The shackles peel away from me
> When desire strikes
> In the shadowed forest of my limbs.

Stanza two evokes a release of feeling, limitless "thunder" in the poet's ears, beyond the mind. He abandons himself to an ecstasy of desire, whose object remains vague. Yet, finally, the third and final stanza approaches a threshold of revelation, as if the seeker was meeting an overwhelming force:

> With closed eyes—
> I stretch forth my ears
> Toward the clangor,
> Toward the resounding steps of the All.[37]

The poet frames his quest in neutral, neo-Platonic terms. Still constrained by the tight, cerebral form, this poetic syllogism reaches toward a greater, perhaps unearthly, unity. Heschel uses concrete, dramatic verbs ("peel away," "strikes," "thunder") to emphasize his aspirations. At the same time, the strong images "clangor" and "resounding steps" bring "the All" closer to the heart. Somewhat obscure, the poem is certainly not specifically Jewish. But it extends the poet's yearnings beyond the commonplace.

A Secret Sorrow

Many students sought Moyshe Kulbak's approval of their poetry, and it was known that two members of the Young Vilna group—Shimshon Kahan, a student at the Real-Gymnasium, and Velvke Hokhman—had recently visited Kulbak with success. They refused to say exactly what he told them about their poems, but they were excited. Heschel's consultation remained an even better protected secret, but he did share it with Nakhte Faynshtayn, his confidant.[38]

One day Heschel sought Kulbak's judgment. The master read some of Heschel's poems and told him, "You will never be a great poet, but you will become an excellent philosopher." This compliment and criticism cut several ways. Perhaps Kulbak found Heschel's verse too cerebral (as did Shlomo Beilis and his group) and suggested that the author direct his energies more to academia than to art. In any case, Kulbak's mixed message had positive results. Heschel continued to write poetry, improving it greatly, eventually publishing an entire book of Yiddish verse.

Kulbak's wider forecast also proved to be correct. After emigrating to the United States, Heschel mastered literary English and became both admired and reproved for his poetic prose. Although esteemed as a philosopher of Judaism, some professionals reproached him for being "a poet"—as if his beautiful style automatically precluded intellectual rigor. They did not understand how Heschel used poetic rhetoric as a means of provoking religious insight. Kulbak's candid judgment must have echoed throughout Heschel's career with a poignant irony.

Leaving Vilna

You are a Psalter spelled in clay and iron.
A prayer in every stone, a melody—every wall.
Moyshe Kulbak, quoted by Heschel
in *Jerusalem of Lithuania* (1974)

At the end of each academic year, students at the Real-Gymnasium were required to pass oral and written tests sent to Vilna from CYSHO headquarters in Warsaw. Heschel probably did not take the national certification examination, the Abitur, since anti-Semitic regulations prevented even those Jews who passed the Abitur from routinely entering European universities. Heschel completed his final examinations on 24 June 1927, the last hurdle before seeking entrance to the University of Berlin.[39]

Graduation took place on Sunday, 26 June 1927, at four in the afternoon, the school's fifth such ceremony. The event brought the entire community together—students and faculty, parents, family, friends, distinguished guests from the outside. The director, Yosef Yashunsky, gave a speech, as did the class valedictorian and representatives from the Vilna TsBK and CYSHO officials from Warsaw. After the distribution of diplomas and prizes, there was dancing—the fox-trot, the tango, maybe the Charleston—with refreshments. It is unlikely that the branches of Heschel's family in Warsaw or Vienna responded to the invitation.

Heschel, still alone, possessed the credentials of a modern education. But he was still seeking a spiritual home for his studies and creativity. His departure from Vilna was probably more solitary than his leaving Warsaw, when he had received blessings, and a warning, from his Hasidic patriarchs. After graduation, Heschel returned home briefly and visited relatives in Vienna before moving to Berlin. There, in the cultural and intellectual capital of the Weimar Republic, his prophetic and mystical vision encountered the rationalism of critical philosophy.

The Essence of Jewish Vilna

By the time he left Vilna, Heschel advanced in his decisive metamorphosis. Yet he wrote virtually nothing about these momentous years. Aware of the complexity of multicultural Vilna and its strangeness to the American scene, Heschel shared his memories of this period only with rare, Yiddish-speaking acquaintances from Vilna such as Leyzer Ran. (The preeminent Yiddish writers Chaim Grade and Abraham Sutzkever came later to the city.) Among his "American" friends, only Wolfe Kelman, a child of Hasidic parents from Toronto and his closest companion at the Jewish Theological Seminary, was aware that Heschel attended the Vilna Real-Gymnasium as preparation for the university.[40]

Heschel as a writer idealized his European experience. His sparse essay on Vilna, for example, preserves its essence as the harmony of religious and secular Jewishness. Five years after emigrating to the United States, he attempted to convey, in general terms, this aspect of Eastern European Jewry in a speech delivered in Yiddish in 1945, at the annual conference of the New York YIVO.[41] "Di mizrekh-eyropeishe tkufe in der yidisher geshikhte" was translated (probably by Shlomo Noble) as "The Eastern European Era in Jewish History" and published in the 1946 YIVO Annual. Heschel's revised and expanded version of the speech, *The Earth Is the Lord's: The Inner Life of the Jew in East Europe* (1950), illustrated with moving woodcuts by Ilya Schor, another refugee from Poland, inaugurated his American career as witness to Eastern European spirituality and moral activism.

Heschel began to retrieve his Vilna experience at that 1945 conference. There he spoke with Leyzer Ran, who in Vilna was engaged in the Jewish Scout Movement (*Hashomer Hatzair*).[42] Reb Leyzer (as he was known familiarly in Yiddish) reminded Heschel of two of their conversations around 1926. At that time, Heschel was amazed that, despite widespread poverty, Vilna Jews had developed such a marvelous culture—religious houses of study, social and political organizations, thriving Jewish educational systems. Students at the Real-Gymnasium captivated him with their serious faces; the school's soul was their dedication to a liberated Jewish future.

Their second Vilna conversation confirms Heschel's persistent fascination with Menahem Mendl, the Kotzker rebbe, his adolescent model of spiritual radicalism. Ran had been reading I. L. Peretz, who interpreted the boldness of traditional Judaism, and especially Hasidism, for secular readers. They discussed Peretz's famous drama, *Di goldene keyt* (The golden chain), in which a Hasidic rabbi refused to make *havdalah* (the ceremony marking the end of Sabbath) for a higher purpose. He defied one fundamental religious law by extending the holy time until the Messiah comes. Heschel demonstrated how this dissident drama was inspired by the audacious Hasidism of Kotzk. To Ran's enthusiasm, Heschel exclaimed, "Ah! You are a Kotzker!"

Leyzer Ran understood—in retrospect, after reading Heschel's posthumously published Yiddish book on Kotzk—that Heschel may not have believed in Kotzk at the time (he was not prepared to fulfill its iconoclastic moral rigor), but he loved it. Heschel's interpretation of Peretz's drama echoed the lesson of the Kotzker Hasid, Yitzhak Levin, who also "violated" a prohibition for the purpose of preserving joy, the essence of Sabbath.

Heschel's first affirmation of his Vilna experience was esoteric, available only to Yiddish speakers. Some years after Heschel's 1945 speech at the New York YIVO, Leyzer Ran began collecting testimonies to commemorate the twenty-fifth anniversary of the founding of Young Vilna. Heschel contributed a poem which he had first published under a pseudonym in 1933 in the Warsaw Yiddish paper *Haynt*. Now in 1955 it appeared under his name in Ran's simple mimeographed booklet. The brochure reproduces the poem with a photograph of Heschel taken later in Frankfurt.[43] In a statement that follows the poem, Heschel claims that he was instrumental in creating the movement, thus demonstrating the personal importance he attributed to his poetry. Although the group as such was not officially recognized until 1929—two years after he left the city—he perceived himself to be a co-founder. He was proud to have participated in its inception.[44]

Heschel next alluded to his Vilna period almost fifteen years later, in 1969, shortly after his first heart attack. In the meantime, Ran had solicited an essay on Vilna from Heschel for his memorial book *Jerusalem of Lithuania*. (It took Ran twenty-five years to publish the three folio volumes; the text is in Yiddish, Hebrew, Russian, and English.) As Ran was approaching the last stages of his opus, he came to Heschel's office with some materials and found him sick and suffering, with a pained expression on his face. But when Heschel started examining the documents, his eyes began to shine. He asked Ran to sit down and began writing something, perhaps the introduction which, some time before, he was invited to contribute. But instead Heschel was drafting a letter, later used to publicize the work.

"How will you sell the book?" Heschel asked.

"I will go to those 50,000 Jews who, I am told, are from Vilna and live in the United States."

"No," Heschel replied, "you will not have much success from them. They may have been born there but they are not *from* Vilna. I am *from* Vilna and I will help you. Every rabbi and every synagogue and school must have this book and understand what Vilna was about."

Almost thirty years after settling in the United States, close to death in 1969, Heschel began drafting his ode to Vilna. His dithyrambic preface to *Jerusalem of Lithuania,* written in Yiddish, typifies his manner of creating a Jewish synthesis of ancient and new. What is more, Heschel absorbs the ethical into the sacred.

Heschel hallows Vilna, transmuting secular virtues into spiritual gold. The essay begins with an epigraph from Kulbak's famous ode, "Vilna," and then he counsels readers: "Only he who has been privileged to behold Jewish Vilna will grasp the full sense of Kulbak's words. Jewish Vilna was an environment whose walls, corners and cellars breathed memories of gigantic intellects, reminiscences of self-sacrifice for Jewishness, of reverence of God and man, of charity and the thirst for knowledge."[45] Ranging over Vilna's Jewish history, he emphasizes modernity: founding of the Bund, the PEN club, and YIVO—all progressive institutions. He lists "prominent scholars, writers and poets" of his own time: Max Weinreich, Zalman Reyzen, Max Erik, Moyshe Kulbak, Chaim Grade, Abraham Sutzkever. He recalls "the Strashun Library, the richest public collection of Jewish books in possession of East European Jews, the publishing house of the Widow and Brothers Rom, which provided Ashkenazim, Sephardim, and even Karaites with books. The most beautiful editions of the Talmud, Babylonian and Palestinian, the prayer book *Ozar ha-tefilot,* and *Midrash Rabbah,* with commentaries and numerous other publications."

Above all, Heschel celebrates the spiritual grandeur of poverty-stricken Vilna Jews. He recounts the story of simple Shimele Kaftan, who made a miserable living by twisting rope and pressing tobacco leaves. Despite his hardships, he collected alms for the poor by walking through the town with a tin cup. "And nobody refuses him. Jews run after him with their pennies." Heschel recalls that a Polish poet wrote a poem about Kaftan, "The Jewish Alms Collector," which Peretz translated into Yiddish. "The poem describes how after midnight Shimele

Kaftan sits in a tavern, bent over a book, chewing a few chickpeas. He ignores the mockery of the people about him. They are drunk, given to buffoonery, and his face is sad, his eyes full of yearning. He is far from there, far from all taverns. His soul soars afar and its destination is Zion." Heschel concludes the story: "'What prompts you to do this?' he was once asked. And his reply was: 'Shapsel the chimney sweep, who donated his house to a yeshiva, retaining for himself the garret, whence he would listen in rapture to the sound of study.'"

In this pluralistic Yiddish-speaking society, as a poet and student at the Real-Gymnasium, Heschel reconciled his Hasidic past with secular Jewish activism: "The readiness of self-sacrifice for justice and the dignity of man, inherited from many holy generations, was also glowing in the modern Jews. So many secular-ist Jews who lived the life of saints and did not know it!" He included within his vision Jewish Vilna's traditional religious scholarship, poverty, compassion, and the radical politics of his teachers and companions. For Heschel, justice and tenderness—as well as higher education—were forms of service to God.

Part Three
Berlin: Europe in Crisis

In the spiritual confusion of the last hundred years, many of us overlooked
the incomparable beauty of our old, poor homes. We compared our fathers
and grandfathers, our scholars and rabbis, with Russian or German intel-
lectuals. We preached in the name of the twentieth century, measured the
merits of Berditchev and Ger with the standards of Paris and Heidelberg.
Dazzled by the lights of the metropolis, we lost at times the inner sight.
Heschel, *The Earth Is the Lord's* (1950)

HESCHEL CONSOLIDATED HIS SPIRITUAL AND INTELLECTUAL IDENTITY IN THE cosmopolitan city of Berlin. When he arrived in the fall of 1927, its intellectual giants were still present, for during the Weimar Republic the sciences, philosophy, and the arts flourished as never before. Albert Einstein and Max Planck in physics revolutionized our conception of the universe; Max Reinhardt, Erwin Piscator, and Bertolt Brecht created avant-garde and politically engaged theater; Arnold Schoenberg composed his twelve-tone music. There was a daily diet of cinema, artistic and literary expressionism, and much more.[1]

Berlin also became a center of Yiddish culture during the 1920s. East European Jewish artists and intellectuals had fled there to escape virulent anti-Semitism, pogroms, the Bolshevik revolution, the civil wars—and poverty. Most prominent among the writers were Der Nister, Dovid Bergelson, Dovid Hofshteyn, and Leib Kvitko. Heschel's former teacher, Moyshe Kulbak, lived in Berlin between 1920 and 1923, publishing poems and novellas while working as a prompter in Piscator's theater. Because inflation made it cheaper for foreigners to do business in Germany, Yiddish book publishing thrived, and at least nineteen Yiddish periodicals appeared in Berlin alone.[2] In 1921, the prominent Hebrew poet and essayist Haim Nahman Bialik moved from Odessa to Berlin and continued his writing and publishing activities there before emigrating to Palestine three years later.

Fishl Schneersohn, Heschel's Warsaw mentor, was also active in Berlin during the early 1920s. Together with David Koigen, a social philosopher whom Schneersohn met while teaching at the University of Kiev, he founded a review called *Ethos* that put forth sociological, religious, and philosophical solutions to post–World War I alienation. Heschel soon formed his own synthesis of Jewish tradition and Western culture both with and against Koigen—and, later, with and against Martin Buber, who was already a leading theological and political thinker as well as an acquaintance of Koigen's and Schneersohn's.[3]

Historically, during this period, the triumph—and the swan song—of Heschel's two worlds, Hasidism and humanism, occurred. At the beginning of his Berlin years, in 1928, the Agudat Israel, the movement defending religious study and Orthodox observance, gathered in Vienna, inspired by Heschel's cousin Rabbi Israel Friedman, the Tchortkover rebbe, and his uncle's close friend Rabbi Abraham Mordecai Alter, the rebbe of Ger.[4] In 1929, at the Swiss conference site of Davos, a momentous debate took place between Ernst Cassirer, the neo-Kantian humanist philosopher, whom Heschel admired, and Martin Heidegger, whose skeptical diagnosis of the mortal condition, *Sein und Zeit* (Being and time), published in 1927, shook the world of optimistic thought.[5]

Heschel answered these crises as a modern thinker, adapting academic disciplines to his Hasidic spirit. The various languages he had mastered mediated disparate worlds. He used German to harvest the university curriculum and *Wissenschaft des Judentums* (historically based or "scientific" Jewish studies). Spiritual foundations were provided by texts in ancient and rabbinic Hebrew and Aramaic—Bible, Talmud, Zohar, and other Hasidic sources. Heschel knew modern Hebrew as well, the idiom of secular and religious Zionism and university-based scholarship. Yiddish, however, remained the instrument of his soul.

6

A Student in Berlin (1927–1931)

*I came with great hunger to the University of Berlin to study philosophy.
I looked for a system of thought, for the depth of the spirit, for the meaning of existence. Erudite and profound scholars gave courses in logic,
epistemology, esthetics, ethics and metaphysics. They opened the gates
of the history of philosophy.*

Heschel, "Toward an Understanding of Halacha" (1953)

HESCHEL ARRIVED IN BERLIN AT AGE TWENTY, IN THE FALL TERM OF 1927, renting a room in an apartment with a Jewish family, as he had in Vilna. His needs were simple—kosher food and a place to sleep. For the first time he entered a non-Jewish world, having left Hasidic Warsaw with its mystical and legendary attitudes and secular Vilna. Although the Real-Gymnasium was alien to his ancestral identity, it was still a Jewish environment; even his left-wing peers deferred to his rabbinic bearing. In Berlin he navigated between vaster possibilities, Jewish and otherwise.

Heschel bolstered his independence while maintaining a deeply loving relationship with his family. He had little money, but he stayed in close touch with his mother and sisters and sent whatever funds he could spare from his meager earnings at odd jobs. Yet he did not maintain his ancestral pattern by renting rooms in the city's predominantly East European Jewish section, known as the Scheunenviertel. This area of East Berlin, not far from the university and near the Alexanderplatz, was populated by Jewish immigrants who maintained the dress and customs of their shtetls. Even many Orthodox students preferred to live elsewhere, while visiting the kosher shops and the many traditional houses of prayer. Heschel took rooms (which he frequently changed for financial reasons) near the university or in the Charlottenburg section to the west.

Yet, at first, Heschel worshipped at a synagogue of Talmud learning recommended by his family, the Hevra Shaas of Rabbi Hayim Moses Feldmann-Postman, located on Grenadier Strasse in the Scheunenviertel. There Heschel prayed wearing a *gartel* (ritual belt) favored by Hasidim. Heschel also worshipped a few blocks away at the Hasidic shtiebl of Boyan, associated with his Friedman cousins, descendants of the Ruzhiner rebbe.[1]

Heschel's university career began officially on 27 April 1928 as he registered at the Philosophical Faculty of the University of Berlin with a *kleine Matrikel* (partial or provisional matriculation) contingent upon passing the general entrance examinations.[2] Heschel's academic tasks were daunting. As a foreign student he was required to take special tests before being allowed "full" matriculation at the university. His diploma from the Vilna Real-Gymnasium, despite its intrinsic merit, was not accredited abroad, nor were Polish graduation certificates considered equivalent to the German Abitur. Resident aliens were required to demonstrate competence in the classics, mathematics, German language, and other aspects of the national culture during their initial four terms of study. Heschel registered at the Deutsches Institut für Ausländer (German institute for foreigners) and mobilized his exceptional capacity for learning. This was not simply a process of collecting information about Western heritage. He had to grasp another vision of reality—literature, art, music, philosophy, and more.

Modern Institutions of Learning

Heschel's geographical center was the area around and including the university, known as the Unter den Linden district, referring to the gracious wide avenue (lined with limewood trees) which crossed the city. He lived at 7 Schröder Strasse,[3] within easy walking distance of the university and the modern Jewish institution where he also registered, the Hochschule für die Wissenschaft des Judentums (Academy of scientific Jewish scholarship), which trained Liberal rabbis and scholars. (Hochschule refers to an institution of advanced education beyond the Gymnasium.)

Heschel maintained informal ties with, but did not register at the modern Orthodox Rabbiner-Seminar (also known as the Hildesheimer Rabbinical Seminary), located nearby at 24 Artillerie Strasse (the Hochschule was at number 31). The Liberal Hochschule and the Orthodox Seminary were both about a ten-minute walk from the university. In 1920s Berlin, the frontiers between tradition and modernity were not so sharply drawn as today, and Heschel passed easily from one community to another. He was comfortable—and uncomfortable—in both institutions, for different reasons. People in the Hasidic prayer houses became cool to Heschel when they learned that he was not studying at the Orthodox Rabbinical institution but at the scientific, Liberal one.[4] They were unsettled by this evidence of Heschel's independence.

These various academies within close proximity mediated Heschel's emergence as European thinker. Foremost among them was the University of Berlin—officially the Königliche Friedrich-Wilhelms-Universität—an outstanding research and teaching institution which attracted students from all over Europe.[5] Established in 1809 by King Frederick William III, it was renamed Humboldt University in 1949 by the East German government to honor the founding rector, the philosopher and philologist Wilhelm von Humboldt. The University of Berlin enjoyed worldwide prestige, along with the universities at Leipzig, Tübingen, Heidelberg, and Marburg, among others.[6] By 1928 there were about 20,000 students enrolled at the University of Berlin, 10 percent of whom were women.

Heschel considered several fields before eventually settling upon philosophy as his major subject. Because university requirements were broadly humanistic, doctoral candidates chose two minor concentrations. After hesitating between psychology and art, Heschel decided upon the history of art and Semitic philology. The study of esthetics sustained his passion for beauty, while ancient Near Eastern languages gave scientific grounding to his pietistic mastery of religious texts.

His real interest was religion, however, and he refined his ancestral insights while mastering contemporary methods. At the university, he enrolled in both the Faculty of Philosophy and Faculty of Theology, the latter a domain defined by Protestant biblical scholarship. In philosophy, he studied primarily with Heinrich Maier, department chairman and authority on Kant, and Max Dessoir, a versatile expert in esthetics, phenomenology, and psychology who became Heschel's dissertation adviser. In the art history department, he worked with Albert Erich Brinckmann.

Heschel developed his expertise in Judaic studies in the university's theological faculty. Among its nine divisions were the department of Hebrew language and Old Testament research, where he worked with Ernst Sellin and Alfred Bertholet. As part of his minor in Semitic philology, Heschel studied with Eugen Mittwoch, director of the Institute for Semitic and Islamic Studies. Heschel also took courses in the department of New Testament research, and the Institutum Judaicum, an interdepartmental entity specializing in comparative Jewish-Christian research which had rejected its former missionary function.

In fact, the Institutum Judaicum of the 1920s emerged as a precursor of Jewish-Christian cooperation that Heschel realized thirty years later in the United States. Its director, Hugo Gressmann, a Protestant theologian and Old Testament expert, enthusiastically collaborated with Jewish scholars. Right before Heschel's arrival in Berlin, during the 1925–26 academic year, Gressmann organized a series of guest lectures by Leo Baeck, Ismar Elbogen, and Julius Guttmann of the Hochschule; Michael Guttmann of the Breslau Jewish Theological Seminary; and Jehuda (Judah) Bergmann, a community rabbi in Berlin and cofounder of the Free Jewish Adult Education Center. Gressmann published these papers in book form as an act of solidarity.[7]

Heschel began his university studies during an uncertain period for Jews. Gressmann's preface to the collected volume, dated 1927, is a courageous protest: "A strong wave of anti-Semitism is passing over our people, and the image of Judaism is being distorted." Gressman went on to praise his Jewish colleagues' exceptional acumen, considered a byproduct of their intimacy with the material: "For true objectivity always requires love, and therefore the Jewish scholar always has the advantage regarding the Jewish religion: by necessity he must know it better than the Christian scholar." Heschel did not know Gressmann, who died during a visit to the University of Chicago in April 1927, but his

Hasidic education prepared him to emulate the Christian scholar's wisdom: "True objectivity always requires love."

Heschel now subordinated his "love" for the Bible to his professors' "objective" methods. His main task, for the first time in his life, was to integrate religious and secular values. In addition to his doctoral work at the University of Berlin, he entered the degree program (which included ordination as a Liberal rabbi) at the Hochschule.

Founded in 1872, the Hochschule trained Heschel in the "higher criticism," a method of Bible analysis based on examination of the text's historical strata. Liberal thinkers considered Judaism to be the product of a complex cultural evolution, rather than of revelation in the supernatural event at Mount Sinai. They rejected Orthodox dogma that the Bible was written by Moses as one document. Their academic discipline applied the theories of Leopold Zunz, who envisioned a historical-philological approach to Jewish religion. The standard of Bible scholarship had been established by Julius Wellhausen, who defined the four different sources of the holy text: J, or Jahwist; E, Elohist; D, Deuteronomy; P, Priestly Code. Judaism was a cultural synthesis, the integrity of which was preserved by scientific research (Wissenschaft des Judentums).

The Hochschule's neutral academic environment, however, was dedicated to Jewish continuity and renewal. Members of the faculty were required to possess qualifications of a university lecturer (the equivalent of assistant professor), and its students matriculated at the university. The Hochschule admitted nontheological students, including women and some non-Jews. To avoid factions and conflicts over dogma, rabbis of any denomination were excluded from its board of governors (the Kuratorium).[8] Graduates became scholars and teachers as well as rabbis.

The Orthodox Seminary, officially the Rabbiner-Seminar für das Orthodoxe Judentum, was founded in 1873 by Rabbi Azriel Hildesheimer to combat Reform Judaism and its undermining of the divine authority of biblical and rabbinic texts.[9] Hildesheimer applied the knowledge he gained from studying mathematics, astronomy, and Semitic languages at the universities of Berlin and Halle to justifying *halakhah* (revealed Jewish law), the backbone of Orthodoxy. The seminary's second period was dominated by David Hoffmann, who exercised a unique combination of Talmudic and secular scholarship.[10] Hoffmann defended the faith by publishing a book faulting the historical method of Wellhausen.

The Hildesheimer Rabbinical Seminary was a sophisticated academic environment, and during Heschel's years in Berlin the faculty consisted of four professors: Samuel Grünberg, Moses Auerbach, rector of the seminary Yehiel Jakob

Weinberg, and Josef Wohlgemuth. Its leading intellectual figure, Wohlgemuth, taught courses on Jewish philosophy, theological subjects (such as free will, theodicy, natural religion, revelation), and practical halakhah.[11] As editor of the scholarly Orthodox monthly *Jeschurun,* Wohlgemuth exercised considerable authority. His widely circulated study of *teshuvah* (repentance) in Max Scheler's philosophy of religion helped disseminate Scheler's thought in Jewish circles— and may have influenced Heschel's choice of a dissertation topic.[12]

Heschel's decision to attend the Hochschule over the Orthodox Seminary was not a momentous spiritual choice, and was mitigated by the fact that students and faculty from both institutions often interacted. Rabbinical degree candidates at both institutions were required to matriculate at the university. At the Hochschule men and women were seated separately at religious services and *kashrut* (Jewish dietary law) was maintained.

Heschel probably chose the Liberal Hochschule—in addition to the University of Berlin—because the other institution trained men to become practicing Orthodox rabbis, and Heschel was curious. He knew what the Orthodox Seminary could teach him—Talmud, codes, midrash—but he wanted to acquire the biblical criticism and theology that he *thought* the Liberal academy might offer. In addition, the Orthodox Seminary was a center of religious authority, with its distinguished rector, Rabbi Yehiel Jakob Weinberg, serving as Germany's foremost halakhic judge. Its approach to sacred texts was of the Lithuanian type, primarily legal, and Weinberg kept in close touch with the world's expert on Jewish law, Rabbi Hayim Ozer Grodzinski of Vilna.[13] The Orthodox emphasis on Talmud and halakhah had sacred status; modern scholarship and philosophy were used to justify the divine origin of the Bible, which they considered to be a unitary document.

At the university, Heschel focused on the Hebrew prophets. Bible interpretation was a freer, though no less theological, discipline. Talmud and halakhah, which he had studied profoundly, were not his primary focus. The Liberal Hochschule, which taught critical methods opposed by the other school, supplemented more appropriately Heschel's concentration on Bible. Independent of Orthodoxy as such, Heschel did not have a vested interest in demolishing historical hypotheses or in using academic techniques to defend rabbinical authority. Yet, in his doctoral dissertation, he did find a method that implicitly justifed the validity of divine revelation.

It is not clear how Heschel spoke of his university studies to his Hasidic relatives. They understood that, like numerous other East European young men (and some women) from traditional families, he maintained an observant life.

Heschel's thinking was progressive, but he sought out Orthodox homes where he could share a Sabbath meal. Heschel was frequently invited by Rabbi Jakob Freimann, who came to Berlin in 1928 to head the Rabbinical Court and who also lectured at the Orthodox Seminary.[14] Years later, some family members believed that Heschel had continued his religious studies in Berlin, associated perhaps with students (such as Joseph Baer Soloveitchik and Menahem Mendel Schneerson) who gathered around the brilliant Talmudic scholar Rabbi Haim Heller, who left Berlin around 1929 to teach at the Rabbi Isaac Elhanan Seminary in New York (later renamed Yeshiva University). It is more likely that Heschel came to Berlin to participate in modern Jewish creativity.

Would the Hochschule become Heschel's academic or spiritual home? There he joined many other East European Jews who continued earlier migrations to the West. When Heschel entered the Hochschule in 1927, most of the sixty-six Jewish students (and thirty-five guest auditors) were German. With candidates from Poland increasing in number, the Hochschule became more cosmopolitan, and the student body more learned in the Jewish classical texts.[15] The next year, among its seventy-one students, twenty-seven were from Germany and twenty-eight from Poland, with thirteen auditors. People with preparation similar to Heschel's continued to arrive.

The Liberal school did not threaten Heschel's faith, as it emphasized method over theology. Heschel did not intend to become a Liberal or Reform rabbi. (German Liberal Judaism can be distinguished from its radical counterpart, Reform, of which there were only two temples in Germany at that time—its principal locus having moved to the United States in the nineteenth century. In addition, Reform worship was mostly in German, and Sabbath services might even take place on Sundays.) Yet, like his peers at both Jewish schools, he confronted Europe's religious crisis of assimilation and increasing indifference to religion.

Cultural Treasures

The world beyond these academic institutions—Jewish and secular—was equally compelling, for Heschel relished literature and the arts. His walks to lectures at the university, the Hochschule, or other places took him through Berlin's thriving center. Heschel recalled, "There were concerts, theatres, and lectures by famous scholars about the latest theories and inventions, and I was pondering whether to go to the new Max Reinhardt play or to a lecture about the theory of relativity."[16] The city itself was an astounding resource.

Along the main avenue, Unter den Linden, there were cafés, restaurants, shops, elegant hotels, the Russian embassy, the Ministry of Science, Art, and Education (Kultur-Ministerium), and other impressive buildings. On the corner of Friedrich Strasse, on opposite sides, were the Victoria-Café and the Bauer. At the same corner were electric tramway and omnibus stops and convenient access to the underground railway system. Using the Stadtbahn (city railway) and Ringbahn one could easily reach other parts of the city and the suburbs.

His reading and research opportunities were nearly limitless. The University Library, reserved for professors and students, contained 678,000 volumes, with its elegant reading room presided over by a large portrait of Frederick the Great. Everyone could use the much larger Staatsbibliotek (Prussian State Library) at 38 Unter den Linden, which, as the Baedeker guidebook claimed, was "surpassed in size by the Paris, London, and Washington libraries alone."[17]

The university, located at the east end of Unter den Linden, displayed its distinguished history. Visitors entering the main gate passed the equestrian monument to Frederick the Great, erected in 1851. The university's monumental buildings, its two long wings, stretched northward. Lecture rooms of the Old Royal Library, a superb example of rococo architecture and also part of the university, were decorated with statues of two rectors, the philosopher J. Gottlieb Fichte and the jurist K. von Savigny. On the opposite street was the Opera House, with over a thousand seats, and Opera House Square.

Heschel could view artifacts from the origins of Western civilization in the remarkable collections adjacent to the university. Museum Island, located between the Spree River and the Kupfer Graben, housed the National Gallery, the Deutsches Museum, the Pergamon Altar Museum, the Western Asiatic Museum, the New Museum, and the Old Museum. The Old Museum, a building in Greek style, contained antique sculptures and halls of Greek and Roman art. The New Museum, in the Renaissance style, included the Egyptian Museum. The magnificent Pergamon sculptures, which had their own building, rivaled the Parthenon friezes in the British Museum.

In the Emperor Frederick Museum, built during 1897–1903 in Italian baroque style, Heschel could enrich his studies of art history. The picture galley on the upper floor featured Dutch and early Italian masters, sixteenth- and seventeenth-century Italian art, and the Spanish school. There was Florentine art, marble sculptures, and works of the high Renaissance. Of special interest were Venetian painters of the sixteenth century, Tintoretto and Titian. Dutch painting was well represented by Frans Hals, Ruisdael, and Rembrandt and his school. Heschel remained partial to Rembrandt's paintings and their subtle emotional depth.

With characteristic independence and passion, Heschel navigated among these institutions and, by dint of intense study and experience, he assimilated these masterpieces of European culture. His inner, spiritual beliefs remained intact as he learned of Liberal Judaism and conversed with humanistic and Orthodox thinkers also facing modernity.

Professors and Personalities

I became increasingly aware of the gulf that separated my views from those held at the University. I had come with a sense of anxiety: How can I rationally find a way where ultimate meaning lies, a way of living where one would never miss a reference to supreme significance? Why am I here at all, and what is my purpose? I did not even know how to phrase my concern. But to my teachers that was a question unworthy of philosophical analysis.

Heschel, "Toward an Understanding of Halacha" (1953)

Within himself, Heschel harbored discontent. He had arrived in Berlin "with great hunger to study philosophy," as he later wrote. Although his basic beliefs had taken shape—a certainty of God's attachment to humankind—he hoped to reconcile them with Western categories of thought. Heschel's professors at the University of Berlin and the Hochschule, and David Koigen, were inspired by the ideals of Wilhelm Dilthey, having reached professional maturity in the early 1900s.[18] They shared the ambition to combine realms of academic research and knowledge that are normally fragmented today. Heschel was thus able to blend psychology, art and literature, and philosophy in his approach to religion and the Hebrew Bible. Although his immediate priority was to pass the state examinations, he attended lectures at both institutions and constructed a broad intellectual foundation while fulfilling his academic obligations.

The University of Berlin

Heschel concentrated on philosophy at the university. Heinrich Maier and Max Dessoir, his two leading professors at the Philosophical Faculty, provided scientific criteria which he evaluated critically. Eventually Heschel subordinated their hypotheses, which were based on psychology and critical philosophy, to his own religious understanding. Heschel used the generally accepted philosophical discourse of his time, but for an uncommon purpose. He developed a biblical approach to ethics, prophetic inspiration, and prayer.

Heinrich Maier, chair of the philosophy department and historian of systems, represented neo-Kantianism, the reigning intellectual ideology of the time. This school held that what we can know is constrained by the limits of reason. Maier began as a psychologist of the mind. He came to Berlin in 1922, after teaching at other universities. He analyzed what he called "emotional thinking" in order to locate the irrational basis of judgment by defining sets of affects, wishes, and intentions that comprise the decision-making faculties. He considered a power of will as the main force. By describing the logical functions of the emotional imagination, he tried to determine through psychological and philosophical analysis the essence of thought.[19]

But it was the versatile Max Dessoir (1867–1947), professor of philosophy and esthetics, who provided the most productive mediation for Heschel's eclectic curiosity. (Heschel eventually chose Dessoir as co-director of his doctoral dissertation.) When Dessoir was a student in Berlin, he had studied with Dilthey and earned doctorates in philosophy and medicine, seeking to establish a verifiable foundation for thought and creative activity.[20] Dessoir also contributed to the field of parapsychology (a term he coined, referring to all sorts of extrasensory perception, including communication with spirits after death). Dessoir's combination of psychology, philosophy, esthetics, and analysis of occult phenomena was congruent with Heschel's several interests.

Dessoir, a precursor of Freud in exploring the unconscious, developed a theory of personality similar to that of Fishl Schneersohn, which delineated multiple "spheres" unified by a "string of memories." Dessoir's notion of "double consciousness" applied to Heschel himself, whose own spheres of thought and action were continuing to multiply: academic and religious study in German, Hebrew, and Aramaic; writing poetry in Yiddish; regular prayer in Hebrew; studying music and the plastic arts; and reading modern literature in German, Yiddish, and Hebrew.

Dessoir also possessed a complex cultural substratum. He was the son of Germany's most admired Shakespearean actor, Ludwig Dessoir (who was Jewish, originally named Leopold Dessauer), but the son renounced his religion and characterized himself as "a quarter Jewish." Only later, after the Nazis moved to dominate the university, Max Dessoir was forced to contend with his background more actively.

Heschel concentrated on Bible at the university's Theological Faculty.

Max Dessoir, Berlin. Portrait by Rudolf Stumpf,
1929. From Christian Herrmann, Max Dessoir:
Mensch und Werk. *Stuttgart: Ferdinand Enke,*
1929.

Heschel's professors included Ernst Sellin, who succeeded Hugo Gressmann as director of the Institutum Judaicum.[21] Sellin came to Berlin in 1921 to join the department of Hebrew language and Old Testament research. Among his books on Old Testament studies and on the Hebrew prophets and a two-volume *History of the Semites in the Biblical Period* (1924–32) was a book on Moses, to which Freud refers in his essay "Moses and Monotheism."

Heschel worked more closely with Alfred Bertholet (1868–1951), who arrived at Berlin University during Heschel's second year. The Swiss-born Bertholet, an ordained Protestant pastor, helped renew Old Testament research through his knowledge of the several civilizations of the ancient Near East. In addition to wide-ranging books on Jewish religion, the history and culture of ancient Israel, and comparative religion, Bertholet published historical commentaries on Leviticus, Deuteronomy, Ezekiel, Ruth, Ezra, and Nehemiah, and the Apocrypha and Pseudoepigrapha (noncanonical books of the Bible). He co-

*Eugen Mittwoch, Berlin, 1936. Photograph
by Herbert Sonnenfeld. From* Monatsschrift
für Geschichte und Wissenschaft des
Judentums *81 (1937).*

edited, with E. Lehmann, a revision of Chantepie de la Saussaye's widely used
Manual of the History of Religions (1924–25).

Heschel probably chose his dissertation topic in conjunction with Bertholet's
courses, while honing his approach in Dessoir's seminars on psychology and esthetics. During fall 1928, Bertholet offered an introduction to the history of religion, a course on the theology of the Old Testament, and a tutorial on interpretations of chapters 40–66 of Isaiah. In spring 1929, he lectured on Semitic
religion, offered an Old Testament introduction, and directed a seminar on the
Hebrew prophets. This Bible scholarship provided a context for Heschel's spiritual task.

To fulfill his minor concentration in Semitic philology, Heschel studied with
Eugen Mittwoch, who, from 1920 to his removal in 1933 by the Nazis, was co-
director of the university's Institute for Semitic and Islamic Studies. (Mittwoch
was an observant Jew.) Born in Schrimm in the Posen province of Prussia, he attended the Berlin Orthodox Rabbiner-Seminar and was one of the first German

Jews to speak modern Hebrew, having visited Palestine and other Near Eastern countries as a student. With Mittwoch, Heschel advanced his scholarly knowledge of biblical Hebrew. Mittwoch, also an eminent Arabist, published books on ancient Hebrew inscriptions, a biography of Mohammed, works on Arabic medicine, poetry, prayer and worship, and analyses of the influence of the Jewish liturgy. Under Mittwoch Heschel probably studied Arabic, a language required for research in medieval Jewish philosophy.[22] Heschel's first academic publications—on Maimonides and other metaphysicians—developed directly from materials in this field.

There were many bridges among Heschel's three academic worlds: Mittwoch himself, from the university, was associated with the Hochschule as co-editor, with Ismar Elbogen and Julius Guttmann, of the *Collected Works* of Moses Mendelssohn. The Christian scholar Alfred Bertholet also crossed over, as it were, on 3 February 1930, when he gave one of the Monday evening guest lectures at the Hochschule on "The Concept of Sacrifice in Religion." Around that time, Bertholet became co-director of Heschel's dissertation on the Hebrew prophets.

While concentrating on Judaism and philosophy, Heschel broadened his humanistic education. At the university he studied esthetics with Dessoir and visited Berlin's museums, concert halls, and galleries. He had the exceptional opportunity to attend lectures by the art historian Heinrich Wölfflin, who was a visiting professor at the university.[23] Heschel's listing of Wölfflin as one of his teachers reconfirms the interdisciplinarity of his thinking, for Wölfflin had studied with Dilthey in Basel as well as with Grimm and Ernst Robert Curtius. Heschel remained attracted to such masters of *Geistesgeschichte* (spiritual and cultural history).

The sponsor of Heschel's minor concentration in art history, Albert Erich Brinckmann (1881–1958), arrived only in fall 1931, during Heschel's third year at the university. This effective teacher used slides to explain masterpieces and offered a full program: major works of German art from Romanticism to rococo, baroque and classical art of the seventeenth century (Italy and France), and exercises in style criticism: sixteenth-century Italian mannerism. By then Heschel had virtually completed his course work and began to prepare his dissertation.

Heschel considered specializing in psychology and was probably drawn to Wolfgang Köhler, a philosopher and experimental scientist who surpassed the usual academic boundaries.[24] (Köhler taught the introductory philosophy course required of all entering students.) Born in Tallin, Estonia, Köhler studied physics at the University of Berlin under Max Planck and psychology under Carl Stumpf. After his pioneering psychological studies of chimpanzees, he became professor of philosophy at the university and succeeded Stumpf as director of the Psychological Institute. Köhler applied to his field Husserl's phenomenological method in addition to concepts from physics and the biological sciences.[25] Heschel probably witnessed Köhler's efforts to establish his school of Gestalt psychology. Köhler later became one of the few established professors to oppose Nazi domination of the university.

The Hochschule's Liberal Jewish Curriculum

The Hochschule's small but distinguished faculty, some of them associated with the university, gave Heschel an overview of contemporary Jewish scholarship. The catalogue summarizes his choices. In 1927–28, during his first year of matriculation, the faculty consisted of Hanoch Albeck, rabbinic philology and Talmud; Leo Baeck, homiletics, Apocryphal writings, and Midrash; Eduard Baneth, nearing retirement as the Talmud specialist; Ismar Elbogen, courses on the foundations of Wissenschaft des Judentums, history of European Jewry in the age of the expulsion, liturgy, and explication of one Talmud tractate; Julius Guttmann, the history of philosophy of religion from Kant to the present, a course on Jehuda Halevi's *Kuzari*, and contemporary philosophy of religion. The faculty chairman, Harry Torczyner, taught biblical exegesis and Semitic philology.[26]

Ismar Elbogen was the school's dominant personality (the chairmanship rotated each year, by alphabetical order, but Elbogen's approval for major decisions was always necessary). He represented both the qualities and shortcomings of German-Jewish scholarship. Born in the Prussian province of Posen, educated at the university and the Jewish Theological Seminary of Breslau (prototype of the American Conservative school), Elbogen appeared to harmonize German and East European Jewish cultures. He combined intellectual incisiveness and wit and a devotion to scholarly methods with a drive to revitalize contemporary Judaism. He found no tension between philological examination of texts, historical criticism, and his belief in an evolved Judaism as a testimony to the reality of God.

Elbogen was admired by generations of students as a dynamic teacher, effective administrator and fundraiser, and a warm-hearted counselor. Elbogen was an authority on prayer and worship, and his major work, *The Jewish Liturgy in Its Historical Development*, first published in 1913, defined its personal and collective aspects.[27] As a chronicler of Judaic scholarship, he wrote the Hochschule's official history. In addition to academic contributions, Elbogen's teaching popularized his broad knowledge of Jewish history and covered a range of subjects.

But Heschel, a former Hasid from Warsaw, could not share his spiritual life with Elbogen, despite the latter's benevolence. Elbogen endorsed the formal

German Jewish liturgy and had little sympathy with, or understanding of, East European manners. After settling in the United States, Heschel, tactfully omitting his teacher's name, deplored Elbogen's prejudiced views: "Describing the way in which the Hasidim prayed, a prominent Jewish historian, in a work first published in 1913 and reprinted in 1931, could write: 'The [Hasidic] movement did not signify a gain for religious life; the asset that lay in its striving for inwardness was more than cancelled out by the preposterousness of its superstitious notions and of its unruly behavior.'"[28] Contemporary Judaism, Heschel went on to note, should reject such stereotypes as it sought to renew itself.

Heschel was drawn to the Hochschule by the prospect of studying with Julius Guttmann (1880–1950), professor of Jewish philosophy who placed doing the mitzvot—which he called "this worldly miracle"—at the center of Judaism while developing a critical approach to systems.[29] A probing thinker and intellectual historian, Guttmann was brought to the Hochschule by Hermann Cohen, Immanuel Kant's eminent interpreter who became professor at the University of Marburg and founder of the neo-Kantian school. Cohen lectured for several years at the Hochschule as a visitor before moving permanently to Berlin in 1912.

With Guttmann, Heschel could clarify his own struggle between philosophy and spiritual insight. Guttmann approached this problem with sympathy for inwardness coupled with a severe objectivity. Although keenly interested in phenomenology and spiritual consciousness, Guttmann restricted himself to a descriptive history of ideas. But he agreed with Kant and Hermann Cohen that "religious truth is a consequence of ethical truth and thus its contents can be deduced from ethical principles."[30] At the same time, Guttmann appreciated the private experience of faith as interpreted by Schleiermacher and others. Guttmann's article on Jehuda Halevi, for example, states that true religious life occurs only "where the certainty of God seizes us with the full force of feeling and personal certitude is alive in us with immediacy." Heschel as a writer in the United States sought to arouse within his readers a similar conviction.

Heschel benefited from his teacher's firm distinctions, even if he did not share them. Guttmann taught that modern Jewish thinkers were expected to establish the validity of religion either "ideationally," by rational argument, or by appealing to a reader's inner life. In that respect, Heschel was closer to Franz Rosenzweig, the Jewish philosopher (and close associate of Buber's) whom Guttmann reproached for compromising both religion and philosophy by "using the language of Judaism to express personal experiences which had no general validity and which a Christian or non-religious thinker could as well express."[31] Guttmann, on the contrary, distinguished objective thought—what he called

*Julius Guttmann. Hebrew University, Jerusalem.
Courtesy of the Leo Baeck Institute, New York.*

"thinking inside Judaism" (*Denken im Judentum*)—from Rosenzweig's "situational thinking" (*Gelegenheitsdenken*). Heschel's self-definition as a religious philosopher—or "situational thinker"—was influenced by these debates.

Heschel formed warm personal ties with Guttmann, whom he graciously thanks, among others, in his dissertation. They often took walks together. Yet many students found Guttmann's lectures to be dry, abstract, and lacking topical relevance, and they considered the person to be distant: "The man standing behind the lectern, usually dressed in an old-fashioned, comfortably loose black or grey 'swallow-tail,' his figure already stooped when he was in his early forties, his head bent toward the right shoulder, was no smooth orator."[32]

Guttmann and Heschel had several intellectual affinities in common. For one, Heschel shared Guttmann's neo-Kantian belief in a priori cognitive categories, for Heschel possessed a "certainty" about the living God. Guttmann's serious consideration of phenomenology—study of the structure and contents of human consciousness—reinforced Heschel's work with Dessoir, leading to his doctoral dissertation on the mental awareness of the Hebrew prophets. On a personal level, Heschel enjoyed visiting Guttmann and his wife on Sabbath afternoons, with other students, at their comfortable apartment near the Tiergarten, Berlin's equivalent of Central Park.

Students appreciated the contrast of personalities in the Guttmanns' happy marriage. The delightful Grete Guttmann, daughter of a wealthy Liberal Jewish family, had a primarily intellectual interest in religion. "Julius Guttmann was pious and lived like an Orthodox Jew although there was nothing ostentatious about his religious practices. Grete Guttmann had an immense capacity for getting along with people, of any kind, especially those who were out of the ordinary. She was the interested and sympathetic confidante to many a bohemian writer, artist, and professor who confessed to her his troubled life."[33]

Heschel spoke humorously of another teacher, the philologist Harry Torczyner, who did not attract him. Early in the semester, Torczyner, impressed with Heschel's mastery of Hebrew, gave him a difficult biblical text to analyze, one that required careful philological, historical interpretation. When Heschel returned the next day with a completed project, Torczyner was amazed and encouraged him to specialize in biblical philology. But Heschel was not interested; he preferred to master this area, if only to reject its premises. The text's final unity was more than the sum of its "sources."

Heschel's more valuable ally was Hanoch Albeck, a specialist in Talmudic philology and Midrash who was educated at the Vienna Theological Seminary and the university. (Albeck's father, also a Talmudic and rabbinic scholar, was born and educated in Warsaw.) Heschel's teacher came to Berlin in 1920 as an independent researcher, and in 1926 began to replace the aging Eduard Baneth at the Hochschule.[34] Because Heschel had mastered Talmud and Midrash as an adolescent, in 1931, at the age of twenty-four, he was assigned as Albeck's assistant to teach advanced Talmud students.

Heschel considered the scholar, rabbi, and philosopher Leo Baeck (1873–1956), the Hochschule's most prominent teacher, to be "the most *educated* man" he ever met.[35] This quintessential German Jew combined piety, intellectual sophistication, and skilled community leadership. Baeck had taught homiletics and Midrash since arriving at the Hochschule in 1913 and was recognized (unofficially) as the chief rabbi of Berlin. At the time of Heschel's matriculation, Baeck at age fifty-four was president of the German Association of Rabbis, a leader of the Association of German Citizens of the Jewish Faith (*Central-Verein*), and several other community organizations.

Ismar Elbogen at a farewell dinner in his honor, Berlin, 1938. Detail of a photograph taken by Alexander Guttmann. Courtesy of the Leo Baeck Institute, New York.

Leo Baeck at a farewell dinner in honor of Ismar Elbogen, Berlin, 1938. Detail of a photograph taken by Alexander Guttmann. Courtesy of the Leo Baeck Institute, New York.

Baeck was a model German Liberal Jewish thinker, a rabbi's son who grew up in Lissa (in Polish, Leszno) in the Prussian province of Posen, meeting ground of eastern and western Jewishness.[36] He studied at the Breslau Theological Seminary and the university, completing secular and rabbinic studies in Berlin: philosophy at the University of Berlin (with a dissertation on Spinoza) and ordination at the Hochschule. Through Baeck, Heschel continued to absorb the legacy of Dilthey, Baeck's professor at the University of Berlin. During the fall of Heschel's first year at the Hochschule, Baeck taught the Apocrypha in light of contemporary approaches, religious pedagogy, and homiletics for beginners and advanced students. In the spring, he offered an introduction to Midrash, a tutorial on Midrash of Song of Songs, and homiletics. Baeck's teaching style was typical of the times. He arrived in the classroom punctually, read from his notes, and left immediately after class. He was formal, but occasionally extended himself generously to students.

Heschel developed a cordial relationship with Baeck, as with Julius Guttmann. And Heschel, along with many students, was received at the home of Professor and Mrs. Baeck for tea on Sabbath afternoons. Heschel may have appreciated Baeck's ability—inspired by Dilthey—to sympathize with the past and Baeck's ambition to establish a philosophical anthropology. But Heschel could not assent to Baeck's rationalism. The critical philosophy of Kant and Hermann Cohen was a decisive intellectual model for Baeck, who considered religion to be derived from ethics.

Breakthroughs and Disappointments

Heschel's intense study during his first two years in Berlin brought success. On 24 April 1929, he passed the supplementary government examinations for foreigners in German language, history, and literature, as well as Latin and mathematics.[37] Possessing unusual competence in the basic curriculum of the Hochschule, he effectively learned medieval philosophy and historical Bible criticism. In December of that year, he completed the Hochschule's intermediate examinations in Hebrew, Bible and Talmud, Midrash and liturgy, philosophy of religion, and Jewish history and literature. He was becoming a modern Jewish scholar.

But he underwent anxiety and pain in the process. Heschel was particularly worried about passing the mathematics part of the government qualifying examination. He sought help from Leo Baeck, who, as a representative of the Berlin Jewish community, knew people in several agencies. Baeck offered to intervene with an official on the Prussian Board of Education, who might exempt him from that test. Heschel was relieved, for he was weak in math and needed the time to prepare the other subjects. But, the day before the examination, the board notified Heschel that mathematics would be required. Heschel ran to Baeck. What should he do? Baeck said nothing to console the student.[38]

Heschel learned the hard way that Leo Baeck, with his keen desire to help, often promised more than he could deliver. Deeply disappointed, Heschel stayed up all night with a textbook, trying to memorize it. The next day he passed the mathematics section. Now he entered the university with full matriculation.

Heschel's third academic year at the Hochschule (1929–30) brought him further success, with some chastening of his pride. The school's ruling spirits— Julius Guttmann, Leo Baeck, and Ismar Elbogen—arranged a competitive essay on "Prophetic Visions of the Bible," which they expected Heschel to win because this topic was related to the university dissertation he had started to prepare. They might even retain him on the Hochschule faculty. A prize would be a feather in his cap, clear encouragement toward his doctoral thesis or scholarly publication. As it turned out, the first prize in the competition went to another outstanding student, Moses Sister, highly qualified, like Heschel, by an East European Jewish education—and an older man who already had completed his doctorate at the university. Heschel took second place.[39]

The Hochschule acknowledged the excellence of both students by according them teaching positions.[40] Heschel became an assistant to Hanoch Albeck, the Talmud professor, as his unusual competence in this field was sorely needed. But when Albeck took a year's leave of absence in fall 1933 and emigrated to Palestine the following year, his position was not offered to Heschel but to Abraham Weiss, who was followed by Alexander Guttmann. When Harry Torczyner emigrated to Palestine in 1933, Elias Auerbach was hired and soon replaced by the first-prize essay contest winner, Moses Sister.

Heschel's academic choices around 1928–30 present instructive contrasts with two other East European Jewish students of philosophy who became prominent in modern Orthodox Jewish life. In July 1930, about two years before Heschel fulfilled his requirements for the doctorate, Joseph Soloveitchik and Alexander Altmann submitted their dissertations to the Philosophical Faculty. (Heschel knew Altmann in Berlin but probably not Soloveitchik.)[41]

When Joseph Baer Soloveitchik (originally Solowiejczyk) came to Berlin in 1925 from Warsaw where he was studying economics, he already had mastered the rigorous Lithuanian Talmudic method of his celebrated grandfather, Rabbi Hayim of Brisk (Brest-Litovsk). He did not matriculate at the Orthodox Rabbinical Seminary but specialized in philosophy at the university, minoring in physics and mathematics. Soloveitchik asked Heinrich Maier to direct his doctoral dissertation on the epistemology of Hermann Cohen, the Jewish neo-Kantian philosopher, and received his doctoral degree in December 1932.[42] This subject and approach helped Soloveitchik to elaborate a rigorous rationale for Talmudic authority and halakhah as the systematic foundation of Jewish life.

Alexander Altmann, who did study at the Orthodox Seminary, chose Max Dessoir to direct his dissertation, which was on Max Scheler's phenomenology of religious cognition.[43] Altmann, who was particularly sensitive to the dynamics of consciousness, explored Scheler's "philosophy of value" and the manner in which emotions may convey insights, both ethical and religious. Altmann remained Orthodox in his practice and used philosophy to justify the integrity of halakhah. Ordained at the seminary, he received the doctorate in February 1931. Altmann then entered community life as an Orthodox rabbi, while furthering his teaching and scholarly research.

Heschel remained betwixt and between his schools, Jewish and secular—the Liberal Hochschule, the Orthodox Seminary, the university—and David Koigen's discussion group (see chapter 7). At the university, however, Heschel remained centered on religious issues. Unlike Soloveitchik and Altmann, Heschel did not devote his dissertation to philosophy as such, but to Bible interpretation. His interdisciplinary subject required a bureaucratic maneuver. Although sponsored within the Philosophy Faculty by Max Dessoir, he needed a co-director from the Theological Faculty, Alfred Bertholet. Bending the university's normal divisions, but within the bounds of academic objectivity, Heschel's dissertation on the Hebrew prophets expressed his personal commitments.

Professionally, Heschel was at a crossroads: would he become a philosopher, a rabbi, or a scholar? He was relatively free to define his vocation—until January 1933 when Hitler's ascent to power severely limited his choices. His predecessors were more decisive. In 1932, Altmann succeeded Josef Wohlgemuth at the Rabbiner-Seminar as lecturer in Jewish philosophy and became rabbi for the Berlin Orthodox community.[44] Soloveitchik married, emigrated in 1932 to the United States, settled in Boston, and commuted to New York where he taught Talmud at the Rabbi Isaac Elhanan Theological Seminary (later Yeshiva University). He became the ranking halakhic authority within the American Orthodox community.

Heschel was still seeking his true community in Berlin. At the university he remained suspended between philosophy, Old Testament studies, and theology; at the "scientific" Hochschule, he was a man of traditional, East European piety. Nor did his Hasidic roots find soil in the Orthodox Seminary, more amenable as it was to Lithuanian legalism. Unsettled in each sphere, he continued to write and publish Yiddish poetry. Inwardly, his religious convictions did not change. His character was too strong, his spiritual autonomy too radical, to compromise his feeling of intimacy with God and his unique responsibility to the Jewish people.

7

A Jewish Philosophical Mentor (1928–1931)

And yet, systematic thinker that he was, he never quite subdued within himself the "situational thinker." Whoever met him had to recognize the simultaneous existence of a naïve soul combined with an energetic philosophical mind.

Heschel, "David Koigen" (1934)

HESCHEL'S MEDIATOR AMONG HIS WARSAW, VILNA, AND BERLIN IDENTITIES WAS A person, not an institution. Helping him integrate his diverse worlds and rise above them was David Koigen (1879–1933), one of Fishl Schneersohn's closest associates. On 30 January 1928, about two months after Heschel's arrival in Berlin, Koigen gave a lecture at the Hochschule entitled "The Structure of the Historical World in Judaism," based on his recently published book.[1] Koigen was a philosopher of history and culture trained in Europe's leading universities who had studied with Wilhelm Dilthey, among other important thinkers. His field was sociology in its broadest sense. He became Heschel's model Jewish thinker. Yet Koigen exercised his calling privately, for he was not part of any university or school faculty. He got by on a government pension thanks to Grimme, the Prussian Minister of Culture, who was noted for helping scholars—although stipends were rarely accorded to Jews. Koigen supplemented this precarious livelihood through invited lectures.[2]

Soon after Koigen's Hochschule presentation, Heschel formed a friendship with him. By 1929 Heschel found a haven at the Koigens' apartment at 3 Mommsen Strasse in the Charlottenburg section of Berlin, almost two miles west of the

David Koigen in Berlin. Courtesy of Mira Zakai, Tel Aviv.

Brandenburg Gate, and he used it as his return address on correspondence. By 1930 Heschel moved into a room at Kant Strasse, just two blocks away.[3] David Koigen brought Heschel into his own cosmopolitan, Jewishly committed community, whose orientation was primarily philosophical. With Koigen and the group gathered around him, Heschel tested ideas and refined his spiritual commitments. Koigen's professional ambition was to analyze cultural activity in all its manifestations. His intimate intention—which Heschel shared—was to rescue the Jewish soul from indifference, assimilation, or alienation.

Koigen's effect on Heschel remained indelible. In the United States, Heschel always alluded to his "teacher, David Koigen" with utmost reverence, a tone he reserved for few other persons. Among the photographs gracing the walls of Heschel's study in his Riverside Drive apartment in New York were portraits of his mother and his father, the Novominsker rebbe—and some remembered a photograph of Koigen.

From Peasant to Committed Scholar

Koigen's Eastern European Jewish odyssey anticipated the journey into modernity on which Heschel was embarked. Koigen was born of rural Hasidic parents and became an internationally educated social philosopher. His exceptional warmth and intellectual passion helped shape Heschel's responses to contemporary needs and values. The influence was concrete and precise, for Koigen's vivid historical autobiography, *Apokalyptische Reiter* (Apocalyptic horsemen; Berlin, 1925) demonstrated how a traditional religious upbringing helped shape his revolutionary commitments and, ultimately, his innovative Jewish thinking.[4]

Students knew their mentor's history. Koigen (the name is a Russian or Yiddish form of Kohen) was born in the village of Wachniaki, near Staro-Konstantinov, in the Ukrainian province of Volynia. He was raised by devout parents and educated in a *heder*. His mother was the daughter of "a peasant learned in Torah."[5] His father, "Mordecai Koigen, animated by ecstatic Hasidism, was a tenant farmer who descended from an old family of Kabbalists; his ancestor was the famous Frankfurt Kabbalist Rabbi Naftali, the son of Isaak ha-Kohen." In addition to this distinguished ancestry, and profound contact with his parents' Habad (Lubavitch) Hasidism, Koigen treasured his closeness to "the Ukrainian soil and its peasants [as] the happiest years of his childhood." Students believed that their teacher's "serene, loving attitude toward his fellow human beings" and "artistic inclinations" were due to these simple origins.

The nineteenth century's turmoils entered Koigen's life at age seven when his father died. His older brother, Fishl, a militant who later supported the Bolshevik Revolution, took over his education.[6] During the late 1880s, David Koigen attended excellent Russian schools in Nemirov and Odessa and acquired a native's knowledge of German, the key to European thought and culture. By age sixteen he was fascinated with economics and was familiar with the writings of Adam Smith, David Ricardo, Léon Say, and Karl Marx.

Yet, unlike his brother, David preferred theory to political activism. From around 1896 to 1901 (between ages seventeen and twenty-one) he studied at the universities of Paris, Berlin, Munich, Zurich, and Berne. In 1900 Koigen earned a doctorate at the University of Berne, with a dissertation on the left-wing Hegelian school.[7] After marrying Helena Sulzmann, who studied Russian literature and shared his philosophical interests, he began his career in Berlin.

As a spiritually committed philosopher of culture (or sociologist, as a practitioner of the nascent discipline was called), Koigen carried forward the intellectual legacy of Dilthey, whose philosophy dominated academic thought before and immediately after the First World War. Dilthey's range of knowledge was astounding, and he contributed major insights to the fields of metaphysics, ethics, theory of knowledge, literature, art, and the history of philosophy. Dilthey ambitiously sought to establish a "philosophical anthropology"—a science of humanity in which all realms of activity fit into a whole.

Koigen's teachers—the generation preceding World War I—shared this harmonious vision of creativity, ethics, and religion. At the University of Berlin alone, Koigen studied with Dilthey, Friedrich Paulsen, Georg Simmel, Gustav von Schmoller, among others. In Berlin, Koigen also met Martin Buber, with whom he continued to correspond.[8]

Friedrich Paulsen wrote on pedagogy and stressed the interrelation of moral and cultural dimensions of personal and public life. The philosopher of culture and religion Georg Simmel, who lectured at Berlin University without full faculty status, was known for his broad, encyclopedic interests—and he was of partly Jewish descent. Simmel made original contributions to the fields of religion, art, literature, and sociology. Koigen, like Buber and many others, was stimulated by Simmel's analysis of religious thought, which resonated with his personal intensity.[9]

Heschel was attracted to this synthetic approach, for it could provide a common foundation for religion, ethics, art, and other forms of knowledge. Heschel, attuned to the inner workings of the mind, was particularly sensitive to Koigen's theory of cognition, which he adapted from Dilthey's analysis. Koigen called it "the culture act," a coordination of data from disparate realms within one cognitive insight. In the 1920s, under the influence of Edmund Husserl, a philosophy of mind called phenomenology was developed, examining the structure and dynamics of human consciousness. A theory of interpretation called hermeneutics was a practical result of this close study of mental and creative processes.

Koigen considered thought to be inseparable from action. The choice of a theory of knowledge held political and moral consequences. In Berlin during the decade from 1903 to 1913, Koigen began his independent scholarship, maintaining his research despite financial insecurity. Inspired by Simmel and Dilthey, Koigen devoted his research to defining common structural laws—from science, politics, and economics to literature, philosophy, and religion. By the time he was twenty-four years old, Koigen had published four books of political and cultural ideology.[10] He was committed to some form of socialism as the new world philosophy; he then returned to Russia shortly before the revolutions of 1917.

Koigen's teachings emerge from intense life experience. Amid the churnings of revolution, the secular theoretician became a thinker with a prophetic mission. In Petrograd, during the summer of 1917, Koigen responded to what he understood was the dying democratic revolution by forming a research seminar, Gesellschaft zur Forschung der Revolution, a study group (or "community") whose purpose was to penetrate the meaning of this history in the making.

Exile from the city provided the laboratory. Threats by the Bolshevik secret police, in addition to physical perils, drove the Koigens and their son Georg (born in 1913) from Petrograd. During their flight across Ukraine toward Kiev, Koigen rediscovered his essential Jewishness and applied it to the present. He learned of horrible pogroms, spoke with survivors, and documented the anarchy following each change of power. He also gained insight into religious faith as he observed simple Jews waiting for whatever would come, strengthened by their certainty of God's existence.[11] Reclaiming the heritage of the Ukrainian countryside of his youth, Koigen found the "authentic Jew" who might cure the ills of modernity.

Koigen then understood that an updated interpretation of Hasidism could provide a vital force for contemporary Jews. The central chapter of *Apocalyptic Horsemen*, entitled "The Land of the Blessed," portrays the Eastern European Jews whose "culture" (their inner, spiritual world) was far richer than their "history" (or social environment). According to Koigen, Hasidism arose after the disaster of Shabbetai Zvi (1626–1676), the false messiah who converted to Islam; Hasidism "erected a new 'Jerusalem' in the soul of every Jew, every common person. The rapid spread of Hasidism, bringing new rituals and new conceptions of

God and humanity, is proof that the Shabbetai Zvi movement was but a pretext for a profound, popular movement."[12]

Hasidism was an essentially democratic movement, Koigen believed, potentially able to renew Jewish life. A truly religious humanism would add to faith a strong moral freedom and responsibility. Koigen praised Habad (Lubavitch) Hasidism—his father's affiliation—which spread spirituality and Jewish learning throughout Russia. As a sociologist, he admired the role of rebbe or zaddik, the charismatic leader who could give his followers self-confidence. Every person, educated or not, was capable of approaching God, of tasting the Divine: "The metaphysical and general value of mankind increased and the individual gained greatly in inner strength."

Koigen formulated a Jewish anthropology, a neo-Hasidic definition of being human—one which Heschel later developed in his own terms. Its common foundation was the holiness of every person as created in the image of God. This was not a parochial vision. Even secular forms of Jewish creativity, according to Koigen, were elevated by Hasidic ways of experiencing reality—invigorating Jewish life even more than the Enlightenment. Jewish music, painting, and literature all propagated the Jewish soul. Koigen had reintegrated his childhood culture into a sophisticated sociology of Jewishness.

Fleeing from Petrograd, Koigen reached Kiev in 1919, where he began to teach philosophy and sociology at the university. He and his family lived in the Jewish quarter, called Podol, a community torn by contradictions. In recent years, Jews from other towns had sought refuge there from pogroms, placing their hopes in various doctrines. Many young people were attracted to the Mussar movement, which was devoted solely to Torah study and a pure and moral life. After the 1917 revolutions, others—without losing their yearning for religious faith—became socialist or communist ideologues or nihilists.

The two men who helped shape Heschel's destiny met in Kiev. Around 1920, Koigen and Fishl Schneersohn, both secularly educated Jews of Hasidic background, met at the university. Schneersohn was teaching pedagogy and medicine; Koigen was professor of social philosophy. Koigen describes Schneersohn as a "descendant of the founding family of Habad" and "a man in whom Hasidism and secular culture carry on a symbolic battle." They became acquainted after Koigen delivered a lecture at a Worker's College. Schneersohn tried, unsuccessfully, to enlist him in a religious Bund or union. Koigen preferred to organize philosophical and religious discussions.

The idea for Koigen's Berlin seminars—which Heschel later joined—was thus conceived. In Kiev, about fifty eager people participated, mostly Eastern

European Jews who preferred general topics—such as the unknown God, the nature of the world, how to define humankind, and the like—rather than specifically Jewish issues. Koigen sought to convince them that the study of science does not inevitably lead to atheism and nihilism. Koigen and Schneersohn, with the Zionist Hayim Greenberg—who had just fled from Moscow—edited *Kadima* (Onward), a Jewish literary and philosophical journal devoted to philosophy and the science of religion.[13] But after two years, Koigen was uprooted again.

In 1921, Koigen and his family escaped from Kiev, for Koigen was suspected of treason by the Bolshevik secret police. They resettled in Berlin, where they had lived before the revolutions. Schneersohn returned to Warsaw and remained in touch.

Koigen applied his Hasidic upbringing and his Russian and German education to construct an up-to-date Jewish world vision. In Berlin, he elaborated a systematic philosophy of Judaism as a key to understanding the destiny of Europe. With no institutional support for his scholarship, he renewed his acquaintance with Martin Buber and requested help in promoting his writings.[14] Koigen mailed him some manuscript chapters of *Apocalyptic Horsemen* for Buber's influential monthly, *Der Jude;* he asked Buber to help find a reviewer for his recent book, *The Moral God,* in the Zionist newspaper *Jüdische Rundschau,* which was edited by Buber's friend and disciple Robert Weltsch. Koigen sought to associate Buber with the Jewish Religious-Philosophical Society he founded with his "young friend," Dr. Fishl Schneersohn, who was soon to lecture on "Neo-Hasidic Motifs in the Present East-Jewish Culture."[15]

Koigen urged Buber to join him in promoting his solution to the historical emergency, one profoundly compatible with Buber's biblical humanism. Both thinkers were sociologists in the large sense of the term—defining humankind in its material and its religious dimensions—and both were transmuting Jewish traditions into a "philosophical anthropology" of liberation.[16] They were seeking to alleviate postwar, postrevolutionary alienation.

Transforming European Culture

By the time Heschel met Koigen in Berlin, the latter was applying the Jewish philosophy forged by the century's major upheavals, the First World War and the Russian Revolutions. Koigen and Schneersohn—Heschel's two modern mentors—faced the historical moment by establishing a redemptive science of humankind. Both men lectured at clubs, private homes, schools, and universities. With Schneersohn and Franz Hilker, Koigen founded a learned review,

Ethos: A Quarterly Journal of Sociology, Philosophy of History and of Culture.
This elegantly printed periodical featured articles on culture, history, philosophy, psychology, and pedagogy.[17]

Heschel's moral commitments were congruent with this spiritual and intellectual challenge to Europe's disintegration. The inaugural editorial of *Ethos* (dated 1925–26) announced the constructive battle in somewhat abstract terms: "The conditions and experiences of disharmony, the atmosphere of continual crisis, and catastrophic events, combine with a mental and emotional awareness of human powerlessness, and simultaneously with a meta-individual, even superhuman, yet undefined force. A doom, a 'historical' fate that we can neither understand nor evade, rules the mind and human existence." The journal's editors sought to cure the human propensity for wars (and victories) by helping the various peoples to live together in unity. If Europe could maintain a common "culture" for one or two generations, there might be peace. *Ethos* challenged the "night view," despair: "May God alone help, if he exists, if he wants to. This means questioning not only the insight, but reality itself."

The specifically Jewish orientation of *Ethos* was central to its mission. The individual became worthless, the preface continued. But religion, a key to interpreting the political dilemma, required both community and personal action. This Jewish perspective might protect individuals from the collectivist ideologies now dominating the European masses. According to Koigen, political cooperation among nations and the creation of a link with God could help civilized Europe survive. Jews in particular, he believed, had to recover their essential spirituality in order to strengthen the free individual and the Jewish people.

At the same time, Koigen drew a grim diagnosis in *Apocalyptic Horsemen*. There he predicted that, after the catastrophes of world war and the revolutions, bad times lay ahead. Germany and Russia, so different from each other, shared the same fate. The masses looked either to communism or to nationalistic ideals of glory and power. When the "cultural" aspect was weakened, the "historical" threatened to overwhelm them. In Germany, racialism and the revival of legendary myths were barbaric consequences of its defeat in the First World War. Throughout postrevolutionary Europe, Jews were uniquely vulnerable.

In *Apocalyptic Horsemen* Koigen went on to explain why Eastern European Jews, who had no "history" of their own (because they owned no territory), sought in the "historical mystery of Russia" the meaning of their own destiny. Jews, he believed, possessed a special need to understand the world around them: "The Jew thus suffers from an exaggerated sensitivity. Whereas others react only to relatively major events, [the Jew] reacts violently even to the smallest incident."[18]

When he and Heschel met, Koigen was recognized as an advanced historical and sociological thinker. At the University of Berlin's Institutum Judaicum, he spoke on "Religious Movements in East European Judaism"; at the Hochschule für die Wissenschaft des Judentums, his topics included "Religion in the Being of Solitude" and "The Conception of the Historical World in Antiquity and the Jewish Middle Ages." He also lectured at the Berlin Society for Jewish Literature and History and in the cities of Guben, Chemnitz, Breslau, and Amsterdam.[19]

Heschel thus met Koigen during the heyday of his mission to effect a "profound transformation" of "philosophy and religion, scientific consciousness, pedagogy, state, and political parties"—in a word, of Ethos. Heschel emulated Koigen's attempts to revive genuine religious feeling in a chaotic world. As a doctoral candidate at the University of Berlin, he prepared himself to share that task.

Koigen's Philosophical Community

This philosopher's conscious, passionate struggle for a justification
of public as well as private history, for a "theodicy of culture" . . . also
expresses an ancient will, which, since the Bible, we find in Jewish think-
ing through the Aggadah, the Kabbalah, and Hasidism.
Heschel, "David Koigen" (1934)

During his third academic year in Berlin, Heschel joined David Koigen's personal seminar that met weekly at his Mommsen Strasse apartment. This study group—called a *Philosophische Arbeitsgemeinschaft*—focused more distinctly on Jewish issues than the journal *Ethos,* which used social philosophy, psychology, and religious thinking to analyze and challenge the "night view" of alienation. For Heschel and its other members, the Koigen Circle (as it was also called) provided common ground between several institutions. It was becoming Heschel's modern Jewish home.

The archaeological strata of Heschel's American writings surface in David Koigen's seminar. Yet the agenda does not provide "sources" of his thought. Heschel derived basic notions from these conversations as well as from academic courses and readings. Most of the issues examined in Koigen's group were current in the 1920s. Heschel's inspiration was deeper, confirmed more from insight and experience, as he framed his perspective during the first four months of their theoretical, but fervent explorations.

Members of this intimate group were degree candidates at the university, the Hochschule, or the Rabbiner-Seminar, or had already earned the doctorate. They were engaged in what we call today "Jewish renewal"—judging present conditions with the goal of making the religious tradition relevant. Heschel was inspired by Koigen's activist theory, which defined "inner laws of Jewish culture" as affected by the First World War and Russian revolutions. He seconded Koigen's rejection of nihilism and utopianism which subverted personal responsibility.

The Koigen Circle fostered a warm family atmosphere, with Helena Koigen participating fully, and their young son, Georg, often in attendance. Koigen chose the participants.[20] In a typical meeting, one person presented a paper, and discussions ensued which Koigen then summarized and analyzed. The meetings normally lasted for two to three hours, starting in either late morning or evening. The night sessions might continue until 12:45 A.M., when the last Stadtbahn train was about to leave. For each meeting a reporter (*Protokollführer*) took notes and typed a summary (the *Protokoll*). The group reviewed the minutes at the beginning of the next seminar to ensure continuity.[21]

Participating critically in these group discussions, Heschel came to realize that, even among these highly educated Jews—most of whom were East Europeans—he was a misfit. They were philosophers; he was a religious thinker—and more. Heschel broadcast his witness in Yiddish poetry. With and against the Koigen Circle, Heschel tested ideas and completed his self-definition.

Although Koigen and his writings held the center of attention, Heschel soon became the circle's most prominent member—other than the leader himself. Heschel gave at least as much as he received, putting his own stamp on the investigations. He did not speak the most, but deftly clarified issues and fortified his approach. Among his peers, he was the least deferential to Koigen, while respecting his master's standing. Heschel was most active during the first six months or so, although he remained involved until the seminar ended in 1933, at Koigen's sudden death.

A sampling of the group's meticulously preserved minutes opens a window to its revitalizing Judaism in times of crisis. One of the first meetings took place on 26 January 1930, from 11:30 A.M. to 1:35 P.M. Participants were listed by title and last name only: Prof. and Mrs. Koigen, Dr. Pless, Borodianski, Heschel, Peysack, Dr. Weinberg, Rosenthal, Poppers. No Protokollführer is indicated. The minutes record this initiative: "Mr. Heschel suggests that the papers given at each meeting be submitted to the record keeper so he will not have to take notes on their content." Dr. Weinberg gave a talk on "The sociological view of religion and anthropo-theology," based on the chapter of the same title in Koigen's book *The Moral God*. Discussions began as Koigen spoke about Rousseau, Hume, and, briefly, Martin Buber.

Among the consistent subjects of debate—and of crucial significance to Heschel—was the relation between ethics (a purely human or rational endeavor) and spiritual insight (implying divine revelation). Heschel in fact opened the next meeting (2 February 1930) with a paper on the "moral structure of religion" according to Kant; the minutes summarize Heschel's analysis of Kant: "1) The religion of the cultivated person has to begin with that freedom which is a fundamental condition of culture itself. 2) Morality is an autonomous realm, independent of God, dominated by the concept of freedom (not dominated by mankind). 3) Religion as complement and support for morality."[22]

Koigen's seminar was the testing ground for Heschel's vehement opposition to "symbolism" (by which he means, broadly, concepts substituted for the ineffable God). Heschel's focus on neo-Kantianism was sharpened by another participant who asked how it was possible to convey verbally the reality of God. The minutes continue: "At the beginning of the discussion, Salomonski says that, strictly speaking, Kant (the starting point of Heschel's talk) as well considers religion to be a 'fiction,' the filling of a void in the construct of reason. Koigen adds to this remark by saying that indeed students of Kant become atheists as a consequence of this doctrine." Koigen seemed to agree with Heschel that "fictions" (that is, mental constructs) are no substitute for divine reality, and he went on to discuss morality, reason, and Kant.

Such vital deliberations continued each week. These were technical analyses dealing with issues of theory, but they held major implications for religious practice. These companions were facing the great divide of twentieth-century religion: Was Judaism a religion of reason or a human response to God's revelation at Sinai? What latitude of interpretation was permissible according to Jewish law? Modern apologists for Orthodoxy, like Samson Raphael Hirsch, attempted to justify the divine purpose of the *mitzvot* rationally. Liberal Jewish scholars, of course, questioned the status of supernatural claims. Heschel navigated these treacherous straits with confidence.

His main concern was not secularism as such, but reductionism, the tendency to explain what he considered to be truly religious phenomena (such as prophetic inspiration) in exclusively human terms. The reigning neo-Kantianism was disputed territory. Another important session was stimulated by Hirsch Poppers's paper on Hermann Cohen, who renewed Jewish philosophy for the twentieth century.[23] The early Cohen derived Judaism from Kant's ethical principles, allowing some of his followers to translate the supernatural religion into a logical system. "Salomonski says that Cohen's dogmatic religion is only marginally different from a biblical religion of revelation. Philosophy must find a more solid basis than theology. Spinoza and Kant have given us something to hold onto."

The issue central to contemporary Orthodoxy was on the table. What was the status of the *mitzvot?* Were they simply human acts or part of a metaphysical process? In this detailed debate, Koigen stated, "The rites are followed because one always wants to be connected to God." Helena Koigen added, "For Cohen, the laws are a kind of religious pedagogy." To which Heschel replied, lifting the analysis to a spiritual level (still according to the minutes): "The chief gain may lie not so much in the actual enactment of rites but in prayer. . . . For the religious person, it is not always necessary to attribute a meaning to every action required by dogma. If one is in love, fulfilling even a whim may constitute a meaningful act." The real value of prayer, according to Heschel, is ineffable, beyond reason, beyond words. Whatever the theory, Heschel appreciated Koigen's practical conclusion: "The aim of our group should be that each one can perform sacramental acts without restriction."

Instead of the Liberal, neo-Kantian paradigm, Heschel preferred to draw upon Hasidic sources. He elaborated this approach to Judaism at the following meeting (2 March), steering the discussion toward the living God.[24] Salomonski first spoke about "the cultural-historical structure of religion." Koigen mentioned his book *The Moral God,* and then discussed the interdependence of culture and religion. Heschel examined the Hebrew term *hesed* (loving-kindness). Koigen discussed it from a philosophical viewpoint while Heschel brought into focus the understanding of God as a concerned Being. Toward the end, Heschel asserted a tenet (derived from the Zohar) that he held for the rest of his life: "An ethical action on our part causes a metaphysical result. Not only is God necessary for us, but we are for God. God acts through us."[25] This Hasidic intuition linked mysticism and moral action.

Heschel focused the debate even more intently as he took center stage for the next four meetings. His approach to William James's *Varieties of Religious Experience* deflected the group's emphasis from philosophy of culture to individual experience.[26] Using James to probe various modes of religious consciousness, Heschel developed a refutation of psychology applied to the Hebrew prophets in his dissertation.

At the 16 March meeting Heschel cited James's case histories, which explore (and perhaps confuse) authentic religious experience and pathological cases. After a searching discussion of sin, forgiveness, psychology of religion, and Hasidism, Koigen summarized his perspective: "Each culture—as does each human being—has different paths to God; each culture constructs its own world and thus its own language; thus, this is a problem of communication. This is reported here: emotions, psychic 'stuff.' We speak in the language of psychology; and yet psychology as a science is belittled because we ask: Is the psychological truth identical with the truth of the whole world? Is psyche illusion or reality? It *becomes* reality if we succeed in anchoring it metaphysically."[27]

The debate was momentous, for these thinkers were attempting to define the truth of religion. Nothing was more urgent. Yet Heschel, despite his recognition of Koigen's real understanding of Hasidic piety, began to dissociate himself from his teacher's sociological approach—that the individual is inseparable from his or her culture. Heschel consistently focused upon the individual who relates to God.

Heschel found a method allowing him to reach people outside the community of faith, that is, the majority: interpret the subtle modalities of emotion. Influenced by analysts of religious feelings such as Friedrich Schleiermacher, Rudolf Otto, and Max Scheler—in addition to Hasidic piety and poetic experience—Heschel stood forth as the philosopher of "radical amazement" he became in the United States.

Exceptionally, the group met two days later (18 March), interrupting Heschel's examination of William James.[28] After a discussion of the Baal Shem Tov as a "Jewish Prometheus" who can challenge God, Heschel clarified some emotions associated with religious insight: "Following Heschel's statement, Mrs. Koigen explicates his terms *Angst* [anxiety], *Furcht* [reverence], and *Scheu* [fear, timidity, shyness, awe—or embarrassment]—of which only the last applies to the position of the Jews in relation to God. The *yirat shamayim* [fear of Heaven, another Hebrew synonym of "piety"] in particular expresses *Scheu* but not *Angst*."[29]

Applying his finesse, Heschel establishes criteria for judging religious knowledge. Cognitive emotions allowed him to displace rational philosophy and psychology. His Yiddish poetry already verbalized intuitions of awe, wonder, and spiritual embarrassment. He now used the American psychologist as a foil against which to judge David Koigen's philosophy of culture.[30] His doctoral dissertation eventually justified a higher "individualism" of the prophet receiving God's initiative.

Heschel's participation reached a climax during intense discussions from

May through June 1930. Rejecting psychological explanations of religious insight, questioning Koigen's metaphysics of collective life, he began to assert himself more forcefully.

It was an event of no return. On 3 June 1930, from nine-thirty to midnight, Heschel questioned the seminar's very purpose.[31] Despite his admiration for Koigen—for his vast knowledge, his passion for Judaism, his sublimated Hasidism, as well as his personal warmth and generosity—Heschel was committed to another path, another teaching. The minutes (written by Fritz Salomonski, to whom Heschel later dedicated a Yiddish poem) review the seminar's work to date and record a decisive debate about theory versus action. We cite verbatim this record of Heschel's bold initiative:

> Since three members of the Circle are absent, some more general questions concerning the program will be discussed.
>
> Heschel suggests that they address the question of how the Circle could move on from the state of theoretical observations to more practical realizations. Every member of the group should work on his suggestions and submit them in writing.—In the subsequent discussion the meaning of this question is addressed.
>
> First Prof. Koigen generally welcomes the question. However, he thinks it conveys a certain discontent.
>
> Salomonski attempts to describe the results of the work done so far. He says: Prof. Koigen found a way to make us understand the value of cultural work in a new way by anchoring it metaphysically.—He did this in order to assure that we would be protected in our private, spiritual activity from the doubts that might afflict us in our materialistically-oriented environment. This in itself constitutes an eminently practical effect of a basically pedagogical nature. Salomonski meets Heschel's demand for [practical] realization with the experience of effect: In each of us, the understanding that results from our reflections will grow roots, it will have its effects in our practical-professional lives, depending on our personal abilities. At this point, however, Salomonski cannot imagine what the joint practical action Heschel suggests should look like.

The group assumed that their discussions, as theoretical as they might be, protected them from distractions. If Koigen acknowledged the benefit to individuals, why would Heschel object to continuing their focus on a metaphysics of culture?

> Weinberg asks Mr. Heschel to express himself more clearly. Weinberg distinguishes two kinds of practical community work: one of a more external na-

ture, like the collecting of *zedakah* [charitable contributions]; the other in the sense of a community way of living, which would, to say it clearly, result in a new *Shulhan Arukh* [the standard code of Jewish law].

Rosenthal thinks that the recognition of hitherto obscured cultural facts is itself of practical significance.—Pless sees the only possibility of practical realization in the passing on of our reflections to others outside the Circle. It is noted that Heschel does not contradict this.

The real debate with Heschel then begins, for Koigen's students rallied about their leader without challenging Heschel directly. Yet, teacher and student did disagree profoundly on the solution to their era's moral, political, and religious alienation. Would sociology or individual spiritual discipline provide an answer?

Prof. Koigen now speaks. First he summarizes the work that has been done so far. Then he outlines a general comprehensive program. It is not accidental that the Jewish problem is at the center of our reflections. *Fatum* [Fate] and the nature-God have collapsed, and the Spirit-God, as Judaism has recognized it, will begin its cultural hegemony. Koigen deliberately opposes Spengler, just as he opposes the conflict between Greek classicism and Buddhism versus Judaism and Christianity. From the spirit of Judaism a cultural Vatican has to emerge capable of taking positions on all questions of life and giving answers that have axiomatic value. In this sense, the group's work should eventually broaden and gradually address all kinds of problems of life, be they of a religious, social, or political nature.

—Contrary to this, Heschel demands that instead of a spreading toward the general and the far future there should be a progressive concentration on the individual, on the concrete human being.—

Koigen sees in this a kind of Prometheanism. [Since] the concrete person exists only in the social group, separation would lead to self-destruction. Thus genuine religious emotion in particular seeks the context of the universal; Prometheus, who wanted only to remain separate, stands against God (the Greeks call this Hubris).

To conclude, Prof. Koigen says: a community world-view is possible, but the experience has to remain private. Whenever somebody through his private experience becomes uncertain, he can—from case to case—submit his doubts for general discussion.

After the discussion was finished, a second programmatic issue is addressed—the distribution of topics for a series of papers on a description of Jewish culture. There are, however, difficulties on matching of topics to speakers, so this is postponed.

Contradictory approaches were defined: Heschel's was to augment personal piety; an all-encompassing cultural theory was Koigen's. According to Heschel, philosophy could not provide a foundation for Jewish renewal, for the living God cannot enter our systems, as consensual as they might become under Koigen's benevolent guidance. People, not codes, would save Judaism.

Heschel thus formulated his notion of Judaism as energized by polarities: the individual and the collective, spontaneity and regular prayer, halakhah and aggadah, and so on. Adjusting the putative "Prometheanism" of the Baal Shem Tov to the contemporary world, Heschel insists that Judaism can be renewed by facing the living God. Hindsight makes clear how Heschel's opposition to his teacher's sociological thinking prefigures his own philosophy of religion: intuitive knowledge can bring us closer to God and transform our moral sensitivities; and Judaism must not be limited to ritual, law, or secular nationalism.

If Heschel felt misunderstood, or even rejected, he did not retreat from his oppositional stance. After all, Koigen and his students were not neutrally pursuing knowledge; together they were striving to establish Jewish community on a religious basis for the ultimate purpose of redeeming the world. Yet, after that meeting, Heschel withdrew somewhat and was often absent. After all, he had many other duties: finishing his courses at the university; preparing for his general doctoral examinations; beginning a thesis proposal. And his work toward a degree at the Hochschule was far from complete.

Yet he remained a loyal participant until the very end. In fact, Heschel encouraged others to join the group, especially East European Jews who, like himself, might find in the Koigen Circle a valuable transition into contemporary European thought. One such instance changed the life of another unusual man.

One afternoon, Heschel was talking with Aaron Brand, one of his classmates at the Hochschule.[32] Born in Ozorkov, Poland, Brand was an observant Jew from a Zionist family who had been educated in Palestine. He returned to Berlin in 1928 to earn a medical degree while also studying philosophy and broadening his love for art and literature. Brand admired Heschel's Yiddish poems, recently published in *Zukunft* found at the Hochschule reading room. Brand memorized several of them. Anxious to share impressions, they walked down Artillerie Strasse to the library, while Brand recited the opening piece, "God pursues me everywhere."

Heschel felt understood. Aaron Brand found no discrepancy between science and poetry, and he was moved by the same "silent shudder" of the holy which sustained this former Hasid from Warsaw. Discussing the poem amid the hubbub of Berlin, Heschel urged Brand to join the Koigen Circle, which he did, also remaining until the end.

Around the same time, Heschel welcomed another East European friend into the Koigen group. Moses Shulvass, born in Plonsk, Poland, attended the Takhemoni Yeshiva in Warsaw.[33] Before studying history at the University of Berlin, Shulvass published essays in various Yiddish papers and periodicals. Heschel advised Shulvass to attend the Orthodox Rabbiner-Seminar instead of joining him at the Hochschule. Both of these men remembered the Koigen Circle with reverence, as did Heschel.

Two Crises Within Judaism

Heschel learned how international Jewish leaders sought to renew contemporary Judaism through Koigen. During the time of their debate, Lily H. Montagu, the indefatigable Honourable Secretary of the World Union for Progressive Judaism and its acknowledged leader, invited Koigen to present a major address at its Second World Conference. (This organization represented Liberal and Reform Jews in Europe and the United States.) Koigen's address, entitled "The Conception of God in the Light of Modern Thought," ratifies the theological goals he and Heschel held in common—though in a strikingly different idiom.[34]

Unfortunately, Koigen could not attend the London meeting; at the last moment his wife fell ill and he remained in Berlin. On 20 July 1930 a summary (in German) of his talk was read at the opening session. Its main idea—the centrality of God—was reported in the *Jüdische Rundschau* five days later: "A metaphysics that cannot be translated into valid currency, into real events of internal renewal and commitment, is empty. Any existence, even a religious existence [*religiose Dasein*], that does not point toward the metaphysical spirit, is blind. And thus every true life, every true religion always points to a meta-religion. And the living principle of this meta-religion is God." Heschel would agree.

Having observed various forms of Jewish life in Warsaw, Vilna, and Berlin, Heschel read that progressive Jewish leaders deplored the lack of an invigorating theology. At the July 1930 conference, after Koigen's contribution was presented, Rabbi Samuel Shulman of New York insisted, "The central fact in religion is Prayer. Prayer expresses the conviction that God is a reality and not merely a wish, and that in some way there will be a real response from Him as the satisfaction of man's needs. The test of the religiosity in anyone is the capacity and the desire for prayer."[35] Twenty-three years later, as a naturalized

American citizen, Heschel issued similar challenges to both the Reform and Conservative rabbinate.[36]

Lily Montagu mailed Koigen a Jewish Telegraphic Agency press release which delineated a problem that Heschel was eminently qualified to confront. Claude G. Montefiore, president of the World Union, stated it candidly in his opening address: "Perhaps the progressive service is too cold and formal, too intellectual, not heartfelt enough. . . . Is the God of the modern world of science and philosophy indeed the God of Judaism? Is there any significance to prayer as such?" Koigen answered Lily Montagu, agreeing with Montefiore's insistence that progressive Judaism needed "an enlightened and modern Hasidism."

Heschel's own mission was soon to provide all Jews, Liberal or Orthodox, with "an enlightened and modern Hasidism." Through philosophical argumentation and literary prose, he cultivated religious emotions, side-stepping rationalism, attacking ideology and dogma, as he trained minds to receive the living God. Heschel's nonpartisan, lived Hasidism remained his principal source of authority. As he wrote to Abraham Liessen, his editor at *Zukunft*: "I had other teachers, other ways, other images."[37]

Heschel in Berlin socialized with diverse people, Liberal and Orthodox, Jew and Gentile. Years later an anonymous Reform rabbi reported that, during this period, Heschel's Hasidic values were challenged in a different way, and within Hasidism itself.[38] This controversy concerns another scion of Jewish nobility, Menahem Mendel Schneerson, who became the Lubavitcher rebbe in the United States. The following encounter—if it actually occurred—dramatizes the ethical core of Heschel's spiritual radicalism, his hallmark during the American civil rights movement and his opposition to the Vietnam War.

Schneerson was living in Berlin with his wife, Chaya Mushka, one of the three daughters of Yosef Yitzhak Schneerson, the Lubavitcher rebbe who moved from Russia to Riga, Latvia.[39] Menahem Mendel was studying natural philosophy at the university, while his wife, registered at the Foreign Students Institute, was studying mathematics. Although Schneerson tended to associate with the Orthodox community, the incident purportedly took place at the home "of a mutual friend," a place where German and East European Jews could comfortably meet.

Two Hasidic perspectives clashed in that setting. A man was praising his converted wife, who kept a kosher home and raised their children in the proper Jewish way. But when he commended the rabbi who had converted her, Jacob Sonderling, spiritual leader of the Reform synagogue in Hamburg (one of the only two truly Reform temples in Germany, Liberal synagogues being more traditional), Schneerson vehemently declared the conversion to be invalid because a Reform rabbi possessed no halakhic authority. The Lubatvitcher rebbe's son-in-law declared that a child of his would never marry into such a family.

The couple was upset, disheartened. Heschel, outraged at the shame Schneerson inflicted, rebuked him. No Jew, especially the scion of such a holy family, Heschel is reported to have insisted, should ever humiliate a person publicly. The teller of this story understood that Schneerson's harshness brought a curse of childlessness to his marriage.

The drama apparently continued after Heschel and the Schneersons reached the United States in 1940. Heschel eventually became a professor at the Jewish Theological Seminary in New York and Schneerson the rebbe of Lubavitch, after his father-in-law's death in 1950. Having remained childless after several years, the rebbe remembered this incident in Berlin and telephoned Heschel, asking how he might contact this couple to ask their forgiveness. Heschel suggested that he call Rabbi Sonderling (who was now in Los Angeles) for information. The rebbe asked Heschel to call Sonderling first to make him aware why Schneerson would contact him. Heschel did so, but the rebbe is said never to have placed the call to California.

This anecdote, as disputable as it may be, convincingly displays Heschel's radical approach to Jewish law. Heschel was a sensitive man who would rebuke such a hurtful public remark. His compassion and Hasidic standing demanded that he speak out, even against the future rebbe of Lubavitch. Public shaming, for Heschel, violated his reverence for each and every human being. In the United States, he often cited the following tenet of Talmudic ethics (in *Berakhot* 43b): "One should throw onself into a burning furnace rather than insult another person publicly."[40] Heschel in Berlin would also esteem the sincere Jewish observance of a Liberal or Reform convert. In emulation of his ancestors the Apter Rav and Levi Yitzhak of Berditchev, "lovers of Jews" who yielded ultimate judgment to God, his application of Jewish law *to others* was lenient. While meticulously following halakhah, his reverence for people remained absolute.

Whatever the details, this incident anticipates how these two cosmopolitan Hasidim, each possessing exceptional religious and secular training, coped with Jewish assimilation: the Lubavitcher rebbe's dynamic, worldwide outreach movement maintained a strict construction of halakhah (which fervent Orthodox Jews call "Torah-true Judaism"), whereas Heschel taught a "ladder of observance" to respect and nurture each person's inner development. Heschel believed that the Jewish paths to redemption were many.

8

Poetic Vision and Prophetic Sympathy (1928–1931)

Thus there arose, as though spontaneously, a mother tongue, a direct
expression of feeling, a mode of speech without ceremony or artifice,
a language that speaks itself without taking devious paths, a tongue that
has maternal intimacy and warmth. In this language, you say "beauty"
and mean "spirituality"; you say "kindness" and mean "holiness."
Heschel, *The Earth Is the Lord's* (1950)

SINCE HIS DAYS IN VILNA, HESCHEL DRESSED AS A MODERN EUROPEAN STUDENT. His hair was thick, black, and wavy; he wore rimless glasses, displayed a pleasant, somewhat reserved manner and a charming sense of humor. In Berlin, he was recognizable as an East European Jew by his accent, for he started learning German in Warsaw among speakers of Polish or Yiddish. He impressed peers with his intelligence and kindness. For example, in Heinrich Maier's seminar in philosophy, a German Jewish student of literature, Ludwig Kahn, willingly sought his help in mastering the difficult subject matter.[1]

While maturing as a German-speaking academic, Heschel preserved his inner identity. Matriculated at two schools and studying intensely, he tended to gravitate toward other East European Jews. He joined Berlin's Organization of East European Jewish Students Living in Germany and kept in touch with Melekh Ravitch and other poets in Warsaw.

Writing Yiddish poetry remained a personal necessity, but Heschel was also ambitious. Actively seeking publication, he contacted Yiddish periodicals in the United States. Publishing his poetry might gratify his desire for recognition, but he also urgently needed the modest fees some periodicals paid their contributors. Heschel was a practical person, well organized and with professional skills, who championed his writings efficiently.

In July 1929, at the end of his second academic year, he initiated his first mature literary publication. Using David Koigen's Mommsen Strasse apartment as his return address, Heschel mailed five new poems to *Zukunft* (Future), the influential Yiddish monthly run by the Forward Association of New York, whose longtime editor was Abraham Liessen, himself a Yiddish poet and member of the socialist Bund.[2]

Heschel had accumulated a body of work of which he was proud. These lyrical pieces continue to express his inmost struggles, but there is a quantum leap in substance and innovations in form. Heschel's new poems surpass the three-stanza syllogisms Melekh Ravitch published earlier; the later poems are varied in theme and subject, and some are long, even expressionistic in style. They all evoke Heschel's hypersensitive moral conscience and his steadfast, but also independent relationship with God.

Heschel's mailing to *Zukunft* was ambitious, for the work of almost every significant Yiddish writer appeared in this progressive journal, which reached Poland, Russia, South America, Palestine, as well as North America. Heschel could share his aspirations with this worldwide Yiddish-speaking community.

He managed the submission process adroitly. Like all neophytes (and many experienced authors), he waited impatiently for an answer. Four months passed without even an acknowledgment. Heschel followed up on 3 November 1929 and inquired diplomatically if the poems had been received.[3] To ensure that they would not be lost, he enclosed additional copies of the five poems ("slightly changed," he wrote) with two new ones. "Please let me know their fate immediately," he added.

Heschel remained in the dark. In the meantime, *Zukunft* sent his poems to an evaluator living in Berlin. The answer reached Liessen while Heschel was renewing his request. The aspiring author would have enjoyed reading this appreciation: "I have read the *lider* [in Yiddish, songs or poems] of Mr. Heschel and find that it behooves us to publish them. They are good and quite good; it has been a long time since I've had such pleasure from such poetry. Please read and reflect upon them. You will enjoy them. They are new, fresh, deep, and genuine. In short, it is true poetry. That is my opinion. I believe it will also be yours."[4]

Only several months later did Heschel learn that the December 1929 issue of *Zukunft* had launched his literary career with four poems that exemplify his unique combination of thirst for God and ardent moral sensitivity. The first and last poems comprise a frame, "God Pursues Me Everywhere . . . " and "I and Thou," and are the finest he ever published.[5] They assert that the religious and ethical dimensions of human experience are one and the same. This sequence of four poems, which remained stable in several later publications, comprises Heschel's mature self-portrait.

Dialogues with God

The opening poem evokes the intuition at the foundation of his biblical theology, anticipating his doctoral dissertation on prophetic consciousness. Within the secular city of Berlin, the poet senses how the Almighty, another Hound of Heaven, takes the initiative. As set forth in Heschel's American theological summa, *God in Search of Man* (1955), the Divine constantly seeks the righteous person, who becomes an *object* of God's awareness:

> God pursues me everywhere—
> Spinning a web around me . . .
> Blinding my sightless back like a sun . . .
>
> God pursues me everywhere like a forest . . .
> My lips are forever astonished, speechless—overwhelmed,
> Like a child astray in an ancient holy place . . .
>
> God pursues me everywhere like a shudder . . .
> I want tranquillity.—He urges: Come!
> And see how visions lie strewn in the streets.

I wander with my thoughts, like a secret
Down a long corridor through the world
And sometimes high above, I discover the faceless face of God . . .

God pursues me in the streetcars and cafés . . .
Every shining apple is my crystal sphere to see,
How mysteries are born, how visions come to be!

Germany's cultural capital became like Vilna's Zakreta Forest—potentially at least—a "holy place." Even tramways rouse his awareness of the living God. The poet's "shudder" (in Yiddish, *shoyder*) recalls Fishl Schneersohn's descriptions of Hasidic ecstasy, an emotional intuition of a meaning beyond the ego.

This inaugural poem also defines the paradox of Heschel's religious art. Writers readily understand that ordinary words can barely convey insights and feelings, while some metaphors have the power, at least suggestively, to overcome the dilemma. Heschel's instruments are his "speechless lips forever astonished." In the United States, he developed the category of the "ineffable" while striving, in rhythmic, ornate prose, to evoke God's presence. Heschel's God is alive, concrete, available, but the essential reality—what he calls God's "faceless face"—defies human understanding.

The second poem, "Millions of eyes are choking on one teardrop . . . ," insists that compassion is inseparable from a vision of the Holy. Echoing the Hebrew prophets (and his ancestor Levi Yitzhak of Berditchev) who challenged God, the poet is an ethical extremist who holds God responsible for nature's normal enigmas. He beseeches the Almighty "to sunder the Gordian knots/ In the loom of every human destiny" and to cure all illnesses. "You must tell every virus: 'Thou shalt not kill . . . '" The poet even threatens to expose divine mercy as a sham: "I warn you, I will make the rounds and scream/ That God forgot and left behind His heart in me." This is not excessive pride, because Heschel is not celebrating his own powers but instead courageously takes upon himself divinely ordained responsibilities.

The next poem, "Evening in the Streets," about a modern city, also addresses God, who remains unseen, "unknown." The poet wanders the streets as if they were "some sacred maze," but the twice-repeated refrain reaffirms his loyalty: "Oh, may I be the first, here,/ To worship with your *nigun*." Heschel recovers the sacred wordless melodies of his Hasidic childhood and youth, placing himself, once again, at God's disposal.

The sequence ends with a poem whose title could not fail to evoke Martin Buber's famous book *Ich und Du* (I and Thou), first published in 1923 while

Avrumele was still studying Talmud in Warsaw. This poem's prominent place in the sequence of four may point to Heschel's "anxiety of influence" (in Harold Bloom's phrase), battling to replace a strong predecessor. Heschel's Yiddish "Ikh un Du" expresses his exceptional intermingling of self and God, surpassing Buber's "dialogue" between separate entities, one human and the other divine.

> Messages proceed from your heart to mine . . .
> Exchanging and blending my pain with Yours . . .
> Am I not—You? Are You not—I?
>
> My nerves' tendrils are intertwined with Yours . . .
> Your dreams meet in mine . . .
> Are we not one embraced in millions?

Heschel's "I and Thou" boldly implies that God lives within him, anticipating his analysis of the prophet's sympathy with "God's pathos," the divine "emotions" responding to human events. Buber envisaged "dialogue" between a human "I" and a divine "Thou" as an existential remedy for the alienation which followed the First World War, as it gave priority to human efforts to communicate. Heschel stresses the priority of Holiness, the divine I, insisting that the person responds to God's initiative. He represents God who is the model of human compassion.

This poem unveils the personal conviction at the root of Heschel's theology of divine pathos. In the Hebrew Bible, the living God seeks out (pursues) the prophet, who responds with "sympathy" (or identification) with God's expressed "feelings." Levi Yitzhak and other Hasidic holy men experienced similar closeness to—and independence from—God. The inspired person then becomes a mediator between God and the community.

The poem continues by raising delicate theological issues. Heschel's intensity feels almost like a fusion of divine and human emotions: "Are we not one embraced in millions?" The poet absorbs within himself God's compassion and pulses with the same galvanic affect. Yet God remains the transcendent origin:

> I live in myself and in You . . .
> Through Your lips words proceed from me to myself . . .
> From Your eyes a tear drop wells up in me . . .
>
> When a need springs up within You—call me!
> When you need someone else—open my door!
> You live in Yourself, You live in me . . .

In exclaiming, "Am I not—You? Are You not—I?" the poet appears to evoke a mystical absorption of his personality into that of the Almighty: the distance between human "subject" and divine "object" seems to have been abolished. Yet closer reading reveals, first, that the poet proposes this intuition of oneness as a question, and, second, that he sympathizes above all with God as a divine Subject attached to human actions. In any case, poetry, which artistically expresses raw, unanalyzed intuitions, is not theology.

Nevertheless, in retrospect, Heschel's poetic insights appear to be the lived source of his theology. His "I and Thou" anticipates his American writings, which strive to re-center the reader's consciousness from the self to God. This poem also initiates his lifelong debate (mostly implicit) with the thought, and soon the person, of Martin Buber, one of Germany's preeminent modern Jewish thinkers. Not long after the poems were published Heschel met Buber, who made frequent trips from Frankfurt to lecture at various institutions in Berlin, including the Hochschule.

Heschel had consolidated his poetic vision. After these poems appeared, a letter finally arrived from the editor of *Zukunft* with a much-needed honorarium, stating that four of his eight poems were accepted. Liessen also asked Heschel if he had been influenced by Rainer Maria Rilke, whose *Book of Hours* was widely read and admired.

This was an opportunity for Heschel to declare his originality. He answered Liessen on 24 February 1930, asking if he could submit new pieces. More important, the twenty-three-year-old poet maintained that his religious poems were inspired not by Rilke's works nor by any other literature but by experience. Should the editor ponder his poems more carefully, he would recognize their native authenticity. "I didn't have to study in Rilke's *heder* to recognize that there is a God in the world. I had other teachers, other paths, other images," he insisted. Heschel's poems were not artistic exercises, but the expression of personal insights. "My explanation is not to be understood as a defense, but as an objective clarification," he went on to say.

Heschel's medium was literary, his message prophetic; he insisted: "There is a God in the world." Alluding to his Hasidic background, some images, he admitted, were inspired by "other teachers, other paths, other images"—from Warsaw, from Medzibozh, from Sinai. To Heschel, his ancestors, his uncle the Novominsker rebbe, words of the Bible, Midrash—perhaps even the divine Presence—existed within him. His verse was indeed "true poetry" (as the evaluator understood), directly speaking from the writer's soul.

Why then did Heschel, despite his academic progress and this literary success in New York, express discouragement to his sponsor in Warsaw, Melekh Ravitch? On 9 March 1930; soon after the December 1929 issue of *Zukunft* and Liessen's letter finally reached him, he wrote "Dear Haver Ravitch," seeking emotional and professional support. Feeling "discouraged and indifferent to publishing anything, despite the fact that, in the meantime, several of my poems have come out in print," he wanted his first sponsor to visit him in Berlin soon. Yet Heschel did insert one poem he had previously promised: "If it is fated to die like millions of other newspaper lines, I prefer it to remain in manuscript form," he claimed, somewhat disingenuously.[6] The young poet was exaggerating his anxieties while urging Ravitch to publish this important testimony to his native city. Heschel craved more recognition from the Yiddish-speaking world.

In the meantime, another message arrived—this one from Tel Aviv in Palestine—which heartened him. Heschel had mailed the first set of poems in *Zukunft,* with some new pieces, to Haim Nahman Bialik, the celebrated Hebrew poet (who also wrote in Yiddish) whom he had met in Berlin. On 18 March 1930, Bialik answered to congratulate Heschel for "the first fruits of your poems presented before the public." Reacting frankly to the manuscript samples, he gently urged Heschel to "correct their minor blemishes." Bialik continued: "After all, you are still a beginner. Sharpen and sharpen your pen until you sharpen it more than enough, until it breaks." The letter's finale was most generous: "And here I am who anticipates your greatness. And I believe in you." Heschel was proud of this sensitive response to his own expressed ambitions and, indeed, he "sharpened his pen," continuing to revise and refine his verse.

Then a third poem of Heschel's appeared in Warsaw, one which translated the prophetic sensitivity of "I and Thou" into secular terms, without mentioning the word *God.* The frustration Heschel had expressed to Ravitch paid off, for the Yiddish editor took good care of the piece, which spoke to a political audience on a topic that was close to its heart. On 25 April 1930, another major poem of Heschel's appeared in the widely circulated *Naye Folks-Tzaytung* (New people's newspaper), the organ of the Jewish Bund in Warsaw:

> I will give to you—o world—
> The lattice of my limbs,
>
> My words, my hands,
> The wonder of my eyes.
>
> Take me as your slave
> And let me serve you.

Send me to banished brothers,
Confined in prisons.

Send me to the languishing mourners
With jugs of fresh tears to console.

With help to the poor.
With healing to the sick.

Take me as a brother—world—
Take me as a slave. . . .[7]

This poem appeared in a left-wing periodical, as did his first series. Heschel's piety was pragmatic, not parochial; it had to affect other people. With an extraordinary proclamation of moral responsibility, Heschel promises to enslave himself to the world's redemption.

Joy, Infatuation, and Moral Judgment

New poems appeared in New York that reveal more conventionally artistic—but also sincerely lyrical—aspects of Heschel's sensibility: fantasy, humor, and a playful desire for love. Liessen appreciated the poems Heschel sent in February 1930, and he featured four of them in the August issue of *Zukunft*, at the conclusion of its literary section. These pieces dwell upon forms of ecstasy related more to the body than to a sober religious-ethical conscience.

The first poem, "Summer," evokes nature's sway over the imagination. Its dynamic couplets thrill to a seasonal storm as the poet plunges joyfully into himself: "Today it rained liquor on the fields—/ A tree went crazy in the woods." He becomes another Pan whose self almost melts into its own bliss, a fainting intoxication: "Branches want to embrace me, straining and dipping / The field, like a brook, comes toward me to kiss." And the poem ends with this bold identification: "Words and breath are stuck in my throat . . . / I am the Nothing, I am the All." Enlarging the simpler quest for the "All" in his 1927 Warsaw poem, Heschel recognizes that within human ecstasy "Nothing" and "Everything" can feel the same.

Heschel implies that this pagan-like imagination might serve as a bridge to authentic religious insight. Readers unfamiliar with Hasidic mysticism might suspect a radically unconventional spirit, but Heschel is not promoting pantheism, where the mystic feels of one substance with nature. The poet makes clear that his fantasy does not claim the status of revelation, but arises from an exceptional summer madness in which he celebrates the world.

The next poem, "I Want So to Be in Love," applies the poet's projections of desire from nature onto a woman, echoing the first poem Ravitch chose for the 1926 *Varshaver Shriftn*. No longer the shy, anxious adolescent yearning for a woman's body, Heschel celebrates the possibility of love (but not a reciprocal relationship); love, here, is an esthetic delight, inspiring the writer.

> I want so to be in love!
> To have someone with whom to wander in dreams.
> Someone to whom to dedicate and address my songs
> Of love from my stormy heart.

This lovely, naïve piece is compatible with a biblical tradition inspired by the Song of Songs, which can be interpreted as an allegory of Israel's longing for God. But Heschel's theme is simpler. The poet's "monotheistic" love (as he calls it humorously) is metaphorical; its object is a woman constructed by desire, not the unreachable God—nor even a female companion within reach.

Two poems asserting ethical values conclude this second *Zukunft* sequence. "Noble Friend" rejects the world's lust for money, power, and hatred—repudiating "Hollywood's clever Bible" of venality and other forms of twentieth-century hedonism: "I would rather stay together with my generation!" In conclusion, "Call Through the Nights"—a powerful six-stanza evocation of urban horror—accumulates visceral, sometimes violent images of degradation and despair. Dated during Heschel's second academic year in Berlin,[8] it reiterates the ethical independence of "Millions of Eyes Choking" (on one teardrop), which reproaches God, and of "I and Thou," in which the poet mourns with the Almighty:

> Sidewalk corpses embalmed in snow,
> Like poor whores the river shivers with cold.
> Heavens weep in my bosom, sinking sinister: No!
> A wind wails weeping, "Help!" As if God were present. . . .
> Why won't You help—You, You?

Humankind is of ultimate value. Debating with God like the biblical Father Abraham over the destruction of Sodom and Gomorrah, Heschel again questions divine mercy. His compassion is painful, his faith militant, admonishing the Creator to follow absolute standards of justice.

The poem's final line summarizes Heschel's amalgam of spirituality and righteousness, as he defines himself: "A poet, a mystic hear luminous God weeping in a *nigun*." Heschel in Berlin is both "poet" (*dikhter*), who expresses the world of imagination, desire, and ecstasy, and a "mystic" (*makubl*), who feels God's presence and represents the divine will.[9] His "songs" include that multiple music, woeful at human pain, indignant at God's distance—but leading to self-affirmation. Morality is inseparable from mysticism, and Heschel shoulders God's aspiration to mend the world.

Prophetic Independence

During the eight months between this publication and his renewed requests to *Zukunft*, Heschel completed his university course requirements to qualify for the doctoral dissertation. He also left the city to visit other places. On 22 April 1931 he wrote again to Liessen in New York, excusing his lack of correspondence by some unnamed "difficulties" he was shouldering. And, thanking the editor for the August 1930 publication of his second poetic sequence, he reassured Liessen that, after his prolonged absence from the city, "I am already back in my Berlin order of things [in Hebrew, *seder*]."

Practical concerns were foremost. In the same letter, asking if more of his "*shirim* [poems or songs] now in your possession" might be published, he added this tactful request for the honorarium he had never received for the poems. His "co-addressee, David Koigen," had notified the bank to forward him the money, but they failed to do so. It was an awkward situation; he continued, "Since I am terribly in need of this money, I ask you most respectfully to send me the money, and I will naturally pay the postal expenses."

The difficulty of finding a dependable outlet for his creations was compounded by his need for the payment which, in any case, could not have been large. Perhaps Liessen would become a "friend," as Ravitch had. But *Zukunft* never again published Heschel's writings, nor did it review his book of Yiddish poetry, which appeared two years later.

Yet Heschel did not feel helpless. He dominated the situation, to the extent possible, by taking action in Berlin. Around 1930, with another Yiddish writer born in Poland, A. N. Stencl, who participated in the Yiddish expressionist movement in Germany, he co-founded an avant-garde Yiddish periodical, *Berliner Bleter far dikhtung un kunst* (Berlin pages of poetry and art), associated with the Organization of East European Jewish Students Living in Germany. Heschel revived his Warsaw peer group, for among the contributors of this short-lived journal (only three issues were published) were M. Zhialovsky and Sh. L. Shneyderman, whose poems had appeared with Heschel's under the heading "Young Poets of Warsaw" in the June 1927 *Literarishe Bleter*.[10]

Now Heschel, co-editor of *Berliner Bleter,* placed a sequence of six of his poems (some of them published for the second time) in the inaugural issue, dated November 1931, which enlarge the New York series.[11] The frame remained unchanged from *Zukunft*, although in reverse order: now "I and Thou" was the first and "God Pursues Me Everywhere" the final one.

That the poet is a witness to God is their ruling theme. God is both near and far; above all, God is real—such is the basic given of Heschel's wisdom. These poems attempt to convey the ineffable meeting, and they confront the abyss—and points of contact—between God, the poet, and the world. During the 1929–30 academic year Heschel had met Martin Buber, so his placing of "I and Thou" at the head of the *Berliner Bleter* sequence reinforced this emblem of his own, independent voice. (Heschel also set his "I and Thou" first in his collection that appeared in 1933.)[12]

For Heschel, human ethics challenges God. After insisting that the poet's compassion derives from the divine pathos, the following poem, "Dusk," gives an example. Heschel evokes city streets in avant-garde style, replete with grotesque expressionistic images of degradation. The poet speaks through the mutilated corpse of a suicide who reproaches God for not responding to millions of other people in despair:

> A dusk star kindles
> Two rows of cloudy gaslights,
> Like dead bodies—yellow tapers at a deathbed.
>
> Night, speak out! Whose laments, whose sighs
> Does the wind bring to my ears
> To pierce our peace of mind and hearts?
>
> In a courtyard under darkened flights of building
> They gather up bloody limbs and remains
> Of a suicide's body——
>
> In the air an echo of his last cry
> Still hangs:
> "I will not pardon You my woe!"
>
> We all serve God absent-mindedly . . .

The poet, who becomes "my thousand begging hands," fearlessly reproaches the Almighty: "Why did You not respond?" The intermingling of human and divine feelings expressed in Heschel's "I and Thou" magnifies the poet's moral autonomy. What remains is his pledge, as the ninth stanza proclaims: "And I have promised, stubbornly, boldly, that I will increase tenderness in the world."

Heschel's struggles with limits emerge in the next piece, "Transformations" (probably composed late in 1929, while he was preparing for examinations).[13] Remembering his youthful proximity to holiness, he opens an inclusive pathway to God, one which recognizes the conflict of worldliness versus sacred yearnings. Ordinary people need personal happiness as well as sanctity: "Between me and the world always stood my God . . . and blocked the world . . . / Then a longing arose and I took hold of you:—real world!"

Heschel's religious vision does not require external authority. As a poet, he does not defend biblical or rabbinic tradition, nor does he uphold revelation from God, as his Hasidic ancestors might have done. His commitments derive from his (often troubling) relationship with humankind and God—not from Jewish law as such. The poem concludes with a pledge to his future task: "So I can only wander on, to find in my heart silent bridges to God."

Heschel was a man of faith, but he speaks to contemporaries through his acute sense of God's distance. The poem "Need" beseeches God once again to help the destitute, adding a subtle awareness ("As silently as a hair growing on me") of the Divine within himself. In today's world, realistic prayer includes an anxious yearning for God who keeps silent:

> My powerful shudders speak to me about You.
> Feelings within me wildly arouse prayer . . .
> And I do not know, I do not understand how to call You.
>
> The danger of unconscious longing
> Frightens me. Cramped feelings in a narrow space
> I choke from not-knowing. Save me—a word!

Heschel reiterates his ethical concern in "The Pauper."[14] Evoking the Midrashic image of God's weeping, he suggests that even the smallest creatures are worthy of compassion: "To the worms crushed beneath our feet/ God calls: 'My holy martyr!'" At the end, however, he returns to pragmatic values, making a radical statement: "The pauper's sins are more beautiful/ Than the good deeds of the rich." Challenging the complacent religious conscience, he points to the Almighty (not to human saints) as the true paragon of morality. The self and God become one in compassion, as the first line insists: "God's tears wet the cheeks/ Of men weakened and ashamed."

This sequence is sealed by Heschel's poetic emblem, "God Pursues Me Everywhere . . . " This coda reasserts the divine source of his calling. This piece, which first appeared in 1929 to announce the poet's mission, now ratifies his self-definition.[15] Heschel's faith in God was not uncertain, nor did doubt darken its glow. But his ethical sensitivity was a cause of anguish. Like his father the Pelzovizna rebbe, he remained afflicted by the enormity of human suffering and by God's apparent inaction.

Heschel's Yiddish poems—most of them written in Berlin, but conceived in Warsaw and advanced in Vilna—express the tense, sometimes distressing crossing of cultures (sacred and profane) within his increasingly complex, and increasingly assertive, personality. Heschel's persistent efforts to publish them—to the point of founding his own review in Berlin—demonstrate his need to externalize himself in writing and to seek confirmation of his vision from speakers of his mother tongue. But he was still a doctoral candidate in Germany forming a Western European idiom for his spiritual and ethical commitments.

9

Paradigm Shift (1929–1931)

Thus, symbolism became the supreme category in understanding religious truth. It has become a truism that religion is largely an affair of symbols. Translated into simpler terms this view regards religion as a fiction, useful to society or to man's personal well-being.

Heschel, "Toward an Understanding of Halacha" (1953)

HESCHEL AS A STUDENT DID EXPERIENCE A CRISIS IN BERLIN. HESCHEL PURSUED his education efficiently and with enthusiasm; he reveled in the city's cultural opportunities. And yet, somewhat unconsciously at the outset, he realized that his religious convictions and passion for truth clashed with his academic studies. At the university he mastered the history of philosophy and theories of knowledge. At the Hochschule, he performed expert philological analyses of the Bible and Midrash and grasped the historical development of Judaism. But as an intellectual he needed to verify the givens of the heart.

Heschel placed great hopes in his humanistic studies, for a sort of inchoate disquiet was driving him to justify his Hasidic confidence, still vitally present in his Yiddish poetry: "How can I rationally find a way where ultimate meaning lies . . . ?/ Why am I here at all, and what is my purpose?/ I did not even know how to phrase my concern. But to my teachers that was a question unworthy of philosophical analysis."[1] His internalized piety—that of his father, his uncle the Novominsker rebbe, and his ancestors—still remained foreign to modern thought.

These difficulties of faith, inherent as they are to contemporary thinking, were historically specific. His professors refused to address religious questions. Heschel felt that the objectivity of German academia distorted their conception of reality: "My teachers were prisoners of a Greek-German way of thinking. They were fettered in categories which presupposed certain metaphysical assumptions which could never be proved. The questions I was moved by could not even be adequately phrased in categories of their thinking." The neo-Kantian theory of knowledge was the accepted standard; scholars examined seriously only what could be derived from sense data as processed by structures of the mind (the "categories"). It was not appropriate to consider the holy (or "supernatural") dimension which nourished Heschel's childhood and youth.

So, Heschel remained profoundly apart. As an observant believer and a Polish Jew, he benefited from his studies at the University of Berlin, which, nonetheless, neither nurtured his piety nor welcomed him as a Polish Jew. The Hochschule, which deemed sacred texts to be historically derived, did not encompass his loyalty to revelation. Nor did the Orthodox Seminary, despite its involvement with philosophy and scientific methods, provide a community. Each institution was, at best, a halfway house.

The Neo-Kantian Paradigm

Heschel's vocation as philosopher of religion emerges from his grappling with his professors' intellectual ideology. His was not the time-honored collision of philosophy against faith, logic against belief. Heschel did not doubt the existence of God. But he felt compelled to distinguish his values from those of the university: "To them, religion was a feeling. To me, religion included the insights of the Torah which is a vision of man from the point of view of God. They spoke of God from the point of view of man. To them God was an idea, a postulate of reason. They granted Him the status of being a logical possibility. But to assume that He had existence would have been a crime against epistemology."

Philosophical idealism provided the catalyst. Heschel formulated the situation in this way: "Kant, who held dominion over many minds, had demonstrated that it is utterly impossible to attain knowledge of the world . . . because knowledge is always in the form of categories and these, in the last analysis, are only representational constructions for the purpose of apperceiving what is given. Objects possessing attributes, causes that work, are all mythical." ("Apperception" refers to a clear perception of sense data and ideas that is adjusted to a mass of previous knowledge. Kant analyzes how sense data are interpreted by the structures of the mind itself, called *a priori* categories.) According to Kant, the mind itself limits our knowledge of "objective" reality; even the concrete "thing-in-itself" is ungraspable; the spiritual is more obviously beyond reach.

Heschel challenged this sanctioned theory of knowledge. The dimension of the holy, literally, did not enter his professors' minds; but they accepted compromise for the sake of moral expediency, as he explained sarcastically: "We must, of course, give up the hope of ever attaining a valid concept of the supernatural in an objective sense, yet since for practical reasons it is useful to cherish the idea of God, let us retain that idea and claim that while our knowledge of God is not objectively true, it is still *symbolically* true." Heschel deplored this bad faith, but he was more alarmed that noble motives might allow thinkers to deflate the Transcendent: "It has become a truism that religion is largely an affair of symbols. Translated into simpler terms this view regards religion as a *fiction*, useful to society or to man's personal well-being."

Heschel faced the crossroads of modern religion: Was God real, as he believed, beyond rational knowledge, or a mental and social construct? Heschel strived to reconcile philosophical idealism with convictions expressed in his Yiddish poems, and which flowed from sacred sources: "Man's dignity consists in his having been created in the likeness of God." Such was Heschel's irreducible premise.

Piety Versus Philosophy

Heschel was one among many thinkers confronting his era's relativism—an intellectual ambiance in which knowledge was dispersed among different explanations which did not, and could not, connect. Thinkers debated what it meant to be human. As Ernst Cassirer summarized it: "Nietzsche proclaims the will to power, Freud signalizes the sexual instinct, Marx enthrones the economic instinct. Each theory becomes a Procrustean bed on which the empirical facts are stretched to fit a preconceived pattern."[2]

Heschel considered whether religion and ethics could be explained by one or more of these innovative disciplines. And, like his teachers, he sought an essence for culture through the multidisciplinary "philosophical anthropology" established by Wilhelm Dilthey. In the late 1920s, Cassirer's neo-Kantian philosophy of "symbolic forms" (as he defined various cultural manifestations) provided an intellectual key. Cassirer dominated the generation influenced by his teachers Dilthey, Hermann Cohen, Edmund Husserl, and Georg Simmel. Cassirer's theory held the possibility of conveying a unified theory congruent with Heschel's religious commitments.

Heschel dreamed of going to the University of Hamburg, where he could study with Cassirer, a humanistic thinker of extraordinary scope.[3] Cassirer began his career at the University of Berlin and moved to Hamburg in 1919, where he was the only Jewish rector of a German university—until the Nazis came to power.

Cassirer could supplement the guidance of David Koigen, for they studied with many of the same professors. Cassirer shared with Koigen the ambition to embrace all forms of culture—including metaphysics, theology, mathematics, biology, and physics—within one system. By examining the symbol-producing powers of the mind, Cassirer justified a rationalistic (what he also called a "spiritual") principle of human freedom and creativity.

Cassirer, the son of a wealthy Jewish tradesman, was also an exemplary modern Jew. Though not observant, he never denied his Jewishness, and contributed essays to Jewish periodicals and was a member of the Hochschule's board of governors.[4] An elegant, refined personality, he had an immense knowledge of the history of philosophy and science. He could cite an astounding variety of European literatures and works of art and music, and develop philosophical analyses—all in a lucid German style. The handsome Cassirer was described by contemporaries as "Olympian" with his silver-white hair and patrician charm.

Cassirer's philosophical anthropology—which confirmed a spiritual unity of art, myth, religion, and science—might bridge the abyss between philosophy and Judaism.[5] Heschel filled notebooks with quotations from Cassirer, whose recently published magnum opus, the three-volume *Philosophy of Symbolic Forms*, elaborated a synthesis of disparate academic realms. Heschel shared his contemporaries' admiration for Cassirer's masterful application of Dilthey's principle of cognitive unity: volume one, *Language*, surveys linguistic theories from Plato to the present, and volume three, *The Phenomenology of Knowledge*, reviews subjective and objective expression, theories of intuition, scientific knowledge, mathematics, and modern physics. Of special interest to philosophers of religion was volume two, *Mythical Thought*, which restores the intellectual dignity of nonrational symbols in several religions and cultures, including notions of space and time, personality, and worship.

Heschel could not study with Cassirer in Hamburg, but, in any case, the philosophy of symbolic forms did not welcome the holy dimension. Symbolic knowledge, in Cassirer's view, remained exclusively a product of the mind: "Human culture as a whole may be described as the process of man's progressive self-liberation. Language, art, religion, science, are various phases in this process. In all of them man discovers and proves a new power—the power to build up a world of his own, an 'ideal' world. Philosophy cannot give up its search for a fundamental unity in this ideal world."[6]

Around this time, in 1930, Heschel's slightly older peer Alexander Altmann recognized that "the central philosophical problem of our time is the question of the impossibility of an absolute metaphysics. . . . It was primarily Dilthey who took up and confirmed anew . . . the standpoint of relativism. His structural psychology furnished new arguments for metaphysical agnosticism in addition to the reasons developed by Voltaire, Hume, and Kant."[7] Heschel would agree. There was no rational basis for his love of God, a system acceptable as an "absolute metaphysics." For neo-Kantians, the divine was a useful mental construct, a piece of symbolic, not objective truth. Even the rooms of Cassirer's magnificent philosophical mansion were wanting in Holiness.

At the brink of choosing a dissertation topic, Heschel went beyond Cassirer and discovered a spiritual force within philosophy. He formulated an alternative paradigm for religious knowledge: "Must speculation and existence remain like two infinite parallel lines that never meet? Or perhaps this impossibility of juncture is the result of the fact that our speculation suffers from what is called in astronomy a parallax, from the apparent displacement of the object, caused by the actual change of our point of observation?" His touchstones were the absolute sanctity of human life and God's concern: "We do not suffer symbolically. We suffer literally, truly, deeply. Symbolic remedies are quackery. The will of God is either real or a delusion."[8]

Heschel found a fulcrum that enabled him to dislodge the edifice of philosophical idealism or philosophy of mind and to clarify "God's perspective." Responding to current discussions of Einstein's theory of relativity, in which scientific judgment can be conditioned by the observer's location, Heschel studied the Hebrew prophets in order to analyze their awareness of God as the source of revelation. His apt metaphor of *parallax* justifies the translation of his dynamic relation with God into analytical categories.[9]

Heschel's philosophical method—adapted from phenomenology—could elucidate his conviction that God is the *Subject*, while human beings are *objects* of divine awareness. Internally, he did not need to justify his faith. Yet his method of analyzing the prophets' consciousness of God would communicate his conviction to those outside the sanctuary. By examining the structure of prophetic consciousness he could at the very least eliminate explanations of revelation that did not give priority to God.

Heschel's theoretical project had vast practical consequences: "The problem to my professors was how to be good. In my ears the question rang: how to be holy. At the time I realized: There is much that philosophy could learn from Jewish life." He was still a rebbe.

A Parable of Jewish Renewal

Yet Heschel, too, required a similar lesson. These contradictions made him miserable, almost depressed. He explained the circumstances to rabbis in the United States in 1953, thirteen years after his immigration. Alarmed at the superficiality of religious observance in his adopted homeland, Heschel put aside his usual reticence and delivered an autobiographical parable which summarized months of inner conflict. At the annual conference of the Reform movement, Heschel defined himself as modern, as he told his audience: "Your problems are not alien to me. I, too, have wrestled with the difficulties inherent in our faith as Jews." He told about the breakthrough, which occurred one afternoon, when he was suddenly reminded that he was still, essentially, a Warsaw Hasid—a pious man bereft of his liturgical community. Condensing months of self-questioning, Heschel's didactic parable culminates in the following account:

> In those months in Berlin I went through moments of profound bitterness. I felt very much alone with my own problems and anxieties. I walked alone

in the evenings through the magnificent streets of Berlin. I admired the solidity of its architecture, the overwhelming drive and power of a dynamic civilization. . . .

Suddenly I noticed the sun had gone down, evening had arrived.

From what time may one recite the Shema in the evening?

I had forgotten God—I had forgotten Sinai—I had forgotten that sunset is my business—that my task is [quoted in Hebrew] "*to restore the world to the kingship of the Lord.*"

So I began to utter the words of the evening prayer.

Blessed art Thou, Lord our God,

King of the universe,

who by His word brings on the evenings. . . .

And Goethe's famous poem rang in my ear:

Ueber allen Gipfeln ist Ruh'

O'er all the hilltops is quiet now.

No, that was pagan thinking. To the pagan eye the mystery of life is *Ruh'*, death, oblivion.

To us Jews, there is meaning beyond the mystery. We should say

O'er all the hilltops is the word of God.

Ueber allen Gipfeln ist Gottes Wort.

The meaning of life is to do His will . . . And I uttered the words,

Who by His word brings on the evenings.

And His love is manifested in His teaching us Torah, precepts, laws:

Ueber allen Gipfeln is God's love for man—.

Thou hast loved the house of Israel with everlasting love.

Thou hast taught us Torah, mitzvot, laws, rules. . . .

How much guidance, how many ultimate insights are found in the Siddur.

How grateful I am to God that there is a duty to worship, a law to remind my distraught mind that it is time to think of God, time to disregard my ego for at least a moment! It is such happiness to belong to an order of the divine will.[10]

Heschel had "forgotten God." This was a common condition for the secularized majority, but astounding for a scion of Apt, Medzibozh, Ruzhin, and Novominsk. Heschel was enthralled with German culture (symbolized by the Goethe poem). But he avoided Reb Bezalel's demand that he chastise his ego. The grave danger of philosophical idealism, and of art and culture—even of his own Yiddish poems—was self-centeredness. Celebration of the human spirit was not enough.

The setting sun revived words of tradition he long knew by heart, the opening of the Mishnah Berakhot: "From what time may one recite the Shema in the evening?" ("Mei-eimatai korin et Shema"; Heschel cited his ancestor Levi Yitzhak's explanation: *eimah* means fear or wonder.) Jewish prayer emerged from his past and flowed over the recently memorized verses from Goethe, celebrating his pagan love of nature. He neglected his habit (and duty) of evening devotion. Now Heschel renewed his pledge of Jewish loyalty to God.

Were these two cultures—secular German and ancient Jewish—now harmonized? The words of the Ma'ariv (evening) prayer infiltrated Goethe's uplifting but naturalistic verse, returning almost spontaneously to negotiate a truce between piety and European humanism. A grace had transpired: Goethe's poem had roused the spirit within halakhah. Ritual obligations—the ingrained habits of Heschel's first eighteen years of life—filled the emptiness veiled by nature's exterior beauty.

Heschel was depressed. His struggles with modernity, starting in Warsaw, took their toll on his emotional well-being. As he explained over twenty years later: "On that evening, in the streets of Berlin, I was not in a mood to pray. My heart was heavy, my soul was sad. It was difficult for the lofty words of prayer to break through the dark clouds of my inner life. But how would I dare not to *davn* [pray]? How would I dare to miss a *Ma'ariv?* . . . 'Out of *eimah*, out of fear of God, do we read the *Shema*.'"[11] What Heschel later called "awe" or "radical amazement," an emotion of reverence before the very miracle of daily existence, reintegrated him into the Jewish way of life.

The study of religious awe, not philosophy, became Heschel's priority. This parable consolidated his vocation: analyze and arouse piety and teach secularized readers the ways of attachment to God through prayer, study, and action. Almost overcome by Berlin's cultural riches, he concluded that "fear of God" reawakened his obligation to pray three times a day. His ancestral attitudes remained potent, reviving his innate reverence for the Creator.

As he explained to the American Reform rabbis in 1953, loyalty to Jewish law overcame his distractions. This was not a crisis of faith but a crisis of attentiveness, a cultural clash. "What was my situation after the reminder to pray *Ma'ariv* struck my mind? The duty to worship stood as a thought of ineffable meaning; doubt, the voice of disbelief, was ready to challenge it. But where should the engagement take place?" As an intellectual of Orthodox background, Heschel understood that halakhah helped him to refocus his studies: "As you cannot study philosophy through praying, so you cannot study prayer through philosophizing."[12]

Now he passed judgment on philosophy. Doing must precede thinking.[13] If there was a battle to be fought between philosophy and piety, he would "give the weaker rival a chance: to pray first, to fight later." Heschel reaffirmed his responsibility to God and to his people: "What I wanted to avoid was not only a failure to pray to God during a whole evening of my life but *the loss of the whole,* the loss of belonging to the spiritual order of Jewish living." The system Heschel was now formulating pointed beyond culture to the divine Voice.

10

God's Active Presence (1931–1932)

We understand the person enflamed by prophetic zeal, who knows himself
to be in emotional agreement and harmony with God. We understand the
power of Him enflamed with anger and Who turns away from His people.

Heschel, *Die Prophetie* (1936)

BY 24 JANUARY 1931, HESCHEL HAD COMPLETED HIS REQUIRED COURSES AT THE university, with a specialization in philosophy and minors in art history and Semitic philology. He continued to write Yiddish poetry, revise old pieces, and create new ones, maintaining contact with editors in Warsaw, New York, and Berlin. (A major sequence appeared in the November 1931 issue of the *Berliner Bleter*, the journal he co-founded.) All the while, he participated in the Koigen Circle, debating his fundamental ideas. Now he concentrated on his doctoral dissertation, which he completed late the following year. Also in 1932, at the Hochschule, he became assistant to Hanoch Albeck, the Talmud professor, while still a degree candidate.

Heschel coordinated his Yiddish and German writings—his personal and academic lives—efficiently. When his thesis was nearly finished, on 10 November 1932, Heschel wrote Dean Hartung of the Philosophical Faculty officially to declare Max Dessoir's and Alfred Bertholet's willingness to be his co-directors. Heschel completed the typescript less than a month later. That same week, on 5 December 1932, he prodded his New York editor, Abraham Liessen, diplomatically: "I am very surprised that my things [poems] have not, for such a long time, found a future in 'The Future' [*Zukunft*]." Heschel's letter, with four new poems enclosed, continues by anticipating his *Promotion* (formal bestowal of the doctorate).[1]

It was a momentous week, full of maneuvering within a bureaucratic labyrinth. On 9 December 1932, the day he submitted his *Inaugural-Dissertation* to Dessoir, he wrote Dean Hartung asking if the doctoral registration fee of two hundred Reichmarks could be paid in installments, "since my economic circumstances do not allow me to pay this sum" at once.[2] Two days later he sent a copy of the dissertation to the dean, the accompanying letter formally requesting admission to the oral examinations. Heschel also included a handwritten *Lebenslauf*, an academic biography listing the names of his professors and his previous diplomas.[3]

Within two weeks, on 21 December, Dessoir read Heschel's dissertation and wrote his evaluation, passing them both to Bertholet, who completed his reading on 5 January 1933. The two sponsors then agreed upon a grade and sent individual reports to the philosophy department, which voted and remanded their decision to the dean. The comments, although confidential, were conveyed in some way to Heschel as he revised his thesis for publication.

Scholarship and Prophetic Insight

Heschel's doctoral dissertation—entitled *Das prophetische Bewußtsein* (Prophetic consciousness)—is a notable intellectual achievement but also a prime autobiographical document. Just as his Yiddish poetry unveils his feelings of intimacy with the Divine, so his study of the Hebrew prophets suggests that he identified with those summoned by God. Its intellectual scope is ambitious: using philosophical terms to analyze the components of prophetic inspiration (God's presence within human awareness) and develop a taxonomy describing this process.[4]

Heschel's dissertation became the foundation of his mature religious philosophy. Written from 1930 to 1932, and conceived, executed, and defended within the confines of academia, his study places his personal vision into systematic categories. The two chapters comprising its conclusion—"Theology of Pathos" and "Religion of Sympathy"—establish the biblical source of his ideal of piety.[5] Speaking years later to an assembly of Jewish day school principals, Heschel claimed that this work inaugurated his life's mission "to maintain a Jewish way of thinking."[6]

A doctoral candidate must distinguish himself from other scholars, and the thesis passes judgment on current issues. Heschel duly cites or alludes to authorities within and beyond his field, painting his interpretation on the canvas provided by Bertholet, Buber, Dessoir, Dilthey, Hugo Gressmann, Julius Guttmann, Koigen, Max Scheler, and Ernst Sellin. (Koigen is cited six times, exceeded only by Bertholet, cited seven times.) European philosophy supplied the neutral language.

Heschel's immediate target, however, was Buber's broadly disseminated theory of "dialogue"—widely appreciated as the "I and Thou" relation between the person and God. Heschel acutely sensed the secularizing potentials of Buber's insistence that God can be spoken about only in the "betweenness" (*das Zwischenmenschliche*) of human and divine. Heschel understood that the "biblical humanism" favored by many of Buber's followers might subtly displace the overwhelming reality of God. Heschel's theocentrism (his emphasis on God's initiative) modified significantly Buberian dialogue that emphasized a reciprocal exchange (and a realistic human initiative). For Heschel, divine revelation validated Jewish law.

Heschel's dissertation clinched a debate on Buber's sociological theory that occurred earlier in the Koigen Circle. On 14 December 1931, he had countered Koigen's description of moral conscience as "dialogic" (a subject-object relationship) with his own paradigm, as noted in the minutes: "Heschel says that one could consider an ethical action from the perspective of the person for whom the action is done, but one could also do something for God, for the universal, against the individual. The positive way in which the mystics treated animals *demon-*

strates this ethics from the standpoint of the universal. The ethics of the prophets was not directed toward the people but toward God" (emphasis in original).[7]

Heschel systematically refuted several other attempts to reduce God's incursion into the prophet's awareness to a social or psychological event. Method was his key to refuting theories that favored secularization. The approach current in 1920s European academia inspired by Edmund Husserl and his disciples—phenomenology—allowed him to surpass Buber's (or Koigen's) metaphysical sociology by focusing on the individual's inner life. (*Phenomenon* refers to what appears to and within the mind, the "contents" of consciousness, originally derived from sensory experience.) In the preface to his dissertation, Heschel explained how he analyzed the structure and dynamics of the prophet's certainty of being addressed by God. His implicit strategy was to label the components of divine revelation and thereby to point to its transcendent Source.

Heschel hoped that his alternative theory of prophetic insight would dislodge the prevailing neo-Kantian rationalism. He implemented his approach, which justified the cognitive value of certain emotions, by applying the thought of Max Scheler, a moral philosopher and phenomenologist who developed subtle analyses of religious experience and author of *The Nature and Forms of Sympathy* (1913; 1923).[8] Heschel, like Scheler, adjusted Dilthey's psychological categories to religious knowledge—but for a less theoretical purpose. For Heschel, the integrity of Jewish tradition was at stake.

Heschel followed phenomenological procedure by elaborating an intuitive method which allows the reader to grasp, through empathy, the prophets' experience of God: "*Verstehen* [comprehension] makes possible, as opposed to *Erkennen* [knowledge], a multiplicity of relationships with the 'comprehended' person. The prophet experiences emotional and intellectual situations, he makes demands, he prays." The footnote to this passage cited recognized authorities to validate his methodology: "The idea of *Verstehen,* introduced into the human sciences by Dilthey, Spranger, Jaspers, can be extremely fertile as a category of theological systematization."[9] Heschel had announced—in this discreet footnote—his ambition to provide an intellectually convincing theology for contemporaries.

This was and remained Heschel's personal conception of scholarship. While respecting academic discourse, he firmly implied that a transcendent God, a real God, is the source of insight. His method was compatible with his religious certainties. Phenomenology (or "systematization," as he then called it) allowed him to preserve, with an apparent objectivity, the integrity of divine inspiration.

His dissertation insulated from relativism the uniqueness of the Hebrew prophets' message: God remains available to humankind. Again, a notable citation named Heschel's preferred authorities—Koigen's paper "The God-Idea in Light of Modern Thought" (London, 1930): "The prophet had to be understood not in terms of ecstasy but in terms of theophany [God's visible manifestation to people]. Theophany is already detectable in the oldest biblical sources; it is, in contrast to ecstasy, a real and original, popularly-based conception in Israel."[10] Koigen ratified Heschel's own conviction that the Jewish people as a collectivity—and not just as individuals—formed its identity through God's presence.

Heschel's theory of knowledge (or epistemology) bridged neutral academia and religious commitment. Again the shadow of Martin Buber appeared as Heschel refined his analysis of subject-object relations within the prophet's described encounters with God. He refuted the analogy to poetic imagination, which is impersonal; a creative writer, for example, undergoes an "object-object-relationship," bringing to awareness a previously unconscious idea. On the contrary, the guiding principle of prophetic thinking was theocentric—giving witness to God as Subject (*das göttliche Subjekt*).

Heschel did not reject Buber's terminology; he transformed it. Without citing Buber, Heschel used the received vocabulary to modify the "dialogical structure" of prophetic communication. God was active while the prophet remained autonomous; their "meeting" contained "a subject-subject-structure: the self-conscious I, the prophet's active I, encounters the subjective reality of Him who inspires [the prophet]. A dialogue between God and the prophet takes place."[11]

This passage continued with a bold assertion of human power and responsibility, an attitude congruent with Hasidic traditions, such as those of Levi Yitzhak of Berditchev and Rabbi Nahman: "The part taken in the dialogue by the prophet can sometimes become the determining factor. And if the prophet's word provokes a different spiritual attitude within the divine Person and obtains a new decision, then we are almost tempted to speak of the prophet's 'co-revelation'" ("*Mitoffenbarung*," Heschel's quotation marks).[12] Even when the human impulse prevails, the living God remains the central judge.

Heschel also rejected current theories of altered consciousness. Returning to the structure of ecstasy, Heschel closed part I of the dissertation by re-centering the event from the person to God: "The authentic reality of revelation occurs beyond prophetic consciousness. The prophet experiences, as it were, that transcendent action as an 'ecstasy of God' Who emerges from the distance and inaccessibility of His person, to reveal Himself to the prophet. It is within the transcendent Subject that the event's intensity occurs and is obviously directed toward the prophet's living experience."[13] Yet God needs persons; divine communication is fulfilled only when the prophet proclaims it to his people.

Divine Pathos and Prophetic Witness

Heschel's 1929 Yiddish poem "I and Thou" demonstrated one person's sympathy with God: "My nerves' tendrils are intertwined with Yours." Part II of the dissertation lifted that intuition to a theoretical level: God's active concern for humankind was the content of prophetic sympathy with the "divine *pathos*" (the Greek word for emotions). It was an ethical reciprocity. God established standards for living: "Whatever occurs in history, [God] feels it inwardly. Events and actions provoke in [God] joy or suffering, acceptance or discontent."[14] God is not aloof from the consequences of human decisions. Theology is inseparable from ethics.

Some technical distinctions reinforced this theocentric perspective. Heschel's nomenclature became somewhat specialized as he further specified the prophet's "feeling-experience" (*Das Erlebnisgefühl*)—his response to God's sorrow, distress, disappointment, love, and so on. Refuting psychological reductionism, he distinguished the prophet's "experience" (*Erlebnis*) from the prior "event" (*Ereignis*) of divine revelation.[15] The initiative came from God's decision or "turning" (*Wendung*) toward the person; God's "direction" (*Richtung*) initiated communication. The prophet's sympathy was an emotional and cognitive imitation of divine concern.

Heschel then embarked on a potentially devastating critique of institutional religion. Hebrew prophecy is the opposite of "theotropism," the human need to seek God; in priestly religion, people systematically seek closeness to God. God's turning toward the human—what Heschel calls the divine "anthropotropism"—is a fuller path to redemption. The prophet is overwhelmed by the Word that arrives at God's initiative. Heschel implicitly warned against the danger that worship, which formalizes our desire for the holy, may become an end in itself.

Theocentrism throws into question the "ethical monotheism" of Liberal Judaism. Heschel rejects the Kantian view that moral law is autonomous, independent even of divine will: "Morality is the norm of the relationship; it is not the structure. . . . If the ethos meant something absolute or ultimate, it would represent the power of a fate hovering over God as a *fatum*. To make in this way morality into something absolute would mean nothing other than enslavement of the divine, to chain God to objective, petrified norms."[16]

Heschel's personality emerges most compellingly in "Pathos as Category *sui generis*" (Part III, sect. 14). This argument seems to paraphrase sources from Kabbalah and Hasidic literature, which elsewhere he locates in the Zohar: "Every event within the world brings with it an event within God."[17] Countering the humanistic projects of his time, Heschel reiterates his ambition to establish a "theomorphic anthropology" or "religious anthropology, as a specific discipline alongside theology"—Heschel's answer to the generation of Dilthey humanists.

The final chapter, "Religion of Sympathy," states his personal judgment most explicitly. Emotions have both cognitive and spiritual force: "For the biblical person who understands the unity of psychological life, in which passions are, as well, an integral part of the spiritual, a cold objective attitude cannot form a religious life. It is an emotional religion of sympathy [with God's pathos], not the practical ritual fulfilled, that corresponds to its psychological structure. Thus the prophets can devote to God their most intimate depths, their enthusiasm and their fervor." The same is true of the author, for whom ritual observance is a means to a higher end, attachment to God.

This would be a rousing finale for a theological essay, but not an academic treatise. A covert confession, toward the end of the dissertation, echoes discussions in the Koigen Circle about religious intuitions: "Sympathy does not mean that we either melt into pity or tremble like a fanatic; it is to be struck with awe [or dismay, *Bestürzung*] and wonder [or perplexity, *Betroffenheit*]. [Divine sympathy] resounds in every word and expression of the prophets, and, although not always formulated, in the unfolding of time it affects the depths of religious responsibility." The footnote to this passage again reveals the author's true sources: "[The study of] religious sympathy in postbiblical Judaism—especially in the Aggadah, the Kabbalah, and Hasidism—would require a special inquiry."[18]

One further detail clarifies a nuance of Heschel's personality as he attempts to rationalize a major flaw in his demonstration: the sparseness of textual evidence. Echoing Helena Koigen's elucidation of religious emotions (at the meeting of 18 March 1930), he suggests that the prophets remain, to a significant extent, reticent: "It is also perhaps through *Scheu* [shyness or embarrassment] that the prophet announces only through slight suggestions that supreme and ultimate feeling [of sympathy with the divine pathos], the best that mankind can produce before God." Heschel, like the prophets, was both blessed and afflicted by spiritual modesty.

Toward the very end of the dissertation, however, the candidate declares his own prophetic passion without abandoning his academic demeanor entirely. The scholastic discourse gives way, in lyrical and intense prose, to a pledge:

We understand the person enflamed with prophetic zeal, who knows himself to be in emotional agreement and harmony with God. We understand the power of Him enflamed with anger and who turns away from His people . . . and the prophet's sharing that lived predicament; and that suffering is of such power, of such obvious value, so unique, that still today a calling remains inherent in its idea, that of being present to demonstrate it [sympathy with the divine pathos] as a form or as a possibility. Perhaps that is the final meaning, the ultimate value, and the ultimate dignity of an emotional religion. The depths of the personal soul thus become the place where the comprehension of God [*Verständnis für Gott*] flowers, the harmony of agreement [*Einverständnis*] with the transcendent pathos.[19]

The final sentence returns to Heschel's "religious anthropology." There he reasserts the sacred character of humankind, for theocentrism is but a golden path to sanctifying ethics: "In that experience [of becoming the object of God's concern] in which [mankind] experiences transcendent attention, the awareness of God is awareness of self." Thirty years later, Heschel closed *The Prophets* (1962), his expanded translation of the thesis, with this paraphrase: "'Know thy God' (1 Chron. 28:9) rather than 'Know thyself' is the categorical imperative of the biblical man. There is no self-understanding without God-understanding."[20]

Academic Evaluation and Approval

Heschel's two dissertation advisors read his typescript with discernment and professional impartiality. Their evaluations anticipate much of the criticism, and acclaim, the author later received as a philosopher of religion.[21]

His first reader, Dessoir, reacting as a psychologist and a philosopher of artistic consciousness, challenged the method. Dessoir's carefully typed report first summarized the dissertation, highlighting its main idea: "The above-mentioned 'pathos' is treated by the author most thoroughly. Pathos is not an essential attribute of God but a reaction to human acts, an appearance, a 'schematism' of the divine transcendent. Without pathos, the personal God would be an unfree God bound by absolute ethical norms. . . . God's sympathy for us is the root of religious feeling."

Then he stated some fair but rather harsh reservations: "To begin an assessment of this study with its external form, I have to say that it is written in faulty German and contains a great number of newly invented, yet quite superfluous technical terms. Much of this will have to be remedied before publication. The internal structure as well gives cause for complaint." Although it was not unusual for a thesis to require significant revision to become a book, some of Heschel's eccentricities as a writer already appear: a tendency to play cleverly with terminology and an unwillingness, or inability, to follow a tidy, linear exposition. Dessoir perceptively judged Heschel's "habit of constantly returning to the same fundamentals instead of making the actually existing basic concept of sympathetic religion into a clearly visible center."

Yet Dessoir also appreciated Heschel's tenacity, even when it contradicted his method. The report went on to state that radical reorganization of the thesis "would go beyond the author's mental strength. His abandoning a psychological approach, i.e., his failing to take into account forces of the unconscious, attests to the author's mental astuteness rather than to his inventiveness." In the end, Dessoir accepted the candidate's "independence particularly laudable in a beginner." Heschel's rejection of other approaches to biblical prophecy was "admittedly only the reverse side of a laudable advantage—by excluding all so-called causal explanations, the author has indeed accomplished a purely phenomenological description."

All in all, Dessoir's conclusion was positive: "The analyses are executed in a clear and consistent manner, so that at least a most appreciable preliminary task has been accomplished in this dissertation, which could be the basis for further study." Hesitating between the grades of *opus laudabile* (with honors) or *opus valde laudabile* (with high honors), Dessoir proposed "honors" but would go higher "if my colleague Bertholet should consider this grade."

Bertholet, the Old Testament scholar, read the thesis, Dessoir's report, and concentrated on the textual exegesis. With balanced and appropriately critical remarks, and some wry humor, he also appreciated the candidate's insights but not his pedantic style: "I am happy to say that generally I agree with the advisor's evaluation. Both the strengths and weaknesses of this study appear to be characterized by the author's following sentence: 'The empirical-functional [aspects] in the multiplicity of facts shall be neglected here; only inspiration as such in its essential qualities determining prophetic consciousness constitute the subject of this inquiry' (p. 9)." In this example of thesis writing at its worst, was Heschel just playing the academic game, or was he truly tangled in his borrowed rhetoric?

Bertholet offered useful suggestions for improvement. While recognizing Heschel's global theory of prophetic inspiration, he named some counterevidence. The learned master of biblical narrative and ancient Near East history also objected to the limits imposed by Heschel's phenomenology, his overly systematic strategy. In addition, he regretted that Heschel examined only the pre-exilic prophets—"Particularly in those cases where for other prophets social conditions would have had to be observed." And Bertholet, like Dessoir, also wanted Heschel to pay "more attention to prophetic phenomena *outside* the Old Testament" and "to translate into the language of modern psychology processes experienced in more primitive states of consciousness." Bertholet concluded: "Altogether I am of the opinion that it would not be appropriate to exceed the grade *'laudabile.'*" So Heschel received his doctorate with honors—pending successful completion of his oral examinations and publication of his thesis as a book.

Neither reader had attacked Heschel's theological agenda, but, as often happens, they criticized the candidate for neglecting their particular areas of expertise. Heschel indeed systematically refused to "translate" into psychology or anthropology the distinctive event of divine inspiration. The dissertation thus inaugurated his lifelong oppositional strategy, his polemical approach to religious and philosophical debate. His tactic was deftly to revise *terminology* in order to discredit his opponent's basic notions.

In practical terms, Heschel passed the penultimate hurdle to receiving the doctorate. Only his oral examinations and publication of his revised thesis remained. But he was not free; political events added to these relatively internal tensions. By December 1932 and early January 1933, while his dissertation was being evaluated, the Nazi party was beginning to dominate Germany's political, social, and academic life.

Most important, Heschel's dissertation on prophetic consciousness bridges scientific and religious perceptions of the world. He had deliberately chosen to elucidate a biblical topic—and not a more easily acceptable philosophical problem. Himself "enflamed by prophetic zeal," amidst the increasing menace to his people, he completed his academic requirements and furthered the vision he conceived as a Hasidic prince in Warsaw.

11
A Year of Grief and Rage (1933)

---

*Evil is not only a threat, it is also a challenge. Neither the recognition
of the peril nor faith in the redemptive power of God is sufficient to solve
the tragic predicament of the world.*
Heschel, *God in Search of Man* (1955)

SORROWFUL EVENTS FELL UPON HESCHEL DURING THE FOLLOWING WEEKS AS HE prepared for his general examinations. Soon after he submitted copies of his dissertation and was awaiting the administration's judgment, he learned that his beloved uncle Rabbi Alter Israel Shimon Perlow—his mother's twin brother and guide of his youth—had died suddenly on 3 January 1933. At fifty-eight years of age, the Novominsker rebbe, although known to have heart disease, unexpectedly succumbed to a stroke. Heschel thus lost the patron of his inmost identity—in Koigen's terms, the prototype of his essential "culture."

We do not know if Heschel took the twelve-hour train ride to the funeral in Warsaw the next day, yet the details of the Novominsker rebbe's death were quickly announced in bold headlines. *Dos Judisze Togblatt,* the Agudat Israel's Yiddish-language newspaper, reported: "Last evening, he did not feel well and the newspaper received a phone call requesting prayers. A short time later we learned that he had died." No one noticed a problem during *Minha* (the afternoon service); then one of his sons saw that the rebbe had fallen down. "Several doctors were called, but it was too late. . . . Messages were sent to all the shtiebls in Warsaw, to the other rebbes and close friends of the deceased. As an act of mourning the Executive Committee of the Agudat Israel interrupted their important meeting when the news arrived." On 4 January at three P.M., a "huge crowd reciting Psalms and studying passages from the Mishnah" made its way to the cemetery from the rebbe's home at 10 Franciszkanska Street.[1]

The community's misfortune was recognized in a way that reflected Heschel's original destiny, when the Novominsker was his ideal: "The present generation—at a time of terrible crisis—is orphaned. [The Novominsker rebbe] was loved not only by his Hasidim, but all others who knew him admired his kindness, his cordiality, his humility, his unlimited love for the Jewish people. . . . Today we are lost sheep without a shepherd."[2] Rabbi Perlow was a leader "able to fortify Judaism in people's hearts through his composure, his modesty, his glance, his words, and his *krekhts* [groan or sigh, an oral expression of suffering and compassion]."[3] Years later, Heschel attempted to capture the essence of that ethic musically: "Sorrow was their second soul, and the vocabulary of their heart consisted of one sound: '*Oy!*' And when there was more than the heart could say, their eyes would silently bear witness."[4]

In Berlin, Heschel was transplanting this legacy. As a biblical scholar (using the German language) and as a poet (in Yiddish), he expressed similar compassion and devotion to God. All the while, he expected the University of Berlin and the Hochschule to certify him as a modern Jewish teacher.

Mourning and Examinations

Less than a week after his uncle's death, Heschel received permission from the dean of the Philosophical Faculty (dated 10 January) to schedule his general examinations. The faculty confirmed the date, 23 February. Heschel was expected to answer questions about everything he had studied at the university during the previous five years.

On 30 January 1933, however, a political calamity transformed Heschel's future—and perverted the course of world history: Adolf Hitler was appointed chancellor of the German Republic. In a stately ceremony, the aged president, Paul von Hindenburg, administered the oath of office. Hitler and the Nazi party swiftly consolidated their power. Within six weeks, at the beginning of March, elections ratified their dictatorship and the German legal system became an instrument of oppression. Heschel's doctorate—necessary to secure an academic post—was also in jeopardy.

Under these stressful conditions—mourning his uncle and witnessing Hitler's incipient triumph—Heschel took his oral examinations on 23 February, answering rigorous questions about his several areas of expertise. The committee covered the spectrum: Max Dessoir and Heinrich Maier represented philosophy, his major subject; Eugen Mittwoch represented his minor in Semitic philology; and Albert Brinckmann, the history of art.

Heschel's university records preserve the event, brief notes on his examiners' questions, and their evaluations of his responses.[5] Dessoir began with the history of phenomenology—particularly the notion of synthesis from Plato through Descartes, Leibniz, Kant, and Husserl; "—The Copernican revolution in Kant, its explication by [Hermann] Cohen.—The material consciousness in Hegel's phenomenology." Maier focused on his own philosophy of emotional thinking and covered a broad area: "Affective and solitary imagination. Syllogism. Theory of imaging. Philosophy of immanence. Realism. Physical realism. Materialism. Metaphysics. . . . Fundamental problems of ethics. The question of telos. Perfectionism and Eudemonism. Kant"—and much more, according to their handwritten summaries.

Dessoir's evaluation of Heschel's answers was both critical and sympathetic: "The examinee lagged far behind what his performance in my seminar had led me to expect. He was visibly nervous and inhibited. Still, *Satisfactory*." Maier's assessment: "Good." Maier had crossed out the phrase, "on the whole" (*Im ganzen*); he originally chose a lower grade but stressed the positive.

Questions about Heschel's two minor areas were also comprehensive. Mittwoch, the Semitics scholar, asked him about the background of the prophets Amos and Hosea, especially Amos chapter 4. He also tested Heschel on Hebrew and Aramaic syntax, on the relation of biblical Hebrew to Aramaic and modern Hebrew, and on modern Abyssinian dialect. Mittwoch judged that knowledge to be "Good." The art history examination was less successful. Brinckmann interrogated Heschel on Andrea del Sarto, Leonardo da Vinci, Correggio and middle Italy, Kamarischen paintings, Baroque spatiality, and paintings of the birth of Venus. But Heschel made some elementary errors and received the grade "Very weakly sufficient."

The examining committee passed Heschel with the overall grade of *Sustinuit* (sufficient)—slightly lower than the average of his four grades. All in all, it was a respectable but undistinguished ranking. As Dessoir reminded his colleagues, he knew the candidate to be superior to his performance—for that was what this audit was, a public display of knowledge under pressure. Heschel probably considered this examination to be a mere procedure, as he decided that neither neo-Kantianism, nor Dessoir's psychologism, nor Heinrich Maier's "emotional thinking" contributed anything essential to his own system. And he was nervous.

In order to graduate, only one step remained: submitting two hundred printed copies of his dissertation (most to be distributed to libraries). It would not be easy. Although candidates could usually find the money to subsidize their first academic book, Heschel had few financial resources. In addition, the situation for Jews in Germany was worsening.

Hitler's authority increased rapidly. Four days after Heschel's examinations, on 27 February, the Reichstag building was set on fire. A Dutch Communist was blamed, and Hitler used flimsy evidence to pass a series of emergency decrees that undermined civil liberties and basic protections for all Germans.[6] The fate of Europe, and Heschel's diploma, were in the balance.

Events shattered his intimate community as well. Less than two weeks after the Reichstag arson, the elections of 5 March brought victory to the National Socialists who, still disappointed at not receiving an absolute majority, won 43.9 percent of the vote. This was an ominous outcome for Germany—and for the world. It touched David Koigen to the quick. In January, Koigen lost his pension from the Prussian Education Ministry and, as one who responded passionately to political events, he was overcome with anxiety.[7] Koigen died two days after the elections.

The 10 March issue of the *Jüdische Rundschau*, Germany's leading Zionist newspaper, announced Heschel's mentor's death:

In his Berlin apartment,
Professor Dr. David Koigen
died suddenly of a heart attack on 7 March.
He was fifty-four years of age.

Within two months of his uncle's passing, Heschel contemplated with profound sadness the black-framed photograph of his Berlin mentor on the front page. Alongside the death announcement was a report on the closing of Jewish-owned stores by storm troopers (the SA). The Nazi party declared officially that this repression was a spontaneous expression of the people's anger, not an anti-Semitic plot. Ironically, Koigen died right before Purim, the joyous holiday celebrating victory over Haman, who had conspired to massacre the Jewish people. Now mourning was the order of the hour.

Robert Weltsch, the *Rundschau*'s eminent editor and a Zionist and friend of Martin Buber's, wrote Koigen's obituary. In an uncanny way, Weltsch's portrait of Koigen also sketches Abraham Heschel's life, past and future—for both men were modern intellectuals of Hasidic ancestry who formed strategies to revitalize Judaism. Weltsch's summary allows one to speculate about Heschel's developing self-definition, by harmony or by contrast.

First, there was Koigen's dynamic personality—"thoughtful, active, vivacious, so interested in all living things." Then, Weltsch praised his intellectual ambitions: "Koigen was a thinker of wide scope. He worked to formulate a strictly logical, scientific basis for his special field of sociology, but his research also covered the fields of history, historical philosophy, and metaphysics."

Abraham Heschel had just completed a doctorate in philosophy at the University of Berlin and, like Koigen, he mastered German language and literature, ancient and European history, and philosophy. But Heschel, immersed until age eighteen in Bible, Talmud, Kabbalah, and Hasidic sources, interpreted contemporary conditions in a different way than Koigen had, with categories drawn directly from Jewish texts and lively spiritual insight.

Weltsch continues by describing Koigen's major professional handicap: "Yet this man, whose rigid style and often very abstract mode of expression, who as a writer remained inaccessible to the larger public, stayed in closest contact with tangible life." Daily events composed the "laboratory" of Koigen's thought and newspapers provided "material for the scientist." Even the advent of Hitler was an opportunity for knowledge: Koigen "was filled with the awareness of standing in the midst of historical upheavals which would yield experimental data for insights into the regularity of social human processes."

Abraham Heschel, like Koigen, was committed to a "personal evaluation of daily events"; as any intelligent European, he read several newspapers and was intensely aware of social and political changes. Yet Heschel's writing style in German was clearer, more concise, and more vivid than his mentor's. Heschel, after settling in the United States, used literary English effectively to convey his moral judgments and the nuances of religious sensitivity.

Weltsch ends the obituary by applying Koigen's philosophic and historical sociology to the fundamental issue of "Who is a Jew"? Up until the mid-1930s, most German Jews considered themselves to be Germans first and Jews second. Koigen seriously examined several possibilities: Are the Jews a "people" dispersed around the world? A "religious" group? A "nation" to be achieved only by establishing a state in Palestine? Koigen and his family, the Zionist editor concluded, had purchased tickets to visit the Holy Land before he died and expected to leave the next month.

Most relevant to Heschel was Weltsch's astute insight into Koigen's cultural incongruities. Such modernized Eastern European Jews, Weltsch averred, could never feel at home: "Koigen was unfortunate in that he—an immigrant in a dual sense of the word—never quite found an adequate sphere of action. Despite the fact that he had been educated in the spirit of the German scientific mind and identified closely with its methods, German universities remained closed to him in this post-War period and intercession of influential Christian colleagues remained without result; even the possibilities for publishing his writings were limited."

Abraham Heschel, throughout his life, also remained an immigrant, despite his successes; his "sphere of action" was never adequate to the country or culture in which he lived. In Hasidic Warsaw, he became a Yiddish poet and budding intellectual; in secular Vilna, he was a Warsaw Hasid in modern dress; now in Berlin he was an observant Polish Jew attempting to construct an academic career in an increasingly racist society.

Two weeks after Koigen's death, on 21 March, Adolf Hitler ceremonially opened the Reichstag at the Potsdam Garrison Church, where Frederick the Great was enshrined. "Hitler, in a cutaway and top hat, with unaccustomed tact and modesty, paid formal homage to the aged President in his field marshal regalia. That very day the first prisoners were brought under SA guard to the Oranienburg concentration camp outside Berlin."[8] Two days later, the deputies passed the Enabling Act, which legally gave Hitler dictatorial powers. Articles of the constitution guaranteeing civil and political equality, regardless of race or creed, were suspended.[9] Within days, thousands of people were taken into "protective custody." Jews noted these events with horror.

Desecrating the Divine Image

In these disturbing circumstances, Heschel urgently tried to find a publisher for his dissertation. He submitted his manuscript to the firm of Salman Schocken, established in Berlin since 1931, but it was rejected. (Later, he learned that one person had blocked this opportunity: Schocken's good friend Martin Buber, whom Heschel had met informally around 1929–30 in a Berlin café and who soon became his teacher and colleague.)[10] This was a severe blow: by 1933, few German firms were allowed to produce and market scholarly books by Jewish authors.

After trying other resources in Germany, Heschel thought of seeking a publisher in Poland, and he planned a trip home. First he needed the university administration to help obtain travel documents. A letter from Dean Hartung to the Polish consular authorities, dated 31 March 1933, certified that the doctoral dissertation of "Herr Abraham Heszel" was accepted and that "*Promotion* [legal graduation] will probably still take place this semester." The dean's generous prognosis quickly helped Heschel obtain the permits.

The very next day (Saturday, 1 April), a government-sponsored anti-Jewish boycott inaugurated a methodical persecution. SA troopers and other Nazi supporters intimidated citizens who tried to enter Jewish-owned stores and professional offices.[11] Nazi loyalists were instructed to place a yellow star with the word "Jew" on windows and doors by ten o'clock Saturday morning at the latest. Storm troopers, carrying inflammatory placards in German and English, were posted in front of these establishments to warn "Aryan" Germans not to enter. It was Germany's first large-scale anti-Jewish attack, and its intent was as much to humiliate the Jews as to undermine their economic stability.

Many citizens, to their credit, refused to obey the Nazis, but most yielded. Heschel's reaction was to write an explosive poem in Yiddish entitled "In tog fun has" (On the day of hate).[12] Heschel's vehement response parallels a series of articles Robert Weltsch wrote for the *Jüdische Rundschau* to inspire resistance. On 4 April, Weltsch published an editorial whose title became a famous slogan for German Jews, *Tragt ihn mit Stolz, den gelben Fleck* (Wear the yellow badge with pride).

Heschel's immediate personal necessity was to publish his thesis soon, lest the university not award his doctorate. The Nazis were quickly dominating Germany's academic institutions, beginning with the law of 26 April 1933 against the "alienization of German high schools, colleges, and universities."[13]

Heschel made his urgent trip to Poland, completing several projects during his five-month stay. He spent the Passover holidays (15–21 April) in Warsaw with his mother and sisters at 3 Dzika Street, where they had moved not far from Muranowska. He contacted the Polish Academy of Arts and Sciences in Kraków to ask if its Oriental Studies Division might publish his dissertation.[14]

In Warsaw, he also arranged for the publication of "On the Day of Hate," the poem he wrote during the Nazi boycott. Editors of the Yiddish daily *Haynt* published Heschel's poem anonymously on 10 May 1933, the very day the Nazis planned to burn Jewish books publicly. A note accompanying the poem informed readers that the pseudonymous author "Itzik"—a derogatory nickname for Jew—was "a world-famous German-Jewish writer whose books found a 'place of honor,' in a bonfire, which burned in the German State." (If the Nazis saw such a poem signed by Heschel, the university could be pressured to deny him his doctorate.) This dramatic poem—the longest and one of the best he ever published—flows from a clash of holiness and abomination, as it opens:

> On the Sabbath day
> At ten o'clock, a filthy-brown mass of people
> Sat on shoulders, on doorsteps, on thresholds.
> Like snakes, grown dumb and large,
> A guard at every entrance—murderously poisonous, a desecrator
> Of genuine lives, and my throat choking with disgust
> The mob spitting laughter on all who go inside.
> . . . .
> *Gut yontif* [happy holiday], pure-bred Germans!
> You hallow hatred on this day, sacred to your precious subjects!
> The people are a drum, beating within them yellow-greed tones
> And within them beats years of hatred and envy.

As a poet, Heschel had only irony as a weapon. He had no legal or political power in Germany—nor in Poland, for that matter. So he greets with sarcasm the "master race," who desecrate at one and the same time the holy Sabbath and God's people. Echoing Weltsch's "badge of pride," he proclaims, "Sacred is the shame of Jerusalem!" in the next powerful stanza:

> On every window pane, the hand spits a burning Star of David.
> How holy the curtains of the desecrated arks
> Gleaming on the entrances of Jewish homes————
> "The Ineffable Name of God," light and dark
> —ITZIK—burns in every window!

Heschel's vision of human sanctity repudiates the evil; here he identifies the accursed "Jew" (Itzik or kike) with the sacred Hebrew term: *Shem Hameforash,* "the Ineffable Name of God." Later in 1933, he published a book of Yiddish poems in Warsaw carrying that title.

The poet, moved by the suffering of his fellow Jews, imitates the "divine pathos." Moral empathy then expands into a prophetic judgment: "I know: God now sees through my eyes./ My every limb is absorbed in the angry 'day of sorrow.'/ Shudders erupt from my hair and lashes." And prayer emerges from rage, anguish, and bereavement: "But suddenly I am gripped by a glowing verse./ Now I write God's *tefillin* with our disgraced blood:/ I believe in God and I believe in the Jew!"

Using the Talmudic image of God as Himself a devout Jewish man praying with phylacteries, Heschel affirms simultaneously the presence of God and his people's future. The concluding stanzas form a call to action, while the two final lines reaffirm the poet's faith. Heschel combines rebuke and forgiveness as he beseeches God to act: "Heal and hallow us in this our life,/ O God of our ancestors and prophets!"

Still in Warsaw, Heschel made progress in finding a publisher for his dissertation. On 15 June he wrote to Max Dessoir, his thesis co-sponsor, asking him to support his request for university authorization to publish his thesis abroad, specifically with the Polish Academy of Arts and Sciences in Kraków. On 5 July, Heschel wrote the dean to help obtain a visa to reenter Germany. The sympathetic official did so, and, without being asked, extended the deadline for submitting copies of the printed thesis to 1 February 1934, even suggesting that Heschel was exempt from attending his *Promotion* in person.

Heschel also tried to advance his literary career, writing to New York to remind Abraham Liessen, the editor of *Zukunft*, about unfinished business: Heschel expressed "surprise" that he had heard nothing about his "things," additional poems submitted over a year earlier. "You were supposed to write me last summer, and I expected to receive a letter soon."[15] Despite Liessen's silence, Heschel sent him by express mail fourteen new poems, with several revised ones. Now he hoped that Liessen would at least support his attempt to publish a book of poems in Warsaw.

Heschel returned to Berlin in August and found a new room.[16] By then, some of his teachers and acquaintances were actively seeking to emigrate. Yet the fate of his thesis was still uncertain. Without the degree in hand, he could not find academic employment—nor qualify for a visa to another country. He submitted the typescript of his dissertation to the Polish Academy in Kraków and began to await its decision. In the meantime, on 4 December 1933, he asked the dean for another extension and, again, requested official permission "to have the dissertation published outside the borders of the country."

Nevertheless, Heschel's five-month stay in Poland was successful. In Kraków, he located a possible publisher for his dissertation—and in Warsaw he arranged to publish his collection of Yiddish poems: *Der Shem Hameforash: Mentsh. Lider* (Mankind: God's Ineffable Name. Poems). In two dissimilar modes—academic dissertation and lyric poetry—these complementary books express two poles of the author's spiritual personality: loneliness provoked by God's distance, and piety, love, and ultimate trust in God. Writing was indeed Heschel's Golden Bough, shielding him on his descent into the depths.

12

A Poet's Self-Portrait (Winter 1933–1934)

The symbol of God is man, every man. *God created man in His image* (tselem), *in His likeness* (demut). . . . *Human life is holy, holier even than the Scrolls of the Torah.*

Heschel, "Symbolism and Jewish Faith" (1954)

HESCHEL KNEW WHO HE WAS, AT LEAST INTERNALLY: A YIDDISH-SPEAKING modern Jew, loyal to the Sinai revelation, with a universal ethical conscience. This process of self-definition originated around 1924 in Warsaw, as he began to write poetry in his "mother tongue."[1] After modest publishing débuts in *Varshaver Shriftn* and *Literarishe Bleter* (1926–27), he placed mature verse in New York and Berlin journals. His literary ambitions did not relent, and he completed his earliest, and perhaps fundamental self-expression in the winter of 1933. Having completed his doctoral studies at the University of Berlin at age twenty-six, he published his collection of sixty-six poems, *Der Shem Hameforash: Mentsh. Lider* (Mankind: God's Ineffable Name. Poems), in Warsaw.[2]

Heschel's first published book consecrates his life's first cycle, from Hasidism into modernity. He addressed Yiddish speakers who could understand his inner struggles and ethical commitments, dedicating the volume to his long-deceased father "of blessed memory." Heschel's 1922 Talmudic analysis had commemorated "my teacher and master, Rabbi Moshe Mordecai Heschel." Since then other men had replaced his father, among them his uncle the Novominsker rebbe and cosmopolitan Jews like Fishl Schneersohn and David Koigen.

Heschel charted his formative moments through dedications of crucial poems: to his Warsaw confidant Yitzhak Levin, who supported his earliest secular studies ("Help"); to Yehiel Hofer, his childhood friend ("Between me and the world . . . "); to his sister Esther Sima ("July Sunday in Berlin"); to Haim Nahman Bialik, the Hebrew and Yiddish poet whom he met in Berlin and who encouraged his writing ("Intimate Hymn"); to Fritz Salomonski, his colleague from the Koigen Circle ("Prayer"); and to David Koigen, recently deceased ("God pursues me everywhere . . . ").

Yet *Der Shem Hameforash: Mentsh* is not simply an autobiographical document. The poet's persona and the author are not identical. A lyrical collection rises above self-expression and becomes an artistic construct. Yet the book's epigraph—"I asked for wonder instead of happiness, and you gave them to me"— depicts Heschel's creative energy arising from *tensions*—between awe ("wonder"), a closeness to God, and an inescapable alienation. As a modern Hasid, he contained both: "You gave *them* to me."

The 1933 collection maintains a continuity with previously published verse. Heschel gathered old pieces, revised some of them, and placed them and new ones into a larger framework in which he advances his joyful sensuality and ecstatic appreciation of nature, and adds poems which probe his loneliness. What emerges from the whole is an ideal portrait of the sensitive contemporary Jew he hoped his readers—and he himself—would emulate.

A Sacred Humanism

The collection's title—*Der Shem Hameforash: Mentsh*—proclaims Heschel's guiding idea. The biblical book of Genesis states that human beings are created in God's image. The Hebrew term *Shem Hameforash* refers to the Tetragrammaton, YHVH; it is "ineffable" and can be pronounced only by the high priest at the Temple in Jerusalem during the Day of Atonement.[3] The poet adds a Kabbalistic emphasis based on humankind as holy, a physical representative of God's Presence. Briefly put, human life possesses ultimate value.

Sacred preciousness touches all dimensions of human experience. Each of the book's six sections defines a different, but equally authentic sphere: "Human Is Holy" establishes the intimacy between the poet and God. "Bearing Witness" beseeches the Divine to reveal its presence further. "To a Woman in a Dream" extends the voluptuous yearnings of Heschel's earliest published poem. "Between Me and the World" returns to ethical themes. "Nature-Pantomimes" finds ecstasy in landscapes that become Jewish. "Redemptions" concludes with a pledge to help God rescue suffering people.

The itinerary begins with the essence of being human. Many of the eleven pieces in the first section—entitled "Human Is Holy" (in Yiddish, *der mentsh iz haylik*)—had been published before. The section opens with his emblem: "I and Thou"—which had appeared in *Zukunft* and *Berliner Bleter*. The poet defines his premise, an emotional reciprocity with a God of pathos: "I live in me and in You." He differs from his "predecessor" Martin Buber in one fundamental respect: Heschel's theology is theocentric (emphasizing God's ultimate mystery beyond the human initiative), but they both emphasize responsibility, the person taking action:

> It is your task to help, O God,
> But You are silent when the needy cry,
> So help me to help! I will fulfill
> Your duty, God, Your debts I'll pay.

So far, the poet reinforces the spiritual radicalism he expressed from 1929 on.[4] Both confident and humble, he challenges divine justice and compassion. While assuming that God cares, he scrutinizes divine inaction, which remains a mystery, while taking God's responsibility upon himself.

The second section expands this theocentric perspective. "Bearing Witness" (in Yiddish, *eydes-zogen*) opens with Heschel's second emblematic piece, "God Pursues Me Everywhere . . ."—also featured previously in *Zukunft* and *Berliner Bleter*. In the poem now dedicated to "My teacher, David Koigen, of Blessed

Memory," he confirms the social philosopher from Kiev as his modern Jewish model. Repeating his pledge to sanctify the world, Heschel endeavors to create places for God's presence.

Also in this section Heschel explores the function of poetry in "The Most Precious Word," a new poem. Language can become a vehicle of divine power, for the vocable "God" is the poet's ground of being: "My All!/ Your name is already a home to me." He continues:

> My only possession is this very word.
> I would more quickly
> Forget my own name
> Than forget Yours.

Writing allows the poet to share his devotion to God, and so poetry itself becomes an act of bearing witness. At the same time, God remains hidden, "ineffable," since words both convey and veil the Transcendent. The concluding poems of the second section add the poet's longing for a distant God to his ethical duties. The poem "Brother God" defines the paradox of modern religion: actions bring people closer to holiness than theology or institutional observance. Religion itself may distance us from the divine Reality:

> God is imprisoned in a jail,
> In the labyrinth of the Infinite.
> Running and coming through all the streets,
> Only Godliness disguises You, O God!

Heschel defines his mission in "Intimate Hymn" (dedicated to Haim Nahman Bialik). He becomes a sort of "human-planet" circulating from town to town, testifying to God's pervasive presence: "I have come to sow vision in the world— / To unmask the God who disguises Himself as world—." Five more poems, among the most melodious and lyrical of the collection, complete this cycle which reaffirms the poet's sacred calling.[5] Years later, Heschel expanded "Palaces in Time" into a graceful essay, *The Sabbath* (1951), exploring through parable, philosophy, and testimony how observance of the holy Seventh Day forms an architecture of eternity.[6]

Longings Sacred and Profane

The "love poetry" of the third section, "To a Woman in a Dream" (in Yiddish, *tsu a froy in kholom*), provides the only chronicle of Heschel's love life.[7] At this point, there is no evidence of any actual romantic involvements. Yet as a student at the university and the Hochschule—and as a guest at Sabbath meals in observant Jewish homes—he had numerous opportunities to meet women socially. But he was poor, absorbed in his studies and writings, and he was compelled to earn money for himself and his family in Warsaw. In any case, the absence of a dedication in this section is noteworthy.

The sensual aspect of Heschel's love poetry ripened, surpassing the adolescent fear of physical intimacy which characterized his earlier efforts. Adding to images of unfulfilled yearning for communion and pangs of solitude, he is bolder than before, more confident in his desires. Some of these pieces are genuinely erotic, dwelling on a woman's physical beauty, but the poet's expressed excitement is characteristically chaste.

Heschel absorbs fleshly desire into a craving that is sanctified. Following the medieval and Renaissance genre of the *blason*, using the woman's body parts as emblems of the man's emotions, the title piece, "To a Woman in a Dream," establishes his technique:

> Your eyes are greetings from God.
> An oasis in desert world is your body,
> Joy you are for homeless eyes.
> Your legs are trees of passion.

This imagined woman may extend traditional interpretations of the Song of Songs; or she may evoke the rabbinic and Kabbalistic notion of the *Shekhinah*, the feminine Indwelling of the Divine; or recall the Sabbath Queen. Whatever the allusion, the poet does not segregate holiness from the female body.

Yet the mysterious woman remains "in a dream"; she is a poetic construct. Both compelling and sublimated, she augments the poet's capacity for spiritual love. As "The Right to Wonder" explains, she is "a poet's proof for God," a carrier of religious insight:

> When for the first time I touched
> Your endlessly tender shoulders
> Like a sky—
> You sweetly sealed
> My right to wonder.

Nevertheless, "In Farthest Intimacy"—the poem that closes this cycle—suggests that the adored woman may be real. This is one of several poems which evoke piano playing as both amorous and artistic inspiration:

Your fingers gently caress the keyboard,
A herd of long, white bird beaks—
I have gathered silence for the eternity
Of my nights and light for your wild secrets.

So I hear that you, my beloved,
Want to quench my thirst for wonder—
And I too can heal your last deep longing
And call your soul—you.
And name my soul—you.

This is another variant of Heschel's "I and Thou." The essence of his beloved "you" is her *neshamah* (the inner soul). The poet harmonizes sensuality, craving for personal communication, and longing for God. Religious emotions (such as wonder) emerge from his search for intimacy, when lovers understand each other "from heart to heart."[8] Whatever Heschel's availability as a lover might have been, or his actions, these poems conjure up a female musician who, at least potentially through art, gratifies his yearning for transcendence.

Heschel's most personal confession, however, and that of the fullest consequence, occurs at the book's structural center.[9] The nine poems of the fourth section, "Between Me and the World" (*tsvishn mir un velt*), portray the writer's irremediable contradiction: his closeness to God distances him from the world. (Only one of these had been previously published.) Complementing his dreams of love, Heschel probes the solitude he carried deep within himself for his entire life.

Heschel's cultural alienation was inevitable because of his own and his family's several emigrations. But as a person who feels close to God, or who just as often craves holy intimacy, he endures a radical ontological rift. He describes his very being as split: the poem entitled "Lonely" juxtaposes two key words— *eynzam* (lonely) and *keynzam* (undefined). Despite the fulfillment of God's presence, he endures an internal alienation: "I cannot say 'thou' to myself" (*keynmol mit zikh nisht af du*). His divine responsibilities bring exquisite anguish, as he lacks the strength to fulfill them: "So much fire, so little light! Oh why/ Have I not enough fervor in prayer to convert my blood to courage?"

The central paradox of Heschel's life—as for many mystics or people of prayer—is that attachment to God can intensify estrangement from the world. Heschel was more than a cultural pilgrim uprooted from his ancestral community. The section's title piece, "Between Me and the World," says it all.[10] The poet is an instrument of divine will, yet his sacred duties insulate him from ordinary pleasures:

> I knew that I kept a message from Heaven in my breast
> For the world,
> That God Himself had requisitioned every moment of my life.
> . . . .
> My eyes in solitary confinement, through bars so narrow,
> How hard for my hands whose desire is bound by the *tefillin* straps.
> God has eternally stood between me and the world, barring me from it . . .

Heschel recognizes the mundane reality. Loyalty to God's vision of holiness can inhibit his enjoyment of life, as stated in the collection's epigraph: "I asked for wonder *instead of* happiness." The devout Jew who prays each morning, wrapping his arm and forehead in phylacteries (*tefillin*), highlights this contradiction. Gifted with "the right to wonder" (which Heschel later called "radical amazement"), he feels quarantined from people who see only a one-dimensional existence.[11]

Heschel's American vocation—giving a taste of genuine Jewish observance to assimilated readers—emerges from these poems, for poetry can integrate different spheres of being. As he states in "Between Me and the World," although he is uncomfortably placed between transcendence and satisfaction, the poet dedicates his imperfect instrument, words, to God's love for humanity: "I can only wander on to find silent bridges/ From my heart to God."

Poetry lifts him above the emptiness and dissatisfaction of his age. The poem "Lonely" develops the powerful emotion of longing (in Yiddish, *benkshaft*), which mediates the contradictory positions of piety, alienation, and compassion. Heschel's sensitivity to God's distance allows him to communicate with those who only yearn for faith: "But I:/ Like a child from mother nurse eagerly/ The thirsty longing for my God." Energized by endless dissatisfaction, the "longing poet" gathers fragments of spiritual fulfillment, sharing them with readers.

Modern also are poems which celebrate the resources available to Jewish immigrants in Berlin. "In the Park" describes how he sits on a bench, while the urban landscape conjures up his Hasidic past. He observes swaying trees that resemble "ascetic mystics [*opgetserte mekubolim*]/ Stopped suddenly in their dance." The trees remind him of Hasidim with their Sabbath fur hats ("windblown *shtreimls*"), familiar from his youth in Warsaw. (As he wrote later, "even the landscape became Jewish.")[12]

The next poem summarizes the ethical and theological foundation of Heschel's religious spirit in a lighter mood. "My Seal" imagines the poet as a "human flower" "to be rich in smiles instead of words." Its final couplet—from which the collection's title was taken—explains that the poet imitates the divine Self. The ineffable God is the person's paradigm: "Tenderness, You, God's Ineffable Name (*Shem-Hameforash*),/ You be my life's image! [*tselem-elokim*]." Human and divine compassion cannot be distinguished.

The section concludes with several poems evoking both the powers and frailty of literature. The poet is "emprisoned in words" and yet he can "celebrate Eternity's birthday/ In a hidden corner of a moment." He is a musician playing God's score, as he says with an appealing mixed metaphor: "Somewhere in the world I live as a piano/ Like a mother's breasts played by childfingers—." The last line states that writing *almost*—and he repeats the word—releases him from anguish: "Almost, I forget the excitement of feeling/ In the cage of words imprisoned."

Rescuing God in Exile

Heschel plays variations on these esthetic, ethical, and religious themes in the two final sections. His task, now, is to inspire: "My songs hang like a *shivisi*/ In some non-place in the temple of words." (This alludes to a wall hanging, usually parchment, placed before the prayer leader and containing the verse: "I shall set [in Hebrew, *shiviti*] the Lord before me at all times.") Heschel wants to display, as it were, his testimony to the ineffable God.

The twelve poems of the fifth section, "Nature-Pantomimes" (*natur-pantomimen*), praise God who speaks through the animate world, adding rural imagery to his city setting. Berlin was not completely bereft of nature—there was the central Tiergarten park—and Heschel's vivid imagery celebrates its gardens, a waterfall, even fields. A delirious tone is set by "Summer," previously published in *Zukunft*, in which drunken trees dance and the poet almost melts into "the All." Heschel dedicated the nostalgic poem "July Sunday in Berlin" to "My Sister Esther," suggesting that he feels forsaken in the cultural capital. The poet is an "émigré" who walks around "forgotten by all," but finally, he hopes, nature can embellish and humanize the metropolis.

The book's final section, "Redemptions" (*tikunim*), retreating from nature's euphoria, features Heschel's prophetic theology. (The Hebrew *tikkun olam* has several meanings: to repair the world, atonement, setting things right—all in all, preparing the world to become the Kingdom of God.)[13] The poet's ethical commitment resounds in these thirteen poems, convincing readers of his loyal but questioning faith.

As before, contradictory impulses release creative energy. The opening piece, "Guilt," laments the poet's hypersensitivity to suffering while thanking

God for bestowing upon him an arduous responsibility. Heschel admits to being afflicted with an uncompromising conscience: "You blessed me God with guilt, solid and immense/ Could I be the most guilty of the generation, of my generation?" The following pieces express his compassion for the underclass, laborers, "whores my outlaw sisters," victims of murder, and a *shlimazl*, a term for a proverbial misfit and victim who is usually a comic figure.

Heschel's most surprising expression of compassion appears in "The Patient," as he probes the mind of a man dying in a hospital, surrounded by his wife and friends, helpless and alone in spite of medical technology. The poem ends by questioning divine compassion. As the patient cries out, "God," the poet wonders if the Divine will grant the victim's prayers or respond to the "screams of millions of bacillae/ Gorged and full with the sick person's blood?" Does Heschel imply that a microbe is as precious to him (or to God) as a human life? That is unlikely, but the poet's radical pacifism demonstrates that God has not yet redeemed the world. He applies the same prophetic standard to human and to divine. Violence and death as such, no matter who or what the victim, is immoral.

Heschel reaffirms human responsibility in a major poem entitled "Prayer," dedicated to Fritz Salomonski, his colleague in the Koigen Circle. Here the poet speaks for and to people bereft of faith, responding to the earlier poem "God pursues me everywhere . . . " dedicated to David Koigen, their teacher. Rebellion against God is an appropriate response to the pervasiveness of undeserved suffering:

> Answer—O God!—our never-ending yearning!
> Break Your vaunted silence, Master of all answers!
> Prisoners of a thousand years beg You: reveal Yourself!
> Show us Your goodness, not Your cleverness, joy instead of magic.
>
> Why do you abuse our trust?
> And mock our pride for You?
> Why do You conceal Yourself before our desire. Oh, see:
> Our sufferings are longings in disguise for You,
> Our sin—our needy thirst for You,
> While Your enduring silence is Hell on earth——

Heschel's double consciousness—joining the ethical and divine dimensions—becomes even clearer in the two grand poems before the end. He still ponders the meaning of suffering but returns to emphasize God's perspective. Images of the *Shekhinah* (the Presence of God dwelling within the world) becomes a symbol of God's exile—and of God's need for human action. Emulating the Kabbalists, who accepted responsibility for liberating the *Shekhinah* from her earthly prison, Heschel reaffirms his task as God's rescuer.

At the same time, the poet accuses God but, sympathizing with the divine dilemma, he helps God Almighty to effect atonement. "Midnight Lament" recalls the custom of *Tikkun Hatzot,* rising at midnight with ashes on one's forehead, lamenting exile from the Holy Land. In Heschel's poem, the *Shekhinah* herself sits shiva, weeps and mourns "on Heaven's lonely threshold." And the poet speaks through a young man in despair who screams: "God and Father, grant me death!" Evil and injustice are "altars of catastrophe" where "God blasphemes Himself." But even the Divine can be redeemed, and so at the end, God confesses to His sins before humanity: "In infinite remorse [God] pleads:/ 'Why am I so ashamed/ To show mercy?'" This image of God wrapped in a prayer shawl and worshipfully contrite is somewhat bitter.

Heschel summarizes his goal, and the theology of pathos underlying it, in "Repentance," the collection's penultimate poem. (The Hebrew term *teshuvah* means "repentance" or "atonement" and can be translated as "turning," or "return" to God.) The poet repeats once again how humankind suffers, recognizing how people lose faith: "God, You great silent one!/ Responding with riddles to our cries."

Heschel does not rationalize the contradiction between God's compassion and God's silence. He refuses to justify innocent suffering theologically. Poetry retains the illogical complexities of experience, not refining them into simpler abstractions (or even into polarities). Heschel justifies his theology of pathos, quite simply, by identifying with God's emotions:

> Yet, sometimes, rain drops like a tear,
> God's confession to the world—
> I feel sad, embarrassed,
> For God Himself and for our own sake.
>
> Still our pain demands: have mercy!
> Instead of tears give help, action not regret.
> Every hope should be Your command
> And every shudder—an alarm.
>
> Let us, men, dogs, and God
> Atone together and return
> Or do penance for one another.
> Forgive us God our sins
> And we shall forgive You of Your own.

Modern religion actively dares God to help—and, actively, to repent. Heschel does not passively shed tears of remorse. The atonement codified in Jewish ritual and the inner experience of prayer provide a meeting ground where God and the person strive—with or against each other—for the sake of mutual redemption. Heschel expresses his love for humankind as a protest against God.[14]

Heschel's poetry indeed combines reverence and rebellion. The poet identifies with the *Shekhinah* Herself who grieves at Heaven's threshold while at the same time he questions God's love for humankind. The collection ends with his pledge, "My Song," first published in 1930 in Warsaw's *Naye Folks-Tsaytung.* There Heschel states simply that he will become the world's servant, its slave. God—or humankind—could ask for no fuller commitment.

Der Shem Hameforash: Mentsh thus complements his dissertation as a model of contemporary religious consciousness. Both are resolutely pragmatic. Heschel's Yiddish poetry, developed over a longer period, itself constitutes an act of prophetic judgment, confronting the enormity of selfishness, evil, and injustice. He tells God to lift the veil of inscrutability and to help the poor and the downtrodden, redeem criminals—to say nothing of preventing the martyrdom of bugs and viruses! These two works reconcile the moral militancy of Yiddish-speaking secularists with his Hasidic mysticism.

Publicly ratifying his pledge to represent God, Heschel's poetry continues a venerable Jewish tradition, starting with Father Abraham, the first patriarch, who argued with God to spare the few righteous mortals left in Sodom. Heschel's maternal ancestor, Levi Yitzhak of Berditchev, as well, beseeched the Almighty in eloquent Yiddish to apply compassion, rather than strict justice, to all sinners. In the end, Heschel remains God's enduring witness, both for and against God. Recognizing that the divine will ultimately remains unknowable, we cannot simply blame God; we must act.

Building a Reputation

Heschel carefully promoted his work. After the publication of his first series in *Zukunft,* he remained in touch with Bialik (now living in Tel Aviv), writing him in Hebrew to solicit his support. He sent Bialik two sets of poems, but received no response. Then, after Heschel sent him a copy of *Der Shem Hameforash,* Bialik finally answered, saluting the author familiarly as "Dear Heschel," and playing with words: "Your poems, in combination with your letters, I have received twice. In the first instance without your signature, in the second instance your name 'right there' [in Hebrew, *hameforash,* easy to spot]. And I was blessed twice."[15]

Bialik went on to appreciate the power of Heschel's emotion, responding to his worries about making a name in the Yiddish-speaking literary world: "You express great 'faith,' with great belief and great strength, the wrath of these days." Bialik congratulated Heschel for "finally finishing" his studies at the university and tried to alleviate his uncertainties: "You are right that the language in which you wrote these poems 'is waxing and waning.' If your soul leaves your body tomorrow it should be a good death, and don't let the fact that the poems are in Yiddish stop you from publishing." Finally, Bialik expressed pleasure that Heschel intended to "publish his ideas on the prophets" in the Jewish national tongue. "I see in your letters that the Hebrew language is with you."

Bialik ended his generous letter by expressing sorrow at the recent murder of Chaim Arlosoroff, a Labor Zionist politician, socialist thinker, and head of the Jewish Agency. (This assassination on a beach in Tel Aviv was blamed inconclusively on right-wing revisionist Zionists.) Heschel was reminded that the turmoil in Germany was matched by political violence among Zionists in Palestine. These two Jewish poets did not separate literary, ethical, and spiritual ideals.

13

Spiritual and Intellectual Biographies: Koigen and Maimonides (1934–1935)

He considered all thoughts to be the reception of a revelation. The cease-less flowing of the divine enters human thought, but also each worldly event, wherever matter acquires its form: that idea was also one of the ways Maimonides found the path to the concrete.

Heschel, *Maimonides: Eine Biographie* (1935)

WRITING BECAME HENCEFORTH HESCHEL'S INSTRUMENT OF FINANCIAL AS WELL as spiritual survival. After *Der Shem Hameforash: Mentsh* appeared in Warsaw, he turned to other nonacademic types of publication in German. His dissertation mapped out the particulars of prophetic inspiration while his Yiddish poetry more directly expressed his aspirations, clarified his churning inner life, and presented religious and ethical models. With his academic career in suspension, still hoping that the Polish Academy would publish his dissertation, he found his essential genre: biography.

In one form or another, Heschel explored a life in its intimate and cultural fullness, from the person's consciousness to the historical context. That year, commemorations of Jewish thinkers inspired him further to clarify his ideals: the first anniversary of David Koigen's death, and the eight hundredth anniversary of the birth of Moses Maimonides (1135–1204). Heschel published an essay on Koigen and a biography of Maimonides, in the process further defining his particular profile as a Jewish intellectual.

A Modern Philosophic Personality

By 1934 Heschel's mourning for David Koigen was completed; he dedicated his poem "God pursues me everywhere . . ." to his memory in *Der Shem Hameforash: Mentsh*, which appeared in Warsaw a few months before. Then, along with others from the Koigen Circle, Heschel also memorialized his mentor in the 27 February issue of the *Jüdische Rundschau*.[1] Because the Nazi government's racist policies increasingly deprived Jews of their economic, cultural, political, and individual rights, writing became a favored mode of resistance. Koigen's community was impelled to broadcast his worldview all the more urgently.

Heschel contributed a portrait of his teacher to the *Rundschau* tribute. This was his first published essay in German. In anticipation, he signed it "Dr. Abraham Heschel," despite the university's postponement of his doctorate; to his mind, the dissertation, though still unpublished, was completed, and he wanted recognition. Heschel's essay probes Koigen's mind, with special sensitivity to his teacher's internal contradictions.

The portrait opens by interpreting Koigen's facial peculiarity, "the exceptional character of his appearance." Because of some nerve damage, one side of his face was normal, the other immobile—a condition Koigen himself interpreted as representing two sides of his nature.[2] Heschel states that his teacher "lived within a curiously tense dialectics of spirit and being, of idea and matter." Koigen's abstruse expository style ("his idiosyncratic, secluded language and mode of thinking"), as well, was countered by his enthusiasm, his ability to communicate "both a naïve and a philosophical stance."

Koigen represents an ideal "philosophic personality"—which included ethics, religious insight, and passionate commitment. Koigen's enthusiasm for life, Heschel wrote, combined intellect and emotion: "From the innermost layers of his being flowed his love and warmth for small, everyday matters, a glance of goodwill and a belief in those with whom he dealt. . . . The world around him was mirrored in his personality and absorbed some of its dignified characteristics."[3] In other words, Koigen sanctified life through his reverence and compassion.

Heschel goes on to champion an existential ethics, anchored in empirical reality. Using Franz Rosenzweig's terms, he avers that Koigen "never suppressed within himself the 'situational thinker' (*Gelegenheitsdenker*)." (This became Heschel's hallmark as religious philosopher in the United States.)[4] He then specifies the subtle dynamics of his teacher's practice of cognition in which Koigen's mind interpreted events in the world, forging the raw materials into what he called a "philosophical act." Heschel then vaunted his teacher's intellectual energy, his contant attention to "processing into mental shapes everything that was given to him by experience and observation."

Koigen's investigations into the "structuring laws" of culture inspired Heschel, who was refining in his own terms that ambitious program.[5] Heschel concludes by claiming that Koigen's social theory advances a fundamental Jewish striving. Koigen was a passionate philosopher who sought to apply the laws of social science in the service of a "theodicy of culture." This essentially religious task, according to Heschel, applied his own deepest textual sources—an ancient will, which, since the Bible, we find in Jewish thinking through the Aggadah, Kabbalah, and Hasidism."

A few months later, another one of Heschel's supporters unexpectedly died. On 6 July 1934 the front page of the *Jüdische Rundschau* announced that the Hebrew poet Haim Nahman Bialik—to whom he dedicated one of his Yiddish poems—succumbed to a heart attack. An article entitled "Grief in Vienna" described the funeral: "Today Bialik's body was displayed in the ceremony hall of the Jewish division of the central cemetery in Vienna. The catafalque was flanked by an honor guard consisting of members of Jewish academic societies and associations. Only a few hours after the corpse was laid out, hundreds of people had already passed by the coffin to part respectfully from the great man."[6]

Heschel's generation was influenced by this dynamic interpreter of tradition, particularly Bialik's famous essay "Halakhah and Aggadah" (translated from the Hebrew by Gerhard Scholem in the same issue of the *Rundschau*). There Bialik stresses the cooperation of law and invention, halakhah and aggadah, in forming Jewish consciousness: "Day by day, hour for hour, moment for moment, it intends to build only one figure: the primal form of the creature, the image of God in man." Bialik goes on to compare the Sabbath with Christendom's great cathedrals: "The children of Israel have their marvellous creation, the sacred and sublime day, 'the Queen Sabbath.' . . . And what is the fruit of this painstaking work of Halakhah? A day which is Aggadah through and through." Heschel expanded similar formulas in his luminous essay of 1951, *The Sabbath.*

Ordination and Professional Hardship

In the meantime, practical considerations were pressing. Heschel had meager funds and few prospects for a career. He continued to seek sources of income. During his early years in Berlin, he earned money from menial labor of an intellectual sort. One such task was to establish an index for an edition of the *Tsena Urena,* a Yiddish-German commentary on the Torah intended for women, which Bertha Pappenheim, the prominent social worker and feminist (and Freud's patient known as Anna O.), was editing in Roman script.[7] Heschel remembered that the now-aged Pappenheim, founder of the Jüdische Frauenbund (Jewish women's movement), was the only person in Berlin who spoke harshly to him of Eastern European Jews, deploring their prominence in South American prostitution rings.

Teaching was more compatible with Heschel's special skills. In 1932, he became Hanoch Albeck's assistant at the Hochschule and taught Talmudic exegesis to advanced students. Heschel also tutored individuals. In the summer of 1934, W. Gunther Plaut, a young German Jew who had just received a law degree from Berlin University, realized that he had no future in his native land. His father suggested that he study Judaism at the Hochschule in order to understand this "bitter junction in history." But to qualify for the degree program, Plaut needed to improve his Hebrew. "The next day a slender, bushy-haired young man appeared with intense eyes and lilting speech, and clearly an East European accent."[8] It was Heschel.

Several times a week, Heschel tutored Plaut. "Heschel was patient and soon we developed a symbiotic relationship. He was then studying philosophy at the University of Berlin and I helped him with his German which, however, was considerably better than my Hebrew." Plaut entered the Hochschule in the fall of 1934. Emigrating the next year to the United States, Plaut studied at Hebrew Union College in Cincinnati and became a leading Reform rabbi and biblical scholar. In fact, Plaut edited the Reform movement's *Humash* (the Five Books of

Moses, with readings from the prophets and commentary), used widely in schools and synagogues.

In July 1934 Heschel completed his degree at the Hochschule, easily passing the culminating examination on Talmud and rabbinics. Heschel was ordained by the new Talmud professor, Alexander Guttmann, since Albeck had recently emigrated to Palestine.[9] To complete certification, Heschel wrote a paper on "Apocrypha, Pseudo-Epigraphic Writings and the Halakhah."[10] About sixteen months had passed since his university examinations for the doctorate.

Heschel now possessed the diploma of an ordained Liberal rabbi familiar with historical analysis—in addition to his Warsaw *smikha*. But he did not intend to practice as a clergyman. Heschel's Jewish certification, in any case, was not useful in Nazi Germany, and his goals were broader. Yet, with these Jewish qualifications, and soon (he hoped) his doctorate in philosophy, he would be eligible for a position in another country. Some organization outside Europe might sponsor his visa.

In the meantime, in the Polish city of Kraków, the fate of Heschel's doctorate hung in the balance. His thesis was not yet accepted for publication. On 8 March 1934, the Oriental Studies Committee of the Polish Academy considered *Das prophetische Bewußtsein* with misgivings "because it is mainly a psychological-philosophical work." Despite this misunderstanding of his method, the committee sent the manuscript to outside experts.[11] There was no response for several months. It was almost rejected, as reported in the minutes of 1 December 1934, and was returned to its author because of its "philosophical-psychological" approach, accompanied by a letter stating that "the question of costs is also not unimportant."

Heschel was not discouraged and acted swiftly and decisively. He set about raising money to cover the printing expenses—a normal precondition for most thesis publications. But his situation was worsening. Lack of income forced him to stay with friends or acquaintances for short periods instead of renting a room. On 6 December, he requested another extension from the dean, without mentioning financial need. The administrator's speedy reply, dated 10 December, was mailed to yet another address on the same street.[12] Within four days, Heschel had moved.

The anguish Heschel must have felt at receiving this official letter was mixed with gratitude for the dean's basic decency: "Dear Mr. Heschel: Answering your request of 6 December of this year, I once more agree to extend your graduation deadline by six months, that is, until 1 July 1935. I would, however, like to remark even now that hereafter you will be unable to submit to the faculty another

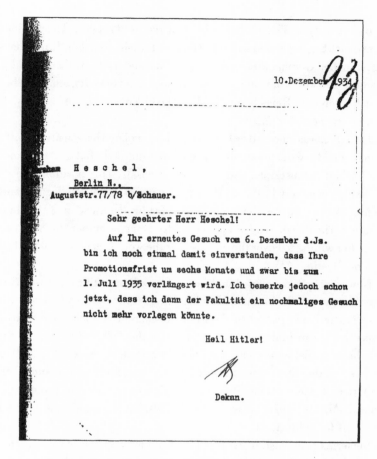

10.Dezember 1934

H e s c h e l ,
Berlin N.,
Auguststr.77/78 b/Schauer.

Sehr geehrter Herr Heschel!

Auf Ihr erneutes Gesuch vom 6. Dezember d.Js.
bin ich noch einmal damit einverstanden, dass Ihre
Promotionsfrist um sechs Monate und zwar bis zum
1. Juli 1935 verlängert wird. Ich bemerke jedoch schon
jetzt, dass ich dann der Fakultät ein nochmaliges Gesuch
nicht mehr vorlegen könnte.

Heil Hitler!

Dekan.

*Letter to Heschel from Dean Hartung, University of Berlin, 10
December 1934. Courtesy of Humboldt University Archives.*

request. Heil Hitler! [signed] H, Dean." We cannot gauge Heschel's response to
this noxious salutation. By then the government required the infamous tribute
to the Führer in significant administrative communications. The University of
Berlin was increasingly controlled by Nazis and their followers.[13]

Heschel battled on several fronts. If the dean's "Heil Hitler!" were not
enough, political developments made it clear that a Jew could no longer become
a professor in Germany. The law of April 1933 established stringent quotas in
all academic institutions. Acts of violence against Jews became common, and
the professional activities of German citizens of Jewish descent were severely
limited or even halted.[14] How could Heschel keep at bay his arbiters in Kraków
and Berlin? He needed time. And money.

By February 1935, Heschel located the required support. The previous year he had met Erich Reiss, a cultured German Jewish publisher. Erich Reiss Verlag published German literature, translations, and books on theater and acting, in addition to works of history, children's books, the fine arts, and some books of Jewish interest.[15] Reiss had published David Koigen's autobiography, *Apocalyptic Horsemen,* in 1925.

The editor was charmed by Heschel and appreciated his sensitivities.[16] Reiss soon invited Heschel to establish a new series entitled "Judaism Past and Present," solicit manuscripts, and evaluate proposals. This position at the Reiss publishing company furthered Heschel's contacts in the intellectual world. Of immediate importance, Reiss agreed to subsidize publication of Heschel's dissertation. The Polish Academy acknowledged that the author "found a [German] publisher willing to cover the expenses, if the work is accepted to the Committee's publications."[17]

Now Heschel's doctorate hinged upon his skill in writing letters—in two borrowed languages. In German, Heschel solicited the Berlin University authorities for extensions; in a Polish idiom that he seems to have learned primarily from books, he began intricate negotiations with the Polish Academy in Kraków. Heschel's sympathetic sponsor in Poland was Tadeusz Kowalski (1889–1948), professor at the liberal Jagiellonian University and recently appointed chair of the Oriental Studies Committee. With the patient support of Kowalski, a specialist in Muslim languages and cultures, Heschel began painstakingly to revise his thesis for publication.

In Germany at least, it was now beneficial to be Polish. As a resident alien, Heschel, ironically, was less vulnerable to the Nazi authorities than German Jews—but only slightly so. Money was the immediate problem. The Polish Academy required Heschel to advance 9,000 zloty before it could begin production. Another officer of the academy, Dr. Stanislaw Kutrzeba, pursued negotiations with Erich Reiss, guarantor of the subsidy, while Heschel managed the operation.[18]

Heschel remained in Berlin but returned occasionally to Warsaw to borrow or raise funds and, when possible, exchange Polish for German currency. In Berlin, writing on 26 March 1935 from the Woisky residence on Kant Strasse, Heschel informed Kowalski that Reiss, who planned to distribute the work in Germany, had not yet obtained permission from the government Financial Exchange Office to transfer money. Heschel expected to arrange "a private loan from acquaintances in Warsaw. *Soon* the last installment of the money will be deposited!" he confidently announced. Heschel's letter to Kowalski concluded

Erich Reiss, New York, 1939. Photograph by Lotte Jacobi.
Courtesy of the Lotte Jacobi Archive, Dimond Library,
University of New Hampshire.

by expressing, in a cryptic manner, a sense of foreboding. Anticipating his imminent departure from Berlin, he informed his Polish sponsor that he expected to receive the doctorate officially "on 1 December, after publication of my work. There are also very serious reasons which make accelerating the printing of my work a very urgent matter."[19] As he later learned, his life would depend on it.

The final date to submit a published thesis was 1 July 1935—and the dean no longer allowed extensions. Was Heschel planning a permanent move, perhaps away from Europe? He may have begun to contact institutions in Palestine, the United States, or other European countries. Whatever the case, he needed his doctorate in hand. Time was of the essence.

By March, Heschel's first scholarly book seemed to be approaching publication. He returned to Warsaw temporarily and obtained 1,000 zloty for his first payment, as he informed Kowalski on 30 April.[20] Meanwhile, at Berlin University, the Nazis replaced the anti-Nazi Dean Hartung, who respected Jewish students, with a staunch Nazi sympathizer, Ludwig Bieberbach. The Nazis so centralized their control that all academic transactions were regulated by the highest political authorities.

A Precocious Autobiography

The ironies of history were harsh. During this period, Nazi racism stimulated Jewish creativity similar to that which flourished during the Weimar Republic.[21] Yet most German Jews possessed little traditional learning, and even those who participated in Jewish affairs tended to identify themselves primarily as Germans. Forced now to rely only upon themselves, seeking to recover their heritage, Jews flocked to synagogues, studied Jewish texts, and began publishing books and periodicals.[22] As an editor for Erich Reiss Verlag, Heschel entered this Jewish sphere while managing his university business and completing requirements at the Hochschule. Heschel taught adults from Berlin's Jewish community, among whom Eastern European Jews played a considerable role.

In this realm too, Erich Reiss was helpful. Reiss was the epitome of the cultured German Jew—or rather "Jewish German" since his religious or ethnic identification was not primary.[23] By 1933, reacting to Nazi propaganda and anti-Semitic legislation, he decided to produce only books by Jewish authors, and even—anticipating Goebbels's decree purifying "Aryan" publishers—to use Jewish printers.

Under these tense conditions, Reiss launched Heschel as an author for the general public. Late in 1934, anticipating the eight hundredth birth anniversary of Moses Maimonides and its numerous publications to commemorate the event, he asked Heschel, almost at the last moment, to write an accessible, popular biography. Heschel replied that he had no time, as he was working several jobs at once in order to pay for publishing his thesis and to send money to his mother and sisters. Reiss took out a five-hundred mark note, gave it to Heschel, and told him to write. Heschel worked night and day on the biography, which he completed in seven months. The royalties for this book, if any, would be welcome.

Heschel's vivid life of the Rambam (as Maimonides is also known) spoke to Jews who had to live in Nazi Germany deprived of their religious culture. It is a "teaching biography." Readers might identify with this rabbi, scholar, and activist, whom Heschel considered to be another "situational thinker" inseparable from his intimate and historical experience. This life story, giving decisive importance to the philosopher's personal events, was also a precocious autobiography, portraying an exemplary sage whose religious and intellectual genius and ethical decisions the author was striving to emulate.

Heschel reveals his bias by systematically opposing the prevailing view of Maimonides as a rationalist and Talmudic or philosophical authority. True to the persona projected in his poetry, Heschel featured Maimonides's ethical and spiritual sensitivities, emphasizing his yearning for contact with God. He even collects evidence for prophetic inspiration. Part one, "Development and Maturity" (chapters 1–15), traces the Rambam's astounding intellectual skills and spiritual insight. Part two, "Renunciation and Fulfillment" (chapters 16–25), explains how the pure scholar and contemplative, after his brother's death, became a healer.

Heschel could write this book quickly because he already possessed considerable knowledge of the field. But he also undertook meticulous research. He wanted this work to be as accurate as possible, and footnotes specify numerous sources in various languages. Even when almost finished, by November 1934, he continued to verify details by writing Max Grünewald, a rabbi, historian, and folklorist living in Vienna.[24] *Maimonides: Eine Biographie* was completed by the following spring.

Heschel, in reviewing his own childhood and adolescence, had many reasons to identify with this child of genius who separated himself from his father's rabbinical court. Maimonides as a youth was guided by his yearning to "grasp God, as much as a human being can do so." Referring to a paper by his teacher Eugen Mittwoch, Heschel describes a prodigy: "Maimonides had such a memory and mental gifts that by age twenty-three he already mastered all the sciences. . . . He read a book once and knew its contents."[25] At age sixteen, Maimonides wrote an introduction to logic; at twenty-three, a mathematical treatise; later, commentaries on the Mishnah; and he elaborated a metaphysics. Heschel's ambitions were more modest, but also comprehensive.

Echoing his description of David Koigen's analytic method, Heschel convincingly anatomizes Maimonides's mind. The Rambam "didn't simply amass a wealth of heterogeneous facts; rather, he grasped everything intuitively, so that all the elements he acquired arranged themselves naturally into the harmonious framework of his understanding." But Maimonides accomplished far more than a "culture act" of rational synthesis. For him as for other medieval philosophers, insight joined the human and the divine: "For him all intellectual labor was a metaphysical process."[26]

Was this the biographer's secret as well? Theologically, Heschel's controversial chapter 3 states that Maimonides believed that "as of the year 1216, the spirit of prophetic illumination would return to the world. Could not Maimonides's intense yearning for prophecy have helped him participate in this precious gift? . . . Only this personal motivation can explain the central place held by the problem of prophecy in Maimonides's philosophy," Heschel insists. In the United States, Heschel later published two major articles, written in Hebrew, which cite hundreds of rabbinic and other post-biblical sources supporting the belief that divine inspiration (or *ruah ha-kodesh,* in English, Holy Spirit) was available even after Malachi, the last Hebrew prophet.[27] This belief, contrary to the majority view of Jewish authorities, implies that Heschel, too, considered himself sensitive to sacred intuitions.

Some of Maimonides's other personal struggles reflect Heschel's own travails. As his narrative follows Maimonides to Palestine and Egypt (chapter 7), Heschel claims, alluding to a statement by Koigen, that the Rambam, unlike the poet Jehuda Halevi, "lacked the 'sacred egotism' of the poet"; that is, the philosopher was not receptive to the landscape's sensuous beauty.[28] Heschel, to the contrary— as poet and philosopher and man of prayer—was drawn equally to pure thought, to religious contemplation, and to stimulation by nature, art, and literature.

The unspoken mysteries of Heschel's bereavements enrich his rendition of Maimonides's depression after the unexpected death of his brother, David, whom he instructed in Bible, Talmud, and Hebrew grammar, and whom he loved deeply: "Seeing him was my only joy." The philosopher's initial reaction was pathological: "Grief crushed him: after his bereavement he contracted a critical heart disease accompanied by fever and a skin disease of nervous origin. He sank into an abyss of melancholy."[29] Eventually, his vision of reality ripened, however, "provoking in his soul a decisive crisis."[30] By forty years of age, Maimonides "had mastered the difficult art of patience and forgiveness."[31]

Heschel was only twenty-eight when he wrote these words. For several years he endured extraordinary stress, losses, and dislocations: his father's sudden death in 1916; his tutor Reb Bezalel's attacks against his self-esteem; leaving for Vilna in 1925; settling in Berlin in 1927; the deaths in 1933 of his uncle and David Koigen—and now, the strides of Nazism, his poverty, political helplessness, and academic uncertainties. Yet there is no evidence in Heschel's life of either reduced capacity for work or psychosomatic illness—quite the opposite.

It may be that loyalty to God stabilized his mental health; it is clear that Heschel surmounted obstacles through work. In contrast to Maimonides's reduced "intellectual activity" during his depression, Heschel dramatically increased his research and writing. As a youth in Warsaw, he was reminded that despair was the arch sin of Hasidism. Now, as he admitted of Maimonides: "He also knew that mourning suspends the gift of prophecy."[32] Heschel, too, was driven by ambitions beyond academic or worldly success.

Part one of the biography, in fact, dwells upon the prophetic elements in Maimonides's intellectual system.[33] The medieval philosopher was fueled by an aspiration to contact God directly. Asserting that we cannot define or know God's *essence*, he developed an approach to God through negative attributes. As Heschel summarizes toward the end: "Maimonides, who from his youth had pursued not only the philosophical but also a prophetic quest for understanding, established his method of meditation with elements of the prophetic."[34] Maimonides appears as a crypto-mystic; his biographer guides readers to the Source.

Inwardness and Activism

In part two of the biography—entitled "Renunciation and Fulfillment"—Heschel makes judgments which promote his own neo-Hasidic and democratic worldview. Again emphasizing the medieval philosopher's spiritual goals, he nevertheless credits "Rashi the commentator" and not "Maimonides the codifier" for shaping Jewish civilization. "It was not the metaphysics of Maimonides that molded the future, but the Kabbalah and Hasidism. . . . Kabbalistic contemplation and Hasidic fervor directed the minds of the Jewish people toward 'the roots of his doctrine,' but in ways quite different from what Maimonides had dreamed."[35] Heschel's version of "Maimonides" lies beyond the historical person.

As he explores the sage's mature years, Heschel speculates that Maimonides's one true disciple, Joseph Ibn Aknin, a young physician, poet, and philosopher, left him after two years because of the master's refusal to share the secrets of prophetic inspiration. Heschel also discusses Maimonides's lack of inward peace in his career as "the supreme head of the Jews" (chapter 18). Opponents "accused Maimonides of poor scholarship in presenting legal rules without indicating their sources, without naming their authors, without citations and proofs."[36] Heschel, too, was later reproached by specialists for not documenting his references in books meant for a general readership.

The asceticism of Heschel's early adolescence finds an echo in his discussion of the Rambam's negative attitude toward sexuality. It was known that Maimonides wanted to conquer erotic appetites: "He constantly cites Aristotle's statement: 'The sense of touch is our disgrace!'" Yet, as the court physician of sultans, Maimonides was required to prescribe aphrodisiacs or discuss "harem matters."[37] Yet Heschel's poetry shows no disdain for the flesh, just a measure of timidity and tact.

Maimonides's apparent dislike for carnal pleasures, according to Heschel, was not fundamental—but it supported his concern to protect his gift of prophecy, which was.[38] In the end, Heschel's Maimonides is an ethical hero—more than an exemplar of intellectual, psychological, or even spiritual struggle. The final chapter, "Imitation of God"—the only part of the book that Heschel himself, years later, adapted and translated into English—celebrates the Rambam's medical service during the last fifteen years of his life.[39] Heschel aptly summarizes the journey: "Maimonides's final transformation: from contemplation to action, from the knowledge of to imitation of God. God was no longer an object of his understanding: He became the model to follow." Worship, thought, and action are one.[40]

Heschel then insists upon Maimonides's deeper, spiritual goal, to make his God-consciousness available to everyone, to sanctify the everyday. Since the "active intellect" forms a constant awareness of God's presence, according to Maimonides, philosophy can unveil the world's holy dimension: "He no longer needs to think of sacred things in order to feel himself close to the sacred." Heschel's English version adds: "Thought itself is holy. Thought itself is the presence of God."[41] No clearer anticipation of Heschel's goal as philosopher of religion can be found.

Maimonides: Eine Biographie, Heschel's first book in German, was praised as a popular success with a scholarly foundation. Soon after it appeared in May 1935, reviewers stressed the author's skillful evocation of the philosopher's life, mind, and prophetic aspirations. They appreciated the lively narrative as "a work of art that combines scientific strictness and noble popular appeal." Reading it was "a thorough delight."[42] A reviewer in Madrid singled out the author's "artistic touch."[43]

Heschel's biography for a general audience was also recognized by the most prestigious journal in his academic community, the *Monatsschrift für Geschichte und Wissenschaft des Judentums*, in the 1935 issue commemorating the eight hundredth anniversary of Maimonides's birth.[44] Sensitive to its literary qualities, but more critical, was the review by its distinguished editor, Isaak Heinemann. The expert appreciated Heschel's psychological acumen, his analysis of the Rambam's "thinking processes," but remained unconvinced that Maimonides believed he was inspired by God: "With diligence the author has studied the sources on Maimonides's life and times and from hard-to-find materials, but also using less reliable information, has presented a credible, colorful, and attractive depiction."[45]

Heinemann astutely delimits Heschel's qualities and shortcomings as an academic writer, anticipating the resistance Heschel later encountered from specialists. He could synthesize vast amounts of information, transform it into a lively narrative, while imagining the person's emotional and spiritual life, whether it be the Hebrew prophets, Maimonides, Koigen—or himself. Strict experts might agree that, while Heschel's portrait of Maimonides was sensitive, the conclusions were too bold. Flexible or sympathetic scholars would support the valuable result: his portrayal had embodied an exemplary Jewish mind and spirit. Heinemann concluded that the author "knows also how to bring closer to the reader the experience of the people of the time." Heschel as biographer indeed strives to make eternal holiness alive in the present.

14

The German Jewish Renaissance (1934–1935)

---

*Heschel knows German culture, he is scientific and schooled in method,
and he possesses the innate Jewish force nourished equally from the deepest, natural feelings and from a special understanding. In ordinary life,
this is a contradiction, but not here. "Only through wonder is the union
of consciousness and unconscious possible."*

F. A., *Der Morgen* (1935)

AS EDITOR AT THE ERICH REISS PUBLISHING COMPANY, DEGREE HOLDER FROM THE Hochschule, and author of a popular biography of Maimonides, Heschel enhanced the community associated with the Berlin Jüdische Lehrhaus, the city's Jewish adult education center. Founded in 1919, the Freie Jüdische Volkshochschule (Free Jewish people's school) emulated Franz Rosenzweig's ideal of introducing practical Jewish knowledge to people without traditional background.[1] Under the leadership of Paul Eppstein and Fritz Bamberger, the Berlin Lehrhaus offered a variety of Jewish—and secular and academic—subjects.

Heschel lectured at the Berlin Lehrhaus in 1935.[2] The catalogue for that year's winter semester (November 1934–March 1935) reads like a directory of the German Jewish renaissance. It includes among its sixty courses Martin Buber on the Bible, Ignaz Maybaum on the prophets, Alexander Altmann on Jewish holidays and festivals, Alexander Guttmann on Talmud, David Baumgardt on philosophy, Rachel Wischnitzer on religious art, Leo Hirsch and Ignaz Meitlis on Yiddish literature, Hans Joachim Schoeps on Kafka, and Robert Weltsch on the Jewish press. Major events were Sunday lectures on "fundamentals" given by prominent figures: Baeck, Elbogen, and Joachim Prinz; Jewish history and faith were represented by Max Wiener on Orthodoxy, Maybaum on the prophets and rabbinics, Buber on Hasidism, Arnold Metzger on Liberal Judaism, and Ernst Simon on Zionism; while Max Grünewald, Margarete Susman, Eppstein, and Bamberger gave lectures on Palestine, German Jewry, and contemporary problems.

This renewal of German Jewish culture was dispensed in many areas, the intellectual periodical *Der Morgen* being one of the most significant. Founded in 1925 and published in Berlin, *Der Morgen* began as a bi-monthly, with scholarly and popular articles about history, philosophy, religion, psychology, literature, and other topics of Jewish interest.[3] Most of its contributors were Jews associated with the Hochschule, the Rabbiner-Seminar, the Berlin Lehrhaus (or the original one in Frankfurt, founded by Rosenzweig and Buber).[4] The journal's most dynamic period coincided with the rise of Hitler after the Reichstag arson of February 1933.

A sophisticated self-awareness emerges from its pages. As Jews were banned from journalism, *Der Morgen* was able to become a monthly and writers responded to the immediate dangers. Before mid-1933, most articles were scholarly. (In April 1933, for example, Cassirer published a paper on Henri Bergson's ethics and philosophy of religion.) After October, every issue began with a five-page commentary on the political situation and a digest of German periodicals and newspapers. Jews still felt free enough to analyze the situation in writing, hoping to brace the community until the Hitler phenomenon went away. The essays became more concise as authors introduced personal judgments.

Contributors to *Der Morgen* gave substance to modern Jewish identity, countering racial definitions mandated by the Nazis. The January 1934 editorial warned that Jews rejected by a perverted Germany would become "existentially adrift in space, time, and spirit" if they did not recover their roots.[5] That search of course began much earlier, with Zionism and the Jewish youth movement, and in the effervescence of Weimar Republic culture. But now mainstream Jews, excluded from their homeland's political and economic life, turned toward a Jewish civilization which was unfamiliar to most of them. One writer noted the grotesque irony that German Jewry, so estranged from tradition, might become entirely assimilated without the menace of Hitler's repressions.[6] Heschel later remarked, "If the Hitler threat went away, I expected a great renaissance of Judaism among German Jews."[7]

Portraits of Heschel

Heschel impressed sophisticated German Jews during this trying but invigorating period. The authorial persona conveyed in his elegant *Maimonides* biography prepared a warm friendship. Late in 1935, a review copy was sent to Stefan Kayser, an essayist, music critic, and art historian writing for the Jewish weekly *Israelitische Familienblatt*.[8] Kayser was struck by the book's attractive binding and typeface, characteristic of Reiss publications, and he savored the opening panorama: "Between the arid Sahara and the Mediterranean sea furrowed with ships, between the solitudes of the Atlantic and ancient Egypt . . . " Kayser wrote a laudatory review which the publisher cited in advertisements.

Kayser asked Reiss to introduce him to Heschel. They became friends and discussed art and literature, Heschel's studies with the Bible scholar Ernst Sellin, and other matters. The art critic was singularly sensitive to Heschel's bearing, which expressed better than words his inner identity. "He was a lovely young man, young in every way. In the way he moved, in his open-mindedness. He behaved with great charm," Kayser recalled with pleasure. Heschel added a unique graciousness to intelligent conversation.

Kayser and his wife, Louise, herself an artist, sometimes invited Heschel to dinner. As a bachelor with little money, he was happy to accept. Although they knew nothing of his Hasidic ancestry, they knew he was observant and carefully adhered to the laws of *kashrut*. (Kayser had an Orthodox upbringing in Frankfurt.) Heschel was an engaging guest, and especially enjoyed speaking with Mrs.

Kayser. One evening they delighted in Heschel's gift of a bottle of Stari Voyak (meaning Old Soldier), a rather expensive Polish brandy. The young scholar, with little money to spend on himself, "knew not only the Jewish side of the Poles, but also their more pleasant side." Heschel was not ascetic; he relaxed with the Kaysers, whose appreciation of fine liquor he shared.

Kayser admired Heschel as a "rounded-out personality," at home in both Western culture and Jewish piety. His artistic sensibility was particularly appealing and Kayser perceptively discerned how Heschel spontaneously "lived the esthetic" from within. He did not approach it intellectually "from the outside, slipping into art." Kayser remembered Heschel's reaction to an illustration of Abraham beginning to sacrifice Isaac. "Heschel was almost moved to tears when he looked at it. He identified with the human drama of biblical story. They were kindred spirits. Heschel lived these things. . . . And he was open to modern trends too."

Learning in all domains was Heschel's primary focus: he mastered German literature and philosophy, and he admired European civilization. At the same time, Heschel was a master of the classical Jewish texts, as Kayser put it, "a *talmid hakham* of the highest order." Yet he carried his knowledge lightly, not reproaching those who were not as well educated.

An accomplished intellectual, Heschel remained strictly observant religiously. One very cold day Kayser offered him an overcoat, for his clothing made his poverty quite obvious. Heschel first examined the coat carefully to see if it did not violate *shaatnez*, the law forbidding the mixture of linen and wool in clothing (see Lev. 19:19), practiced among meticulously observant Jews. Fortunately it was "kosher."

At the same time, there was a troubling nuance within Heschel's sober, energetic personality, which Kayser keenly sought to define. Heschel was extremely sensitive—as attentive to daily events, which pained him, as he was to art and literature. But he showed little evidence of suffering. He appeared to be "one of the most self-contained personalities" Kayser had ever met. During that anguishing time (Kayser left Germany early in 1936), Heschel did not appear upset or disoriented. He seemed to accept the difficult conditions in Germany and made the best of it. Heschel was hiding his turmoil, keeping his feelings to himself. The "rabbinic bearing" his companions in Vilna had noticed a few years before appeared to Kayser as self-possession and courage. Still, Heschel must have felt lonely and vulnerable.

Clearly, he had no future in Germany. Most of Heschel's teachers at the Hochschule were emigrating and by 1935 the faculty was reduced to a bare minimum. The Talmud professor Hanoch Albeck took a leave of absence in 1933 and settled in Palestine the following year. Heschel's philosophy professor, Julius Guttmann, was invited to the Hebrew University in the winter of 1934, and was replaced by Berlin rabbi Max Wiener. The Hochschule's "permanent faculty" now consisted of Elbogen, Baeck, Sister, and Wiener.[9] According to his résumé, Heschel instructed advanced students in Talmudic exegesis in 1934, as he had two years earlier, but there was no faculty position for him.

Heschel sought to establish himself more deeply within the larger Jewish intellectual community. During that time Martin Buber, the acknowledged leader, with Leo Baeck, of Jewish cultural resistance to the Nazis, taught courses at the Berlin Lehrhaus and the Hochschule. When in January 1935, Buber began a series of guest lectures at the Hochschule on "Problems of Biblical Messianism," Heschel renewed their earlier, brief contact.

A chance for Heschel to publicize his work presented itself. In this unstable period, when German Jews were reshaping their identities, he was appreciated as an East European representing "authentic Jewishness." Since the 1920s, a number of relatively assimilated German-speaking Jews—such as Rosenzweig, Franz Kafka, and earlier Martin Buber—were attracted to Hasidism and other forms of traditional religious culture. That idealized image of East European Jewry (a form of "Orientalism," attraction to the exotic) still engaged the German brethren.[10]

Heschel's poetry was promoted by a colleague who taught Yiddish literature at the Berlin Lehrhaus, Leo Hirsch, a poet, playwright, essayist, and journalist who wrote books on Jewish observance and cultural history.[11] Heschel had much in common with this observant Jew, who, like Baeck and Elbogen, was born in the Posen province. Hirsch was a frequent contributor to *Der Morgen*, publishing essays on Nietzsche, Disraeli, Ferdinand Lasalle, Sholem Aleichem, Leibniz and Spinoza, and contemporary fables in an ironic, Midrashic style.

The editors of *Der Morgen* recognized that Heschel's religious and ethical vision might provide an alternative to Jewish alienation—what he called the *seelischer Luftmensch* (a spiritually empty person) most German Jews had become.[12] In Hitler's time, even before Jews were forced to wear the yellow star, many parents were too ignorant to help their children retrieve the religion of their grandparents. In the March 1935 issue, Heschel's book of Yiddish poems, *Der Schem-hameforasch—Mentsch* (as it was spelled in German), was praised by the reviewer F. A. (probably Fritz Aronstein, who taught courses on the Hebrew press at the Berlin Lehrhaus), as "modern poems from a Polish Jew."[13]

Heschel's composite identity was a virtue. The reviewer portrayed him as a former Hasidic Jew, educated in Germany, able to communicate religious insight in a pertinent idiom—tradition tuned to modernity without losing its spirit.

Heschel's "scientific training," he went on, lent credence to his "innate Jewish force nourished equally by the deepest, natural feeling and by a special understanding." This sampling of Yiddish culture could help preserve German Jewry against assimilation.

Heschel's Yiddish poetry was a form of "situational philosophy," building bridges between secular and religious thinking. The reviewer accordingly featured the practical consequences of Heschel's religion by quoting the collection's powerful concluding piece: "I give to you, o world, / The lattice of my limbs / My word, my hands, / The wonder of my eyes." This activist Judaism might inspire moral courage and self-respect: "The *Schem-hameforasch—Mentsch* is the man who forever lives under [God's] call and strives, through the greatest difficulties, to give answers."

Was Heschel aware that he successfully represented a form of "enlightened and modern Hasidism"—as it was called at the 1930 World Conference for Progressive Judaism? At this point, in any case, Heschel felt ready to engage Martin Buber, interpreter of Hasidism for modern Europe. The relationship was hatched in June 1935, when Leo Hirsch's German translation of Heschel's Yiddish poem "I and Thou" appeared in *Der Morgen,* three months after F. A.'s friendly book review.

Heschel's poem (already published in Yiddish three times) was an implicit appeal—both positive and critical—to Buber, whose *I and Thou* marked an era after its publication in 1923. (Hirsch, a long-time acquaintance of Buber's, had contributed an essay on his Hasidic works to a 1928 volume honoring the master's fiftieth birthday.) That same month, Heschel mailed his first substantive letter to Buber. In addition, Heschel hoped that publishing this poem in *Der Morgen* would inaugurate a German translation of the entire collection.[14]

However, Heschel published nothing in *Der Morgen* after his Yiddish "I and Thou" appeared. Instead, in 1936, he began regularly to publish book reviews, and some religious essays, in the widely circulated Berlin newspaper, *Gemeindeblatt der jüdischen Gemeinde zu Berlin.* These brief writings provided some income. In 1937, Leo Hirsch continued to import Heschel's spirit into Nazi Germany by publishing in *Der Morgen* a laudatory review of Heschel's dissertation when it was published in book form.

Books of Jewish Renewal

During this period, Heschel, as editor for the Reiss series "Judaism Past and Present," formed a community of Jewish scholars. His biography of *Maimonides* was the first to appear, and its dust jacket anticipates several projects: a book entitled *Jews of the World* by historian Mark Wischnitzer (husband of art historian Rachel Wischnitzer-Bernstein, who contributed an essay to his ephemeral Yiddish journal, *Berliner Bleter*);[15] a biography of Philo of Alexandria by Edmund Stein, professor at the Warsaw Institute for Jewish Studies; a book on Rashi by Elbogen; and three anthologies (beautiful Jewish poems, Jewish letters, and Jewish art history). Heschel also announced the imminent appearance of his dissertation with the provisional title *Die Propheten* (The prophets). But events halted this flowering. Only Wischnitzer's and Heschel's books actually appeared.

As editor, Heschel furthered his mission to capture the spirit of East European Jewishness. He helped publish *The Son of the Lost Son*, the first novel of Soma Morgenstern, a journalist from Vienna and friend of Walter Benjamin's.[16] A distant descendant of the Kotzker rebbe, Morgenstern returned to Jewish commitments after years of assimilation and marriage to a Gentile woman. His autobiographical story of the son of an apostate Jewish doctor (the lost son), living in Vienna, who rediscovered his Hasidic roots in the Ukraine, appealed both to non-observant Jews and the Orthodox. The novel's rendition of the cultural rifts within contemporary European Jewry struck its readers deeply.[17]

Morgenstern's book must have awakened Heschel's most formative memories as well. Among its vivid depictions of the 1928 Agudah Congress in Vienna are portraits of the assembled Hasidic leaders, among whom were Rabbis Israel Friedman, the Tchortkover rebbe (son of Dovid Moshe), and Abraham Mordecai Alter, the rebbe of Ger. Heschel informed Morgenstern that his book was praised in a Frankfurt newspaper by Jacob Rosenheim, leader of the Agudat Israel, who wrote, "This is our book!"

Heschel's first meeting with Soma Morgenstern in Vienna typified his mixture of ease and isolation as a worldly but observant Jew.[18] One day Heschel telephoned to say that he was in town visiting relatives, and the Morgensterns invited him to their home. As Morgenstern remembered: "He arrived at tea time, a very young man with an ascetic expression and the credulous eyes of a free-mannered, good-hearted, open person. When invited to sit down to tea, he drank a few cups, but didn't touch anything else. We spoke of many things on that first visit, particularly Martin Buber and the sad condition of German Jewry. The conversation lasted until evening, but when my wife invited him to dinner he declined politely, and with some awkwardness. I realized that he would have been happy to remain had he been assured that we observed the dietary laws."[19]

Heschel's scholarly book of Jewish renewal—his doctoral dissertation on the

Hebrew prophets—remained in limbo. Still without official permission to publish in Poland, he continued to grapple with the university administration. German respect for rules gave Heschel an advantage. On 21 May 1935 the Nazi sympathizer Dean Bieberbach sent him a copy of his appeal to the Reichsminister of Science, Art, and Popular Education (and a copy to the university rector). The bureaucracy worked well. The dean's answer of 18 June assured him of official support: "By the decree of 6 June 1935—WIF no. 2238—the Reichsminister has made an exception and authorizes the publication of your dissertation abroad."[20] Some emotional door opened within Heschel, for that very day, 18 June 1935, he wrote a letter to Martin Buber which inaugurated their alliance.

In the meantime, Heschel labored to improve his manuscript for publication, even while its status remained precarious. Virtually assured of the doctorate, he needed to request further extensions, beyond the 1 July deadline. After the Nuremberg Laws were promulgated on 15 September 1935, he no longer expected judicial protection from Germany. "Jews were definitely robbed of their citizenship. Next the swastika was made the flag of the Reich and Jews were forbidden to display any but the 'Jewish blue-white colors.'"[21]

For a scholar, expressly for one without a position, these revisions and corrections were indispensable. Recognizing the dissertation's technical shortcomings, he edited meticulously. Writing to Tadeusz Kowalski on 17 September, in unusually large handwriting he announced proudly that, the manuscript completed, he had mailed it that very day. Heschel hoped that his numerous corrections would please his sponsor; he had already become an expert editor of his own work: "Less important details, wordiness, repetitions, and other minor flaws have been removed. The cutting down was quite considerable. On the other hand, additions and supplements, which strengthen the base of the work, were added."[22] Heschel's postscript requested a title change, from *Das prophetische Bewußtsein* (Prophetic consciousness) to the less technical *Die Prophetie* (On prophecy), a more dynamic invitation to readers.

The university's deadline was approaching, and the fate of his doctorate depended upon his speed and efficiency. Everything must be right: the text, the title, the details of presentation. He must assure the quality of this book, which might earn him an invitation to another country—and the prospect of a new life. The tension must have been enormous. At last, the printer was ready to set the book in type. But slight problems remained. Kowalski responded with further suggestions for revision, advising Heschel that a page was missing from his manuscript. On 27 October, Heschel sent the errant leaf with an apology, inquiring as well if they had received money from an unnamed "Warsaw acquaintance."

QVOD FELIX FAVSTVMQVE SIT

VNIVERSITATIS LITTERARIAE
FRIDERICAE GVILELMAE
BEROLINENSIS

RECTORE MAGNIFICO

WILHELM KRUEGER

MEDICINAE VETERINARIAE DOCTORE IN HAC VNIVERSITATE ANATOMIAE VETERINARIAE PROFESSORE
PVBLICO ORDINARIO

EX DECRETO ORDINIS AMPLISSIMI PHILOSOPHORVM
PROMOTOR LEGITIME CONSTITVTVS

LUDWIG BIEBERBACH

PHILOSOPHIAE DOCTOR IN HAC VNIVERSITATE PROFESSOR PVBLICVS ORDINARIVS
ACADEMIAE SCIENTIARVM BORVSSICAE SOCIVS

ORDINIS PHILOSOPHORVM H. T. DECANVS

VIRO CLARISSIMO ATQVE DOCTISSIMO

ABRAHAM HESCHEL

VARSOVIANO

POSTQVAM EXAMEN PHILOSOPHIAE RITE SVSTINVIT
ET DISSERTATIONEM LAVDABILEM CVIVS TITVLVS EST

-DAS PROPHETISCHE BEWUSSTSEIN-

AVCTORITATE ORDINIS PROBATAM EDIDIT

PHILOSOPHIAE DOCTORIS
ET ARTIVM LIBERALIVM MAGISTRI

ORNAMENTA ET HONORES

DIE XI. M. DECEMBRIS A. MCMXXXV

RITE CONTVLIT

COLLATAQVE PVBLICO HOC DIPLOMATE

PHILOSOPHORVM ORDINIS OBSIGNATIONE COMPROBATO
DECLARAVIT

Heschel's doctoral diploma. Courtesy of Humboldt University Archives.

Finally, Heschel received the galley proofs of *Die Prophetie*. On 18 November he replied lyrically in formal Polish, including his first corrections of the proofs: "I cannot hide the heartfelt expression of gratitude which the music of your goodness in each of your letters evokes in me every time." Technical emendations continued for some time, as did the payments.[23] He corrected additional errors in the proofs and asked Kowalski to date his preface "Berlin, Fall 1935." Everything was completed.

Finally, on 11 December 1935, a full three years after finishing his dissertation, Heschel received the doctorate. Considering the Nazi domination, the university had been remarkably fair, for Heschel was allowed to submit unbound copies of his book rather than completely bound volumes, as originally stipulated. The Latin diploma in the name of "Abraham Heschel Varsoviano" (of Warsaw) was signed by the University Rector, Wilhelm Krueger, professor of veterinary medicine—a Nazi stooge referred to contemptuously as "the four-legged rector"[24]—and Ludwig Bieberbach, dean of the Philosophical Faculty. While still expected to submit 200 bound copies of the book eventually, he officially became Dr. Abraham Heschel.

15

Alliance with Martin Buber (June–December 1935)

It was at an early stage of my studies at the university that I came to realize: If God is a symbol, He is a fiction. *But if God is real, then He is able to express His will unambiguously. . . . The will of God is either real or a delusion.*

Heschel, "Toward an Understanding of Halacha" (1953)

ON 18 JUNE, WHILE CORRECTING GALLEY PROOFS OF HIS BOOK, HESCHEL received the dean's final extension beyond which the university could no longer admit his doctorate. That same day, overcoming months—perhaps years—of inhibition, he initiated a decisive exchange with Martin Buber, intellectual hero at the center of German Jewish cultural renewal.[1] Heschel had debated Buber's philosophy in the Koigen Circle and in his dissertation. He now felt free to engage the man directly. Contrasting his perspective with Buber's, Heschel completed his self-definition as a religious thinker and declared his autonomy.

Even at this early stage of his career, Heschel had many reasons to feel affinity (as well as rivalry) with Buber. They first met in Berlin during the 1929–30 academic year, perhaps through Koigen, who knew Buber since their student years.[2] Heschel spoke several times with Buber during his lectures at the Hochschule and the Berlin Lehrhaus and, in effect, already lived within Buber's wide sphere of influence. Heschel was associated with other contributors to *Der Morgen* and the Zionist newspaper *Jüdische Rundschau* in which Buber also published.

He admired Buber's enormous learning in a myriad of fields, later praising him "as the most erudite man he ever met," similar to his judgment of Leo Baeck.[3] More to the point, Heschel knew that Buber was renowned for translating the spirit of Hasidism into a literary idiom. He wanted to form an alliance with Buber while preserving his independence, a delicate task for a young man without an academic position—and without Buber's inherited wealth and well-earned international prestige.

There were practical reasons as well to become involved with Buber. In addition to providing spiritual support, Buber was a valuable professional contact. He communicated with leading writers, academics, and activists in Europe, the United States, and Palestine. As director of the Frankfurt Jüdische Lehrhaus and the Center for Adult Education, Buber might help Heschel find a paying position in Germany. Braced by his own achievements, and recognizing Buber's ability to consider criticism, Heschel finally defended his divergent view.

Although their perspectives were not fundamentally opposed, Heschel asserted himself by questioning Buber's interpretation of divine-human "dialogue" in the Hebrew Bible. Heschel admired, but was also suspicious of, the Dilthey-inspired philosophical anthropology of his teachers' generation. (Baeck, Buber, Koigen, Dessoir—among many others—studied with Dilthey at the University of Berlin). Buber and Koigen, both of whom attended the universities of Vienna, Leipzig, Zurich, and Berlin, were sociologists in the large sense, investigating Jewish and other cultural productions in order to construct an encom-

*Martin Buber around 1930. Courtesy of Maurice
Friedman.*

passing theory of civilization. Heschel warned against the secularizing potentials of their thought, as religiously motivated as it might be.

Holiness Versus Symbolism

In June 1935 Heschel's poem "I and Thou" appeared in *Der Morgen* and, assured that his revised dissertation would soon appear as a book, Heschel boldly
decided to establish himself on stronger footing with Buber. On 18 June, reminding Buber of a recent lecture of his he had attended in Berlin, he wrote to
express regret that he could not afford the trip to Buber's home in Heppenheim,
near Frankfurt, to continue their conversations.[4] Both circumspect and determined, Heschel initiated this first debate—and partnership—diplomatically.

At age twenty-seven, Heschel was at the precarious beginning of his career—
without the prospect of employment. Buber, at age fifty-two, was a venerated author and lecturer. As was customary, Heschel addressed his senior with an almost exaggerated courtesy, asking the "highly respected Professor" (*Hoch*

verehrter Herr Professor) if he would be willing to examine his dissertation: "I feel that it might verge on hubris to bother you with the reading of this manuscript. . . . Please do not consider this suggestion as an imposition. I wanted, with this letter and also by sending you my *Maimonides. A Biography,* simply to give you a favorable reminder of myself." Heschel also informed Buber that his manuscript on the prophets was on its way to publication.

Heschel's request was tactically astute. While soliciting Buber's opinion, he mentioned his recent biography of Maimonides as proof of his prowess as a scholar and writer. Buber would appreciate its erudition and graceful quality; he might tell other people about it and help find reviewers. But Heschel's real, most personally urgent, concern was his forthcoming study of the prophets.

Heschel now attempted to resolve his hurt and anger at Buber's almost catastrophic dismissal of his dissertation when it was submitted about two years earlier to Schocken Publishing House in Berlin. Somehow, Heschel learned that Buber had advised the editor, Salman Schocken, who was also Buber's publisher and good friend, *not* to accept Heschel's manuscript; this rejection jeopardized his doctorate, forcing him to seek publication abroad.[5] Now that the book was forthcoming in Poland, Heschel felt fortified enough to test Buber's opinion about his foundational work. It was a very touchy negotiation.

Buber answered Heschel immediately and enclosed a recent offprint, "Symbolic and Sacramental Existence in Judaism."[6] Presented the previous summer at the second international Eranos conference in Ascona, Switzerland, Buber's essay was a comparative analysis of prophetic inspiration and Hasidic spirituality. That subject matter addressed the substance of Heschel's dissertation—and touched his heart. A month later, Heschel responded thoughtfully, and challenging what he considered to be Buber's disagreement with his God-centered perspective.

It is remarkable how sturdy Heschel remained throughout this frightful period. His challenge to Buber took place while his life was agitated and his university diploma uncertain. Heschel rarely stayed long at the same address in Berlin. His first letter (18 June) carried the return address 150 Kant Strasse; his second letter, on 24 July, came from no. 160 on the same street.

Heschel's second letter to Buber, analyzing "Symbolic and Sacramental Existence in Judaism," constitutes the clearest rebuttal of what Heschel regarded to be his era's theological compromises. As early as 1935, he declared his lifelong tendency to correct regnant ideas, usually by drawing a polemic contrast between them. While striving to foster a productive relationship with Buber, Heschel politely but firmly insisted upon their divergent theories.[7]

He came quickly to the point. After thanking Buber for his letter of 22 June and the reprint, he objected to Buber's interpretation of the prophet's behavior as "symbolic." Instead of accepting Buber's contention that the "symbol" is concrete evidence of a covenant between person and God, Heschel claims that Buber's essay considers the prophet to be the prime reality:

> The focus on the category "sign" is certainly very important and will clarify many things. But it seems questionable to me when you define, in this sense, the totality of prophetic experience ("he lives symbolically . . . he himself is the sign," p. 350). Is that not a generalization, instead of determining its prevailing uniqueness? Yet, not only methodologically, but also in principle, I would like to object to a conception according to which the prophet's existence *in toto,* as well as the particulars of his activity, should have no intrinsic value, but only value as sign.

Heschel attempted a precise dissection by citing passages from Buber's essay that could, in his judgment, lead to a humanistic explanation of the prophets. While admitting that Buber's emphasis on the prophet's "symbolic" behavior, directed toward the people, was "very important and helps clarify many things," he dwells upon Buber's apparent refusal to consider God's behavior.

Heschel feared that Buber's anthropological account of the effects of divine revelation implied a basic theological compromise. Forthrightly, Heschel rejected Buber's notion, as he understood it, that the prophet's claim to divine inspiration was "a mere illustration"—not a supernatural revelation in itself, but only a "*sign* of meaning" (Sinn*bild*, as underlined by Heschel). Was Buber actually guilty of explaining away the mystery, the transcendent origin, of divine revelation, as Heschel implied?

Buber, in fact, asserted the reality of God's initiative, but he focused more than Heschel upon relationship, what he called the "betweenness" of human and Divine. Whatever the reason for Heschel's insinuation that Buber did not take God's reality seriously enough, he had acutely located the fissure of twentieth-century religion. He feared that a view of prophecy as "symbolic action" might be used to justify a purely humanistic religion. His real target was philosophical anthropology without God, which Buber himself would deplore.

There were grave theological implications. Concerning biblical exegesis, Heschel warned Buber that he, as a Jewish thinker, perilously associated his theory of symbolic "incarnation" with a Christian typology whereby the Hebrew text can be read as predicting the coming of Christ. Heschel again highlights the key phrases:

"Biblical man, and with him the biblical God, craves for the spirit to express itself more perfectly, more substantially than in the word only, but that it [i.e., the spirit] become incarnate," p. 347.

But what is the advantage of such an incarnation? Is the ~~reproduction~~ image more perfect than the ~~original~~ being?

You presuppose a need for signs and symbols. Then why should we not incarnate God himself and symbolize him?

Christian exegesis undermines the uniqueness of the Jewish covenant. Although Judaism rejects incarnation of the Divine, Heschel himself was walking a tightrope, since his own Yiddish poetry expressed an "intermingling" of God's emotions with his. His Hasidic piety seemed in practice (if not in theory) to be "incarnational," for the rebbe or zaddik must be a living symbol of Torah. But incarnation was not the essential problem.

Perhaps Heschel suspected that Buber's stress on symbolism, which fostered constructive conversations with the non-Jewish world, would compromise the authority of the Sinai revelation—the divine origin of Judaism and the mitzvot? At the 1934 Eranos conference on "East-West Symbology and Spiritual Direction," Buber was the Jewish representative—along with Erwin Rousselle from Frankfurt-am-Main who spoke on Chinese mythology; J. W. Hauer of Tübingen on Indo-Arab symbolism of the self; Heinrich Zimmer of Heidelberg on Hindu mythology; C. G. Jung on archetypes of the collective unconscious; Mrs. C. A. F. Rhys Davids of London on mandala (wheel) symbolism; Friedrich Heiler of Marburg on the Madonna as religious symbol; Swami Yatiswarananda of Madras on Hindu symbolism; and others.

Yet, as the words Heschel crossed out in his letter make clear, he opposed the reductionism of Buber's dialogical religion by claiming that the essay substituted a "reproduction" or a human image for the "original," the Divine. (Speaking elsewhere, Heschel considered Buber's description of prophetic inspiration to be a "vague encounter" since he refused to admit that God communicated rules of behavior.)[8] Buber's emphasis on the prophetic relationship to God and to the people, despite its recognizing the initiative of the "Eternal Thou," might dwell upon the human encounter to such an extent that thinkers could replace revealed religion with existentialism. Indeed, Buber's *I and Thou,* speaking universally and to assimilated Jews, presents an ontology of inter-human relations, and as such does not rely on a specific religious idiom.[9] Stressing the immediate experience, Buber did not illustrate his theology of dialogue with Hebrew sources.

For Heschel, the Bible is our primal witness to the living God. Heschel's dissertation, pointing repeatedly to the God of pathos, systematically refuted anthropological or psychological accounts. Instead it highlighted through structural analysis the "essence" of inspiration, the divine incursion into the prophet's awareness. Again quoting Buber's text, Heschel reproached the master for interpreting Hosea's marriage as a symbolic performance, a "'representation of an experience of God, of his experience with Israel' (p. 349)." The danger of such interpretation, Heschel surmised, was to subordinate God's overwhelming reality to its human imitation: "Now what is the advantage of incarnation in the sign compared with the empirical experience of the actual history?" Claiming that Buber substituted a "symbol" for the transcendent Subject, Heschel concluded, as would any courteous scholar, by asking Buber to correct his possible misinterpretation.

The closing remarks in this comprehensive letter of 24 July 1935 reveal Heschel's intimate agenda: he was trying to establish mutual trust. Recalling Buber's initial opposition to his manuscript, Heschel alluded to his "everlasting grief" (*unvergänglicher Schmerz*). And, again, he enclosed further proof of his accomplishments, his book of Yiddish poetry:

> On this occasion I send you my poems. For many years I wondered if I dared to do so—I would be happy if you like them.
>
> Your relation to my prophetological work is still my everlasting grief. I still don't understand the reason. It would be very important for me to find out.[10]
>
> Perhaps I shall be able to see you soon. Your presence is so unique.

Intending to establish a completely honest relationship, these three brief paragraphs mix a heady stew of contradictory attitudes: hope, flattery, anger, sadness, respect, veneration, and affection. After sending Buber his biography of Maimonides, Heschel admits to having hesitated for several years before sharing his poems. Now he hoped that Buber would ratify the authenticity of *Der Shem Hameforash: Mentsh*. Better still, Buber might enlist him in his movement of Jewish renewal—and secure him an academic position.

Heschel never discovered why Buber played a role in the rejection of his manuscript on the prophets, and we can only speculate on the possible reasons. Buber did not really know Heschel at the time. He may have misread the young man's focus on the prophet's consciousness of inspiration as another form of the intensely inward "*Erlebnis* (experience) mysticism" he himself repudiated during the period leading up to the composition of *I and Thou*. Just as Heschel feared that Buber's dialogical theology might foster a humanistic existentialism, so Buber may have considered Heschel's "religion of sympathy" with God's pathos—the prophet's claim to perceive divine emotions—to be a form of gnosis, in which the human ego substitutes itself for a transcendent Voice.

Whatever the tangled reasons, neither interpreter changed his judgment. After settling in Palestine, Buber published his book, *The Prophetic Faith* in Hebrew (1942) and, in a footnote referring to Heschel's by then published dissertation, he rejected its testimony to God's pathos: "And Hosea does as he is bidden. But this does not at all mean that he 'feels with God,' as some think,* [note to *Die Prophetie*] but the sensation assailing him is the sensation of his own love and suffering, but in feeling it he feels that he is following the divine footsteps."[11]

Each man misread the other for a good cause. For Buber, Heschel's implicit claim to "know" divine "emotions" from the God-side was perilous. For Heschel, the sacred origin of the mitzvot justified their legal and ritual authority in Jewish religious life. Buber, for his part, refused to assume that human beings can experience God's "feelings," just as he did not consider the mitzvot to be prescriptive expressions of God's will. For each thinker, the hermeneutical conflict had immediate implications for Jewish continuity.

At the time of this personal debate, it was well-known that Buber was not an observant Jew. Although Buber assumed the reality of the divine Thou, he subordinated the Law to human initiative, and in his early discussions with Franz Rosenzweig he insisted that the person should feel "called" by the Law in order to accept its obligations. Heschel was more militantly loyal to the divine Subject; he wanted to justify regular observance as a path of return to Judaism. Heschel gave priority to God. Even the human self (the I of I-Thou) was not, in itself, complete, but "something transcendent in disguise."[12]

Such was the complex inauguration of a dialogue which continued long after Buber chose Heschel, the following year, to succeed him in Frankfurt-am-Main as educator at the Mittelstelle (abbreviation for Center for Jewish Adult Education) and the Jüdische Lehrhaus. Heschel was correct in trusting Buber to accept their differences—which remained unresolved.

A Spiritual Archaeology

Yet the paucity of references to Buber in Heschel's books and essays is surprising, despite many parallels in terminology and ideas. One explanation is that Heschel, on principle, rarely criticized "one of his teachers" publicly or even privately. Instead of systematically refuting opposing views with carefully documented argumentation, Heschel became an "irenic polemicist" who transformed the terminology of opposing thinkers (usually without naming them), so as not to impugne their positive contributions.[13] That way he disputed their ideas while advancing his perspective. This ethic both weakened and enhanced Heschel's reputation in the United States. Although philosophers and academic critics deplored the lack of extended analysis in Heschel's writings, he generally preferred an affirmative, relatively seamless narrative, with few footnote references, as the more effective way to communicate.

There is an intriguing biographical substratum to Heschel's and Buber's mutual ambivalence. Buber "discovered" Hasidism as a child, before Heschel was born, and from a modern perspective. In his widely read essay of 1918, "My Way to Hasidism," Buber explained how he was raised in Lemberg (Lwow) and in Galicia by his grandfather, Salomon Buber, a wealthy businessman and observant Jew adept at Western thought who published critical editions of the Midrash. The boy also spent summers at his father's estate in the Bukovina, where he visited, as he wrote, "the dirty village of Sadagora."[14] The coincidence is amazing. For this "decadent" Hasidic court—as Buber called it—was the home of Heschel's paternal grandmother, Leah Rachel Friedman, whose father, Sholem Joseph, was the rebbe of Sadagora.

During his gradual attraction to Hasidism, Buber as an adolescent touched upon Heschel's ancestry even more deeply: "Then I came after many years to a newly-inherited estate of my father, in the neighborhood of Tchortkov, a village which is the place of residence of a collateral line of the same dynasty of zaddikim. As there still lives in Sadagora the memory, handed down by generations, of the great 'Ruzhiner' . . . so in Tchortkov there still lives today the direct recollection of his son Dovid Moshe. Unfortunately I received nothing of him at that time."[15] Heschel's father was raised in Tchortkov, at the Hasidic court of his stepfather, Rabbi Dovid Moshe Friedman.

Unfortunately, Buber retained raw, mostly negative impressions of Heschel's roots: "The legendary greatness of the grandfathers has certainly disappeared in the grandsons and many are at pains to preserve their power through all kinds of petty magic; but all their carryings on cannot darken the inborn shining of their foreheads."[16] Although Buber's childhood encounters led neither to religious commitment nor to an intellectual interest in Hasidism, he remained fascinated by the "inborn shining" of the rebbe's charisma.

Unlike Heschel, Buber became immersed in Hasidic spirituality much later, as a European thinker whose promptings were not primarily Jewish. Buber returned only after working through his alienation: "I had been seized by the fermenting intellectuality which is often characteristic of the decisive years of youth and which puts an end to the natural seeing and experiencing of the child." Buber experienced a decisive insight by reading a "little Hebrew book," the *Zevaat Rivash*, the testament of the Baal Shem Tov: "I experienced the Hasidic soul. The primally Jewish opened to me, flowering to newly conscious expression in the darkness of exile: man's being created in the image of God I grasped as deed, as becoming, as task."[17]

Buber interpreted Hasidism in universal terms. In the next line, he carefully noted that "this primally Jewish reality was a primal human reality."[18] Unlike the Hasidim themselves, including Heschel, who were scrupulously devout, Buber translated their strictly observant tradition into a primarily cultural and ethical idiom. Hasidism was Buber's Hebrew humanism, not the authoritative word of God, as it was for the Hasidim themselves.

Buber began to share this understanding through a literary recasting of the *Tales of Rabbi Nahman*, published in 1906. The following year, when Heschel was born, Buber's *Legend of the Baal Shem* appeared. Buber advanced this project over the years, leading to his classic *Tales of the Hasidim* (1947–48), which revitalized for modern readers that neglected Jewish culture.

Heschel had absorbed these traditions from his earliest years when prayer and oral legends were as vivid as texts. The opposite was true for Buber, who came to Hasidism through philosophy, literature, and European politics. In addition, Heschel averred much later that Buber was "not at home in rabbinic literature," particularly the Talmud, which even contemporary Judaism must integrate.[19] Such were the seeds of a divergence (though not as radical as Heschel claimed in 1935) which made their spiritual brotherhood a sibling rivalry as well.

Nevertheless, Heschel considered Buber's writings on Hasidism to be the best available source for readers unfamiliar with the original sources. A witty anecdote he told in response to a question about a book on prayer by Friedrich Heiler (a large academic tome) explains why.[20] Heschel once related how a man asked a matchmaker for a wife who was beautiful, intelligent, and young. The matchmaker found the right person, but the man was not satisfied. He asked, "But I also want a woman who will love me!" The matchmaker replied, "That I can get you, too."

Heschel's point was that Professor Heiler's historical and psychological study of prayer was not intended to inspire faith; it was a work of scholarship. But readers might also find God there. For Heschel, Buber's retelling of Hasidism, which ignored their consistent fidelity to Jewish law, remained capable of inspiring a sacred yearning and authentic Jewish commitment. But for Heschel, the entire cloth of traditional Judaism must survive in the contemporary world. Substitutes should be examined with suspicion, rejected, or applied with caution. Too much *shaatnez,* mixture of disparate fabrics, would destroy the garment.

It was an ironic event of intellectual history: Buber rejected Heschel's theology of divine pathos for being a form of subjective existentialism—and that seemed to be Heschel's objection to Buber as well. On a personal level, however, Heschel and Buber, acknowledging a divergence of theory, formed a spiritual alliance that enriched Western religious and moral life for decades to come.

16

Mission Defined (January–September 1936)

*The Temple was burned down, but a new power arose out of the ashes
which reshaped the spiritual and moral substance of the Jewish people
into a new form. . . . The creator of this metamorphosis was Yohanan ben
Zakkai. . . . Instead of sacrifices at the Temple: studying Torah
at the Lehrhaus.*

Heschel, "Persönlichkeiten der jüdischen Geschichte:
Jochanan ben Zakkai" (1936)

WHILE SUBMERGED IN DETAILS OF GETTING HIS WORK PUBLISHED, HESCHEL WAS becoming an educator for the public. The university accorded him the doctorate and now, as soon as possible, he must fulfill his obligation to deliver two hundred bound copies of the dissertation. He negotiated a diplomatic minefield: in Nazi Germany, he was a Jew subject to Aryan exclusionary laws. The pressures upon him increased. As 1935 ended, he had no steady job, virtually no money, and he could barely meet payments to the Polish Academy of Arts and Sciences to print his book.

On the verge of publishing his first scholarly work, he was defenseless. He could not find a distributor, as Nazi laws made it hard to sell "Jewish books" in Germany; by now "Aryan" stores were forbidden to carry them. Even from Warsaw, he received a discouraging note from the distributor of the Polish Academy's publications, refusing to sell the monograph on a commission basis.[1] Making final corrections on galley proofs, he justified the delays to impatient university officials.

On 30 January 1936, with these obstacles in mind, he wrote again to Dean Bieberbach: "Very complex corrections led to the fact that my dissertation will be published only during these days." He went on to request further consideration, pleading to reduce the quantity of bound books required: "Sending a large number of copies would cause great expense, which to my regret I would be unable to cover since I do not have any fixed employment; besides, I would be unable to pay for these copies because of foreign exchange regulations." Would the university allow the Polish Academy to distribute some copies, saving him expense? The dean's refusal, dated 6 February, typed for the first time in Gothic script, was swift and unswerving.

Despite the exceptional constraints of his situation, Heschel's letters to the authorities in Berlin and Kraków are forthright, dignified, devoid of self-pity. He simultaneously worked on finishing his book and promoting his biography of Maimonides, while beginning another major scholarly project on Ibn Gabirol and medieval Jewish philosophy.

Promoting Prophetic Consciousness

With meticulous care, Heschel supervised the printing of his foundational Bible interpretation. He wrote Tadeusz Kowalski at least once a week during February and March. Numerous little tasks remained: rectifying further typographical errors, choosing a format for the cover and title page, and composing an abstract of the thesis in Polish—a language in which he was not at ease. He continued to investigate possible outlets for the book in Germany, other than the firm of Erich Reiss, itself threatened with liquidation by the Nazis.

The political crisis magnified the expected pressures of bringing to fruition an intricate academic tome. Heschel promised Kowalski on 3 February that he would mail his Polish abstract soon, and shared his difficulty in finding an "Aryan bookstore" to carry the work. He solicited support from the Polish Consular Mission. The next day Heschel wrote again to explain that, "because of the race of the author," he needed a special affidavit to get permission from the Germans: "It can be granted if the Polish consulate certifies that sale of this book published by the Polish Academy of Sciences is beneficial and will add to the 'betterment' of relations between Polish and German scholars. (The above phrase is not the best one.)"

There was no time to lose. Immediately after receiving the required statement, he rushed it to the Polish officials. The following week, Heschel wrote to ask a professional favor "at the request of my mentor" Max Dessoir. Could Kowalski arrange a lecture for Dessoir during his upcoming visit to Poland? Although only part Jewish, Dessoir was made miserable by the Nazi authorities at the university, and he wanted to become more independent.[2]

Heschel's correspondence with Kowalski reads like transcripts of telephone conversations about textual details, sales, and distribution. On 16 February Heschel apologized for his delay in sending the corrections, owing to the fact that his only copy of the proofs was with the Polish Consulate. Negotiations with a possible German distributor fell through, so perhaps the "foreign firm" of Gebethner and Wolff of Warsaw could obtain "a formal permit" to sell in Germany.

Other problems remained. On 21 February, he asked Kowalski to correct grammatical or idiomatic errors in his Polish abstract: "The feeling of uncertainty in the Polish language, caused during the past years of not using it, produced this very sad delay. I apologize." These were not merely the concerns of a scholar who wanted his work to be impeccable. Heschel was bereft of a national identity. His correspondence in Polish brought this anxiety to the surface, as he explained: "In my letter I used an expression for which I am sorry. In fact, it was a literal translation of the letter of support written by Professors Dessoir and Bertholet regarding permission for printing my work abroad. It is also a phrase which can be commonly used here. The feeling that the use of those words was a *faux pas* leaves me highly disturbed. Therefore I ask for your forgiveness." Polish was not his native language; in his linguistic struggle Heschel acknowledged his homelessness, pinpointing his political, cultural, and spiritual exile.

At the same time, aware that the Nazis might prohibit its distribution, he promoted the new book with energy and sophistication. Familiar with the art of culling phrases for publicity purposes, the postscript to this same letter asks the Polish Academy to excerpt some laudatory reviews of his *Maimonides:* "I am enclosing the relevant text." More than personal ambition was at stake; it was a matter of professional survival.

By March 1936 the revisions were virtually complete. Concentrating on final details, Heschel's long letter of 8 March demonstrates unusual astuteness as he justifies his request that the publisher's name (Polska Akademja Umiejetnosci) should be translated, on the cover of copies distributed in Germany, Verlag der Polischen Akademie der Wissenschaften. To guarantee that German readers could understand its scholarly sponsorship, two separate editions, each with a different cover and title page, were printed. The volume for general sale was printed in Kraków by the presses of the Jagiellonian University. The cover and title page state in Polish the name of the Academy followed by "Memoirs of the Oriental Commission" in both Polish and French. In the middle, in handsome capital letters, appears: "ABRAHAM HESCHEL *DIE PROPHETIE.*"

The German copies were printed for the university by a press in Berlin. This title page gave Heschel's *Inaugural-Dissertation* its original name as it appeared on the diploma—*Das prophetische Bewußtsein*—followed by the dates of his *Promotion* (11 December 1935) and oral examination (23 February 1933). The author was identified as "Abraham Heschel aus Warschau" (from Warsaw). The next page named his advisors: Professor Dr. Max Dessoir, Geheimrat Professor Dr. Alfred Bertholet. A printed *Lebenslauf* (curriculum vitae) followed.[3]

Heschel was euphoric. It had taken three years and two months to consummate publication.[4] On 23 March 1936 he sent Kowalski this succinct note of appreciation: "I received today the first copies of my book about prophecy. I remember very clearly your careful attention to my case. The mere words 'thank you' do injustice to my true feelings. Therefore, I can only say that I think about you with great respect and that I have always read your words with gratitude and reverence."

Heschel's credentials as a biblical interpreter and theologian of "divine pathos" were secured. He sent Kowalski a copy of *Maimonides* for his personal library, and Kowalski returned the compliment, telling Heschel that a colleague was so interested that he borrowed the copy. This correspondence continued for two years, henceforth concerned largely with soliciting academic and popular reviews of *Die Prophetie*, obtaining copies for distribution, and marketing the remaining volumes.[5]

Heschel proved to be a keen publicist. He provided names and addresses of learned journals and Jewish community newspapers and periodicals to receive review copies of *Die Prophetie* and closely monitored its distribution. On 11 April 1936, using the Erich Reiss Verlag as his return address, Heschel politely asked "the honorable Academy" to send copies to "relevant journals." He especially wanted to obtain reviews in Poland.[6] Heschel had been away from Berlin and he impatiently awaited clippings.

The first review arrived on 7 May. Heschel immediately sent a postcard to Kowalski, sharing his delight at a short essay by "Dr. Feuchtwanger, a famous scholar." Ludwig Feuchtwanger, professor in Munich and brother of the novelist Lion, was associated with Martin Buber's Frankfurt Lehrhaus and later collaborated with Heschel.

The next month, a French translation of Heschel's *Maimonides* was published in Paris by Payot in its fine historical series.[7] Entitled *Maïmonide,* the French edition carried a flattering preface by Bernard Chapira, professor at the Ecole Pratique des Hautes Etudes, praising Heschel's "remarkable gift of intuition" and his "original conclusions, revealing new aspects of Maimonides's life."

The French scholar also highlighted the biography's contribution to Jewish spiritual resistance. Speaking boldly in a manner forbidden in Germany about parallels with the ongoing political crisis, Chapira stressed how Heschel's story of Maimonides could fortify European Jews menaced by assimilation or tyranny: "A powerful breath became necessary, the enlightened authority of a superior person, to revive minds and return the faith of those who did not possess enough energy within themselves to resist the evil." This was major recognition for a young scholar with no university position.

Heschel was already working on his new research project. He applied his mastery of Maimonides's philosophy to an intricate study of Solomon Ibn Gabirol, a controversial eleventh-century metaphysician also appreciated as a poet and mystic. In November, Heschel solicited Kowalski's expertise in Islamic sources to ask about available manuscripts of Gabirol's *Fountain of Life:* "I allow myself to ask you whether you think it possible to find somewhere fragments of the Arabic original? For example, in Leningrad?"[8] Gabirol's central work was available only in Latin translation (the *Fons vitae*) with renditions in Hebrew and German. Scrupulously following the rules of academic thoroughness, Heschel wanted to establish a valid text.

Gabirol himself reflected Heschel's many interests—philosophy, theology, poetry, prophecy, and prayer. Yet Heschel did not treat Gabirol as another historical alter ego, as he did with Maimonides. Instead, Heschel mapped out the system, his philosophical vocabulary.[9] There is little evidence of personal commitment in the dry monographs he produced on Gabirol's neo-Platonic sources and metaphysics. As would any aspiring academic, Heschel was building a reputation, strengthening his record in the key discipline of Jewish philosophy.

Heschel also found medieval philosophy to be intellectually stimulating, gratifying his need for rigor. This was theology that provided common ground with those outside his community of faith, as it had during the Golden Age among Muslims, Jews, and Christians. Heschel used his knowledge of Gabirol, the prophets, Maimonides, and later Abravanel to construct his contemporary Jewish theology and ethics. Emulating these defenders of Jewish faith, Heschel found other ways to bring secularized individuals into the experience of reverence, prayer, and moral audacity.

Sympathetic scholars admired Heschel's commitment to sacred values in an age of crisis. Henry Corbin (1903–1978), a French Islamic expert impassioned with spirituality and German existential philosophy who was pursuing research in Berlin, excitedly read *Die Prophetie* as soon as it appeared. Heschel's phenomenology of the Hebrew prophets resembled Corbin's personal approach to Islamic mysticism, and Corbin immediately asked Henri Jourdan, director of the French Institute in Berlin, to arrange a meeting with the author. On 5 May 1936, Jourdan wrote to invite Heschel to his home, because the German authorities disapproved of contacts with Jews in his office.[10]

These two young scholars, meeting in Berlin that Sunday afternoon, formed an alliance and a substantial friendship. Two days later, Heschel presented Corbin with an inscribed copy of his book.[11] Their conversation was mutually gratifying. They discussed Corbin's translations of Heidegger (the first in French), new editions of Kant's works, and the French translation of Heschel's *Maimonides,* soon to be published in Paris. It was a pleasant personal encounter as well, for Corbin was a dynamic personality, and his smart and vivacious wife, Stella, shared her husband's intellectual interests.

There were deeper affinities as well, for Heschel and Corbin were similarly driven by fervent longings. Corbin, like Heschel, experienced early bereavement when his mother died when he was ten years old. Corbin then received a comprehensive Catholic education in boarding schools and began seminary studies, intending to become a priest. But his interests were broader. So in 1925, with a diploma in Catholic theology and medieval philosophy, Corbin began learning Arabic at the Ecole des Langues Orientales in Paris, where he became friends with Georges Vajda, a Hungarian-born Jew who specialized in medieval Jewish spirituality. Corbin became an authority in Persian texts, interpreting them using phenomenological methods inspired by Max Scheler, Husserl, and Dilthey.

Henry and Stella Corbin at Ferney-Voltaire, 1954.
L'Herne, *1981. Courtesy of Stella Corbin.*

Corbin was anxious to continue his conversations with Heschel, and the feeling was reciprocated. After the Corbins returned to Paris in June, Henry Corbin and Heschel corresponded. Heschel wrote to Corbin with unusual ease and familiarity. In June Heschel shared some esthetic impressions of his recent visit to Switzerland and Northern Italy: "It has been two weeks since I have returned to Berlin. My stay in Abbazia and in the Engadin, at the Adria and in the Alps was a gain for my soul and spirit. Venice too was an enrichment: Sometimes one gets upset there, but more often one is moved. (Tintoretto!)" He asked after Corbin's "charming wife" and inquired about his translations of Heidegger.[12]

Heschel then enlisted Corbin's help to advance his ambitions: "Meanwhile my book on Maimonides was published by Payot. I would place immeasurably more importance on a French edition of *Die Prophetie*. I would be very much obliged if you would write me about that." Heschel imagined his first two German works conveying his vision of Judaism to French-speaking communities.

Heschel's insights into the prophets eventually entered Corbin's wide sphere, which included leading philosophers and religious scholars in France and in Germany.[13] In Paris, Corbin developed interpretations of Persian mysticism, published translations of Heidegger and Karl Jaspers, and began teaching at the Ecole Pratique des Hautes Etudes. After Corbin published selections in French of *Die Prophetie* in 1939, the careers of both men—and world events—changed significantly before they renewed their correspondence.

Education and Spiritual Resistance

During this tense period, as Berlin prepared to host the Olympics, Heschel developed a less scholarly, but no less inspirational, livelihood: writing essays and book reviews for the Berlin *Gemeindeblatt,* the widely circulated newspaper of the city's Jewish community.[14] Heschel inaugurated his journalistic activity with a series of brief essays on rabbinic leaders of Talmudic times. After evoking the crisis of medieval Judaism in *Maimonides,* he returned to an even earlier time to distill his vast knowledge of its formative, classical period, the first centuries of the Common Era, when the Jews of Palestine under Roman domination created their religion.

Heschel's biographical sketches, appearing from February to August 1936 under the general title "Personalities of Jewish History," were acts of "spiritual resistance to the Nazis," implicitly addressing the situation of Jews in Germany.[15] For him, the Tannaim (meaning, teachers) constitute a dynasty of holy men whose lives could hearten readers with a sense of divine purpose.[16] Confidently addressing a popular readership, he opens each essay with a survey of the historical situation, describes each rabbi's mission, then narrates the individual's life. Summaries put the era into a larger context of developments in Judaism.

Heschel's first essay in the series, "Johanan ben Zakkai," appeared in the 23 February 1936 issue—while he was feverishly correcting galley proofs of his book, dealing with rules at the university, and seeking help from Kowalski and the Polish Consul. Heschel took this opportunity to publicize *Die Prophetie,* for on the same page as the essay he included a composite chapter entitled "Religion of Sympathy" followed by an announcement that the work, published in German by the Polish Academy of Arts and Sciences, could be purchased at Erich Reiss Verlag in Berlin.

Heschel's story of Rabbi Johanan ben Zakkai speaks to German Jews threatened with expulsion from their cultural home. He begins by evoking the Roman siege of Jerusalem and the Jewish zealots who resisted the despised government cooperating with the oppressors. Johanan was Hillel's youngest student. His life, according to Heschel, illustrates "how a political catastrophe can turn into a moral and intellectual salvation."

Parallels with the Nazi menace were obvious. Realizing that the zealots would lose, Johanan escapes and obtains from the Roman general Titus permission to build "a *Lehrhaus*," a religious center in Yavneh: "The Temple burned down, but a new power arose out of the ashes which molded the spiritual and moral substance of the Jewish people into a new form. . . . Instead of sacrifices at the Temple: study of the Torah at the '*Lehrhaus*.'" The ancient connection with God was preserved by study, since now individual Jews—deprived of their geographical center—carried the people's future in their minds.

The 8 March issue of the *Gemeindeblatt* contained Heschel's essay on Rabbi Gamliel II, who succeeded Johanan ben Zakkai as Patriarch of the Sanhedrin (High Court) at Yavneh. Jerusalem was now destroyed and Rabbi Johanan's Lehrhaus lost its importance after his death. The followers of Hillel and those of Shammai, two scholarly factions, entered into conflict. Gamliel II was determined to reunite the two competing camps and appeal to both educated and observant Jews and ignorant ones who do not keep the laws of Torah. At first too strict and repressive, he eventually learned to rule wisely. The division of the Jewish people was an especially serious threat in times of political danger.

Heschel's saga of Israel in exile continued with Rabbi Akiba, the profile that appeared on 29 March. During his time, Judaism was at a turning point: the Temple, the state, and the Jewish aristocracy were destroyed. Akiba believed that every word, every letter, every comma, every ornament of the Torah had a specific function and meaning. It was due to Akiba that Talmud study found so many devotees. Heschel then recounts Akiba's support for Bar Kokhba's revolt against the Romans and his martyrdom. Tortured atrociously, his students asked why he showed no signs of pain. Akiba replied that all his life he yearned to love God "with all his soul." Flayed alive by the Romans, he died while pronouncing the very last word of the *Shema Yisrael*—"the Lord is One."

On 5 April, to prepare assimilated readers for Passover, Heschel published two brief reviews: one of a picture book about the holiday, the other a book on "how to perform the Seder."

The following week, during the observance, Heschel published an essay on another Talmudic rabbi, Shimon ben Gamliel II, taking readers beyond the collapse of the Bar Kokhba rebellion. In Shimon's time, Jews in Palestine were not allowed to practice their religion or study the Torah. Many emigrated to other countries, including Syria, Egypt, Asia, North Africa, and most of all, Babylonia. When the Romans finally lifted the restrictions, it was Shimon ben Gamliel II who reorganized intellectual and spiritual life. Many returned from exile. His emphasis differed from that of Akiba: deeds were more important than study (or contemplation).

Two weeks later, on 26 April, Heschel published an essay on Rabbi Elisha ben Abuyah, who became a heretic. Elisha challenges readers with the question of Job: Why does God punish the just? The Hadrianic persecution (the prohibition to keep the laws of the Torah) was aimed only at pious Jews; the unfaithful were released. This great sage and scholar despaired about the fact that God-fearing and good people were punished, while evil ones often prospered. This gross injustice made him doubt the existence of God. The tormented Jews of Germany might find him a historical companion.

Heschel published more book reviews in May, along with a brief "Fable from Rabbi Meir," describing the complexity of repentance.[17] Another rabbinic biography followed, that of Rabbi Jehuda Ha-Nassi (31 May), the consummate religious leader and redactor of the *Mishnah*.

That summer the world witnessed a confusing spectacle. On 2 August 1936, the headline of the Sunday *New York Times* read: "100,000 Hail Hitler; US Athletes Avoid Nazi Salute to Him/ Frantic Greeting for Fuehrer Resounds on His Entrance for Olympic Opening/ Dazzling Scene Unfolds." As if responding to these current events, Heschel's final essay, on Rabbi Chiyah (16 August), stresses the continuity provided by the Talmud for Jewish civilization. Rabbi Chiyah, one of the great scholars who returned to Jerusalem from Babylonia, did not aspire to fame and submitted to Jehuda Ha-Nassi. He was a modest man who preferred to teach the common people, not the learned élite.

Heschel's skillful narratives do the same.[18] Enriched with biblical quotations, these inspirational sketches of spiritual leaders who lived during the Roman domination of Jewish Palestine trace the energy of classical Judaism for German Jews who did not have a traditional education. His readers, preparing for an uncertain future, must henceforth carry their culture within. Heschel became a teacher and guide for a persecuted public.

A Rebbe for Moderns

During the following month, as the High Holy Days approached, Heschel took on the role of spiritual leader, both admonishing and inspiring his community. Remembering, perhaps, Franz Rosenzweig's decision to become a learned and observant Jew during the Day of Atonement, Heschel published two theological essays, also in the *Gemeindeblatt* (in which his series on Talmudic sages had appeared).[19] He welcomed readers to the solemn ten-day period of self-examination and repentance beginning on Rosh Hashanah eve, which in 1936 fell on 16 September. These "Days of Awe," he declared, were a spiritual opportunity. In two essays (which are more like sermons), he probed the spiritual condition of German Jews, whom he considered to be handicapped by assimilation and indifference.[20]

"The Power of Repentance" (Die Kraft der Buße), the first sermon, appeared in the 13 September *Gemeindeblatt*, forthrightly calling to God in a secular age. Heschel begins with a parable about the creation of atonement and the possibility of remorse. Instead of consoling victims, he challenged Jews to look within and root out self-deception. Then he introduces a favored analogy, one he is said to have used with Menahem Mendel Schneerson, the future Lubavitcher rebbe. Contrasting divine and human clemency, Heschel cites Rabbi Eleazer who admonished those who had insulted a person publicly. According to Jewish law, the aggrieved person is not allowed to forgive if the aggressor had not first asked and had been granted forgiveness from the witnesses. Divine clemency is astoundingly broader. "If a person stands and mocks and blasphemes against God, God will say to him: Repent in private and I will forgive you."

Heschel insists that the Jewish people must stand ready before the living God in order to be redeemed. German Jews in particular must now take full responsibility: "God will appoint a king over them who will instill harsh edicts, then they will atone and turn to the good. All deadlines calculated for the coming of the Messiah have passed, without it ever happening. Now it depends upon our good deeds." The holy day requires a historical decision.

"The Marranos of Today" (Die Marranen von Heute) appeared on 16 September, the first night of Rosh Hashanah, when even "three-day Jews" (as Leo Hirsch called the non-observant) assemble before Judgment. Heschel considered his German brethren—forced to recognize their origins—to be a new breed of Marranos: Jewish on the outside, spiritually empty within. Dwelling upon the primary reality of God, he pushes readers toward theological thinking: "The world has fallen away from God. The decision of each individual and of the many stands in opposition to God. Through our dullness and obstinacy we, too, are antagonists. But still, we ache when we see God betrayed and abandoned." Human feelings of vulnerability and sorrow cannot be compared with those of God.

Heschel now uses his "re-centering of subjectivity" from the person to the Divine, expressed in his Yiddish poetry and analyzed in his dissertation, to address German Jews who are preoccupied (quite understandably) with their own troubles. But while expressing his sympathy with God, he insists upon their compelling responsibility for overcoming self-centeredness: "These days are dedicated to establishing God as King within us. . . . The deepest human longing is to be a thought in God's mind, to be the object of His attention." With brutal honesty, Heschel demanded authenticity, despite the painful situation: "Some people, in moments of enlightenment, believed they saw in the year 1933 an awakening to God and of the community, and hoped that Jews would be heralds of repentance. Yet we have failed, those who stayed here just as much as those who emigrated. The enforced Jewishness still sits so uneasily in many of us that a new wave of desertions could occur at any moment. The apostasy of the past is matched by the superficiality of today."

Heschel proclaimed his unshakable standard for the German Jewish population. The Orthodox share with assimilated Jews the danger of confusing essential Jewishness with exterior behavior. Heschel insisted that God is present and must be allowed to enter our awareness: "There is no return to Judaism without repentance before God. Faithfulness to Him and to the community to the point of utmost readiness remains the fundamental idea of Jewish education." Authentic Jews act as a beacon to the wayward people, helping others to resist Hitler's edicts. Willingness is all. "Utmost readiness" before God—which was Heschel's "fundamental idea of Jewish education"—remained his life's mission.

As Heschel became a rebbe for the modern world, personal loss marked the holy season. On Rosh Hashanah (17 September), the day after this essay appeared in the Gemeindeblatt, his uncle Rabbi Yitzhak Meir Heschel, the rebbe of Kopitzhinitz in Vienna, died. The rebbe's son and Heschel's first cousin, Abraham Joshua Heschel (also husband of Heschel's sister Sarah), then assumed dynastic leadership.[21] Heschel, soon to leave Berlin, continued to transmit and transform their Hasidic legacy through his writings and teaching.

Part Four

Frankfurt, the War, and Exile

Our goal must be to enable the pupil to participate and share in the
spiritual experience of Jewish living; to explain to him what it means
to live as a likeness to God.
Heschel, "The Spirit of Jewish Education" (1953)

FRANKFURT-AM-MAIN WAS THE BACKDROP FOR THE FINAL STAGE OF HESCHEL'S journey from Hasidism into modernity. It was the perfect culmination, for Frankfurt was Germany's second largest Jewish community, and where traditionalists struggled with reformers and overcame them. In the nineteenth century, Rabbi Samson Raphael Hirsch recognized that "Torah-true Judaism" (as Orthodoxy was called by its proponents) could not survive the pressures of liberalism without accepting some aspects of civil life. Reacting to Reform and to Abraham Geiger, the leading exponent of the scientific study of Judaism, Hirsch gave rational justifications for divine revelation, the Bible, and Orthodox observance.

The dominant force in the Frankfurt community became the moderate Orthodoxy of the chief rabbi, Nehemiah Anton Nobel, who defended Jewish law and traditional practice while embracing modern culture.[1] Nobel was a mentor to the philosopher Franz Rosenzweig, who belonged to the second current for which Frankfurt was famous—in general terms, the Rosenzweig-Buber movement of Jewish renewal, reaching out to Jews who were lacking in religious knowledge.

In 1920 Rosenzweig established the Jüdische Lehrhaus and launched a revolution in Jewish culture: a dynamic pedagogy to counter the German standard of aloof, scientific specialists. Martin Buber joined him the next year. They introduced assimilated Jews to the classic texts—Bible, the prayer book, Midrash, and Jewish literature and philosophy. Instead of dry professorial lectures, there were seminars and discussions, and personal contact between teacher and pupils. Courses were given on all areas of Jewish learning, from literary, philosophical, historical, and sociological perspectives. The "new Jewish thinking" (as Rosenzweig called it) attracted alienated Jews, revitalizing the tradition for them.[2]

Around 1925, Buber and Rosenzweig, hoping to make scriptures available to the majority who did not know Hebrew, began a monumental translation of the Bible that attempted to capture, in a robust, literary German, the oral rhythms of the Hebrew text. After Rosenzweig's death in 1929, the Lehrhaus stopped operation while Buber continued writing, lecturing, and teaching.

After Hitler came to power in January 1933, German Jews were in crisis as they were deprived of their civil status and many were forced to emigrate. Preservation of an informed community was imperative. In November 1933, Buber reopened the Frankfurt Lehrhaus under the auspices of the Center for Jewish Adult Education (Mittelstelle für jüdische Erwachsenenbildung bei der Reichsvertretung der Juden in Deutschland), an umbrella organization. Buber's collaborator was Ernst Kantorowicz, a sociologist, jurist, and professor at the Institute of Vocational Education in Frankfurt.

Heschel soon joined these activist scholar-teachers, contributing directly to this cultural and religious renaissance. Buber and other Lehrhaus teachers traveled widely, bringing Jewish knowledge to Frankfurt, Berlin, other German cities, and small towns—in synagogues, community centers, and other public gathering places. But Buber had long planned to emigrate to Palestine, and by 1937 his departure was imminent. For Heschel, Frankfurt provided an enriching—and quite precarious—transition from the dead end of Berlin to his own open-ended future.

In retrospect, it is difficult to fathom why relatively few Jews recognized, even during the early years of Hitler's dictatorship, what Leo Baeck announced as early as 1933: "The thousand year history of Jews in Germany has come to an end."[3] But that was not the general perception of events. Heschel (with countless others) expected the Hitler phenomenon to pass. In the meantime, as a writer and educator he contributed to Jewish spiritual resistance while shaping his theological system.

17

Teaching in Times of Crisis
(September 1936–December 1937)

What moved [Abravanel] most was not a mystical beatitude within God,
or within an active intellect emanating from Him, but the historical
betterment of mankind.
Heschel, *Don Jizhak Abravanel* (1937)

HESCHEL REMAINED IMMERSED IN MYRIAD PROJECTS IN BERLIN, HOPING ALL THE while that Buber would invite him to Frankfurt. He continued to publish reviews, and on 22 November two brief religious parables appeared in the Berlin *Gemeindeblatt.*[1] On 31 January 1937, he reviewed Buber's new, expanded edition of *The Kingdom of God* (originally published in 1932) in an essay entitled "On the Meaning of the Teaching." Heschel pointed to the book's "unusual richness of thought" and expressed "eagerness to see the following volumes."

For the Bubers in Frankfurt, the final months of 1936 and the following year were arduous.[2] While continuing to direct the Jüdische Lehrhaus and the Center for Adult Jewish Education, Buber was preparing, after years of uncertain negotiations (begun in 1927), to establish himself in Jerusalem. Although supported by friends at the Hebrew University, he endured indignities from hostile factions influencing the administrative hierarchy. Labor leaders found him too "religious," while rabbinical authorities questioned the authenticity of his "Jewishness"; for specialists Buber was not "scholarly" enough. To top that, authorities in Poland required him to resolve financial problems connected with his father's estate, and he was planning to visit there in September. A lecture tour in Poland was being organized.

Around that time Buber decided to offer Heschel a responsible position at the Frankfurt Lehrhaus. They now communicated frequently during Buber's trips to Berlin, for a substantial alliance had formed after Heschel criticized his elder's theory of symbolism and admitted his hurt at Buber's rejection of his dissertation.[3] Buber valued Heschel's knowledge of classical Jewish sources, his training in European philosophy, and his authentic Hasidic piety. Heschel's essays on Talmudic sages and on prayer and repentance—published that year in Berlin—also confirmed his potential as educator of adults.

While Ernst Kantorowicz continued as co-director of the Mittelstelle and supervised its pedagogical program, he lacked knowledge of Judaism.[4] Heschel, a modern Hasidic scion, was the perfect associate and, as an observant Jew, he could better respond to the community's religious needs.

Buber wrote to Heschel on 23 November to start the process. For Heschel, moving to Frankfurt meant a job, the possibility of joining a spiritual and intellectual community, and, especially, direct access to Buber himself. Heschel quickly made up his mind after receiving the invitation and answered the next day: "I am absolutely willing to accept your proposition."[5]

On 22 January 1937 they met in Berlin and struck a deal.[6] Two days later Heschel wrote to thank Buber for the discussion: "The idea of being able to talk with you more often gives me great joy. After a conversation with you something like a glowing remains with me."[7] Particularly elated at the prospect of personal contact, he could move to Frankfurt as early as 15 February.

Buber and Heschel shared a mission to preserve and enhance Judaism in a state of emergency. Heschel's letter of 24 January begins the collaboration on that common ground. He solicited his mentor's opinion about various manifestations of "Tradition." Heschel went on to explain that not only were written records of "historical events" important, but also the theoretical reality of tradition "as a structural component of Jewish culture." Using the terms of David Koigen's sociology, Heschel solicits Buber's dynamic approach to the issue.

Their written exchanges were intense. Buber wrote Heschel twice again, and Kantorowicz added his support. On 20 February, Heschel informed Buber that he would arrive in Frankfurt on 1 March, signing his letter, "In admiration and devotion" (*In Verehrung und Ergebenheit*). Henceforth, Heschel directed his energies toward advancing Buber's program of Jewish renewal.

Heschel at Home

Heschel was thirty years old when he moved to Frankfurt on 1 March 1937. (Buber had celebrated his sixtieth birthday on 8 February.) As he did in Berlin, Heschel rented a room with an Orthodox family, where he could eat kosher food and fulfill his ritual duties. For almost a year, he lived in the large apartment of Jacob Simon, his wife, Amalie, and their two young daughters, Rosie and Ruth. The Simon residence at 5 Hansa Allee was near the Orthodox Unterlindau Synagogue where Rabbi Jakob Horovitz, who also taught at the Frankfurt Lehrhaus, officiated. Heschel became close to the Horovitz family and was often invited there for Sabbath and other meals.

Heschel was steadfast in his new responsibilities. He had barely placed his baggage in his room on 1 March when he consulted with Kantorowicz at the Mittelstelle. The very next day, instead of using the telephone, he wrote to Buber that at Kantorowicz's suggestion he had agreed to "draft a circular about the prayerbook." He would seek Buber's advice on the matter of their meeting at Buber's home in Heppenheim the following Sunday and signed the letter: "With reverential greetings."[8]

Heschel could hardly control his enthusiasm. He wanted to remain constantly in touch with his sponsor. Anticipating their meeting five days hence, he also telephoned Buber. The following day, 3 March, Heschel again felt impelled to write about the booklet on prayer he was preparing: "I want to mention my anticipation about the talk with you and my gratitude for today's conversation." The letter was signed: "In admiration, Your sincerely devoted, A. Heschel."[9]

Despite the necessary formalities of written communication, Heschel was at ease in this open environment, where people shared their ideas honestly and with passion. Late in March he described a successful conference at the Mittelstelle, which had drawn people from different parts of the country.[10] He was delighted to "develop a friendship" with Ludwig Feuchtwanger—"a very spiritual man" who was closely associated with the Frankfurt Lehrhaus and a professor in Munich and who had been the first reviewer of *Die Prophetie*.[11]

Heschel was stimulated by Buber's disagreements with his approach. In a letter dated 26 March 1937, Heschel describes how Buber criticized the draft of his essay on prayer, advising him to focus on practical matters: "It's a level too high! The part on the prayer [text] is good, the part on praying does not belong in the circular."[12] Heschel countered, "The assignment is not to learn how to read the text but to learn how to pray," and summarized other reactions: "Friendly quarrel. Buber pushed Eduard Strauss into the discussion by saying, 'Heschel is a lovely youngster, but so stubborn!' This discussion went on so that I long joyously for the next one." The dialogue between these two "stubborn" thinkers lasted throughout their lives.[13]

For some time after his arrival in Frankfurt, Heschel continued drafting guidelines on teaching and studying the prayerbook. Since Buber and Heschel could speak with each other easily, few letters remain from that period. But they did write occasionally for specific business. Buber tapped Heschel's vast knowledge of Judaica bibliography, and after consulting booksellers outside the city, Heschel mailed Buber a list of Hebrew titles relevant to his work on Hasidic masters, some of them old and rare, others quite recent.[14]

Heschel also began to tutor "his teacher" in modern Hebrew, the language in which Buber was expected to lecture in Jerusalem. Of course Buber knew biblical, rabbinic, and Hasidic Hebrew, but he could not yet speak and write the current idiom. Heschel was fluent in Hebrew and he could speak and write the everyday language. Buber, with his extraordinary linguistic gifts, made rapid progress with Heschel's guidance.[15]

Heschel was a European intellectual who looked the part. An identification photograph taken in Frankfurt shows him to be slightly stocky, clean shaven, wearing a double-breasted suit with vest, white shirt and tie, his black wavy hair combed back, and wearing small rimless glasses. His lips almost rise to a smile—but not quite—and his eyes convey determination, confirming the impression of earnestness he made on others.

At the Simon home where he lived, Heschel was an unusually congenial and discrete presence. Rosie, the Simons' fifteen-year-old daughter, astutely observed this quiet boarder, a private, controlled person who was nevertheless warm and generous. Heschel made practically no noise, and he charmed the family with his cheerfulness and impressed them with his intelligence and piety.[16] To the teenaged Rosie, he appeared to be living and thinking on a higher plane. Rosie remembers him as a "God-fearing man so Orthodox that he referred everything to the One above us, even when he relished some good bread or a sweet roll or a good piece of cake." Heschel never spoke negatively about anyone or anything.

Even to this observant family, Heschel seemed to be exceptionally religious. The day of his arrival, he asked Mrs. Simon for a container of *negelvasser* ("finger water") to place in his bedroom. (Devout East European Jewish men dip their fingers in water right after waking up, before reciting morning prayers.) Each night he brought a bowl or glass to his room, placing it near the bed. When Mrs. Simon asked if she could do this for him, Heschel refused her offer graciously.

Heschel's charm was a powerful force as well, for his "mannerisms" (as Rosie describes his wit) highlighted their little pleasures. He praised and admired Mrs. Simon's excellent cooking and her fine pastry. Occasionally he joked and laughed, saying that *Ha-Shem* (God) had given Mrs. Simon the recipes or helped her keep the house so pretty! But through his smiles he remained serious.

Heschel's good humor was greatly appreciated during this ominous period. The previous year, Jacob Simon had been fired from his job and he was depressed and worried. Already many Jews were leaving the country, disappearing suddenly, one after the other. Heschel was sensitive to these tensions and did not appear to be disheartened. Negative emotions he kept inside.

But Heschel made no secret of his attachment to his own family, and he anxiously awaited mail from his mother and sisters in Warsaw. To Rosie he appeared as a most devoted son. He often spoke of his mother, telling the Simons how courageous and wonderful she was, how much he admired and revered her. In his few conversations with Rosie, Heschel also praised her father.

At the same time, the young woman noticed Heschel's emotional distance. He was an attractive, eligible bachelor, but Rosie sensed a certain aloofness in his bearing. He was "super polite, always courteous," almost like a superior being. When Rosie and her father deliberated about Heschel's personal life, they could not picture his getting married. More to the point, he seemed to have no friends. He never brought anyone home. Heschel exuded a sort of remote loneliness that his special magnetism could not dissipate.

Heschel in Frankfurt. Courtesy of the Ratner Center for the Study of Conservative Judaism, New York.

Heschel worked hard, participating fully in the Mittelstelle's pedagogical outreach.[17] While preparing curricular materials under Buber's directives, he would take a train to small towns around Frankfurt or beyond, giving lectures of general interest, such as how to read a passage from the Bible, Jewish philosophy, or Talmud for students without special preparation. Typically, he visited the local Jewish community center (*Gemeindehaus*) and lectured informally, wearing a tie but often without his jacket. In town, he offered courses under the auspices of the Frankfurt Lehrhaus; such gatherings were usually held in the Westend Synagogue, the Unterlindau Synagogue, or the Haupt Synagogue.[18] The Simons attended his lectures at the nearby Unterlindau Synagogue. Two evenings a week he addressed about fifty people about such subjects as mysticism, Jewish culture, Maimonides, and ethics. Although his themes were beyond Rosie, his positive impact as a lecturer remained in her memory.

Heschel's goal as teacher was to awaken a personal involvement with the sacred text. This was also Rosenzweig and Buber's intent for the Frankfurt Lehrhaus, where classes took the form of seminars rather than lectures. The new education avoided formality and hierarchical structure, typical of the German system where students listened passively while a professor sat at a desk and read a prepared lecture, often without looking up. Modern Jewish teachers cultivated a warm group atmosphere and appealed to an individual's inner life.

Although Heschel's classroom style was not as dramatic as that of the other religiously observant lecturer, Ernst Akiba Simon, he inspired listeners. Ernst Simon, a Zionist who had emigrated to Palestine but returned to Frankfurt for a period to help Buber, was an excellent orator, dynamic and well organized. Heschel's presentations were more directly to the subject and somewhat drier.

Yet Heschel successfully communicated his knowledge and, more important, influenced listeners with his reverence for the text. During a retreat with Jewish youth leaders, most of them secular left-wing Zionists (known as *Werkleute*), in 1938 at the Westend Synagogue, Heschel was introducing a passage from the Bible, *Ki Tissa* (Exodus 30:11–35), which includes the episode of the Golden Calf.[19] The activists, disrespectful of religion, started to scoff. But the devoted teacher made his point: we must take the Bible seriously. This was not just a fairy tale or a myth, but a Jewish story that concerned them personally. They became quiet, shaken at being shown the profound meaning of the biblical text.

Heschel insisted upon an approach to Bible study that was obvious to liter-

Heschel teaching, around 25–30 June 1937, Gemeindehaus, Kreidel Strasse, Gleiwitz. Courtesy of Mrs. Egon Lowenstein, Jerusalem.

ary interpreters, but unfamiliar to young readers: key words change meaning according to their context. A concordance explains the Bible's multiple associations and values. For example, the German word for table is *Tisch,* an ordinary table where you eat. The Hebrew *shulhan* is not just a useful piece of furniture; every Jewish "table," where one follows the Torah's laws, can become an altar "set before the Lord" and transforms the participants.

This particular lesson, unexceptional in itself, influenced a young observant Jew from Frankfurt, Fritz Rothschild, who heard Heschel speak two or three more times during that retreat. The futures of both men later became intertwined. After a painful emigration to Northern Rhodesia in 1938 and finally to the United States, Rothschild again met Heschel—this time at the Jewish Theological Seminary in New York, where he studied under Heschel. After Rothschild joined the seminary faculty he became his teacher's most acute exponent and interpreter.[20]

Germany was now a frightful place for Jews. Living under the pall of possible disaster—the magnitude of which could not yet be imagined—Heschel joined the multitudes who searched for opportunities to leave. He began to study English, helped by his landlord, Jacob Simon, who knew five languages, having formerly been a foreign representative for a metal firm. Heschel asked his host to translate his biography of *Maimonides* into English. This task diverted Jacob Simon from his own discouragement at being without work, in addition to helping Heschel prepare for his own emigration.[21]

As Heschel studied English newspapers, he was shocked by a report in *The Times* of London extolling the 1937 Annual Nazi Congress in Nuremberg. He later recalled sarcastically, "I rarely read anything so glowing, so beautiful, so enthusiastic as about this marvelous meeting of the Nazis."[22] This was graphic evidence that people were blind to the evil in these grand spectacles. Fascism had dangerous esthetic appeal, and brute power and pageantry spellbound normally critical minds.

Heschel took up the challenge of inspiring his fellow Jews in another popular biography. As a writer, he considered life stories to be theology in action, models of situational thinking. Biography was also a natural outcome of what he already composed. His Yiddish poetry was patently autobiographical and provided personal confirmation for his analysis of the Hebrew prophets, their closeness to God and their radical ethics. His narratives of post-biblical Jewish figures (such as Maimonides and the Talmudic sages) encouraged resistance to tyranny. All these writings were guides to Jewish self-examination, as his 1936 Rosh Hashanah sermon explained: "For many years we have experienced history as a judgment. What is the state of our repentance, of our 'return to Judaism?'"[23]

This time Heschel developed another historical parallel, the golden age of Spanish Jewry as similar to German Jewish high culture. The five-hundredth anniversary of the birth of Don Isaac Abravanel (1437–1509), Jewish Portuguese and Spanish statesman, financier of kings, biblical exegete, and theologian provided a dramatic case. A hopeful perspective on the 1492 expulsion from the Iberian peninsula might hearten German Jews on the brink of mass exodus.

Abravanel's destiny offered a timeless guide to the present, as stated by the author's italicized editorial comment: "*The Jewish question is a question of God to us.*"[24] The Prussian Jewish Community commissioned and subsidized Heschel's lucid essay (thirty-two pages, including copious source notes), which became one of the final works Erich Reiss managed to publish before the Nazis liquidated his company.[25] To publicize the book, Heschel placed a summary in the Berlin *Gemeindeblatt* of 7 February 1937.

At the outset, Heschel stressed the biography's theological significance: "History is the encounter of eternity and temporality. Just as the word is the cloak of revelation and a testimony of prayer, so history forms a vehicle for God's actions in the world."[26] Heschel saw Abravanel as a modern Jewish thinker: "He was at home in the fields of Jewish literature, in Halakhah and Aggadah, in religious philosophy and exegesis, and also in Christian theology and Islamic philosophy."[27] His historical approach to Bible study justified his title as "the first *Humanist* of Judaism" and the "founder of *Wissenschaft des Judentums*."[28] At the same time, while lauding Abravanel's worldliness, Heschel stresses his opposition to secularism: "Abravanel was not the herald of new ideas, but, rather, the trustee of the right belief. He was not possessed by a philosophical eros. The teachings of revelation were to him an answer, not a problem." A detail reflects Heschel's internal struggle with self-involvement, always unstated. Abravanel's lack of a "philosophical eros" echoes Heschel's remark that Maimonides lacked "the poet's sacred egotism"—both expressions refer to individual curiosity driven by esthetic pleasure or narcissism. Both Maimonides and Abravanel—according to Heschel—counterbalanced their "egotistical" or "erotic" drives by devotion to the *mitzvot* and centering their concern on *God's* will. A hypersensitive person such as Heschel must strive harder to remain in touch with the community.

Here Heschel implies that loyalty to Judaism will help Jews overcome despair. At one point his evening prayer in Berlin, flowing over Goethe's pagan poem, renewed his connection to God and to the Jewish people. Loyalty was also Abravanel's "strongest human quality, the very source of his spiritual approach and his entire style of life"; such devotion could strengthen "spiritually empty" German Jews, the "Marranos of today" menaced in all areas of life.[29]

In order to emphasize the moral message, Heschel contrasts Abravanel's pragmatic view of knowledge with Maimonides's apparent preference for the contemplative life. Abravanel was a genuine historical thinker "mainly concerned about the future of the people Israel and of mankind. His mind's central interest was the messianic kingdom, which he expected in the near future, and in this world. What moved him most was not a mystical beatitude within God, or within an active intellect emanating from Him, but the historical betterment of mankind."[30]

Historical irony, however, takes center stage toward the end: "Abravanel served a royal court in which the Grand Inquisitor Torquemada, the Queen's confessor, provoked hatred of the Jews. It was there that the project of exterminating Jewry was forged. The tragedy of Abravanel's brilliant career is nowhere more evident than here: His experience and talents were put to use toward an undertaking the consequence of which was catastrophic to Spanish Jewry."[31] The concluding sentences anticipate the exile of German Jews. With forceful irony, Heschel observed how the unhappy destiny of Spanish Jewry, from a moral perspective, might provide some consolation:

The Jews, who had played a leading role in the politics, economics and social affairs of their country had to leave their Spanish homeland. The conquest of the New World was achieved without them. Had they remained on the Iberian peninsula, they would surely have participated in the deeds of the Conquistadores. When the latter arrived in Haiti, they found over one million inhabitants. Twenty years later only one thousand remained.

The desperate Jews of 1492 could not know what they were spared.[32]

Readers were deeply stirred by Heschel's penetration of history's incongruities.[33] The destiny of Abravanel and his people suggests that expulsion yielded spiritual gifts. By implication, at the very least, Jews rejected by Nazism would not share responsibility for its barbarities. Heschel's sardonic suggestion that moral dignity might emerge from persecution proved to be appallingly correct.

The following year, Heschel's small volume was translated into Polish, subsidized by the Friends of the Hebrew University, perhaps with Buber's influence.[34] Jews in Poland as well were beginning to foresee inquisition. *Abravanel* might provide them all with a lesson of grim but abiding hope. Nevertheless, in Germany the word *extermination*—even as Heschel mourned the natives of Haiti decimated by the Spaniards—had not yet been pronounced.

By July 1937, the Simon family with whom Heschel boarded had to find smaller quarters, and Heschel moved to the residential Eschersheim suburb, taking rooms at the home of the Adlers at 11 Adelheid Strasse. His routine was not affected. While advancing several projects at the Mittelstelle, he distributed copies of *Die Prophetie*, and on 22 July he wrote Tadeusz Kowalski about some "serious troubles" he was having with currency exchange. Still dogged by problems of idiomatic Polish, he apologized: "A language mistake in my letter to you unfortunately created a very sad misunderstanding, namely, regarding permission for sending money from Poland." Borrowed languages provided fragile support in this state of international crisis.

Heschel ended the year 1937 by thanking Buber, who sent his German translation of the Book of Proverbs, replying that "while reading it I gained all sorts of insights into the 'vital antithetic.'"[35] He craved Buber's spiritual companionship as this difficult year came to a close: "With my heart I received the words, given to me in Proverbs, a great gift and for which I have been longing for some time. May it be given to me to prove myself more and more worthy."

Heschel was indeed found "worthy" by scholars, who generally praised *Die Prophetie* in learned journals and community newspapers in Europe and the

United States. In Kraków, the Polish Academy of Arts and Sciences eagerly collected reviews by Protestant and Catholic, as well as Jewish experts.[36] Heschel was a substantial figure in the world of biblical scholarship, and his book became one of the Polish Academy's most widely reviewed publications.[37] He continued to shore up his position in a world preparing for war.

18

A Prophetic Witness (December 1937–March 1938)

The will of God is to be here, manifest and near; but when the doors of this world are slammed on Him, His truth betrayed, His will defied, He withdraws, leaving man to himself. God did not depart of His own volition; He was expelled. God is in exile.

Heschel, *Man Is Not Alone* (1951)

[1]

DURING THE NINETEEN MONTHS HE LIVED IN FRANKFURT, HESCHEL ANNOUNCED his theology of history—and became the witness to the living God he remained throughout his life. He continued to publish reviews in the Berlin *Gemeindeblatt* of a variety of books, a prayerbook, a Bible concordance, and Yiddish stories. And he developed an idiom for conveying his message to the general public.

In the Hanukkah *Gemeindeblatt* issue of 29 November 1937, Heschel responded to crisis with a parable entitled "Lights over the Sea" (Lichter über dem Meer), which evoked Germany's waning Jewish culture. In the story, three Jews on a sea voyage "trying to begin a new life" remember Hanukkah. But only the eldest remembers how to light the candles and recite blessings. It ends with ambiguous hope: "In distant days, there was a light that shone for eight days, though it could have lasted only one. Eight days? All three of them thought, in eight days we will reach our destination. Our destination? We are at the beginning." Heschel was counting on miracles.

But he also continued pressing on several fronts. Despite the growing Nazi threat, in addition to his journalism, he distributed his books on the prophets, on Maimonides, on Abravanel—and advanced his new scholarly project: monographs on Solomon Ibn Gabirol, eleventh-century Spanish poet and philosopher.[1] These technical studies of medieval philosophy validated him as a specialist in this seminal field and might lead to a book. Although his future was in doubt, Heschel was establishing a body of work to qualify him for a solid academic appointment. He was a prime candidate as a published scholar; he could teach Bible, Talmud, medieval philosophy, Hasidism, and modern Jewish thought.

Yet career possibilities for Jews no longer existed in Germany, and few if any European or North American universities announced positions in Judaic studies. Nevertheless, Heschel discovered that he was freer as a writer. Already a master of German prose, he was tempering Jewish classical sources with up-to-date perspectives of Scheler, Rosenzweig, Koigen, Buber, and others—renovated by his personal vision.

Scholarship and Prophetic Witness

Prospects for French translation of *Die Prophetie* looked favorable in December 1937. Heschel renewed contact with Henry Corbin, through the good offices of Else Adler, in whose home Heschel was renting rooms. Mrs. Adler visited Corbin during a trip to Paris, delivering greetings from Heschel and some questions. Upon her return to Frankfurt, Heschel was pleased to hear that

Corbin's translation of Heidegger's essay "Hölderlin and the Essence of Poetry" had appeared in the French journal *Mesures*.[2] The next year Corbin's translation of Heidegger's *What Is Metaphysics?* would be published by Gallimard.

Corbin advocated Heschel's authentically Jewish interpretation of prophecy. He wrote Heschel, confirming his intention to translate selections from *Die Prophetie*. Heschel was delighted. An elegant version of his *Maimonides* was available in Paris, and he was excited by the prospect of his major biblical interpretation appearing on the French horizon.

Yet Heschel's answer of 18 January 1938 summarized his discouraged state of mind as well as his aspirations. Addressing Corbin as "Lieber Freund" (dear friend), Heschel exposed his sense of isolation, concealed from his Frankfurt acquaintances, as it begins: "Your letter contains so much genuine expressiveness that I experienced reading it as a conversation. It will be quite natural for me to write you in the same way." Then he candidly revealed his private sense of isolation: "It is depressing and quite a drawback that spiritually one has to fend for oneself here, that there is no company which could inspire and enrich one spiritually. I don't know how long I will stay here."[3]

Was this the loneliness Heschel expressed in his Yiddish poetry? In Frankfurt, where he hoped to combine his spiritual and intellectual commitments, conditions apparently were not propitious for developing intimacy. Although Heschel appreciated the tradition of the Frankfurt Jews—and often spoke of it later in highest terms—he longed for the East European warmth he knew in Warsaw, and perhaps in Vilna, and among friends in Berlin. Most of his close collaborators had emigrated or were preparing to do so. Heschel had many reasons known to him alone to keep his feelings to himself.

It was not surprising that Buber did not provide adequate companionship. Their religious ideas were seriously divergent. Besides, Buber was a busy man—he was an eminent author, lecturer, and teacher, and for decades he maintained a worldwide correspondence. Heschel, for all his qualities, was a new arrival in Buber's immense community. During this period, as well, the Bubers were preoccupied with preparing for emigration to Palestine. Heschel felt closer to another teacher at the Lehrhaus, Eduard Strauss, the biochemist whose courses on the Bible had, for over a decade, inspired hundreds of students and auditors.[4]

Heschel's letter to Corbin continued by describing his work on Ibn Gabirol, for Corbin understood medieval Islamic (and Christian) thought and mysticism. To strengthen his credentials, he was placing his studies of medieval metaphysics (all written in German) in publications associated with German Liberal and Orthodox and American Reform institutions. "The Concept of Being in

Gabirol's Philosophy," Heschel's first study, appeared in the Festschrift honoring the seventieth birthday of Dr. Jakob Freimann, rabbi and lecturer at the Orthodox Rabbiner-Seminar in Berlin whom Heschel knew well.[5] (Contributors included Alexander Altmann, Leo Baeck, and Ismar Elbogen.) The second study was published in the distinguished *Monatsschrift* (1937–38), and the last one, "The Status of the Thing in Gabirol's Philosophy," appeared in the *Hebrew Union College Annual*—in 1939, after Heschel was invited to join its faculty in Cincinnati, Ohio.[6]

By 1938, however, metaphysics (medieval or modern) was not Heschel's essential concern, nor was building an academic career—nor obtaining an exit visa from Germany. He told Corbin of the newer project closest to his heart: essays on prayer as preparation for a book on religious consciousness. Two months before, he had begun an essay on "the nature and the reality" of prayer: "Maybe I shall have the strength to continue my research," he continued.[7] Heschel's pedagogical guide to worship, criticized by Buber for being too focused on the sacred *experience* (what Heschel called "the reality" of prayer), had blossomed into a lifetime enterprise.

In Frankfurt, Heschel defined his unique role: to establish piety as the foundation of a living Judaism. "Piety," as he understood the term, was a distinctively Jewish form of consciousness—the word in Hebrew is *Hasidut*. Piety, he stressed, touched the inner life of individuals as well as behavior. Piety combines faith, belief, attachment to God, observance of the mitzvot, loyalty to the Jewish people—all leading to practical action in the world. At this early stage, however, Heschel called his modern interpretation of piety a "systematology."[8]

His immediate concern was to communicate the spirit of the Hebrew prophets. His letter to Corbin lists the chapters of *Die Prophetie* he should translate for the special issue of *Hermès,* a journal of religion and philosophy the Frenchman was editing, published in Brussels and distributed in Paris. Heschel ends by sealing their spiritual alliance: "The whole time I have thought with pleasure of our meeting in summer 1936 and, again and again, I wanted to continue contact at least by writing. Maybe now this correspondence will make a good start." Heschel bolstered his hopes by sharing their passion for philosophy, Jewish and Islamic mysticism, and beauty. But their constructive friendship, grievously, was interrupted by world strife.

In February 1938, Heschel took an opportunity to judge the significance of the impending war in a speech to Quaker leaders. Initially Martin Buber had been invited to address the group by Rudolf Schlosser, a German Quaker and pacifist recently returned from the Second World Conference of Quakers held in Swarthmore, Pennsylvania. But Buber had influenza and designated Heschel to take his place.[9] Among those present were Rudolf and Amalie Schlosser and the widow of Franz Rosenzweig. "Buber's assistant"—as Heschel was described— impressed the audience as "a very serious young man, with strong inner concentration, [who] attempted to fathom the meaning of this new persecution of the Jewish people."[10]

Speaking to a predominantly non-Jewish audience, Heschel interpreted the crisis in theological terms. He applied his Hasidic perspective and formulated a call to action. Just as his Abravanel biography sought theodicy in Spain's expulsion of the Jews, so now he found a message in Germany's campaigns of terror. Entitled "Search for a Meaning" (Versuch einer Deutung), his speech opened dramatically with a symbolic scene:

> Carved over the gates of the world in which we live is the escutcheon of the demons. It happens in our time that the peoples are forging their sickles into swords and their scythes into spears. And by completely inverting the prophetic words, the peoples turn away from the words that come from Zion. Our lot is that we must face that world. We learn how the prophets' vision is fulfilled by our distorting the two characteristics of the human face, the likeness to the Creator and the mark of Cain, of which the latter shows more and more clearly and threatens to wipe out the former more and more thoroughly.[11]

Heschel's judgments were bold and confident. He felt connected to his audience—Jews and Quakers who heroically saved Jews and others from the ravages of disease, poverty, and persecution in Germany, Austria, and England. His listeners would understand that religious people are particularly sensitive to the true meaning: "It is a basic fact of the world that HE, the invisible, is in the habit of emerging from His distance and concealment to announce His opinion to mankind." Like Buber, Heschel spoke in abstract and solemn biblical style, but Heschel's images are more concrete, vivid, concise—and focus upon God as Subject.

Heschel's theocentrism highlighted humanity's inescapable responsibility; it was not passive or fatalistic. Calling upon his tradition, Heschel cites a dictum of "Rabbi Baal Shem, the founder of Hasidism" to explain how Nazi evil serves a judgment on both Christians and Jews: "If a person sees something evil, he should know that it is shown to him so that he may realize his own guilt—repent for what he has seen." People of conscience can recognize radical evil within everyone (including themselves) and oppose the torturers more vigorously.[12] His 1936 sermon on repentance was addressed to everyone, scapegoats and perpetrators alike.

Heschel, in fact, judged contemporary civilization as a whole. In particular, he targeted not secularization as such but the failures of institutional religion, trivialization of belief, and diminished moral courage. People lost contact with the ultimate and replaced "God's Name" with idols: "Through the millennia, His voice has wandered throughout the world. How it was trapped and imprisoned in the temples! How it was misunderstood and distorted, cheated and disfigured!—And now we behold how this voice gradually withdraws, grows faint and is muted." According to Heschel's interpretation, human indifference can inhibit the Divine.

For a believer, this was a grim diagnosis. God is in exile, imprisoned even "in the temples." The present was no different from Bible times, when God hid the Face and withdrew compassion from the people.

Heschel then enunciated what he later called "depth theology," his attempt to evoke "pre-conceptual" moments of religious insight.[13] Accepting the fact of human anguish, he trusted God, even against evidence of God's silence, for he believed that the very tension between the world's horror and our yearning for deliverance can awaken prayer—and may give us strength. This theology of distress assumes that a questioning faith can infuse human beings with new energy. If we face reality courageously, prayer may arise and release us from immobilizing terror:

> It occurs sometimes that the Name erupts from our heart like a cry. Then this happens not just as an event within us but as a miracle before us: this word is there, mighty and holy, the Name of One who is more than cosmos and eternity, and we cannot grasp it, and we know that this word is infinitely more than our life and our heart from which it has erupted. In such tension our prayer matures, and the right to call Him by His name.

Assuming a certainty in the existence of a God of pathos, Heschel's empathy with prophetic consciousness helped him to clarify the liberating tensions of realistic, self-critical prayer. This theory of prayer as a dialectic of confidence and anguish makes plausible his trust that the Divine might spontaneously emerge.

Heschel became a prophetic witness that evening in Frankfurt. With his distinctive blend of faith and ethical courage, he defined a model of realistic religion. His historical assessment was sound: Jews must leave Germany. His listeners could emulate his faith even at the brink of despair: "Perhaps we are all now going into exile. It is our fate to live in exile, but HE has said to those who suffer: 'I am with them in their oppression.' The Jewish teachers tell us: Wherever Israel had to go into exile, the Eternal went with them. The divine consequence of human fate is for us a warning and a hope."

The message was of immediate import. Because he believed that God accompanied humankind in suffering, a people with faith is a strong people, dedicated to the world's redemption. Heschel's perspective recalls the rabbinic and Hasidic view that "the *Shekhinah* lies in the dust";[14] the Divine is in exile and we, human beings, even in our exile, are accountable for God. Religious people have a sacred responsibility.

Heschel's talk so heartened Rudolf Schlosser that, at great personal risk, the Quaker leader distributed hundreds of mimeographed copies in Germany. Later in the United States, Heschel translated and revised the speech and, in 1943, announced to American readers—still relatively unresponsive to the catastrophe—"the meaning of this war."

Abolishing European Jewry

Heschel further intensified efforts to find an academic position outside Germany. He made extensive inquiries and realized that there were virtually no positions available. Yet, soon after his speech to the Quakers, he mailed a copy of *Die Prophetie* to Louis Finkelstein, president of the Jewish Theological Seminary of America, the Conservative rabbinical school in New York City, in the hope that the seminary might sponsor an invitation. That same month, he was invited to join the faculty of a rabbinical academy that the Jewish community in Prague, Czechoslovakia, was attempting to establish.[15] He answered immediately to express interest.

Then, in one horrifying week, any sense of security that Heschel, or any European Jew, might still have possessed, was shattered. On 12 March the Germans invaded Austria. The very next day, the Anschluss (annexation) was completed and all Austrian citizens, including Heschel's relatives in Vienna, became "Germans" subject to Nazi control. That very day, as well, Martin Buber and his wife left Frankfurt for Palestine.[16]

The following week Heschel received two hopeful responses: Louis Finkelstein's letter, dated 16 March 1938, cordially acknowledged receiving his book "of which I have read several reviews. . . . I hope to read it in the course of the next few weeks," he promised.[17] On 17 March, the Prague Jewish community wrote to thank Heschel for his "expression of willingness to enter into negotiations" for a position in their school.[18]

Heschel maintained himself in two discordant worlds: remaining personally defenseless, his intellectual and spiritual life flourished. He pursued teaching, research, and publications, further promoting *Die Prophetie* with Kowalski's help, eagerly awaiting reviews from around the world.[19] In Frankfurt, he and Kantorowicz supervised the work of the Mittelstelle, keeping Buber informed by mail. All the while, Heschel remained acutely distressed by the suffering his families endured in Warsaw and Vienna.

Where could he or they go? The American quotas were filled. At this point, only clergymen and certain professional people were eligible for the few remaining non-quota visas.

After the Nazi Anschluss, Jews in the Austrian capital were deliberately terrorized.[20] Among them were Heschel's sister Sarah, her husband, Rabbi Abraham Joshua Heschel (now rebbe of Kopitzhinitz), and their ten children. Also living in Vienna were Heschel's sister Devorah Miriam Dermer and her husband; and his brother, Jacob, with his wife and three-year-old daughter, Thena. There were also Friedman cousins, the rebbes of Boyan and Tchortkov and their families.

Acts of violence increased. Thousands of Jews escaped or were deported. The German SS and Gestapo did not spare Heschel's pious family, and his brother-in-law, the rebbe of Kopitzhinitz, and his nephew Israel were badly beaten by Nazis and other hoodlums. Despite it all, the rebbe refused to emigrate, insisting on his duty to remain with his Hasidim.[21]

Nor was the distinguished elder spared one of the Nazis' favorite tortures. His youngest son, Meshullam Zusya, remembers how one day the Nazis herded together a large group of devout Jewish men in order to cut off their earlocks (*pey'ot*) and beards. Most of the men panicked, but the rebbe had an extraordinary reaction. He pointed to his beard and told the Nazi soldier, "*Bitte,* please cut off my finger but leave this on." The astounded SS officer paused and burst out laughing. "Don't bother this dumb Jew," he told the other SS men. The rebbe was spared.[22]

The rebbe's heroic defense of Jewish law (the obligation not to shave) probably saved the family's lives. From then on, since Rabbi Heschel was one of the few bearded Jews left in Vienna, the Nazis habitually photographed him to depict a typical Jewish man. Zusya remembers that "nearly every day my father was dragged out of the house and forced to march in front of the jeering Austrian Nazis and made to mop up a freshly painted swastika on the street. Initially my father insisted that he could tolerate this ordeal, that it wasn't that terrible an ordeal. But then they came each Shabbes [Sabbath] and the trauma and hurt of having to desecrate the Shabbes or yontev [festival day] was more painful to him than any torture. So finally he relented on not leaving Vienna."[23]

The Heschels were not able to emigrate until almost a year after annexation. In February 1939 Rabbi Abraham Joshua Heschel of Kopitzhinitz, his wife, Sarah, and several children left for the United States. The same month Heschel's brother, Jacob, managed to reach London with his family, sharing an apartment with relatives who also escaped. Eventually nine of the Kopitzhinitzer rebbe's children—Israel, Chava, Batsheva, Mira, Miriam, Malka, Chaya Pearl, Moses Mordecai, and Zusya—settled in the United States. Only their sister Leah Rachel died in the Holocaust with her husband, Ephraim Fischel. The Friedmans of Vienna, the Tchortkover rebbe and his family (Jacob Heshel's in-laws), emigrated to Palestine the same year, settling in Tel Aviv.[24] Dozens of other relatives later perished.

Heschel had no choice but to remain in Frankfurt, as he had no invitation from abroad and no money. However, he sought help from contacts in the Frankfurt Jewish community. He was invited frequently to the home of Leni Rapp, the wife of a prominent doctor, daughter of a leader of the Frankfurt Jewish community, and a niece of Rabbi Jakob Horovitz. Leni Rapp was highly educated in both Jewish and general culture, and as the only child of Professor Aron Freimann, librarian of the Stadtbibliotek and a distinguished Jewish academic, she had personal contacts with leading Jewish scholars through her father. She was a woman of practical insight and gave Heschel advice in various areas.

Heschel spent many Sabbath evenings at the home of Rabbi Jakob Horovitz, in whose synagogue he worshipped and whose two children soon emigrated—Ruth to London, and Menahem to Palestine. Later in London, Ruth Horovitz helped Heschel depart for the United States.

Heschel remained in close touch with his mother and sisters in Warsaw, as well as with writers and academic colleagues. In Poland there was relatively less foreboding about the future. He thought about returning there if a teaching position were offered. Despite growing tensions between Poland and Germany, one could travel between Warsaw and Frankfurt with the appropriate documents. Under these volatile conditions, he did not panic nor succumb to depression. Although the letters to and from his mother and sister in Warsaw caused him much anguish, they helped them to maintain some hope, stressing the rare good news. His sister Gittel wrote, "Each day that we receive a letter from you is a holiday for us."[25]

19

"Out of the Depths" (March–October 1938)

If God is alive, then the Bible is His voice. No other work is as worthy of being considered a manifestation of His will. There is no other mirror in the world where His will and spiritual guidance is as unmistakably reflected.

Heschel, *God in Search of Man* (1955)

HESCHEL'S INTENSE WORK COUNTERED THE PAINFUL UNCERTAINTIES OF HIS immediate future. We do not possess his correspondence with his family and friends, which certainly points to his fruitless efforts to help them. The documents available in public archives point, rather, to his efficient oversight of what he could do—administer several projects—in Berlin, Frankfurt, Warsaw, and Kraków. Mastery of banal intricacies helped shield him from the ever-present chaos of world politics. Despite the frightful events and frequent dislocations, he maintained careful records of the distribution of *Die Prophetie* and kept the Polish Academy informed. While Austrian Jews—including members of his own family—were being brutalized, for example, Heschel wrote to Kraków on 7 April 1938 for an account of the inventory.[1] All the while, his new project on prayer and piety remained his greatest instrument of hope.

Heschel's letters to Martin Buber in Jerusalem provide an accurate glimpse into this excruciating period. Despite the formality he fittingly maintained with his elder, it is remarkable how closely they kept in touch, sharing personal feelings in addition to ideas and reports on activities. Heschel found in Buber crucial support during these months, as he devoted himself to Jewish renewal in Germany even while contriving means to emigrate. Their hermeneutical controversy mattered less than their spiritual collaboration.

The Depths of Sorrow

Heschel briefly returned to Warsaw, his native city, and he could hardly endure what he saw. In a letter to Buber on 25 April 1938, from his mother's apartment at 3 Dzika Street, he poured out his anguish, explaining that "many internal things hindered my ability to communicate in writing." Poland was in the grip of an "epidemic of despair," a sense of disorganization, and succumbing to "spiritual lethargy." He did not anticipate being able to undertake "anything durable here within the near future."[2] Heschel realized that, if he could keep his anxieties at bay, he would focus his energies on research.

Poland was becoming hazardous because of nationalist, anti-Jewish politics, while economic conditions were desperate. Heschel was gloomy, but he advanced his projects. He apprised Buber of his teaching, reassured him that the condition of his mother, "Ryfka Rojza *Heszel*," was the same, and that he expected to begin his lectures immediately upon his arrival in Berlin the next day. There he planned to meet Kantorowicz as well: "After my return to Frankfurt I will report more in detail. Besides, the situation there has aggravated within the last weeks." And he ended by associating himself with Buber's own future: "I regret not to be in Jerusalem tomorrow, but I wish you well 'out of the depths' [*aus Tiefen*]."

Heschel's citation of Psalm 130, "Out of the depths I cry to Thee," alludes to Buber's recently published anthology of the same title. Appearing in Schocken's Bücherei series, this arrangement of twenty-three psalms (printed in Hebrew with Buber's German translation on opposite pages) sought to inspire Jewish speakers of German who were despairing of their future.[3]

Buber avoided Nazi censorship by using the ancient text to confront present adversities. These psalms in Buber's translation address contemporaries directly. A careful reader might slowly meditate on the sequences, pondering their varied, powerful emotions—progressing from agony to faith and confidence. From the initial imploring "Out of the depths I cry to Thee, O Lord! Lord, hear my voice!" (Ps. 130), questioning the purpose of Jewish suffering ("O God, why dost thou cast us off for ever?" Ps. 74), the Psalmist pleads: "Deliver me from my enemies, O my God . . . and save me from bloodthirsty men" (Ps. 59). Buber also broadcasts the pressing question of faith, that of God's silence: "Why dost thou stand afar off, O Lord?/ Why dost thou hide thyself in times of trouble?" (Ps. 10). Heschel, too, as a Yiddish poet, acknowledged God's distance—but under less severe circumstances.

Buber's task was to brace the Jewish spirit, and thus the collection ends on a positive note—"O Lord, my God, in thee do I take refuge;/ save me from all my pursuers, and deliver me" (Ps. 7)—without denying lethal suffering: "For my days pass away like smoke,/ and my bones burn like a furnace" (Ps. 102). The final prayer still challenges the survivors: "Be merciful to me, O God,/ . . . in the shadow of thy wings I will take refuge,/ till the storms of destruction pass by" (Ps. 57). Who could have predicted the demonic realization of these agonies of Bible times?

In addition to teaching adults, Heschel was exerting considerable managerial skill to distribute *Die Prophetie,* his testimony book in academic form. From Warsaw he returned to Frankfurt on 28 April and the next day wrote to the Polish Academy, acknowledging receipt of one hundred copies. He asked that the remaining books be sent to his sister, "Pani [Mrs.] Gitli Heschel, Warsaw, 3 Dzika, apt. 103." Heschel also informed the Polish Academy, which exhausted its stock, that potential customers might order the book directly from him in Frankfurt. He gently denied any economic motive: "Of course, I am not referring to material [profit] but rather to moral concerns. The publishing house of Erich Reiss in Berlin, which was supposed to carry out this sale, is currently undergoing liquidation." Goebbels was neutralizing Heschel's Berlin patron.

Heschel continued to share thoughts with Buber about intellectual as well as personal matters. He followed the events surrounding Buber's installation as professor of social philosophy at the Hebrew University, on 25 April. (The Orthodox faction denied him a chair in religious studies, despite his expertise in Bible.) Buber mailed Heschel the text of his inaugural lecture, "The Demand of the Spirit and Historical Reality," which declared the primacy of brave activism over allegedly disinterested academic scholarship.[4]

Buber's survey of social thought echoed Heschel's own pragmatic orientation. Buber first traced a brief history from Henri de Saint-Simon, through Siegfried Landshut, Max Weber, and Ferdinand Tönnies, and then insisted that philosophers should strive to grasp "the *meaning* of social existence and events."[5] He contrasted Plato's notion that humankind possesses its own power with Isaiah's recognition of God's sovereignty. It is the responsibility of religious judgment to challenge corrupt political leaders: "None but the powerless can speak the true King's will with regard to the state, and remind both the people and the government of their *common* responsibility toward this will."[6]

The following month Heschel, still yearning for direct conversations, again declared his solidarity: "Often I appreciate memories of the times when I could see you and speak with you more often as a deep joy."[7] And he seconded Buber's rebuff of morally neutral learning: "Perhaps we may hope that your demands, not only of the present but of the future, will find emulation in scholarship [*Wissenschaft*] and in life. Those who look into the depths [*die Tief-schauenden*] will hear your call." Buber was advancing in Palestine a "science" of the Jewish spirit which David Koigen did not live to realize in Berlin.

Heschel, for his part, subordinated "objective" scholarship to elucidating a Judaism that was both spiritually sensitive and ethically engaged. His letter continued by explaining to Buber, as he had to Corbin, that his "Wissenschaft" monographs—as he put it, "works in the style of my Gabirol studies"—were nothing more "than a preparation." Aware that Buber knew at least one of his technical studies on Gabirol, Heschel suggested that medieval thought (Jewish, Islamic, and Christian) was a groundwork for his own philosophy of religion. His heart was elsewhere, beyond philosophy. His subject was piety.

Heschel continued his contributions to the Berlin *Gemeindeblatt*. In the 22 May issue alone, he published reviews of a talk on Zionism and overseas emigration, a review of Shmuel Joseph Agnon's collection, *The Days of Awe*, and Hans Kohn's biography of Martin Buber. Heschel also published a moving essay, "Children Outside in the Sun," describing a healthy retreat for malnourished, poverty-stricken children from the east and north sections of Berlin about two hundred miles from the city. He concludes: "The children sleep without rocking, tired from playing and the fresh air. Some of them might dream how beautiful it is here. . . . Perhaps their entire life here is a dream for each child—and the dream ends very quickly."

Heschel's letters to Buber became even more frequent, as if they were speaking on the telephone each day, for mail often traveled rapidly between Frankfurt and Jerusalem. On 21 May, before Heschel finished writing Buber about bibliographical references to the notion of "community," with quotations in Latin from Thomas Aquinas and Aristotle, he stopped to open a letter from Buber, sent from Jerusalem on 17 May. The next day Heschel added a long postscript response to Buber's suggestion that he return to Warsaw. While visiting home he rejected that option: "I saw that there cannot be any inner development in that dreary environment, full of resignation and depression," he answered. He now made a direct request: "I would certainly consider the possibility for scholarly work in Jerusalem as *the* way for me."[8] Buber was well-connected and might offer advice or write letters of recommendation.

Heschel was attracted to Palestine, but his immediate interest was prompted more by his predicament than by political or religious Zionism. Unlike Buber and other intellectuals of Buber's circle, he had not planned long in advance to settle in the Holy Land. Heschel knew that Buber himself, for many years, was frustrated in his attempts to obtain a post. Even so, Heschel wished that Buber could help find him something in Jerusalem.

More realistically, Heschel placed his hopes in American Jewish institutions, about which he was well informed. Identifying himself as a "modern" candidate, he lucidly assessed job possibilities at the (Reform) Hebrew Union College in Cincinnati, Dropsie College in Philadelphia, and the (Conservative) Jewish Theological Seminary and (Orthodox) Yeshiva University (then the Rabbi Isaac Elhanan Theological Seminary) in New York. His letter to Buber names the influential people: "Decisive for these institutions seems to be Cyrus Adler, then also [Alexander] Marx, Finkelstein and others."[9]

For the next six months (from May through October 1938) Heschel wrote to Buber almost weekly, continuing to share details of his pedagogical work and his search for a haven. He asked for letters of recommendation, even calculating their time of arrival to keep track of their receipt. Conditions were so unpredictable that even one single letter from Buber might guarantee his future.

But Heschel did not remain preoccupied with himself. Under these harsh conditions, he was mapping a curriculum that might save, and enrich, Jewish civilization menaced on all sides. While maneuvering for emigration, he drafted a booklet, of his own conception, on studying the Bible. And with Ludwig Feuchtwanger and Erich Guttmann, Heschel advanced work on a bibliography of Jewish sources that Buber had begun to compose, a "Catalog of Books for Jewish Youth."

On 17 June, in his only letter to Buber typewritten on the Mittelstelle stationery, Heschel commended this curriculum for Germany's newly committed Jews: books on a myriad of relevant subjects such as the Bible, Jewish history, Jewish literature, Palestine, Zionism, exemplary biographies, the study of Yiddish and Hebrew languages, and even a "systematology of Judaism."[10] He asked Buber to write a preface, which he expected to be "not only a gain for the catalog itself but also an important increase in spiritual guidance for us all."

Heschel expressed sadness in a letter written two days later that Buber might not be able to visit Frankfurt as expected.[11] He then repeated calculations about possible jobs in the United States, boiling down to the Reform rabbinical school in Cincinnati, Hebrew Union College (which he called "a purely scholarly [or scientific] institution"), or the Conservative seminary in New York. Where, if anywhere, could Heschel fit ideologically?

His choices, under these conditions, were necessarily prudent. He knew that American Reform was less receptive to his traditional values than German Liberalism. But more to the point, which institution might hire him? The vulnerable citizen of Poland organized his conjectures, as he asked Buber once again for letters of support. Heschel was well informed and wrote that the Reform Hebrew Union College "is well supplied with lecturers," whereas the Conservative institution, the Jewish Theological Seminary in New York, "has no lecturer for Jewish Religious Philosophy." Cincinnati would be his pragmatic "starting line," since it appeared that other places might be more appropriate, for whatever reasons. "This starting line would be the diagonal in the parallelogram of the forces: 1 and 2. I therefore wish to ask you to write to C[incinnati]."

Heschel knew that he had no real choice. According to his geometric metaphor, without the diagonal, the parallelogram—an unstable oblong—would collapse. Already he decided that Hebrew Union College was only "a starting line." What might be perceived as opportunism was simply a will to survive in these dangerous circumstances. His male relatives in Vienna already made applications for special visas based upon their status as rabbis.

Heschel's future was at stake, not his theological references.[12] He ends this letter by recalling his most intimate priority: "I was not able to continue my work on prayer during the summer, because I was busy with the problem 'Jewish education.'" First and foremost, Heschel assured Buber, was his commitment to reviving piety in a troubled world.

The following week Heschel mailed Buber an outline of his booklet on reading the Bible and, expecting to see him in Germany, he wished Buber and his wife "a good trip" on their customary vacation in Switzerland.[13] Toward the end of June, informed that his family received the remaining copies of *Die Prophetie*, Heschel returned to Poland.[14] On the way back to Warsaw he stopped in Krynica, a resort village near the Czechoslovakian border. On 4 August he visited Warsaw, then left for Berlin, and a few days later arrived back in Frankfurt.[15] Although his travels were governed by need, Heschel was not immobilized.

History at a Crossroads

During the summer, Heschel and Buber communicated weekly. Working under extreme stress, Heschel wrote on 12 August about his "methodological reflections," probably his extended project on prayer. He had taught many courses, and those "duties" were "not without value." Nevertheless, in addition to so many activities, the lack of a "quiet environment" made it impossible for him to advance his "other work."[16] He was also still frustrated in his struggle to obtain a visa. But Heschel did expect to spend one academic term, starting at the end of September, at a Quaker college in Woodbrooke, England, recommended by Buber's friend Rudolf Schlosser, the Quaker leader who strongly supported Heschel.[17]

A few days later, informed by Buber's secretary that bad health caused the Bubers to postpone their vacation, Heschel gave friendly advice. Knowing that Buber was, as we say today, a "workaholic," Heschel breached the normal formality of their relationship, "with some presumption and love," by urging the Bubers to find ways to relax.[18] Heschel had become somewhat paternal, for reasons of simple, tender concern.

There was discouraging news two weeks later. Heschel wrote that the Quaker college in England deferred its invitation. He shared another saddening comment from a friend in Germany: "Apparently it is a consensus *gentium Judaeorum* ['Jewish opinion' in ironic Latin] to complain about an abundance of '*Geist*' [spirit]."[19] This evidence that contemporary Jews lacked openness to the religious dimension remained one of the disappointments of his life. The letter closed by informing Buber of a "not-uninteresting" article on the Book of Job, asking Buber to interpret a "*drash*" (he wrote the Hebrew term for textual homily) which he read the day before: "In the words 'I have not come to *dissolve* but to fulfill' (Matthew 5,17) lie the awareness and the intention of Jesus to redeem the world from the decomposing forces (ferment of decomposition)."[20]

Heschel shared Buber's interest in New Testament studies, although he remained grounded in Jewish sources. It appears that no extended discussion developed from Heschel's comment on Jesus. The weighty symptoms of decline and collapse—social, political, moral, religious, economic—of the world around them impelled both thinkers to develop religious alliances wherever they could be found.

In September, Heschel could see Buber or speak with him on the telephone, perhaps from Switzerland. He was aware that Buber and his wife overcame "all sorts of difficulties," and, thanking Buber for his advice, he cited Franz Rosenzweig's dictum on courage: "Today, however, I recalled throughout the day the words you told me in January: faith and humor . . . "[21] Heschel's confidence—and the confidence of all religious people—was being severely tested. A sense of humor could help.

It was probably during this period that Heschel debated with a group of students of Karl Barth, the Protestant theologian who lived in Basel, Switzerland, about the role of the churches during the rise of Hitler. Discussing the relationship between religious and political truth, Heschel insisted that people of faith must act. The Barthian disciples, on the other hand, stressing the intrinsic evil of humankind, refused to mix theology and politics. (Barth's theology confirmed an absolute distinction—or dialectic—separating the world from God.) When Heschel criticized this approach and argued that Christianity must respond to current catastrophic events, they accused him of being an atheist.

Heschel also visited a more sympathetic Christian, the Protestant socialist Leonhard Ragaz, Buber's close friend and pastor at the cathedral in Basel. Ragaz also taught theology in Zurich and edited the activist journal *Neue Wege,* to which Buber contributed several articles.[22] Unlike the conservative Barthians, Ragaz told Heschel how he favored the Hebrew Bible over the New Testament because of its emphasis on ethical concern.

Through letters, Buber's presence continued to sustain Heschel's courage and devotion. Anxious and disappointed about not having received an invitation from abroad—and an immigrant visa—Heschel again regretted that "the people whom I have addressed so far have failed in an astonishing way." A tourist visa might be obtainable, however. In any case, he had to wait two more weeks and master more technicalities in the event that he would decide to leave. Reiterating his desire for Buber's well-being, Heschel ended by pointing to the spiritual fracture caused by the present horrors: "It is not easy to work or to think with a whole heart. Maybe God has pity for the world. I yearn for you very much and pray that God will protect and love you."[23]

Heschel understood, for some time, that the world was at a crossroads. Two days after Yom Kippur, on 7 October, Heschel published an essay in Berlin's *Jüdische Rundschau*, "David Koigen's Interpretation of Jewish History" (David Koigens Sinndeutung der jüdischen Geschichte). In this second memorial tribute, Heschel summarized his teacher's conception of the Jewish destiny as a beacon to civilization. Recalling Koigen's death in March 1933, and elements of his Jewish philosophy published posthumously in *The House of Israel*, he traced Koigen's idea of universal justice and compassion from classical antiquity to the covenant with God when "Hebraic existence redefined itself as part of God's existence, of divine history."[24]

Heschel's summary of Koigen was an urgent, if somewhat abstract, message for contemporaries. Ranging over the Jewish past, he examined several "complete revaluations of power." After the prophets, "the concept of morality underwent a redefinition in favor of the disinherited and the oppressed. Suffering was experienced as purification and the insight emerged that God is closest to the humiliated." According to Koigen, after the Talmudic period, Judaism's essential polarity emerged. One was the "prophetic will" leading to a messianic redemption of the world; the other, the Pharisaic-Talmudic individual and popular will, directed more toward personal responsibility and individual spiritual growth." Heschel concluded with the basic choice: he countered assimilationists who urged Jews for decades "to live like everyone else." Now the Jewish people must consciously, and courageously, accept responsibility for their own survival.

The next letter Heschel wrote to Buber, dated 24 October 1938, was his last from Frankfurt. It was factual and terse. His situation was unchanged. Heschel continued to discuss pedagogical activities, the cancellation of a lecture of his at the Lehrhaus, and a retreat in the Bröl Valley he was organizing. Then, reminding Buber to send comments on his text (Heschel called them "glosses"), he discreetly inquired whether or not Buber would help him publish his pedagogical essay, "Method for Reading the Bible."[25]

Concluding his letter with an allusion to Buber's supportive advice, Heschel hinted at his own efforts to overcome despair: "Only Psalm 2:4 gives me comfort" ("He that sitteth in the heavens shall laugh:/ the LORD shall have them in derision"). When Martin Buber opened this letter in Jerusalem, about a week later, Heschel, with thousands of other Polish Jews, had been expelled from Germany.[26]

In his letter of 2 May to Professor Kowalski in Kraków, Heschel was right to anticipate "a possible change of my address in the future"—but not in the way he imagined. In Frankfurt, on 28 October, two agents of the Gestapo arrested Heschel in his room and ordered him to pack two bags. He took clothing and manuscripts, but had to abandon most of his books and papers. With exquisite contempt couched in politeness, and outwardly respectful of the law, the agents made Heschel carry his heavy luggage. Together they slowly walked to the police station, where he was held overnight.[27] The next morning he was crammed into a sealed and guarded train with hundreds of other Jews, standing all the way during the three-day journey to the German-Polish border.

Saved by Expulsion

Heschel was one among thousands of Jews with Polish passports driven into trains and shipped to the border between Germany and Poland.[28] All over the Reich, Hitler's police carried out an expulsion which, despite the panic, still did not hint at the possible destruction of European Jewry. For Heschel and terrified multitudes, it meant only that escape was necessary.

This crisis was hard to imagine, but not entirely unexpected. On 31 March 1938 the Polish government passed a law requiring all its Jewish citizens who had been residing abroad for more than five years to renew their passports or lose their right to return to Poland. Very few of the approximately 70,000 "Polish" Jews living in Germany and Austria—many of whom were born there and did not even speak Polish—actually completed the forms.

As the 31 October deadline approached, the Germans found a legal pretext to dispose of these "foreigners." Emigration of Jewish citizens of Germany had been encouraged, but foreign Jews remained relatively free. Before dawn on 28 October, police agents entered the apartments of Jews in several German cities, made them carry the bare essentials, took them to pre-arranged gathering points, and put them on trains to the German-Polish border.

But thousands of refugees were refused entrance at the German border town of Neu-Bentschen or at the Polish town of Zbaszyn some forty miles beyond. People sought shelter in the no-man's-land between the two places, some in open fields. Heschel was among the crowds allowed to enter a detention camp in Zbaszyn. Others tried to find rooms or lodged in makeshift shelters. The chaos, panic, and suffering of these thousands attracted reporters from around the world who broadcast the facts.

The refugees were still allowed to communicate with the outside. Those who could get official invitations might leave. We do not know the details of Heschel's temporary confinement, but he did not remain long in Zbaszyn. Contacts in Warsaw helped him return home by the first week of November. He found shelter with his mother and sisters, near the neighborhood where he had grown up.

20

Struggling to Escape (November 1938–July 1939)

I speak as a person who was able to leave Warsaw, the city in which I was born, just six weeks before the disaster began. My destination was New York; it would have been Auschwitz or Treblinka. I am a brand plucked from the fire in which my people was burned to death.

Heschel, "No Religion Is an Island" (1965)

NOW IN WARSAW, "ABRAHAM HESZEL" (AS HIS POLISH DOCUMENTS READ) WAS seeking a job and a visa, as he continued to teach, write, ponder, and pray. He was thirty-one years old. Although the full extent of danger in Poland was not yet obvious, members of Heschel's clan were attempting to emigrate. (Several of the Perlows from Warsaw had settled in the United States in the 1920s. And Heschel's brother, Jacob, had relinquished Polish citizenship when he moved to Vienna, so he and his family, officially stateless, were not deported to Poland.)[1] Anti-Semitism was increasing in Poland, yet many Jews still perceived no grave danger. Some rabbinical leaders, in fact, hoped that accommodation with Polish nationalism was possible, and many rabbis counseled Jews to remain.[2]

On 9 November 1938, Heschel wrote Buber of the appalling event that halted his career in Germany. He did not lose his equilibrium. Instead of succumbing to fear, he again coped with pernicious conditions by focusing on his educational mission. He answered Buber's letter of 2 November by stating that the recent disaster had struck him as well: "Together with thousands of Jews from all over the Reich, I was driven out of Germany. I wanted to spare you this news until now." Then immediately Heschel returned to their pedagogical work. As soon as Buber would return the manuscript of his essay on the Bible, Heschel would send it to Kantorowicz, who, in turn, "will hand it over for publication to the Reich's Committee of the Jewish Youth Association."[3]

Writing and reflection provided stability. Heschel's brutal uprooting did not divert him from seeking Buber's reaction to his essay on teaching the Bible to Jews who were unfamiliar with classical texts. Although compelled to stay in Poland, he communicated regularly with Kantorowicz who, in Frankfurt, had to deal with the Nazi commission monitoring the Mittelstelle's pedagogical program. Heschel continued to share his ideas with Buber as well as technicalities related to his search for a safe country.[4]

During that time, another Polish Jew whose parents were deported from Germany on 28 October, seventeen-year-old Hershel Grynszpan, fared worse. Enraged by the suffering his parents endured in Zbaszyn, he entered the German Embassy in Paris where he was studying, seeking revenge. He shot an official, Ernst vom Rath, who was seriously wounded. The Nazi newspapers in Germany called for swift punishment. When vom Rath died on Wednesday, 9 November 1938, the government found an excuse to carry out a vicious scheme.

The day after Heschel wrote Buber, one week after the mass expulsion of Polish Jews, Hitler sent a forthright message to the world. The details of what came to be known as Kristallnacht were broadcast immediately. The facts were available to the concerned public. As early as June 1933, the American Jewish Committee in New York published a handbook detailing Hitler's anti-Jewish campaigns and legislation. After the November 1938 pogrom, they established a bimonthly digest, the *Contemporary Jewish Record,* consisting of press reports from Europe and Palestine, many translated into English from newspapers in German, Hebrew, and Yiddish—and original articles relevant to the refugee situation.

On Thursday, an unprecedented wave of anti-Jewish violence, arson, looting, and destruction broke out all over Greater Germany. The *Contemporary Jewish Record* reported: "Beginning in the early hours of the morning, in Berlin at 2 A.M., and continuing through the entire day, wrecking crews of Storm Troopers and Nazi Party members in uniform, in many cases under police protection, carried on a systematic and thorough campaign of pillage and destruction of Jewish-owned stores and synagogues in virtually every town and city in the country. . . . The destruction of stores and shops was accompanied by the burning of synagogues throughout the country, while fire-fighting units took precautions only to prevent the fires from spreading to neighboring buildings." In Vienna, all of the twenty-one synagogues were attacked and eighteen were wholly or partly destroyed. A total of seventy-five Scrolls of the Law were dragged from the Vienna synagogues and desecrated in the streets.[5]

Numerous Jews were arrested, beaten, and sent to concentration camps, and many committed suicide. The pogrom of 9–10 November—called "Bloody Thursday" at the time—was vigorously condemned in Britain, France, and the United States: "Riot, bloodshed, terror, economic discrimination. . . . Throughout the world, in every democratic-minded nation, a wave of outrage swept over all the people. Newspapers, organizations, individuals, responded as if on a single impulse, expressing their horror and indignation over the events in Nazi Germany."[6]

It was almost fortunate that Heschel had been deported from Germany, for he was spared this barbarism. The aggression coordinated by Goebbels, subsequently known as the Kristallnacht pogrom (night of the broken glass), was far more sinister and destructive than the sanitized image of crystal suggests. This well-orchestrated violence ended the German policy of expelling its Jewish citizens or pressuring them to emigrate. It anticipated the later policy of extermination.

This was to be one of the most harrowing weeks of Heschel's life. Four days after Bloody Thursday, his friend and benefactor, Erich Reiss, was arrested in Berlin and sent to the Oranienburg concentration camp.[7] That was only the beginning. This is what Heschel, with countless others, could have read about in the space of less than a week in the *Contemporary Jewish Record:*

11 November

Headquarters of Zionist Organization in Berlin completely destroyed. 1,000 Jews arrested in Vienna and sent to Buchenwald Concentration Camp. 40 others are sent to Dachau.

14 November

Jews reported to have been beaten to death in Buchenwald Concentration Camp; 20 Jews commit suicide in Berlin. 300 wealthy Jewish families of Berlin given 24 hours to pay share of fine imposed upon Berlin Jews. . . . Library of Vienna Jewish Community reported burned.

17 November

Jewish children driven from Jewish orphan asylums which were subsequently wrecked. The chief rabbi of Duesseldorf is reported to have been lynched by Nazi mob. Wife driven insane at sight of body. Heinrich Himmler, Gestapo head, threatens to annihilate imprisoned leaders of German Jewry unless Jews abroad cease anti-Nazi propaganda. At funeral rites of vom Rath in Duesseldorf, Foreign Minister von Ribbentrop blames "World Jewry" for assassination; states Germany understands the challenge and accepts it. U.S. Consulates besieged by Jews who plead in vain for asylum, fearful of further reprisals after funeral. . . . President Roosevelt caricatured in *Der Stuermer,* as a brainless Jew slave. Official circles enraged by [New York] Mayor LaGuardia's appointment of a guard of Jewish policemen to protect the German Consulate.[8]

That very week, numbed by the savagery, Heschel shared his grief with Buber: "It was difficult for me to write you during the last days. I still do not possess the sixth sense of what has occurred. The thought of our people there [in Germany] doesn't leave me in peace. What shall we do?"[9] He told Buber that he no longer sought a research position in Jerusalem, as he was about to receive a temporary lectureship in Warsaw.

Polish Jewish Scholarship

Three weeks after expulsion from Germany, Heschel was invited to join the faculty of the Warsaw Institute for Jewish Science (Instytut Nauk Judaisty-cznych), a modern academic institution located at 5 Tlomackie Street, in back of the "Great Synagogue" and in the same building as the Jewish Library. This was the neighborhood of the Yiddish Writers and Journalists Association, at 13 Tlomackie, where the adolescent Heschel submitted his first poems to Melekh Ravitch. Linked with the University of Warsaw and the modern Orthodox Great Synagogue, the Warsaw Institute pursued cultural and historical research in Polish Jewry. Had there not been a war, it might have become Heschel's most compatible academic home.

Substituting for the eminent rabbi and historian Moses Schorr, Heschel was hired as a lecturer (*Dozent*) to teach Bible and Jewish philosophy.[10] Elected to the Polish Academy of Sciences in 1928, Schorr preached as a rabbi at the Great Synagogue and taught Semitic languages and Ancient Near East history at the university.[11] It was a prestigious accomplishment for Heschel to replace Schorr, who now expended his energies protecting Jewish rights in the political arena; since 1935, he was a Jewish representative to the Polish Parliament (Sejm). In his native city, Heschel earned a faculty position not available in Berlin, and one compatible with his eclectic skills.

The Warsaw Institute for Jewish Science had been founded in 1928 by Schorr and the historian Mayer Balaban, among others, combining scientific research, a broad conception of Judaic studies, and openness to spiritual issues.[12] Its four-year program had two divisions: one preparing teachers of Hebrew language and Judaic subjects; the other training rabbis in academic critical methods. Teachers-to-be concentrated on modern Hebrew literature, while rabbinical students concentrated on Talmud. Most of the lectures and seminars were conducted in Hebrew, with only Mayer Balaban and Ignacy Schiper, the other historian, lecturing in Polish. Students were required to enroll at the University of Warsaw for at least a master's degree.[13]

Heschel was in distinguished company. During what proved to be his final year in Warsaw (the academic year 1938–39), the Institute's rector was Edmund Menahem Stein. (It was probably Stein who helped Heschel obtain the post; as editor at the Erich Reiss Verlag, Heschel planned to publish Stein's biography of Philo of Alexandria.) Born in Galicia, Stein received a traditional religious upbringing, combining advanced yeshiva education with secular learning. He earned a doctorate in classical philology from the University of Kraków and received his rabbinical degree from the Hochschule in Berlin. Publishing works in Polish, Hebrew, German, and Latin, he entered the Warsaw Institute at the time of its founding, offering courses on Jewish history, Midrash, Jewish philosophy, and Greek and Roman history.

The previous rector was the Talmud scholar Abraham Weiss, who shared with Heschel a precocious mastery of Talmud and Jewish legal codes, preparing for university studies by attending a secular gymnasium in Poland. In 1921 he received a doctorate in history and classical philology from the University of Vienna while matriculated at the Vienna Rabbinical Seminary, where he was ordained. When the Warsaw Institute opened he was appointed lecturer in Talmud. (Weiss was the only member of the Institute's regular faculty to survive the Holocaust.)[14]

The Institute's other leading figure was Mayer Balaban, the preeminent historian of Polish Jewry and a pioneer in both secular and religious learning. Balaban received a doctorate from the University of Lwow (Lemberg) and taught in secondary schools from 1909 to 1914. During the war he was a rabbi in the military, and in 1920 the Warsaw Jewish community invited him to help found a progressive Orthodox rabbinical seminary, the Takhemoni Yeshiva, which he directed until 1930. Called to found the Institute of Jewish Science, he joined its faculty and published or supervised the school's most productive and comprehensive scholarship.

Such was the modern academy Heschel joined when he began his lectures on the evening of 24 November 1938. Heschel had just received a letter from Buber, and he replied the very next day, committing a Freudian slip on the return address; he first wrote "Frankfurt-am-Main," which he crossed out and corrected to Warsaw. "I thank you with all my heart for your words of 15 November. What shall we do at this hour? I am sorry that I cannot help those many good people. I receive much news from G[ermany]. If only I could answer with deeds!"[15]

Heschel's feelings of powerlessness were justified, for he could do nothing against military force. But as a thinker, he might free people's ideas. His letter to Buber continues: "Perhaps this affliction will teach us something. The unrest is there, but the direction is missing. Concepts suddenly regain their clarity—also for everyone. Maybe we can now bear relativism to its grave."

Amid Europe's collapse, his own insecurities, as well as those of his family and of all Jews, Heschel analyzed the emergency. German outrages against humanity were an opportunity to repudiate moral relativism. Europe could not survive if any ethical system was deemed, at least partially, valid. Heschel's theocentric view of the Hebrew prophets was a radical antidote: the Bible's living God provided an absolute moral standard.

Heschel considered his intellectual work—a combination of scholarship and prophetic judgment—to be of acute consequence. To use Koigen's and Schneersohn's terms, he opposed the "night view" by countering skepticism and resignation which undermine the moral will. Research and writing were Heschel's most instrumental responses. His letter to Buber accordingly deplores the fact that "almost all [his] manuscripts" remained in Frankfurt. But he needed a haven: "—I cannot do any real research here! Perhaps at least my preparations for my lecture on systematic religious philosophy will bear fruit."

This was Heschel's goal. By 1938, he was already constructing the "systematology" he elaborated during his first decade in the United States. After studying the prophets, Maimonides, and other ancient and medieval religious thinkers, he formulated a phenomenology of prayer—as he mentioned to Henry Corbin in January. To make his moral and theological authority felt, Heschel began to contribute exploratory essays on the inner life of piety to academic collections.[16] Scholarship must include a prophetic commitment.

Paperwork of Escape

The mail link between Warsaw and Jerusalem remained active as Heschel informed Buber about himself while reacting to Buber's recent writings and public talks. On 27 December, Heschel wrote that he could not obtain a visa either to the United States or to London: "The stay here is in no way beneficial to my work. Fate does not decree me to carry out my contemplated plans."[17] Aware that Buber was planning to visit Poland, Heschel invited him to lecture at the Institute, asked for a recent reprint, and finished by asking again about "volume 2 of *The Kingship of God*" (Heschel had reviewed volume one in January 1937), a work on Job, and Buber's striking German translations of the Bible.[18]

Heschel was deeply discouraged as 1939 began, despite his intellectual endeavors. He continued lecturing at the Institute and maintained research, though he suffered from the absence of his Frankfurt library. But he remained too agitated to send a letter to Buber for over a month.

The New Year brought havoc to Martin Buber as well. He learned from Swiss newspapers that the Nazis had ransacked his house in Heppenheim, demolished the furnishings, and destroyed the remaining three thousand volumes of his library. Imposing retroactively a 27,000 mark exit tax, the German Finance Office summoned him to return temporarily to supervise the sale of his Heppenheim property.[19] Buber steadfastly refused, defying the Nazis who wanted to avoid public disclosure of their repulsive demands. Buber's publisher in Berlin, Schocken Verlag, was closed during that period, eventually to be transplanted to New York and Palestine. (Salman Schocken emigrated to Palestine in 1934.)

On 1 February, Heschel thanked Buber for a number of essays, apologizing for the emotional turmoil which prevented him from answering sooner—"my guilt and inability continuously to advance on my way, despite my resistance."[20]

Feelings of shame and powerlessness were shared by most people; action was the only appropriate response. Heschel attempted to disseminate Buber's thoughts by publishing a speech of Buber's in Yiddish translation or in Hebrew, but he failed to do so, he explained, because of a general indifference to spiritual thinking in Poland: "Here, people still orient themselves exclusively politically, although one senses quietly that also politics stands in a space that should be recognized." Heschel inquired again about Eduard Strauss, Buber's friend and close associate.

Heschel was at a low point. Again recalling his precarious circumstances— personal, professional, civic—he asked Buber for more letters of recommendation to the United States. Again he stated how his own writing, which helped him survive spiritually and emotionally, was inhibited: "I am not progressing at all in my work. Everything here is terribly disordered and without atmosphere." And he added: "On February 8 I will think of you with great love." The date was Buber's sixty-first birthday.

In a postscript, Heschel thoughtfully asked Buber to help another colleague, a fellow graduate of the Hochschule who had emigrated to Palestine that fall: "Dr. Sister, a very diligent philologist, will probably visit you soon." Moses Sister, who beat out Heschel for a prize essay on visions in the Bible, was safe. Ismar Elbogen, guiding spirit of the Hochschule, emigrated to the United States in September 1938.[21] Heschel's turn to leave Europe had long passed. Perhaps Buber could protect them all.

Heschel lucidly coordinated his myriad activities. He advanced the possibility of a job at Hebrew Union College in Cincinnati, the Reform rabbinical seminary. For several years already, its president, Julian Morgenstern, supported by his board of governors, dedicated himself to saving as many European Jewish scholars as possible. He called this notable group his "College in Exile."[22] Heschel did not yet know that Morgenstern had completed intricate negotiations with the U.S. State Department, enabling him eventually to invite Heschel and several others.

Heschel was still allowed to travel. At the beginning of March he planned to visit Germany for about three weeks, but he delayed his departure in order to meet Buber in Warsaw on 9 March. Accompanied by his wife, Paula, Buber began an extensive lecture tour in Poland.[23] But Heschel and Buber failed to meet up and, finally, the disappointed Heschel prepared to leave Warsaw and retrieve his books and papers in Frankfurt.

After Heschel's arrival in Germany, a serious game of mail tag began. On 13 March, about to leave for Frankfurt, Heschel wrote Buber from Berlin to express regret at missing him. Again urging Buber to lecture at the Warsaw Institute, he told him to expect calls from Edmund Stein or Mayer Balaban. But Heschel also pointed to the Warsaw community's lack of spiritual discernment: "The society whose guest you are encompasses a socially one-sided class." Heschel was deeply discouraged, as he later wrote to Eduard Strauss: "The things I got to know here [in Germany] are unspeakable and weigh me down until this very day."[24]

When he learned that Buber would soon be in Poland, Heschel's emotional prison opened. On 20 March, in Frankfurt, Heschel, responding to Buber's recent letter, joyfully anticipated their planned face-to-face conversation, soon to take place in Lwow: "My heart is overflowing. It is easier to remain silent than to speak appropriately. It is . . . reunion with you."[25] Before Heschel sealed the envelope, however, even more promising news arrived: Heschel announced that he had "unexpectedly" received "a formal appointment as a Research Fellow in Bible and Jewish Philosophy" from the president of Hebrew Union College, Julian Morgenstern, and "on relatively good terms," he admitted with reserve. And the final understatement: "I am very happy about it!"

There was bad news too, as Heschel also explained. The American Consulate in Frankfurt informed him that he must wait another year before receiving a quota visa. He realized that, sadly, had he been able to submit his application in Stuttgart, he might already have received it. Heschel still felt inhibited, he admitted to Buber, about asking Morgenstern directly to get a visa, even though he realized that one might be obtained more directly through Washington, D.C. So he decided to take a chance and try in London. Heschel was planning to visit London, where his brother recently emigrated, to await the visa. His future was in the hands of an unsympathetic U.S. State Department.

Heschel returned to Warsaw on 2 April, and the next day informed Buber that he had completed his business and had arrived in Warsaw the night before, adding, "It will not take a little cunning to experience the joy of the celebration."[26] That day, Passover began at sundown. Buber's letter of 28 March was forwarded from Frankfurt to Warsaw, and Heschel could easily meet him that week in Lwow, three days later. They met and Heschel learned that Buber's lectures in flawless Polish were admired by people in several towns where he spoke.[27]

About three weeks later, Heschel received official confirmation from the president of Hebrew Union College of a position as a research fellow in Bible and Jewish philosophy. His salary would be $500 a year, in addition to board and lodging in the college dormitory. Finally he could justify his application for immigration to the United States.[28] Yet in a memorandum to Polish officials written in both English and Polish, dated 18 April, American Vice Consul William H. Cordell explained that Heschel, who was registered in the Warsaw Consulate office as "a non privileged immigrant in the Quota," must wait an additional nine months before his documents could even be examined. The line in front of him was long.

Heschel responded to Morgenstern on 30 April from his mother's Dzika Street address, expressing gratitude for the appointment to Hebrew Union College. Writing for the first time in English, he responded with almost unbearable emotion: "It was very kind of you to think of me and to help in this sorrowful time. I respect your invitation too much to remain unmoved by your proposal. But I must be reserved to my feelings. Allow me solely to express that my gratitude for you is a cordial and deep one. I wish to render my thanks by my thruthful [sic] service on the Jewish science." Heschel went on to explain the "enormous difficulties" he was encountering in getting a visa: "As there are nearly no prospects here, I intend leaving for another country to try and get a visa there."

Heschel was mastering the intricacies of emigration; his future depended on it. London, where he might get a visa, was Heschel's immediate goal. He was in touch with his brother, but Jacob had no money and no civil status in England. Tragically, Heschel's mother and sisters in Warsaw were not qualified for a visa. Only if Heschel left for another country was there hope to get them out as well.

A friend from Frankfurt who also resettled in London was a possible source of help. Heschel wrote to Ruth and Menahem, children of Rabbi Jakob Horovitz, whose home he had often visited. Ruth Horovitz urged Heschel to contact the Chief Rabbi's Religious Emergency Council for German and Austrian Jewry, a British organization established after the November 1938 pogroms for saving rabbis, cantors, and teachers of all affiliations. If the British authorized a transit visa, Heschel might procure an immigrant permit from American Consular authorities in London.

Connections were crucial, for Ruth was friendly with Judith Hertz, eldest daughter of Rabbi Joseph Herman Hertz, chief rabbi of the United Hebrew Congregations of the British Commonwealth and one of the first graduates of the Jewish Theological Seminary in New York. Hertz was an active Zionist and energetic defender of foreign minorities, but also a firm supporter of Orthodoxy in England against Liberal Judaism. This network could save Heschel's life.

Through Ruth Horovitz, Heschel negotiated with the Religious Emergency Council. She wrote Heschel, asking him to name a financial guarantor in London. Heschel's reply was evasive, and he wrote on 2 April, addressing her formally in German as "Sehr gelehrter Fräulein Doktor" (she was unmarried with a doctorate in German literature), explaining that "I want to use my time in England to continue my philosophical work. In Warsaw this is unfortunately impossible. I don't have money, but when I get to England, I won't need any financial help. I read English books quite well and hope to speak English during my stay."

Ruth prevailed upon Judith Hertz, who in turn consulted with her fiancé Rabbi Solomon Schonfeld, who was principal of the Jewish secondary schools movement, rabbi of the Orthodox Adath Yisrael Synagogue, and a German member of the Agudat Israel directing the Emergency Council's day-to-day operations.[29] Thanks to their repeated efforts, Heschel's transit visa to London was approved by the Home Office. By 20 June he received confirmation from the British Consul and could at last leave Warsaw.

But there was still no way to enter the United States. Heschel's correspondence with Julian Morgenstern in Cincinnati became increasingly desperate. The president of Hebrew Union College continued to exert extraordinary efforts on behalf of his "College in Exile."

For Heschel it was a day-to-day struggle. Morgenstern received Heschel's plea on 15 May and wrote to him in Warsaw, explaining that "since sending off our letters to you difficulties have arisen in the matter of securing visas for the scholars whom we desire to bring over to the Hebrew Union College."[30] He expected to visit Washington, D.C., to negotiate personally with the Chief of the Visa Division of the Department of State.

Before he received this discouraging prognosis, Heschel wrote Morgenstern again on 1 June. He was feeling panic and wanted to be assured that Morgenstern understood how precarious his situation was. After quoting in German Buber's encouraging words to him, Heschel wrote: "I hesitated for a long time, whether I may trouble you with the question as to my visa to US." Grateful enough for the possibility of escape, a sense of delicacy restrained him from requesting additional help.

Heschel again explained how his application from the American Consulate in Stuttgart (where he was number 615 on the Polish quota) was referred to the Warsaw Consulate after his October 1938 expulsion: "That is to say that I am compelled to wait for the visa longer than a year. Such a postponement might destroy my prospects and could have intolerable consequences for me. The stay here is almost impossible." Morgenstern, who did not receive the letter until after his unsuccessful trip to Washington, D.C., marked that passage in the margin.[31]

These struggles affected Heschel's ability to write Buber, himself hardpressed in Jerusalem. On 20 June, the same day his transit visa to London was approved, Heschel finally overcame his compunction and admitted, using a Hebrew phrase, that he was almost overcome by a "low spiritual level and heaviness." Again, work boosted his morale, and he felt invigorated by "two short papers" on prayer he was "forced to submit" for publication.[32]

Heschel's ability to work was not impaired. Invited to submit two essays (or, as he claimed, "forced") by two prestigious institutions, he completed methodological reflections on prayer, one written in Hebrew: "'Al mahut ha-tefillah" (On the essence of prayer), intended for the Mayer Balaban Festschrift in Warsaw; and the other in German, "Das Gebet als Äusserung und Einfühlung" (Prayer as expression and empathy), solicited by Leo Baeck for the *Monatsschrift* in Berlin. Trying again to enlist Buber's support for his spirituality, Heschel hoped that the elder would judge these personal efforts "positively."

Their communication remained friendly. After sharing the good news of his transit visa, Heschel caught up with mutual concerns, asking Buber about the emigration of Eduard Strauss and his family to the United States, a historical work by A. Mieses on Jewish religion, and news about a symposium "under the highly original title, 'The Eternal People,'" as Heschel wryly noted.

Responding to events in Palestine, Heschel shared Buber's anxiety about the Arab revolt and the British attempt to arrive at a partition agreement between Israel and the Palestinian Arabs. Heschel also pondered Buber's "Answer to Gandhi," an open letter which rejected the Mahatma's suggestion that Jews remain in Germany and practice nonviolent passive resistance (*satyagraha*) even unto death.[33] Buber's vivid testimony reanimated their face-to-face encounters: "I didn't read, I heard the words and the tones."[34]

Above all, Heschel confirmed once again his devotion to Jewish spiritual renewal, although teaching in Warsaw did not advance his larger project. Disheartened by his own progress, and pessimistic about the condition of Polish Jewry, Heschel wanted to enlist Allies to resist the alarming forecast. Perhaps Buber, in Palestine, would show the way: "I hope that your influence in the land grows more and more. It is so necessary!" Heschel's final letter from Warsaw ends with that courageous thrust.

Heschel decided to leap. Even without a visa to the United States, he would embark for London and there continue his efforts. There were few if any American quota visas remaining. Only some clergy and academics sponsored by institutions might qualify for non-quota visas. Seeking help for himself formed an unhealable wound, the pain of which cannot be imagined. Heschel feared that exit permits for his mother and sisters in Warsaw were impossible to obtain. He did not vent his feelings in words, but kept his most intimate anguish to himself.

21

Departure and Deliverance (1939–1940)

Dark is the world to me, for all its cities and stars, if not for the breath of compassion that God blew in me when He formed me out of dust and clay, more compassion than my nerves can bear.

Heschel, *Man Is Not Alone* (1951)

HESCHEL, NOW A THIRTY-TWO-YEAR-OLD REFUGEE, REACHED LONDON ON 13 July 1939, welcomed by his brother, Jacob, who had settled there with his wife and daughter in February. Without delay Heschel mailed a note to Jerusalem, sharing yet another defining moment with Martin Buber: "A few hours ago I arrived here, and I feel the need to connect with you in my thoughts. The first impression is already a gain. It has style, this city. Whatever is behind it remains to be looked at more closely." Rhapsodic, Heschel nevertheless remained suspicious of appearances. Amid overwhelming uncertainties, his mission was intact: "Prospects for work here are rather gloomy. But I am glad finally to be here."[1]

During his nine months in London, Heschel consolidated his role as moral and religious witness—despite his lack of institutional support, stable community, or even a national identity. Enduring the pain of leaving his mother and sisters (and many others) behind, he continued the pedagogical mission he shared with Buber, while gathering the strands of his life and seeking a visa to the United States. What preserved the core was his foundational project on prayer and religious consciousness.

Heschel first stayed in the small apartment of his brother, Rabbi Jacob Heshel (as he anglicized the family name), three rooms plus a kitchen and bath.[2] Jacob's young daughter, Thena, shared her parents' bedroom, while other refugees in transit slept on cots in the sitting room, which served as the rabbi's study, or in the dining room, which held another bed. After Heschel rented a room and moved out, cousins from Vienna arrived—Israel Heschel and his sister Mirel, two of the Kopitzhinitzer rebbe's children. Sadly, Israel Heschel, as a "German national" from annexed Vienna, was deported to Australia, almost dying on the boat for refusing to eat nonkosher food.[3] Both Israel and his sister Mirel eventually reached the United States.

Partaking of the family talent for languages, Jacob Heshel began learning English after his arrival and made rapid progress. But five-year-old Thena had a firmer grasp of the idiom. The basement apartment was inhabited by a lovely, very English family, the Watsons. One day Mrs. Watson told Thena, "Do tell your father that he doesn't need to address me as Mrs. Watson, Squire."

"Uncle Avrumele" (as Thena called him) brought cheer to his hosts, and his playful sense of humor lightened their distress. When he arrived, everyone brightened, for the brothers easily created a happy atmosphere, joking and laughing. At Sabbath meals, they sang *zemirot*, Jewish table hymns cherished by their tradition. Once little Thena locked herself in the sitting room and could not get out, refusing to slip the key under the door. Uncle Avrumele saved the day when, amid great merriment, he crawled into the room from a small window on the porch. He teased his niece with his electric shaver, a novelty item which made a loud buzzing noise. Unlike Jacob, who wore a very little beard, Abraham was clean shaven. (Traditionally, Orthodox Jewish men do not use straight razors but can trim their beards with scissors or clippers.)

A Vision and a Visa

Heschel, mindful of his precarious status, sought out influential members of the London Jewish community. He attempted to visit the distinguished scholar Herbert Martin James Loewe, reader in rabbinics at Cambridge University, considered to be a foremost representative of Jewish studies in England.[4] Heschel probably knew of Loewe's negotiations with Leo Baeck and other associates of the Berlin Hochschule to move the institute's library, professors, and academic programs to London. With Baeck's cooperation, Loewe began to transfer the Hochschule's holdings to Britain, but, exhausted by these efforts and his exertions to save refugee Jewish scholars, when Heschel arrived at the professor's home, he was too ill to receive the visitor.[5] Loewe died the following year.

Heschel associated with Rabbi Joseph Hertz, chief rabbi of the United Hebrew Congregations of the British Commonwealth, whose daughter Judith had helped obtain travel documents for him from the Chief Rabbi's Emergency Council. (Hertz, incidentally, opposed the idea of moving the Hochschule to London, which would create a Liberal Jewish academy to compete with the Orthodox Jews' College in London.) Heschel attended Sabbath services at the synagogue where Rabbi Hertz, now retired from the pulpit, sometimes spoke, and he was invited regularly on Sabbath and holidays to the home of a Rabbi Hirsch.[6]

Among the German Jews Heschel met in London was his former teacher from the Berlin Hochschule, Leo Baeck, who was accomplishing many tasks in the city. Heschel, as did many others, attempted to convince the great leader to remain in safe territory. But Baeck insisted upon returning to care for his flock. (Baeck stayed in Berlin until deported in January 1943 to the Theresienstadt concentration camp. He survived and was liberated in 1945.)

Unlike Baeck, Heschel was helpless, with his mother and sisters remaining in Warsaw. Heschel had no pulpit in Germany, no job, no community responsibilities. Despite his Polish passport, he was essentially stateless. Unable to liberate even his closest family, he advanced his two negotiable priorities: obtain a nonquota visa for the United States and contribute to Jewish intellectual and spiritual enrichment.

Heschel sought Buber's emotional support. Worried that some letters were lost, he wrote Buber again barely two weeks after arrival: "I am longing for a few lines from you. Inwardly, I have not been feeling well, for some weeks now. I dream to immerse myself in a larger piece of work. Maybe this dream will come true."[7] Heschel maintained some emotional cohesion by intensifying his focus on a spiritual goal, his far-reaching writing project.

He set to work learning English and apprised Buber of his rapid, insightful assessment of British Jewish life. He was shocked at the apathy (he called it "dreariness") in London. The British community, he felt, succumbed prematurely to Europe's political and moral collapse: "Among the intellectual people, desperation over the fate of Jewry is very fashionable. They are all passive, [but] maybe also receptive to an idea." He diagnosed the disease and was preparing to inject an antidote, his own religious perspective, an "idea." The present influx of German-educated Jewish refugees might revitalize British Jewry, just as migrations of East European Jews, after World War I, brought new energy to the community in Germany.

By mail, Heschel kept up his conversations with Julian Morgenstern of Hebrew Union College in Cincinnati and Martin Buber in Jerusalem. His letters to both men became more frequent and dealt with complex bureaucratic hurdles. He told Buber that, due to the enormous difficulty of obtaining an American visa, he might be forced to remain in London longer than expected, and asked Buber about lectureships for which he might apply.

Heschel received a letter three weeks after it was sent from Cincinnati, dated 5 July and forwarded to London from Heschel's Warsaw address. President Morgenstern explained that, in order to qualify for a nonquota visa as a professor, Heschel must certify two full years of teaching at a comparable institution: "Apparently neither you nor Dr. Rosenthal can comply with this requirement at the present time. I do hope earnestly that I am mistaken in this opinion. It is, however, a matter upon which the American Consul will have to rule." (Franz Rosenthal, orientalist and specialist in Aramaic studies from Berlin, was also stranded in London.) Morgenstern urged Heschel to apply for a quota visa, if he had not already done so.

Holding tight to this lifeline, Heschel replied the very same day (28 July), explaining his situation. His detailed three-page letter shows a surprisingly firm grasp of English, with the inevitable flaws of a nonnative speaker. The refugee rallied all his powers of concentration to master the American rules and regulations.

He first explained to Morgenstern how his two previous years of teaching experience (in Frankfurt and in Warsaw) qualified him for a visa.[8] And he concluded by announcing his intention to write "a philosophical book on the prayer." Referring to his two essays, one in Hebrew, the other in German—already mentioned to Buber—he reminded Morgenstern that "two chapters therefrom will be published before long." And signing off: "With feelings of the most profound respect and gratitude for all you have done for me, I remain, Your most obedient, Abraham Heschel."

A month later, on 1 September 1939, German forces invaded Poland. Hitler's true intentions could no longer be denied. Two days later, on 3 September, Britain declared war on Germany, and a few hours later so did France.

London was in turmoil. Thousands of Jewish children—including Thena Heshel and classmates at her Jewish school—were evacuated to the countryside, where they roomed with families and attended classes. Thena returned home within six weeks while most of the others remained away.

Heschel had escaped from Warsaw just in time. As he stated twenty-five years later, evoking an image from Zechariah (3:2), he felt like "a brand plucked from the fire of an altar to Satan on which my people was burned to death."[9] Reaching London "just six weeks before the disaster began" was his second deliverance; the first was his expulsion from Germany one week before the Kristallnacht pogrom. But there was no solace. While Heschel sought an immigrant visa in London, the German bombardment was destroying his native Warsaw.

There is no way to fathom Heschel's pangs of moral responsibility and desolation. He was cut off from his family; there were no visas for his mother and sisters to join Jacob Heshel in London or to follow his sister Sarah's family, which arrived in New York in February 1939. There were no other sponsors. Heschel himself was not yet authorized for any destination and risked deportation from London. His sorrow deepened, echoed only years later in a written prayer, embedded in his book of religious philosophy: "God, I am alone with my compassion within my limbs. Dark are my limbs to me; if not for Thee, who could stand such anguish, such disgrace?"[10]

It was a dismal end to the Jewish year. On 10 September he wrote to Eduard Strauss, deploring the destruction: "It is shameful that the world could not find another solution."[11] Rosh Hashanah 5700 began three days later. Heschel sent brief, warm greetings to Julian Morgenstern: "As the year is drawing to a close, I beg to express you my most cordial wishes, [Hebrew abbreviation: New Year's greetings]! God have mercy on His world!"[12]

Heschel's Europe was being demolished. He learned the details from newspapers, radio broadcasts, conversations with other refugees. Reports swiftly reached the United States, such as this one.

18 September

Report Hitler orders towns with over 25% Jewish population bombarded. Warsaw Jewish quarter destroyed by Nazi bombs. Jews of Orlowa, Bogumin, Oswiecim and Chrzanow ordered by Nazis to leave homes within eight days.[13]

Abraham Weiss, Heschel's colleague from the Warsaw Institute, contributed this account:

> On Wednesday, September 27, the eve of the Feast of Tabernacles, the heroic defense of Warsaw came to an end, and the city bowed before the invader. With that surrender began a new chapter in the Book of Martyrs, a chapter concerned more especially with Jews. Warsaw lay in ruins. Among the Jews, it was impossible to find a single person who had not been bereaved of relatives or friends. The dead lay unburied in cemeteries. Many were still concealed beneath the debris, and to this day, not all of the bodies have been recovered. One stumbled over the wounded and dying at every step and did what one could to remove them to hospitals. Most of the latter, however, have been destroyed, and the few which remained were without water or light, and lacked food and medical supplies.[14]

On 29 September, under the German-Soviet partition agreement, Poland was divided into a German area, a Soviet area, and "Poland-in-Exile."

Henceforth inseparable in Heschel's consciousness were two irreconcilable realities: the destruction of the cultures which nurtured his spirit and trained his thinking—and his loyalty to the God of pathos. Heschel's American mission emerged from that contradiction. "This is the task," he wrote years later, "in the darkest night to be certain of the dawn, certain of the power to turn a curse into a blessing, agony into a song."[15]

Joining the College in Exile

The world anticipated even greater devastation during the next weeks. Meanwhile, president Morgenstern of Hebrew Union College, patient but unswerving, lobbied for his stranded "College in Exile." Morgenstern visited Washington, D.C., several times to obtain visas to rescue these scholars.

Heschel's case was advancing. Morgenstern mailed two letters dated 21 September 1939, which Heschel received in late October. Responding to the State Department's demand that only teachers (not researchers) could qualify for a nonquota visa, Morgenstern changed the title of Heschel's appointment and augmented the initial annual salary of $500. Morgenstern's personal communication explained that the American Consulate in London had "received positive instructions to issue no more visas"; Heschel should apply for a visa in Dublin, Ireland.[16]

Morgenstern's official letter of appointment—which saved Heschel's life—listed the particulars:

> It gives me very great pleasure to extend to you, in the name of the Hebrew Union College, located in Cincinnati, Ohio, a call as teaching member of the Faculty, with the title of Instructor in Bible, for an indeterminate period, at a salary of $1,500.00 for the first year. By the term "indeterminate period" I mean that it is our intention that this appointment shall be permanent, subject of course to the rules and regulations of the Hebrew Union College regularly governing the appointment and permanence in office of members of its Faculty. I am sending a copy of this letter to the American Consul in Dublin by this same mail. I would urge therefore that you contact the Consul immediately in order to expedite as much as possible your departure for the United States.

More than two months passed before Morgenstern was able, arduously, to rectify Heschel's visa predicament. In September, the HUC President informed the American Consul General in Dublin, Henry H. Balch, that full-time teaching positions were extended to Heschel and Franz Rosenthal, both temporarily residing in London. Balch answered on 13 October, stating that he referred the cases back to London, since the Dublin office possessed no record of their applications. Morgenstern, skillfully wielding influence and polite intimidation, responded by mentioning his personal conversations with the "Hon. A. M. Warren, Chief of the Visa Division, Department of State, Washington, D.C."[17]

While these bureaucratic maneuvers were taking place, the horrors continued:

2 October

Mass suicides of Jews reported from Warsaw following the city's surrender.

6 October

Eyewitness accounts report high Jewish casualties as result of Nazi attacks on Jewish districts. Hundreds of thousands reported fleeing to frontiers. Fear expressed for safety of Chief Rabbi Moses Schorr and members of Warsaw rabbinate.

An epidemic of typhus and cholera in Warsaw reported from Berlin. Moving pictures of Polish Jews being harshly treated in labor camps shown in Berlin, according to Kaunas, Lithuania, report.

Aged religious Jews executed as "snipers," according to photographic evidence by Polish Jewish refugees in Rumania ... Courtyards of Warsaw apartment houses reported to have been turned into burial grounds for lack of space in Jewish cemeteries. Warsaw famine-stricken Jewish quarters not aided, while Nazis feed Poles and Germans.[18]

On 1 November, Heschel wrote to Morgenstern, explaining that he had heard from the consul in Dublin and completed his visa application in London. By now Heschel's immigrant English had nearly reached a level of eloquence, despite the usual errors of prepositions and usage, as he humbly expressed his gratitude: "I beg to acknowledge the receipt of your letter of September 21 and the letter designed for presentation to the American Consul. I am struck with admiration of your indefatigable efforts for the sake of Jewish Learning. I am very much sensible of your kindness. It is at once a great encouragement and a great responsibility to enjoy your confidence."

Heschel, too, exerted "indefatigable efforts for the sake of Jewish Learning." By the end of 1939, he began to organize what he called an "Institute for Jewish Learning" in London, similar in conception to the Mittelstelle program in Frankfurt. On 22 November, in an uncharacteristically small script, Heschel wrote Buber about his projects, implying that he had overcome despair:

In this life on the narrow border between grief and confidence, it is hard to write a letter. The pain at what is happening and what took place is still so intense that one must struggle quite hard not to become enslaved by agony.

I need not tell you that hardly a day passes when my thoughts do not turn toward you. It is a great pity that I know nothing of your statements and your influence.

I am now trying to initiate an educational project for the roughly 1500 people who are here *Hakhsharah* [in Hebrew, preparation for Palestine]. I do not quite have the chance to do any concentrated work.[19]

He then explained his responsibility for a considerable project, preparing over a thousand young people for emigration to Palestine, the *Hakhsharah*. But he complained that these and other pedagogical tasks diverted him from his own relfections. Yet, still affiliating himself with Buber, Heschel's post-script requested copies of Buber's final lecture at the Frankfurt Lehrhaus, entitled "The

Election of Israel," and other writings to distribute in London.[20] Education was an answer to, if not the remedy for, hopelessness.

Three weeks later, from this increasingly "narrow border," Heschel faced the abyss. His mother and sisters were overwhelmed in the war's cruel beginning. The September invasion of Poland was followed by the German bombardment which destroyed most of Warsaw. The Nazi occupation brought disease, starvation, looting, and systematic persecutions. In November widespread epidemics were reported. On 13 December 1939, he confided to Buber the anguish of his first private, war-related loss: among the countless dangers, his sister Esther Sima was killed in a bombing raid.[21] His three-line message ends warmly, expressing his feelings of isolation: "I would like so much to talk with you!"[22] A telegram from his mother had informed him of the personal catastrophe. Heschel's brief message to Buber interweaves gratitude, intolerable sorrow, and the solace of abiding friendship. How delicate their understanding remained for Heschel thus to confide his grief.

There is no hierarchy within Heschel's complicated sorrow. His Yiddish poem of 1933, "On the Day of Hate," saw God's Ineffable Name desecrated, but how could one anticipate to what extent? His Hasidic world, as well as his family, was shattered. An article in the New York Yiddish newspaper the *Forward* (1 December 1939) describes what Heschel knew from many sources:

> Warsaw is a city in ruins, a large village, destroyed as if by a hurricane—a city in which there are more ruined structures than whole ones.
>
> The silence of a cemetery hovers over it. Streets are deserted, for those who still remain are afraid to leave their apartments. The Germans seize them on the streets and draft them for hard labor. . . .
>
> Pulling and cutting off the beards of Jews has become a daily occurrence. No Jew is spared. Even the oldest rabbis of Warsaw had their beards cut off. This disgrace is being inflicted by members of the Gestapo themselves who are instituting a reign of terror in the Polish capital. . . .
>
> Even the rabbi of Gora Kalwaria [the Gerer rebbe] was not spared. His house was searched by agents of Gestapo, the beard of the great saint was shorn off, and for four hours he was tortured in a most inhuman fashion. Regarding the raid on Rabbi Kahane, I was told that the first time several Gestapo agents entered his house, they cut off his beard and ransacked his house. They did their job thoroughly. Books were flung from the shelves and trampled on. "This is Jewish dirt," they taunted the rabbi. "In these all evil is to be found. They must be utterly destroyed." Then they took out a Holy Scroll [of the Torah] from the rabbi's synagogue and ground their heavy boots into it, at the same time mocking and jeering at the rabbi.[23]

Heschel as a boy knew the Gerer rebbe, Rabbi Avraham Mordecai Alter, his uncle's close friend and ally and Jewish Poland's most influential spiritual leader. The age of Hasidism—Heschel's formative culture—had reached this ignominious end.[24]

Jews were being killed, imprisoned, or herded into walled districts in cities controlled by the Germans. The year 1939 finished as the neighborhood where Heschel spent his childhood and youth was enclosed in the Muranow Ghetto: "Cruelties inflicted upon the Jews of Warsaw assumed unbelievable proportions. After driving Jewish residents into a ghetto early in November, the area was barricaded from the rest of the city and German soldiers barred from entering. . . . Refugees from the city revealed (Dec. 17) that an average of 500 Jews died each day as a result of disease and starvation."[25]

How could a bystander remain sane? How could Heschel continue his religious teaching? Could he justify his faith that God cares about humankind? Without being able to penetrate that mystery, only naked facts can suggest the impasse he faced while preparing to leave for the United States:

> As a consequence of Nazi atrocities more than 2,500 Jews were reported (Dec. 17) to have committed suicide. About 1,300 were residents of Warsaw and 600 of Lodz. . . . About 17,000 Jews and Poles were executed by order of German military courts, and 23,000 arrested in the period between the outbreak of the war and the first week of December, a Paris dispatch of Jan. 7, 1940, disclosed. Altogether, about 250,000 Jews were estimated to have been killed by disease, starvation and Nazi firing squads, according to the Jewish *White Book* issued by the World Jewish Congress on Dec. 17 [1939]. The *White Book* also estimated that 30,000 Jews had perished in Warsaw during and after the Nazi occupation, and that a majority of the 40,000 Jews who attempted to escape during the bombardment were also killed.[26]

A London Lehrhaus

On his thirty-third birthday, 11 January 1940, Abraham Heschel, essentially alone, faced personal peril and inconceivable loss. Amid the collapse of his European homes, suspended between possible death and certain exile, he somehow kept his spiritual world intact. While awaiting final word on his visa, he succeeded in establishing an adult education program.

The purpose of Heschel's "Institute for Jewish Learning," as announced in London's leading community newspaper, *The Jewish Chronicle,* was "to introduce all ages and classes of Jew to the history and tradition of their forebears, by means of a cultural approach through lectures by reputed scholars."[27] Heschel's organizing abilities seemed to be at their peak.

Heschel gathered for his "Lehrhaus" a distinguished group of Judaic scholars and leaders, some of them refugees, others established in England.[28] They included the important British scholars Arthur Marmorstein, a specialist in rabbinic theology and professor at Jews' College in London since 1912; the prolific scholar Norman Bentwich, a prominent Zionist, lawyer, and diplomat who served on the League of Nations Commission for Jewish Refugees from Germany; and the British author and editor Joseph Leftwich, who translated works by Yiddish authors.

There were also East European Jews such as the neo-Kantian philosopher and Talmud specialist, Samuel Atlas, who had taught at the Warsaw Jewish Institute and emigrated to London in 1933 (Atlas joined the faculty of Hebrew Union College in Cincinnati a year after Heschel);[29] Aaron Steinberg, a cofounder of the Berlin YIVO in 1924 who moved to London in 1934; Leo Koenig (pseudonym of Leyb Yaffe, a Yiddish author and journalist, who lived in London; Salomon Adler-Rudel, director of the Welfare Organization of Eastern Jews in Berlin, who moved to London in 1936 where he administered the Central British Fund and helped rescue countless Jews; and Heschel's former professor at the University of Berlin, Eugen Mittwoch.

The Institute opened on 30 January 1940 with two speeches: Heschel inaugurated the program with a lecture entitled "The Idea of Jewish Education."[30] The other speaker was the prestigious Selig Brodetsky, mathematician and Zionist, professor at the University of Leeds, and head of the political department of the Jewish Agency in London. The audience was very responsive, though opinions were mixed.

But the next day, on 31 January, the American Consulate in London granted Heschel a nonquota visa and he declared his intention to become a U.S. citizen. That very day, he joyfully informed Morgenstern: "I am very much delighted with the prospect of being soon in Cincinnati. I will lose no time in arranging my journey and I will see to start as soon as possible."[31]

Heschel also resolved his relationship with Buber. This was a propitious time for Heschel, graciously but firmly, to reassert his autonomy in relation to his mentor. The following week (7 February) Heschel sent Buber his final letter from Europe.[32] As he had in July 1935 when *Die Prophetie* was about to appear, Heschel candidly confronted the philosopher of dialogue. First he reacted to an essay on the prophet Amos which Buber published in Leonhard Ragaz's journal:

Many thanks for your letter of 4 January and your essay from the *Neue Wege*. In it you present a theology of Amos as seen from the concrete situation. (What you had said about these things in the winter of 1934/35, when you first spoke to me about my essay on prophecy, became clear to me.) I found many excellent things in it. Some issues, though, should also be clarified, even for a reader like me, as for example the very important term, the "unity of justice and subsistence." The wealth of thoughts you have placed only into subordinate clauses deserves a better lot, i.e., to be told in more detail. I allow myself to say all this because I myself would be so happy to have soon in hand your work *The Prophetic Faith* completed!!! (By the way: The sentences in parentheses substantially hinder the process of reading. Maybe you should add them to the footnotes.)[33]

Heschel overcame any inhibitions persisting after Buber's initial rebuff of his thesis six years earlier as he recalled their discussion on the prophets, around December 1934–February 1935. Appreciating Buber's historical approach ("seen from the concrete situation"), he also points to the elder's sometimes severe difficulty in achieving clarity of expression, and he urged Buber to improve the style of his new book. Having passed far beyond hurt and resentment, Heschel's almost patronizing advice still appears to be at least potentially aggressive.

Then Heschel confessed the feelings of vulnerability that his assertiveness served to cover. With candor, he thanked Buber for his subsequent support, all the more appreciated because of his own self-doubt: "Now I may reveal to you that I was feeling quite insecure when you appointed me to Frankfurt. I was worried about failing pedagogically and that out of kindness you would not immediately dismiss me. . . . Today I know now that you never dismissed me at all, and you even wrote to C[incinnati], which also had its effect."

Heschel then returned to their common task of spiritual renewal. Enclosing a list of lectures planned for his Institute for Jewish Learning, he deplored some negative reactions to his religious point of view:

My opening lecture, "The Idea of Jewish Education" (which I myself consider to be very good!), caused indignation, because I supported an inherently Jewish-spiritual concept of education. Those standing on the "left" found "reactionary thinking." For me, the ignorance and blindness of these people is the wonder of the century. I was a bit angry. Others understood the implications. Brodetsky is working energetically toward a quick printing.— The lectures themselves are well attended!

Echoing his Rosh Hashanah sermons from Berlin—which challenged German-Jewish "Marranos" to pursue inner Jewish integrity—Heschel's spiritual perspective offended some listeners. (In 1936, he wrote: "There is no return to Judaism without repentance before God. Faithfulness to Him and to the community to the point of utmost readiness remains the fundamental idea of Jewish education.")[34] He felt confident in his oppositional mode of teaching and hoped that his program would survive his departure: "If I were an *erlikher yid* [in Yiddish, an honest or genuine Jew], I would stay here to preserve this important institution in the mental desert of London."

But the Institute ceased to exist after Heschel's departure. The first series of lectures was to end on 20 March. By then Heschel already boarded his ship. He transported his "idea of Jewish education" to yet another "mental desert"—the United States.[35] Heschel's final letter from London concludes with a mixture of hope and terror, anticipating his new life: "I will venture onto the sea and think of the sea of suffering in Poland. Best wishes and goodbye! *auf Wiedersehen!*"

Legacies of Renewal

During Heschel's transit, in November 1939, Henry Corbin's French translations from *Die Prophetie* appeared in *Hermès,* its issue devoted to Islamic mysticism.[36] Corbin's preface, dated October (barely a month after the Nazi invasion of Poland), proclaimed the need to "unveil" the transcendent Source of ultimate meaning, challenging "the abyss, where one might be annihilated." He enlisted Heschel and others to discredit nihilism by reconciling the Abrahamic religions—Judaism, Christianity, and Islam.

Heschel's two essays on prayer, combining academic analysis and personal testimony, summarize his German and Polish legacy. He contributed "Prayer as Expression and Empathy" to the *Monatsschrift,* epitome of Wissenchaft des Judentums in Germany. He prepared "The Essence of Prayer" for a volume honoring Mayer Balaban, co-founder of the Warsaw Institute of Jewish Science.

Seeking to convey the reality of piety, "Prayer as Expression and Empathy" delimits the "essence" of spiritual consciousness, as did his doctoral dissertation.[37] This sometimes graceful, sometimes demanding essay lauds the potential of liturgical words: "Praying means grasping and holding on to a word, the end of a string, so to speak, that leads to God. . . . The purer the willingness, the deeper the word penetrates."[38] Regular worship achieves its potential when the person's *empathy* with the inherited text generates spontaneous *ex-*

pression. Echoing his 1938 speech to the Quakers, he trusts that God emerges when contact with transcendent reality feels impossible, "like a cause of discontent generating a counterforce."

"The Essence of Prayer" also justifies the power of piety as a metaphysical "event" transforming our vision of the world. The praying person is "heroic," for, "intentionally or not, he puts his life in danger. He surrenders himself to the One to whom his being and essence belong; he makes a decision, he accuses God, gives notice, confesses himself, makes a vow, accepts the yoke of His rule, pawns his soul, accepts an acquisition, and seals a covenant."[39] Prayer is a total commitment, affecting God as it affects the person.

This was Heschel's "idea of Jewish education" and his testimony to a shattered world. He was assured that prayer could connect us with God, the ultimate source of human energy. Both publications were confiscated by the Nazis and proved to be the swansong of his teachers' generation. Yet the destruction of European Jewry, which he learned about after he arrived in the United States, only inspired him to expand the scope of his mission.

All of Heschel's European writings anticipate his two foundational books in English, *Man Is Not Alone* and *God in Search of Man:* "We have to press the religious consciousness with questions, compelling man to understand and unravel the meaning of what is taking place in his life as it stands at the divine horizon. By penetrating the consciousness of the pious man, we may conceive the reality behind it."[40]

Entering the United States

Heschel's first thirty-three years in Europe made him the religious philosopher, biblical interpreter, and social activist he became in the United States. His theology of divine pathos was complete by 1933, and when he left Warsaw in July 1939 he had formulated his philosophy of prayer and piety. Yet only speakers of Yiddish could share his truly autobiographical self-portrait, *Der Shem Hameforash: Mentsh,* which expressed his deepest aspirations. His commanding theme was repentance—readiness before God.

In Europe, had the Second World War not occurred, Dr. Abraham Heschel might have become a notable professor, writing for specialists as well as general readers. His book on the prophets was praised in Europe and on the American continent. His studies of Bible, medieval Jewish thinkers, Hasidism, and phenomenology of religious consciousness frame a philosophy of religion. And his popular biographies of Maimonides, Talmudic rabbis, and Abravanel made tradition relevant to contemporaries. Associated with Martin Buber, he was advancing German Jewish renewal.

He now faced the task of adopting a new culture and a new language. Headed for the United States, on 9 March 1940 "Abraham Heszel" boarded the Cunard White Star liner *Lancastria* at Liverpool, England.[41] Among the 480 passengers, approximately 360 were classified as German Jewish refugees. The ship's manifest outlined Heschel's tangible identity: "Occupation—professor; Nationality—Polish; Race or people—Hebrew; Complexion—dark; Hair—black; Eyes—brown; Height—5′6″; Final destination—Cincinnati, Ohio."

During the twelve-day crossing of the Atlantic, in this period of impending world war, there were terrifying moments. Violent storms battered the vessel, and waves smashed through several portholes with tremendous noise. Crew and passengers alike feared that a torpedo was detonating.

On 21 March the *Lancastria* docked in New York. Heschel was met by his cousin, Mordecai Shlomo Friedman, the Boyaner rebbe who emigrated from Vienna, and his son Israel, then a social worker in Harlem. Heschel resided for almost three weeks with the family of his sister Sarah and her husband, Rabbi Abraham Joshua Heschel, the rebbe of Kopitzhinitz, at 132 Henry Street on the Lower East Side of Manhattan. (Sarah's family had arrived from Vienna the year before.)

Within hours of landing in New York City, Heschel wrote to Hebrew Union College president Julian Morgenstern, using the ship's stationery. He informed his benefactor, "I have just arrived in New York! *Barukh Hashem!* [in Hebrew, Thank God!] I would like to make my respects to you. Thank you very much." He could hardly find the words to acknowledge his deliverer. The next day was Heschel's first Sabbath in the United States.

The festival of Purim began two days later. For these Hasidic refugees, joy at the Persian Jews' deliverance from Haman highlighted their grief at loved ones recently deceased in Europe and their anguish for those left behind. Heschel's sister Esther Sima had perished in Warsaw and his mother and other sister Gittel remained in the city's Ghetto. Another sister, Devorah Miriam, and her husband still lived in Nazi-dominated Vienna.

There was no way for Heschel, himself without status, to help his family in Europe. But he began immediately to do what he could, build his independence as a future American citizen and assemble an academic network. Receiving mail at the American Express office on Fifth Avenue, he explored libraries and contacted prominent figures—among them the biblical scholar William Foxwell Albright of the Johns Hopkins University and Louis Finkelstein, president of the Jewish Theological Seminary.[42] The latter contact eventually proved to be most fruitful.

Shortly before midnight on 9 April 1940, Heschel boarded an all-night train to Cincinnati, Ohio. He arrived at Hebrew Union College the next afternoon and settled in a dormitory room, the lodgings Morgenstern had promised.[43] Sheltered in the heartland, he was now "Abraham Heschel, Instructor in Bible," rebuilding a life and a career.[44]

22
Epilogue

All this has come upon us, Though we have not forgotten Thee, Or been false to Thy covenant. Our heart has not turned back, Nor have our steps departed from Thy way . . . for Thy sake we are slain. . . . Why dost Thou hide Thy face?

Psalm 44, quoted by Heschel, *The Prophets* (1962)

HESCHEL WROTE VERY LITTLE ABOUT HIS LIFE IN EUROPE, AND VIRTUALLY nothing about his personal losses. But the bare facts point to a heavy burden of good fortune. Three times he barely eluded death or extreme peril. In November 1938 he missed "Bloody Thursday"—the so-called Kristallnacht pogrom—by being expelled from Germany the week before. In July 1939, he reached London from Warsaw "just six weeks" before the Nazi invasion. Now sheltered in Cincinnati, a symbolic bridge to his cherished world was destroyed.

The Cunard liner *Lancastria*, which carried Heschel to safety, returned to Europe, where it was rededicated as a troop transport. Ten weeks after Heschel's arrival in New York, on 17 June 1940, as a bitter epilogue to his escape, he was spared yet another catastrophe. On 26 July, the *New York Times* reported that the ship that had saved the lives of thousands had been bombarded and sunk by German and Italian planes.[1]

> More than 2,500 British soldiers, women and children went down aboard the old Cunard cruise ship Lancastria to die in a blazing sea of oil, singing "There'll Always Be an England," on June 17 during the evacuation of the British Expeditionary Force from France.

The *Lancastria*'s devastation was the worst disaster in shipping history to date.[2] About 5,300 people waited on board the liner at the Saint-Nazaire anchorage. British service personnel were being withdrawn from France in anticipation of the advancing German troops. About 3,000 people were killed by bombs or machine-gun fire, drowned in thick oil, or burned to death by incendiaries. The ship capsized in fifteen minutes and quickly sank. The following day France surrendered to Hitler.

From 1940 on, piecing together his life, Heschel learned of the deaths of many people he loved. Heschel's mourning for individuals remained private, memorialized in silence.

Max Erik (1898–1937)
He settled in the Soviet Union in 1929, following the party line. Arrested in 1936, he was exiled to prison in Siberia where he perished the following year.

Moyshe Kulbak (1896–c. 1940)
After emigrating to Minsk in 1928, Kulbak became an official "Soviet" writer. He was arrested in 1937 and perished in a prison camp.

Moses Schorr (1874–1941)
After the German invasion of Warsaw, he fled eastward and was captured by the Russians. Transported to prison, he died in Uzbekistan.

Hillel Zeitlin (1872–1943)

While preparing for deportation to Treblinka, wrapped in his tallit and tef-filin and clutching his copy of the Zohar, Zeitlin was shot by the Nazis on the eve of Rosh Hashanah.

Rabbi Menahem Zemba (1883–1943)

Heroic rabbi of the Warsaw Ghetto, supporting the uprising against the Nazis. He was shot and killed leading his five-year-old grandson by the hand across the street.[3]

Yosef Yashunsky (1881–1943)

He left Vilna in 1929 to become director of ORT, joining the Judenrat in the Warsaw Ghetto. When he refused to give the Gestapo lists of Jews, his sons were shot before his eyes; he and his wife were deported to Treblinka and murdered there.

Edmund (Menahem) Stein (1895–1943)

He remained in German-occupied Warsaw, where he organized cultural events and lectured on Greek thought. His wife and son were deported to Treblinka and killed. He was deported to Trawniki, near Lublin, and mur-dered.

Leo Hirsch (1903–1943)

He died in a labor camp.[4]

Heschel did acknowledge his intimate pain in dedications to some of his books. The epigraph of his central work of activism—*The Prophets* (1962)—is from Psalm 44 ("Why dost Thou hide Thy face?"), and he dedicated the book "to the martyrs of 1940–45." Instead of emphasizing the horrors, Heschel pro-claimed the prophets' antidotes to cruelty and racism: fervent devotion to holi-ness, compassion, and ethical responsibility.

But only for those who knew Hebrew and Yiddish—the languages of his es-sential identity—did he memorialize the names of people closest to his heart. In 1962, he dedicated his study of Talmud, *Torah min ha-shamayim* (The theology of ancient Judaism), written in rich rabbinic Hebrew, to his martyred family: "To the memory of my saintly mother, Rivka Reizel, and to the memory of my sisters, Devorah Miriam, Esther Sima, and Gittel, who perished in the Holocaust, May their Souls Be Kept Among the Immortals."[5]

In 1942 Heschel learned that his mother had died of a heart attack when the Nazis stormed the apartment on Dzika Street. His sister Gittel also died in the Warsaw Ghetto. Devorah Miriam, another sister, was deported with her husband to Theresienstadt in 1942 and in 1944 was murdered in Auschwitz.[6] Of his sis-ters, only Sarah, who had moved to New York, survived.

Heschel reviewed his European life in dedications to his final work, written in Yiddish and published after his death, *Kotsk: a gerangl far emesdikeyt* (1973, Kotzk: The struggle for integrity). He never forgot his gratitude for these people who supported his decisive transitions:

Bezalel Levy, May the Lord Avenge His Blood
Yitzhak Levin, Blessed Be His Memory
Professor David Koigen, Blessed Be His Memory
Erich Reiss, Blessed Be His Memory
Leo Hirsch, Blessed Be His Memory
Professor Levi Ginzberg, Blessed Be His Memory[7]

These companions were gone. But in a way his internal battle as a ten-year-old in Warsaw never stopped. He remained a man divided between faith and anguish, between confidence in God and abhorrence of human weakness and deliberate evil: "To live both in awe and consternation, in fervor and horror, with my conscience on mercy and my eyes on Auschwitz, wavering between exaltation and dismay? I had no choice: my heart was in Medzibozh, my mind in Kotzk."[8] What was subsequently called the Holocaust only magnified his fervor for social justice and his reverence for the divine human image.

During his thirty years in the United States, Abraham Joshua Heschel defended human sanctity against our resolute mediocrity and barbarism. His European writings, in fact, had been conceived during periods of widespread economic and political danger: poetry in Warsaw and Vilna between two world wars, and a doctoral dissertation expressing his prophetic vision during the consolidation of Nazi dictatorship. His subsequent biographies of Maimonides, rabbinic sages, and Abravanel all confront the threat of imminent expulsion. In the United States, he maintained his spiritual courage. The triumphs—and the painful defeats—of his prophetic witness revealed the truth of a Hasidic teaching about mourning that Heschel often repeated: "He who stands on a normal rung weeps; he who stands higher is silent; but he who stands on the topmost rung converts his sorrow into song."[9]

Notes

Introduction

1. Reinhold Niebuhr reviewed Heschel's *Man Is Not Alone* in the book review section of the *New York Herald Tribune* (1 April 1951). Kenneth Woodward of *Newsweek* magazine confirmed Heschel's universal appeal: "To recover the prophetic message of ancient Judaism, Heschel has built up a rich, contemporary Jewish theology that may well be the most significant achievement of modern Jewish thought" (31 January 1966).

2. Heschel 1950, *The Earth Is the Lord's*, 91. The next two quotations from 103–4.

3. Heschel 1962, *Prophets*, 5.

Part One. Warsaw

Note to epigraph: Heschel 1971, "In Search of Exaltation," 227.

Chapter 1. Heschel's First Home

Note to epigraph: Heschel.1973, *A Passion for Truth*, xiii.

1. Granfield 1967, 73. For information on Heschel's ancestors and family see Rabinowicz 1989; Bromberg 1963; Shedletsky 1977; Alfasi 1986.
2. Copy obtained by Yitzhak Meir Twersky from the old Sadagora rebbe, R. Israel Sholem Yosef Friedman, in Israel. Heschel Archive, Jewish Theological Seminary.
3. Rabinowicz 1989, 99, also 99–103. In an article, Heschel cites the wedding contract of the Apter rebbe, stating that he was called "Yosheya Heshil" after his ancestor, the rabbi of Kraków, and the name Abraham was added later. ("Unknown Hasidic Documents," 1952; typescript translated from the Yiddish by Zanvel Klein.) Also Rosenstein 1990, 948–49 for anecdotes.
4. Diary; Rabinowicz 1989, 138; cf. Buber 1948, 118, 107–22.
5. Rabinowicz 1989, 99.
6. Heschel 1973, *A Passion for Truth*, xiii. The spelling of Medzibozh has been changed in the text for reasons of consistency.
7. Ibid. "The earliest fascination I can recall is associated with the Baal Shem, whose parables disclosed some of the first insights I gained as a child. He remained a model too sublime to follow yet too overwhelming to ignore" (ibid., xiv).
8. Rabinowicz 1989, 161–66.
9. Heschel's mother thus carried the *yikhus* of Ostillo, Koidanov, Chernobyl, Karlin, and Berditchev.
10. Wunder 1990, 111. Also cited by J. Heshel 1967, 349–52. See also Buber 1948, vol. 2.
11. They were married in 1849. Wunder 1990.
12. Moshe Mordecai Heschel had three brothers: Israel Sholem Joseph (1853–1911), rebbe of Zinkov; Yitzhak Meir (1861–1936), rebbe of Kopitzhinitz, and Meshullam Zusya (1871–1920), rebbe of Medzibozh. Their sisters—Gittel, Chava, and Devorah (whose birth dates were not preserved)—all married rabbis. Chava and Devorah may have been born of her second marriage to her uncle, Dovid Moshe Friedman, the Tchortkover rebbe. (The dates vary in different sources.)

    Israel Sholem Joseph was born in Zinkov, before the family moved to Medzibozh. His name combined two prominent forebears: Israel of Ruzhin and the Ruzhiner rebbe's eldest son, Sholem Joseph of Sadagora, his mother's father. Israel Sholem Joseph Heschel became the rebbe of Medzibozh in 1881, after his father's death, remaining there exactly thirty years—as had the Baal Shem Tov. Israel Sholem Joseph died in 1911 at age fifty-eight.

    Meshullam Zusya was born in Medzibozh and enjoyed an auspicious beginning. His wife was descended from a student of the Baal Shem Tov. After his father's death, Meshullam Zusya inherited the room of the rebbe of Apt. But in 1920, during a pogrom, he was mortally wounded and was buried in Medzibozh. He was the only one of his brothers privileged to rest in the last home of the Baal Shem Tov. Alfasi 1981, 169–71, 178–80, 189–90; Wunder 1990, 735–36.
13. Halkowski 1992, 224.
14. J. Heshel 1967, 352. His grandmother's somewhat rapid remarriage was not unusual, since traditional Jews consider it of highest priority to protect and support widows

and their children. Dovid Moshe had been widowed from his first marriage to Feige Twersky around 1880. His niece Leah Rachel, who already had a large family to care for, lost her husband soon after. Nor was it odd that she married her uncle—and that Dovid Moshe became his own father's son-in-law. Leah Rachel, for her part, then became her grandfather the rebbe's daughter-in-law.

15. Dresner 1985, xxviii, note 35.

16. Interview with Khone Shmeruk: "Heschel *behaved* like a rebbe."

17. Rabinowicz 1988, 269–70. Dates inconsistent, cf. Rabinowicz 1989, 289–95. Jacob Perlow formed his identity from *his* three ancestors: Mordecai of Neshkhitz, whose compassion was such, it was said, that he could feel the birth pangs of a woman in labor within a fifty-mile radius; Mordecai of Lekhovitz, who prayed with such fervor that doctors said he tore a hole in his lung. His blessing was not to fool God, not to fool others, and especially not to fool oneself. Asher of Karlin/Stolin, the son of Aaron the Great of Karlin, the founder of Lithuanian Hasidism, was the third.

18. See Dresner 1974; Buber 1947, vol. 1, 203–34; Rabinowicz 1989; Diary for Heschel's putting on Rabbi Levi Yitzhak's tefillin.

19. This and the next anecdote from Bromberg 1963.

20. Coffin 1977, 289–90. Interview with William Sloane Coffin, Jr.

21. According to Rottenberg, Moshe Mordecai might have married a daughter of Rabbi Eliahu, who had managed the house of his father, Isaac, the rebbe of Zhidachov, and had taken over after he died. It was understood that he wanted to marry his daughter into the house of Ruzhin, and so Moses Mordecai was a perfect candidate. Eliahu was poverty stricken, but learned and deeply pious. He was completely dominated by his mind and lived in a state of permanent *devekut* (attachment to God). Interviews with Rottenberg.

22. Letter from Harry Rabinowicz, 27 February 1992.

23. Heschel's letter to Hofer's widow, dated 3 March 1972, published in the original Yiddish and Hebrew translation in Hofer 1976. Details of neighborhood from Szulim Rozenberg, who knew Hofer in Warsaw and in Russian prison camp. The following descriptions are cited or paraphrased from Hofer, "*Milkhome*—1914" (War—1914), published in *Zukunft* (1967), 381–87.

24. Interview with Thena Heshel Kendall, daughter of Heschel's brother, Jacob.

25. Conversation with Yitzhak Meir Twersky.

26. Interview with Bernard Perlow, son of Nahum Mordecai Perlow and grandson of the Novominsker rebbe, Heschel's uncle.

27. Bromberg 1963, 115.

28. Interview with Thena Heshel Kendall; also de Pomiane 1985, 123.

29. Hofer 1967. Rabbi Israel Hopstein, the Maggid of Kozienice (born 1733 in Opatow, after his mother was blessed by the Baal Shem Tov), died in 1815. Rabinowicz 1988, 114–20.

Note to epigraph: Heschel 1942, "An Analysis of Piety," 302; repr. Heschel 1950, *Not Alone*, 287; repr. Heschel 1996, *Grandeur and Spiritual Audacity: Essays*, ed. Susannah Heschel.

30. "It was because of the advice of his spiritual mentor, Reb David Moshe, his uncle, the rebbe of Tchortkov, son of Reb Israel of Ruzhin, that he took up residence in Poland" (Heschel 1973, *A Passion for Truth*, xiii). The following story is cited from Alfasi 1981, 169–71.

31. Heschel 1972, "Hasidism as a New Approach to Torah," 21. Quotation slightly edited; repr. *Moral Grandeur and Spiritual Audacity*, 38.

32. Diary.

33. Heschel 1942, "Analysis of Piety," 301; cf. Heschel 1951, *Man Is Not Alone*, 286; 1996, *Moral Grandeur and Spiritual Audacity*, 312.

34. Interview with Yehiel Hofer.

35. Interview with Thena Heshel Kendall.

36. Hofer 1967, 81.

37. Heschel 1969, "Teaching Jewish Theology," 5.

38. This and the next quotation are from Hofer 1967.

39. Singer 1984, 6.

Chapter 2. Early Studies and Catastrophes

Note to epigraph: Heschel 1950, *The Earth Is the Lord's*, 47.

1. Heschel's curriculum vitae prepared for Hebrew Union College in 1939 provides the only documentary evidence of his childhood education: "From my earliest youth I have received a thorough Hebrew and general Jewish education (especially in the Hebrew language, Bible, Talmud and Talmudic literature) under tuition of distinguished teachers and privately at various schools in my native town, foremost among them being, the Rabbinical Seminary 'Messiwtha'" [*sic*]. Heschel Archive, Jewish Theological Seminary.

2. When Shlomo Hayim was sixteen, he wrote a treatise entitled *Tosafot Hayim* (The commentaries of Hayim) on minor tractates of the Talmud, which he sent to distinguished scholars for their approbation. Impressed, they endorsed the work, believing that the author was a ranking scholar. It was never published because his father, Jacob Perlow, learning of the ruse, did not allow it to appear in print during his lifetime. Even afterward, out of respect for his father's earlier wishes, Shlomo Hayim kept this work in manuscript form.

  Shlomo Hayim married his first cousin, a daughter of his uncle Joshua Heschel Perlow, rebbe of Bolekhov (in Polish, Bolechow). After his father-in-law's death, he became rebbe of Bolekhov, loved and honored, "for he was a person of great gifts and piety, full of Torah and holiness, humility and simplicity and love for every Jew." His manner of prayer followed the style of Stolin and Koidanov, in the sense of "all my bones speak." "His voice was sweet, drawing the hearts of the worshippers to their Father in Heaven. His *hitlahavut* (ecstasy) and outcries were common even during the ordinary weekday *Minha* (afternoon) service." His house was open to the poor.

He fulfilled the admonition literally: "Let the poor be welcome into our house, receiving them with love." Wunder 1990, 252–55.

3. S. Heschel 1996, *Moral Grandeur and Spiritual Audacity*, ix.

4. Interviews with Mrs. Joel Teitelbaum (Nehama Perlow, a daughter of the Novominsker rebbe) and Jacob Perlow.

5. Interview with Israel Heschel; see Roskies and Roskies 1979; Zborowski and Herzog 1952, 88–104, "From the Kheyder to the Grave."

6. Heschel 1950, *The Earth Is the Lord's*, 89.

7. Interview with Jacob Perlow, the present Novominsker rebbe.

8. Interview with Yehiel Hofer, 1960.

9. The other Gerer *shtiebl* on Nalewki was much larger, where about two to three hundred students gathered to learn. Interviews with Israel Heschel, Rabbi Cywiak. The following information has also been gathered from Abraham Zemba, "Shtieblakh in Warsaw" (in Hebrew), in Mirsky 1956, 355–63.

10. Heschel 1950, *The Earth Is the Lord's*, 46.

11. See Kaplan 1996.

12. Gold, "Religious Education in Poland," in Gutman et al., 1989, 272–82.

13. Even the youngest boys remained in school for ten to twelve hours a day, five days a week and a half day on Friday, before the Sabbath. Serious students would spend extra hours Thursday night to make up for the time spent on Sabbath celebrations that began Friday afternoon.

14. Heschel 1969, "Teaching Jewish Theology," 4–5.

15. Heschel 1951, *Sabbath*, 66.

16. Heschel 1950, *The Earth Is the Lord's*, 9.

17. Diary, 13.

18. See the excellent book Schachter-Shalomi 1991.

19. The following observations from Diary, 39.

20. This and the following quotation from Heschel 1950, *The Earth Is the Lord's*, 52.

21. Heschel was especially fascinated with *Midrash Rabba* (in the Vilna edition, two folio volumes) as a young boy. Interview with Marshall Meyer.

22. Diary.

23. Schachter-Shalomi 1991, 94–95.

24. Heschel 1933, "*Palasn in der tsayt*" (Palaces in time), Schachter trans., 31.

25. This and the following are quoted or paraphrased from Hofer 1967.

26. Alfasi 1981: "The regular schedule of the court was changed at that time, so that any draftee would get immediate entry to receive a blessing from him. He prayed and gave them amulets to protect them. They left with full confidence. Years later the Hasidim said that not a single man who saw the rebbe before he was sent to the front died there." Cf. Rabinowicz 1988.

27. Elbogen 1944, 453.

28. Heschel 1967, "The Moral Outrage of Vietnam," 56.

29. Yitzhak Meir Heschel married Gittel Friedman, daughter of Mordecai Shraga, rebbe of Husyatin, one of the Ruzhiner rebbe's six sons. Advised by his uncle, Dovid Moshe of Tchortkov, to remain in the region, Yitzhak Meir Heschel moved to Kopitzhinitz. Wunder 1981, 733–34. Alfasi 1981, 180–86. A daughter of Heschel's uncle Sholem Joseph Heschel, Chava Sarah, married Mordecai Solomon Friedman, rebbe of Boyan. From Vienna they emigrated to New York City around 1926, settling on the Lower East Side of Manhattan. When Heschel reached the United States in March 1940, they met him at the boat. Interview with Israel Friedman, a son of the Boyaner rebbe. See also Mintz 1992, 13–20.

30. Letter from his son Rabbi Nahum Mordecai Perlow to Abraham Isaac Bromberg, quoted in Shedletsky 1977, 143.

31. Cited in Bromberg 1963, 153; see Perlow 1969.

32. Diary, 41–42, and Perlow 1969; also Bromberg 1963, vol. 20, 141–49 for the Novominsker. In the United States, Heschel renewed ties with the middle brother, Rabbi Yehuda Aryeh Leib Perlow (1877–1960). This uncle was also greatly learned and received *smikha* (rabbinical ordination) from three of the greatest non-Hasidic authorities of the time, among whom may have been Rabbi Hayim Soloveitchik of Brisk (Brest-Litovsk), founder of a rigorous method of Talmudic exegesis. Yehuda Aryeh Leib served as rabbi and head of the rabbinic court of Voldova (Wlodawa), near Brisk, but he was soon forced by poor living conditions to emigrate. The family of Yehuda Aryeh Leib Perlow reached the United States in 1924 and settled in the Williamsburg section of Brooklyn.

33. Perlow 1969, which contains a description of the daily customs of the Novominsker by his son Nahum Mordecai; Bromberg 1963, 142.

34. Interview with Israel Heschel (1911–1994), son of Abraham Joshua Heschel, the Kopitzhinitzer rebbe of New York. Susannah Heschel writes that it was the influenza epidemic, *Moral Grandeur and Spiritual Audacity*, ix–x.

35. Located at quarter 47, row 22, Jewish cemetery in Warsaw. On page 165 of the typed book at the cemetery, there is an error in the transcription of the date. The opening word "Tsiyyun" (in Hebrew, marker or monument) is taken from a phrase in 2 Kings 23:17. Photographed by "Our Roots," Gryzbowski Square, Warsaw; the *ohel* (monument) has been preserved by the Lauder Foundation, thanks to the generosity of Rabbi Israel Heschel.

36. It is possible that a younger Heschel boy, born after Abraham Joshua, whose memory has been effaced, also died in this epidemic. Reported by Thena Heshel Kendall, daughter of Heschel's brother, Jacob, but without confirmation.

37. Heschel 1969, "Reflections on Death," 533; repr. *Moral Grandeur and Spiritual Audacity*, 366–78.

38. Heschel 1942, "Analysis of Piety," 307; Heschel 1951, *Man Is Not Alone*, 296; *Moral Grandeur and Spiritual Audacity*, 317.

39. This and the next quotation from Heschel 1973, *A Passion for Truth*, xv.

Chapter 3. "The Blessings of Humiliation" and Triumphal Adolescence

Note to epigraph: Heschel 1973, *A Passion for Truth*, 215.

1. Heschel also published excerpts in Yiddish in *Di goldene keyt*, 1969; earlier at the annual convention of the Rabbinical Assembly (Conservative), vol. 23 (1959), he delivered, also in Yiddish, a talk on the Kotzker rebbe. The two-volume Yiddish book on the Kotzker was written in the idiom of the Gerer Hasidim that Heschel knew intimately in Warsaw. The English version, a much shorter adaptation which includes a systematic comparison with Kierkegaard, is aimed toward an American readership. Both books did not appear until after his death, in 1973. See Shandler 1993.

2. From interviews with Nehama Perlow Teitelbaum; Bernard Perlow; Jacob Perlow, February 1979. The German occupation ceased a year later when Poland gained control over its own people and became a nation: 3 November 1918, Proclamation of the Republic of Poland.

3. Interview with Thena Heshel Kendall, as told to her by her father, Jacob Heshel.

4. The first Gerer rebbe greeted Rabbi Jacob Perlow, Heschel's maternal grandfather, during his emigration from Belorussia, before settling in Novominsk. The family possesses a letter from the Warsaw Gerer rebbe to Alter Israel Shimon the Novominsker, indicating that the Gerer consulted with him on the occasion of the former's second marriage (to his niece) after his wife's death. This letter, beyond discussions of Torah and communal affairs between these two men, testifies to their close relationship. The original letter is in the possession of Rabbi Jacob Perlow of Brooklyn, grandson of the Novominsker rebbe. A copy of it, courtesy of his brother, the late Bernard Perlow of Chicago, is in the Heschel Archive, Jewish Theological Seminary.

5. Rabinowicz 1989, 274–81, also 173–78; Rabinowicz 1988, 258–59, 262–70, 304, 387, 393, 394. And interview with Rabbi Jacob Perlow of Brooklyn, 15 November 1987. The Gerer rebbe had helped prepare the founding of the Agudah at the Bad-Homburg Conference in 1909 and he played significant roles at the Agudist conferences of 1923, 1929, and 1937 at Vienna and Marienbad. "It was widely known that the rebbe from Ger did not waste time, and he would not even take a minute to speak about a secular matter. But he would talk with the rebbe of Novominsk for an hour or more about Torah and piety. . . . The Gerer rebbe once told Rabbi Jacob Rosenheim of Frankfurt, the president of the Agudat Israel beginning in 1929, 'The ideal spiritual guide for the Agudah in Poland would be the rebbe of Novominsk, but he would not accept the position since he is too preoccupied with prayer and learning.'" Bromberg 1963, 155–56.

6. Rabinowicz 1989, on Rabbi Yitzhak Meir of Ger, 173–79. Rabinowicz 1988, 227–39, same text. Baedeker Guide, *Russia* (1914), 29–30.

7. See Heschel 1973, *A Passion for Truth*, 233–34. Also Faierstein 1983, and the novel of Opatoshu 1938, *In Polish Woods* (pub. orig. in Yiddish and Hebrew, 1921).

8. Diary, 38–39.

9. Conversation with Heschel.

10. Diary, 38. Text of Diary stops before the end of the sentence. This information was confirmed by conversation with Heschel.

11. S. Heschel 1996, *Moral Grandeur and Spiritual Audacity*, ix.

12. This and the next anecdote from interviews with Jacob Perlow, son of the Novominsker rebbe of Williamsburg.

13. Green 1979, and Weiss 1985, 44–55, 252–69.

14. Conversation with Heschel, confirmed by Arthur Green.

15. Heschel 1973, *A Passion for Truth*, 215, and note 2.

16. Ibid.

17. Ibid., xv.

18. Conversation with Heschel, confirmed by Arthur Green.

19. Conversation with Heschel, c. 1970.

20. Heschel 1973, *A Passion for Truth*, 97.

21. Interview with Bernard Perlow, 17 February 1981.

22. It was said that the Novominsker rebbe combined within himself several qualities of his forebears: "From R. Shlomo Hayim of Koidanov, prayerfulness; from R. Levi Yitzhak of Berditchev, love of humanity; from R. Pinchas ben Avraham Shapiro of Korets, love of music; and from his father, diligence and a phenomenal memory," Rabinowicz 1989, 294.

23. Interview with Sarah Perlow (Mrs. Moses Eichenstein), daughter of the Novominsker rebbe, eleventh of the twelve Perlow children.

24. Conversation with Heschel. As a child, Heschel had learned to distrust exterior acts of devotion. For example, his father would not follow the Novominsker's custom of reciting the special phrase "In honor of the holy Sabbath" before taking food on the Seventh Day. In later years, recalling these standards, Heschel did not defend such spiritual rigor. "If too much remains within, it can be forgotten—and only that which is external will remain" (Diary, 42).

25. The Novominsker rebbe's brother, Yehuda Aryeh Leib, was reputed to have received ordination from Rabbi Hayim Soloveitchik of Brisk, among other authorities.

26. Diary and interview with Sarah Perlow (Mrs. Moses Eichenstein). Soloveitchik once brought a famous Polish specialist, a non-Jew, to his home. Despite his illness, Rabbi Perlow was sitting and reciting passages from the Mishnah with gusto. Thinking that he was having a seizure, the Polish physician asked Soloveitchik to quiet him down. "No," said the latter, "once he stops his devotions and study, he will die!"

27. Heschel remarked that Hasidim preferred this to the more correct expression, "*Seudah Shlishit*" (the third meal). He explained that from the abundance of food at Friday night and Saturday noon meals, one might be deluded to think that it was the food and not the spirit at the Sabbath meals that was essential. Therefore the Hasidim called the third meal—at which little was eaten and the songs and Torah were in

abundance, clearly a meal of the spirit—"*Shalosh Seudos*" (the three meals), to include the other two meals as well.

28. Diary, 29 (17).

29. While others might judge a person by their clothes, their wealth, their learning, "the Besht could tell what a man was by the way he sang a nigun. The nigun is in reality a *Vidui*, a confession." Diary. Among the traditional songs at the Novominsker's Tish we find: *Askinu Seudasa*, "Prepare Thy table"; *Mizmor le-Dovid*, "The Lord is my shepherd"; *Atah ehad*, "Thou are one, Thy name is one, and who is like our people, unique in all the earth"; *Yedid nefesh*, "My soul's beloved, merciful Father"; *Leit atar*, "There is no place where Thou art not, no thought that can grasp you"; *Yah ehsof*, "O Lord, how I yearn for Thee" (the song of his ancestor, Aaron the Great of Karlin), "Have mercy on our exile," "Teach us O Lord Your ways"; *El mistater*, "Oh hiding God"; *Yom shabbaton*, "O Sabbath day."

30. Heschel 1942, "An Analysis of Piety," 299; cf. Heschel 1951, *Man Is Not Alone*, 282; reprinted *Moral Grandeur and Spiritual Audacity*, 310.

Note to epigraph: Heschel 1950, *The Earth Is the Lord's*, 215.

31. SD reports that the first day he put on tefillin was in Heschel's room at Hebrew Union College. Heschel told him that was the very day he had first put on tefillin and that they had brought him those of Rabbi Levi Yitzhak of Berditchev for the occasion.

32. Interview with Marshall Meyer, who heard it from Wolfe Kelman. Interview with Pearl Twersky, daughter of the Kopitzhinitzer rebbe and Heschel's sister Sarah.

33. We do not know the date of Heschel's early ordination by Rabbi Zemba. Only a nephew recalled the rabbi's name. Interview with Israel Heschel.

34. Rabinowicz 1988, 308–11; Rabinowicz 1989, 333–37.

35. From a draft CV prepared by Rabbi Jacob Heshel in London; papers of Thena Heshel Kendall. Abraham Zemba, "The Mesivta in Warsaw" (Hebrew), in Mirsky 1956, 363–75. The following discussion is taken from this important article.

36. Eisenstein 1950, 72; also Zemba 1956, 363–75; Piekaz 1990, chap. 5.

37. Founded in 1893, the journal ceased publication during World War I, and was revived in 1919—the year Mesivta began—by the founder's son, Israel Isser Feigenbaum.

38. The *Bet Midrash* supplement was started in 1922 and edited by Rav R. Shlomo Altman, head of the Bet Din (Rabbinical Court) of Kikel, located in Warsaw. See Mandelbaum 1976, *Index to Sha'arey Torah*, from which much of the following is taken.

39. In the yeshiva world, two main approaches can be distinguished, emphasizing either (1) formulating the right questions (the "Brisk School" of Rabbi Hayim Soloveitchik), the dialectic of analyzing texts and ideas, or (2) striving for satisfactory answers to explain all the difficulties. It appears that the young Heschel emphasized questions over answers.

40. The first piece cites *Bava Kama* 62, and then Rashi, who examines a Mishnah that deals with how far down a person can dig between a boundary if the roots of another person's tree are coming up on your side.

41. "Avraham Yehoshua Heschel" joined his peers, such as Mordecai Dov Treuse from Kalich, Avraham Engliser from Warsaw, Tzvi Zrulens, and students from Warsaw and Kielicz, Kuzmir, Berditchev, and other towns.

42. Heschel 1950, *The Earth Is the Lord's*, 53–54.

43. Interview with Bernard Perlow of Chicago, son of R. Nahum Mordecai Perlow and grandson of the Warsaw Novominsker rebbe, 17 February 1981. Conversations with Heschel; also death certificate, "Madame Gitla Perlow," Mairie du 5e arrondissement, Paris, 10 March 1959; dossier décès no. 498.

44. Conversation with Heschel.

45. Only after settling in the United States did Heschel marry, at age thirty-nine, on 10 December 1945. His wife was Sylvia Straus of Cleveland, Ohio, a concert pianist.

46. Interview with Khone Shmeruk, whose mother had taken him for such a consultation.

47. Heschel acknowledged the influence of Fishl Schneersohn and remained in close touch with him for the remainder of his life. Conversation with Sylvia Heschel.

48. Interview with Nehama Perlow Teitelbaum.

49. Hofer 1976.

50. See Reisen 1956, 755–57; Hofer 1976, 474–82. Schneersohn emigrated to Palestine in 1937. Schneersohn is not mentioned in the *Encyclopaedia Judaica*.

51. Excerpts are from the English translation which appeared a year later, Schneersohn 1929. See Paul Tillich, *The Courage To Be* (New Haven: Yale University Press, 1954), for a similar analysis of existential anxiety in historical, religious, and ontological terms.

52. Schneersohn 1929, 40. Minor modifications in this and other quotations.

53. Ibid., 168; the next quotation from 191.

54. See Heschel 1951, *Man Is Not Alone*, and 1955, *God in Search of Man*. Kaplan 1996, chaps. 6, 9, "Mysticism and Despair," "Modern Judaism and the Holy Spirit."

55. Schneersohn 1929, 169–70.

56. Interview with Marshall Meyer.

57. Granfield 1967, 84.

58. Heschel 1951, *Man Is Not Alone*, 174.

Chapter 4. Expanding the Self Through Literature

Note to epigraph: Heschel 1951, *Man Is Not Alone*, 254.

1. See Heschel 1936, *Die Prophetie;* 1935, *Maimonides;* and his monographs 1945, 1950; Heschel 1996, *Prophetic Inspiration After the Prophets*. See below, chap. 10.

2. Rabinowicz 1989, 294; see Bacon 1989, "Agudat Israel in Interwar Poland," in Mendelsohn et al., 20–35.

3. Interview with Nehama Perlow Teitelbaum.

4. Interview with Ephraim Shedletsky.

5. Rosenstein 1990, vol. 1, 479–82. Heschel, at his own request, was buried next to

this uncle, Yehuda Aryeh Leib, in a Long Island cemetery. Interview with the present Novominsker rebbe, Rabbi Jacob Perlow, Nahum Mordecai's son.

6. On South Ninth Street. See Rosenstein 1990. Interview with Bernard Perlow, son of Nahum Mordecai, 1981.

7. USA Petition for Naturalization, no. 210036, dated 29 November 1935. His brother, Aaron Perlow (1902–1963)—a close friend of Heschel's and also an ordained rabbi—eventually left for Antwerp, arriving in New York in 1930. In America, Aaron Perlow and Abraham Heschel remained close.

8. From a typewritten draft of a CV by Jacob Heshel provided by his daughter, Thena Heshel Kendall, with her additional information and interpretation.

9. It may be that Gittel Heschel, too, married and moved to Vienna, but returned to Warsaw after the divorce. This information confirmed by Thena Heshel Kendall in an interview, 28 June 1992.

10. Interview with Nehama Perlow Teitelbaum; also Rabinowicz 1988, 307–8; Holtz 1966; Holtz 1970–71; Waldoks 1984.

11. As one participant described it: "Zeitlin was regarded as a heretic by the ultra-Orthodox and a hypocrite by the *maskilim*. Yet to his home . . . flocked *hasidim, mitnagdim*, writers, politicians, Agudists, Bundists, and Zionists to listen and to learn from this modern 'prophet.' He was no demagogue. He spoke quietly with eyes closed, apparently oblivious to the people around him. Yet every public appearance brought eager crowds to hear him" (Klepfisz 1983, 30). Heschel wrote a luminous essay in Yiddish (1948, "After Maidanek") on Aaron Zeitlin's poetry; see Shandler 1993.

12. Quoted by Holtz 1966, 58, and note 14: "For Zeitlin on Bialik, see *ha-Tekufah*, vol. 17 (Warsaw 1923, 436 ff.). Compare Bialik's own ideas on 'The Explicit and the Allusive in Language,' in the Dvir edition of the latter's collected works, pp. 191 ff."

13. Quoted by Holtz 1966, 61.

14. Heschel 1973, *A Passion for Truth*, 307.

15. Years later, Heschel recommended this radical thinker to a rabbinical student at Hebrew Union College. Interview with Arnold Jacob Wolf.

16. His collection of Hasidic legends appeared in 1910 and his Yiddish writings in 1912; see Mintz 1989.

17. Opatoshu 1938, *In Polish Woods*. See Faierstein 1983, "The Friday Night Incident in Kotzk," 184–86.

18. The anthology included 544 pages. Prager 1982, 164.

19. Ibid., 107.

20. Ravitch 1947, 21–23.

21. *Illustrirte Vokhe*, vol. 3, no. 20 (whole no. 73), erroneously dated "1924" in the *Leksikon fun der nayer yidisher literatur*. Heschel's piece is accompanied by a photograph of an eighty-year-old Hazzan, Borukh Kinstler, taken by O. Bereneszteyn from Kremenits. Ravitch was probably responsible for this first literary publication of Heschel's.

22. See Wiesel 1972, *Souls on Fire;* Green 1979, esp. 142–50; 162–67; Fishbane 1994, "To Jump for Joy."

23. Heschel 1973, *A Passion for Truth,* xiv.

24. Heschel 1926–27. *Varshaver Shriftn,* Warsaw. Translated by Sylvia Fuks Fried. *Note to epigraph:* Heschel 1955, *God in Search of Man,* 414.

25. The following anecdotes are from conversations with Heschel and/or with Heschel's relatives when no specific sources are given. See Dresner 1985, xxvii–xxix.

26. Letter from Wolfe Kelman, 4 May 1982.

27. Diary, 40.

28. For other sources see Dresner 1981, 119–75, esp. 169n8.

29. Heschel 1955, *God in Search of Man:* "Observance has, at times, become encrusted with so many customs and conventions that the jewel was in the setting. Outward compliance with externalities of the law took the place of the engagement of the whole person to the living God" (326). See Heschel 1966, *Insecurity of Freedom,* 198.

30. Rabbi Mordecai Josef, a disciple of the Kotzker rebbe, wrote that under special circumstances one could violate the Torah. He based his interpretation on the Talmud's rendering of Psalm 119, verse 126: "It is time to act for the Lord, for they have broken Thy Law," as "There are times when breaking Thy law is acting for the Lord" (B. Berakhot 54a and Rashi); Faierstein 1989, 36–39. See Heschel 1973, *Kotsk* (in Yiddish), 543.

31. "To Yitzhak Levin, May his Blood be Avenged." The Hebrew abbreviation indicates that he had been murdered in the Holocaust. Heschel once remarked that one of the few things he brought with him from Europe were letters from Yitzhak Meir Levin, that they should be published. If they still exist, they remain in the custody of the Heschel family.

32. Diary, 40.

33. The following anecdote is from Dresner 1985, xxxviii. There is no confirmation that Aaron Perlow or any other son of the Novominsker rebbe attended the Vilna Real-Gymnasium.

34. Later, Heschel was sitting at the Tish of his brother-in-law, the Kopitzhinitzer rebbe, Abraham Joshua Heschel, on Henry Street on the Lower East Side of Manhattan. His cousin said to him: "We hoped that you would be the Levi Yitzhak of our generation and save Hasidism. And I thought I would be your Hasid. Alas, you have come to sit at my table." Diary, 1946.

35. Perlow 1931. Thesis accepted by the dean, H. Delecroix, 3 December 1930, written under the direction of professor Adolphe Lods of the Faculté des Lettres, Université de Paris, with the support of professor A. Back of the Ecole rabbinique de France. Information on file at the archives of Le Rectorat de Paris, at the Sorbonne and the Archives nationales, Série RJ 16: no. 4803*, and carton 5010. Sorbonne library, HF uf 136 (381). Excerpt from the death record: Married and divorced from Lucien Léon

Wattécant, married to Paul Gaston Monthéard. Gitla Perlow, died 10 March 1958, 1:30 P.M.; 14, rue Henri-Barbusse, Paris 5th.

36. Sheindel Brakha Perlow; see Rabinowicz 1989, 364.

37. Interviews with David Roskies and Sarah Perlow (Mrs. Moses Eichenstein).

Part Two. Vilna

Note to epigraph: Heschel 1974, *Jerusalem of Lithuania*, vol. 1, xxi; Yiddish, xi.

Chapter 5. A Rebbe Among Revolutionaries

Note to epigraph: Heschel 1950, *The Earth Is the Lord's*, 103–4.

1. The following anecdote from Diary and interview with Israel Heschel.
2. Interview with Shlomo Beilis and 1980 article. Interview with Benyamin Pumpiansky.
3. Telephone interview with Dobruszkes.
4. This chapter on the Vilna Real-Gymnasium is based, in large part, on the accurate and heartfelt series of essays written in Yiddish by Azario Dobruszkes. Also articles by Pupko, Giligitsh, Abramowicz; correspondence and telephone conversations with other graduates: Benyamin Pumpiansky (class of 1926), Minsk and recently of Tel Aviv; Abram Lewin ('27), Paris; Esther Selz Zajac ('26), Paris; Benjamin Wojczyk ('27), Brussels; Lezer Yankelovich Aron ('30), Vilnius, Paris; Dina Abramowicz ('26), New York.
5. Defying anti-Semitic government edicts, the Real-Gymnasium refused to compromise its mission by teaching some courses in Polish. The school was finally certified in 1930.
6. Dobruszkes article, September 1986.
7. Letter from Azario Dobruszkes, citing Wojczyk. The following information is based on conversations with Benjamin Wojczyk, Abram Lewin, and Azario Dobruszkes.
8. Faynshtayn emigrated to Paris in 1933. *Le Monde*, 26 July 1967; *La Presse nouvelle*, August 1967. Information provided by his son, Michel Fansten, Paris.
9. Shenkman 1960–61, 12; D. Abramowicz 1946.
10. Giligitsh 1968–69.
11. Dobruszkes, September 1986.
12. Dobruszkes, October–December 1986.
13. D. Abramowicz 1946.
14. Dobruszkes, April–June 1987.
15. Telephone interview with Benjamin Wojczyk, 1992.
16. Dobruszkes 1970.
17. Reisen, *Leksikon* 1960, 3:600–606; Ravitch 1947, 227–29; introduction by Rachel Ertel (1982) to the French translation of Kulbak's novella, *Lundi*, vii–xxv. Original: *Montog*, first published in 1929 (750 copies) by the Kultur Liga in Warsaw.

18. Sh. Niger, "A New Beginning" (published in 1921), reprinted in *Yidishe shreiber in soviet rusland* (New York, 1958), 69 passim. Cited by Ertel 1982, x, n7.

19. They included Baal-Makhshoves (pen name of Isidor Eliashev, 1873–1924), Dovid Bergelson (1885–1952), Hersh-Dovid Nomberg (1876–1927), Niger (pen name of Samuel Charny, 1883–1955), Peretz Markish (1895), and Der Nister (pen name of Pinhas Kaganovitch, 1884–1950, born in Berditchev). See Liptzin 1985.

20. Interview with Leyzer Aron, Paris, 1992.

21. Boris Kletskin was Vilna's leading Yiddish-language publisher. This and the next quotation are from D. Abramowicz 1946. Now librarian at the New York YIVO Institute, she has helped generations of researchers, including the present authors; see *The Book Peddler* (1996) for a tribute to this remarkable person.

22. Heschel 1939, "Das Gebet"; revised and translated as "Prayer as Empathy and Expression," *Quest*, 1954. See chap. 20.

23. Abramowicz 1946.

24. Heschel 1966, *Insecurity of Freedom*, 249.

25. Because the Polish government limited the hours per day that Kulbak was allowed to teach, and because he declined to accept Polish citizenship, he was required to maintain his Nansen passport, a temporary visitor's document subject to stringent labor regulations.

26. This and the next quotation are from Dobruszkes, October–December 1986.

27. Giligitsh 1968–69; Dobruszkes, October 1970, and conversation, 21 June 1992; conversations with Abram Lewin, 9 June 1992; Benjamin Wojczyk, June 1992.

28. Telephone interviews with Eydelzon and Wojczyk.

29. Interview with Dobruszkes.

30. Giligitsh 1968–69.

Note to epigraph: Heschel 1974, *Jerusalem of Lithuania*, vol. 1, xxi.

31. This information taken from interview with Shlomo Beilis, and Beilis's article on Yung Vilne in *Di goldene keyt* 1980: 18–19. Reference thanks to its editor, Abraham Sutzkever.

32. Heschel 1950, *The Earth Is the Lord's*, 19.

33. *Varshaver Shriftn*, 31–32. Each brochure featured a single genre—prose, essays, or poetry, each issue numbered from page one.

34. Heschel 1951, *Man Is Not Alone*, 266; see the entire section, "The Holy Within the Body." Also Dresner 1981, 161–62, 174n69, and sources in Heschel cited there.

35. From *Literarishe Bleter*, 3 June 1927, no. 22, 417. This progressive paper serialized essays by Maxim Gorky (translated into Yiddish). Fishl Schneersohn, who contributed an important novella, "The Last Are the First," might have urged Heschel, before leaving Warsaw, to visit its editorial offices at 2a Nalewki Street, not far from his home. "Di letste kenen zayn di ershte" appeared in three installments: *Literarishe Bleter*, nos. 34–36, starting on 26 August 1927. Consulted at the Hebrew University, Jerusalem.

36. Telephone interview with S. L. Shneyderman.

37. Translated into French by Itzchok Niborski (Paris), into English by Yossel Birstein (Jerusalem), revised slightly.

38. Faynshtayn wrote about the incident years later in the Paris newspaper *Naye Presse*. Alexandre Derczansky, a man of remarkable memory who read the article several years ago, told EK about it. The remaining comrades at the *Naye Presse*, particularly "Anna Vilner" (pen name of Khana Kuritsky, RG class of 1930) and her husband, Itshe Brudno, also remembered the article—but no one, after much effort, succeeded in finding it.

Note to epigraph: Heschel quotes only these two lines from Kulbak's poem, "Vilne," in his preface to Ran 1974. The poem first appeared in the 1926–27 *Varshaver Shriftn* that includes Heschel's first poem; Kulbak's piece is reprinted in *Di goldene keyt*, no. 101 (1980): 8–10. For a translation see Howe, Wisse, and Shmeruk 1987: 406–10. Heschel does not quote the transformed refrain in the third stanza: "You are a psalm, spelled in clay and iron. The letters fading. They wander—stray" (408). Perhaps he felt that by omitting Kulbak's realistic assessment he was helping prevent the "letters" of Vilna's Jewishness from fading even more.

39. S. Heschel 1996 (x) dates 24 June 1927 for the final examination. Heschel's CV gives 27 June as the date of graduation. There is no copy of Heschel's diploma from the Real-Gymnasium at the Humboldt University Archives. According to its records, he did not take the Polish Abitur. Other student records from the Real-Gymnasium allow us to reconstruct his probable program. YIVO Institute for Jewish Research, New York.

40. Even Heschel's essay in Ran's memorial book on Vilna does not mention the Real-Gymnasium. Yet his records at the University of Berlin state that he received his diploma from the Real-Gymnasium in June 1927. And in 1939, he included this information on the CV sent to Hebrew Union College in Cincinnati. And he regularly listed his Real-Gymnasium degree in various editions of *Who's Who in America*.

41. The annual meeting began on 5 January 1945 in the Hunter College auditorium; Heschel spoke on Sunday, 7 January; see *Newsletter of the YIVO*, no. 7, February 1945. A Yiddish expansion of his talk appeared in 1945 published by Schocken Books, New York; see Heschel (1945; 1946; 1950). For an excellent analysis of these and other issues, see Shandler 1993, and Neusner 1981, 82–85. Heschel was a member of YIVO's board of directors.

42. Interview with Leyzer Ran, 11 December 1987; Pumpiansky letter.

43. Brochure on Young Vilna 1955, 45; copy in YIVO, New York.

44. The announcement was made in the 11 October 1929 issue of the *Vilner Tog*, a Yiddish newspaper. Among the first participants were Leyzer Wolf, Shlomo Beilis, Moshe Levin, Moshe Bassim, Aron Puetsch—and Shimshon Kahan, the only other student from the Real-Gymnasium (class of 1926). Haim Grade and Avraham Sutzkever, perhaps the best known to posterity, arrived later. In a special issue of the Yiddish peri-

odical *Di goldene keyt,* no. 101 (1980) commemorating the fiftieth anniversary of the founding of Yung Vilne, Beilis describes it as a "brief episode" in Heschel's life. According to Leyzer Ran, Heschel insisted that he be listed as a co-*founder,* not just a member.

45. All the following quotations from Heschel in Ran 1974.

Part Three. Berlin

Note to epigraph: Heschel 1950, *The Earth Is the Lord's,* 105.

1. See Gay 1968; Mander 1959; Brenner 1996.
2. Alt 1987.
3. Fishl Schneersohn began to correspond with Martin Buber in 1922; Schneersohn's letters can be found in the Martin Buber Archive at the Jewish National and University Library, Jerusalem, Ms. Var. 350/699. Koigen's letters to Buber, which start around 1907, are from the same collection, Ms. Var. 350/379.
4. See S. Morgenstern 1946, 63–65, 79, 93–102.
5. This paradigmatic debate deserves a book of its own: in French see E. Cassirer and M. Heidegger, *Débat sur le kantisme et la philosophie (Davos, mars 1929)* (Paris: Beauchesne, 1972), with complete bibliographical references to sources in German, French, and English; for example, Carl Hamburg, "Discussion: A Cassirer-Heidegger Seminar," *Philosophy and Phenomenological Research* 25 (1964): 208–22. Franz Rosenzweig, in a little-known review of posthumous writings of Hermann Cohen, "Reversed Fronts" (a translation of "Vertauschte Fronten," from *Zweistromland* [Nijhoff, 1984]: 235–37), describes this debate as between the old thinking (represented by Heidegger's denial of human freedom) and Cassirer's "new thinking." In Barbara Galli, *Franz Rosenzweig and Jehuda Halevi: Translating, Translations, and Translators* (Montreal: McGill-Queen's University Press, 1995): 479–82.

Chapter 6. A Student in Berlin

Note to epigraph: Heschel 1953, "Toward an Understanding of Halacha," 386–87.

1. Interview with Leon Feldman.
2. Heschel's university records state that he remained registered at the Philosophical Faculty from 27 April 1928 to 24 January 1931. Student number 5252/118. Humboldt University Archive: Abraham Heschel's *Matrikelbuch* (student registration book).
3. Berlin North 7 District, near Garten Strasse. This is the address in his university student file, although the date is not certain: "Anschrift während des Studiums" (*during* his studies). Humboldt University Archives.
4. Interview with Leon Feldman.
5. See Schnädelbach 1984, esp. 21–32, on the university system. This book is invaluable for interpreting intellectual currents in Germany during Heschel's time.

6. Information taken from *Minerva Jahrbuch der gelehrten Welt,* a guide to the academic institutions of Berlin at that time, and university catalogues: *Verzeichnis der Vorlesungen der Königlichen Friedrich-Wilhelms-Universität,* 1927–33. Heschel's academic records can be found at the Humboldt University Archives.

7. Article on the Hochschule by Volker, in Walravens 1990, 200–205. Gressmann quotation from Gressmann, ed. 1927, 1–2. See review article of Louis Finkelstein 1929–30.

8. Fuchs 1967, 5; see also Elbogen's history of the school.

9. Eisner 1967, 32–52. Also *Encyclopaedia Judaica,* s.v. "Wissenschaft": some of the dates in this entry are inconsistent with the articles cited.

10. Jung, ed. 1958, 363–419; Alexander Marx (Hoffmann's son-in-law) 1947, 185–222.

11. *Jahresbericht des Rabbiner-Seminars* 1928.

12. Wohlgemuth's paper on Scheler was published in the 1931 Festschrift in honor of Jacob Rosenheim, of the Agudat Israel. The paper was circulated and discussed well before publication. Thanks to Alexandre Derczansky (Paris, France) for this important reference. See Mendes-Flohr's introduction, "Theologian Before the Abyss," in Altmann 1991, 149n45.

13. Hoffmann and Schwartz 1991, and Shapiro 1995.

14. Heschel, among other Liberal and Orthodox scholars, contributed a paper to the Festschrift published in Freimann's honor in 1937.

15. Statistical and factual information can be found in the various yearbook-catalogues, or Berichte, published by the Hochschule.

16. Heschel 1953, "Toward an Understanding of Halacha," 389. See full context.

17. Founded in 1661, the State Library, which held more than 1,777,000 volumes (and Jewish manuscripts), also housed the Academy of Sciences, the Information Bureau of German libraries—with the general catalogue of Prussian libraries—and the America Institute, established to promote exchange of books and knowledge of the United States. *Baedeker* 1923, 53; see 51–124 for descriptions of the area's museums.

Note to epigraph: Heschel 1953, "Toward an Understanding of Halacha," 388.

18. The *Lebenslauf* attached to Heschel's 1933 doctoral dissertation states that his principal professors were Dessoir, Maier, Brinckmann, Liebert, Wölfflin, Baumgardt, Köhler, Schmidt, and Hochstadter, among others. The *Eisler-Lexikon* (1912) surveys Heschel's professors at least a decade before he met them in Berlin. See also Asen 1955. Arthur Liebert (1878–1946), professor of philosophy at the Institute for Commercial Sciences in Berlin, was appointed in 1925 to teach courses on epistemology at the university. Liebert was a prominent neo-Kantian, editor of the periodical *Kant Studien,* and he also lectured on history of philosophy and religions. David Baumgardt (1890–1963) taught Greek philosophy, phenomenology, and Hegel's esthetics. Erich Hochstetter (1888–1968) taught medieval European philosophy. Ferdinand Jacob Schmidt (b. 1860) taught the history of recent philosophy and, in the Peda-

gogical Institute (Margaretenschule), an introduction to the history of pedagogy. Schmidt was especially concerned with the process of cognition, an analysis of "experience." Heschel's 1939 CV states in English: "Among my professors were: Dessoir, Maier, Wölfflin, Brincmann [*sic*], Mittwoch, Albeck, Baeck, Elbogen, and Koigen."

19. Maier published a three-volume study of Aristotle, *The Psychology of Emotional Thinking* (1908), and a three-volume *Philosophy of Reality* (1926–35), which Heschel purchased in Berlin and preserved in his personal library after his immigration to the United States.

20. Among Dessoir's several books, *The Double Self* (Das Doppel-Ich, 1890), *A History of the New German Psychology* (Geschichte der neueren deutschen Psychologie, 1894) and *From Beyond the Soul* (Vom Jenseits der Seele, 1917) gave solid evidence of his originality. See also *Eisler-Lexikon*. Dessoir was editor of the *Zeitschrift für Ästhetik* (Journal of esthetics). Heschel, in his doctoral dissertation, refuted theories of poetic inspiration and other forms of psychological reductionism as explanations of biblical prophecy.

21. Curiously, Heschel's CV and his university file do not name Sellin—nor did Sellin became an adviser for his thesis. Heschel did tell Stefan Kayser about his work with Sellin; see chap. 14.

22. Schwab 1964, 97–98.

23. Wölfflin was at the University of Basel when Bertholet was there. The renowned author of *Renaissance and Baroque in Italy* impressed him, as had the historian's *Principles of Art History* (1915). Conversation with Heschel, 1971.

24. Listed on Heschel's *Lebenslauf* by last name only. See Cummings on Wolfgang Köhler in Edwards 1972; c. 1969; see also Deutsch 1997, chap. 8, "The Philosophy Professors of the University of Berlin."

25. Köhler boldly sought to develop positions in the fields of biology, physiology, physics, and chemistry, and he made significant contributions to philosophy, in particular, epistemology, and ethics or theory of value. It may be that Köhler's ideas of "requiredness" and "value" influenced Heschel's later works—although these issues were generally shared by interdisciplinary thinkers of that time.

26. Fuchs 1967, 12; also Baron and Marx 1943.

27. Rosenthal 1963, 18–19, quotes from Elbogen's *Studien zur Geschichte des jüdischen Gottesdienstes* (1907); Elbogen's encyclopedic study of Jewish liturgy, *Der jüdische Gottesdienst in seiner geschichtlichen Entwicklung* (first published in 1913, with additional notes in 1923 and 1931), after being translated into Hebrew, was translated into English in 1993, dated, dull, but still authoritative.

28. Heschel 1948, "The Two Great Traditions," 421.

29. See Guttmann 1959, "Principles of Judaism"; Guttmann's father, Jacob, was a distinguished historian of Jewish philosophy. See Bamberger 1960, 3–31.

30. Bamberger 1960, 16–18. The professor's masterwork, *Philosophies of Judaism*, was

originally published in German in 1933. See introduction to English translation (1964) by R. J. Zwi Werblowsky; also critical review of trans., A. Altmann, *Conservative Judaism* 19:1 (Fall 1964): 73–80.

31. This quotation from Bamberger 1960, 21, slightly edited.

32. Bamberger 1960, 12.

33. Ibid., 22.

34. Albeck taught advanced and introductory Talmud courses and, together with J. Theodor, published a critical edition of the Midrash *Genesis Rabbah* (1926–36), and a commentary on the Mishnah (1952–59).

35. "Educated" (*Hochgebildet* in German) to be distinguished from "cultured" (Cassirer), or "erudite" (Buber), Heschel's other (nonreligious) superlatives. Interviews with Fritz Rothschild and David Novak.

36. Baker 1978; Altmann 1956.

37. This information on examinations from Heschel's candidacy book (Doktoranden-Buch) no. 68, journal no. 238, Humboldt University Archives, and Heschel's CV.

38. Anecdote related by Fritz Rothschild.

39. *Bericht der Hochschule* 1931 (printed in 1932), 12.

40. From memorandum on the Hochschule by Mrs. Ismar Elbogen [née Regine Klemperer], dated 8 June 1956. Original at the Leo Baeck Institute, New York City. Some details corrected according to information in Hochschule Yearbooks. See Heschel's CV: "In 1931–32 and 1934 I was invited by the staff of the 'Hochschule für die Wissenschaft des Judentums' to give a course of lectures on Talmudic Exegesis to the advanced students of the College."

41. Conversation with his son Haim Soloveitchik, December 1995. We know that Heschel and Joseph Soloveitchik met in 1962, when the latter was involved briefly with preparing Jewish position papers for the Second Vatican Council. While completing his degree at the university Soloveitchik did not take courses at the Orthodox Rabbiner-Seminar, but joined Rabbi Hayim Heller's group of Talmud students in Berlin. See Goldberg 1989; Lehman 1964; Deutsch 1997, *Larger Than Life*, vol. 2, chap. 4.

42. Josef Solowiejczyk, *Das reine Denken und die Seinskonstituierung bei Hermann Cohen* (Berlin: Reuther & Reichard, 1932). The dissertation was submitted in July 1930 and the degree awarded in December 1932.

43. Alexander Altmann, *Die Grundlagen der Wertethik: Wesen, Wert, Person. Max Schelers Erkenntnis und Seinslehre in kritischer Analyse* (Berlin: Reuther & Reichard, 1931). The dissertation was submitted in July, and the degree awarded in February 1931. Mendes-Flohr preface to Altmann 1991, 148n31.

44. In 1935, Altmann founded a Rambam Lehrhaus which sought to "integrate and coordinate" historical and supernatural conceptions of Torah. As he stated in his opening address: "We have not a static structured theology but a dynamic-unsystematic one, born out of the living reciprocal relationship of God and Israel [the Jewish people]" (Mendes-Flohr in Altmann 1991: xxxvii). See Altmann's opening address, "The

Teaching Methods in *Lehrhäuser:* Some Basic Considerations" (1935), ibid., 88–99; next quotation from 92.

Chapter 7. A Jewish Philosophical Mentor

Note to epigraph: Heschel 1934, "David Koigen," 4–5.

1. *Der Aufbau der sozialen Welt im Zeitalter der Wissenschaft* (The construction of the social world in the age of science) (Berlin: Carl Heymanns Verlag, 1929).
2. Interview with Moses Shulvass.
3. Address from Heschel's letters to A. Liessen, editor of *Zukunft,* 3 November 1929, was 56a Kant Strasse, c/o Pasemann; also, return address of a letter Heschel wrote in Yiddish to Melekh Ravitch, dated 9 March 1930.
4. Koigen's typed academic résumé from the Central Archives for the History of the Jewish People, Jerusalem (Hebrew University, Givat Ram campus), box P196; donated by Koigen's granddaughter, Mira Zakai. Also the biographical essay by Ernst Hoffmann in Koigen 1934, *Das Haus Israel,* 75–78; this slim volume remains the only available anthology of Koigen's writings relating specifically to Judaism. See also Hoffmann in *Jüdische Rundschau,* 27 February 1934. Additional details provided by Weltsch, and articles by Heller, *Jüdisches Lexikon* (1929), and Richard Popkin, *Encyclopaedia Judaica,* s.v. "David Koigen."
5. Hoffmann 1934, introduction to *Das Haus Israel.*
6. There was a third brother, Nathan, who, after emigrating to the United States, remained Orthodox.
7. The thesis became his first book, *Zur Geschichte der Philosophie und Sozialphilosophie des Junghegelianismus* (Bern, 1901).
8. Koigen's letters to Martin Buber, Jerusalem, Schwadron autograph collection, Koigen file, 1–6, dated 1907–08, addressed to "Herr Doktor." Koigen's letters to Buber from 1921 on: Ms. Var. 350/379: 10–12, 15–18.
9. See Mendes-Flohr 1989.
10. Koigen's four major books: his doctoral thesis, published in 1901, on the young Hegelians; *Die Kulturanschauung des Sozialismus: Ein Beitrag zum Wirklichkeits-Idealismus* (The cultural conception of socialism: A contribution to reality-idealism) (Berlin, 1903), a sympathetic interpretation of socialism as a solution to the world's turmoil; *Ideen zur Philosophie der Kultur: Der Kulturakt* (Ideas on the philosophy of culture: The culture-act) (Munich and Leipzig, 1910); and *Die Kultur der Demokratie: Vom Geiste des volkstümlichen Humanismus und vom Geiste der Zeit* (The culture of democracy: From the spirit of popular humanism and from the spirit of the times (Jena, 1912).
11. Koigen 1925, *Apokalyptischer Reiter,* 117, 127; see 147 for the incident of a town being spared, quoted by Heschel in a 1945 YIVO speech and Heschel 1950, *The Earth Is the Lord's,* 84–86.

12. This and the next quotation from Hoffmann 1934, introduction to *Das Haus Israel*, 73–74.

13. Articles on Fishl Schneersohn in Deutsch 1997, 49, 124–34; for original sources see (in Yiddish) *Leksikon fun der nayer yidisher literatur* 8:755; in Hebrew, *Leksikon ha-saffrot ha-ivrit bedorot ha-achraynim*, 1965. Hofer 1976. See Hayim Greenberg, "A Meeting with Yahalal," in *The Inner Eye: Essays*, vol. 2 (New York: Jewish Frontier Association, 1964), 244–53.

14. Martin Buber Archive, Jerusalem, Ms. Var. 350/379:1–6.

15. Letter of Koigen to Buber, 20 May 1922, inviting Buber to attend Schneersohn's lecture.

16. There were, indeed, deep affinities between Koigen and Buber. Their university educations were similar. Buber had studied in Vienna, Leipzig, Zurich, and Berlin, and he applied his cosmopolitan knowledge and experience to resolving contemporary Jewish problems.

17. *Ethos: Vierteljahresschrift für Soziologie, Geschichts- und Kulturphilosophie*, co-edited by Koigen, Fishl Schneersohn of Warsaw, and Franz Hilker of Berlin. They published analytic book reviews, summaries of sociology conferences around the world, and other items of professional interest. Only two volumes appeared: the first dated 1925–26 and the second 1928. The first issue featured articles by Schneersohn on "The Psychology of the People and the Masses" and Koigen on "History and Culture."

18. *Apokalyptischer Reiter*, quoted by Hoffmann 1934, introduction to *Das Haus Israel*, 70, 72.

19. Koigen's CV and interview with Mr. Grüngard, son of friends of Koigen and Schneersohn. In the fall of 1928 at the University of Hamburg (where Ernst Cassirer was rector), Koigen spoke on "the construction of the social world," the subject of his recent book. At the German Sociology Conference in Vienna he spoke on "Democracy and the Coming into Being of the People." In 1930, he was invited to give the opening address at the Second Conference of the World Union for Progressive Judaism in London on "The Idea of God in Light of Modern Thought."

Note to epigraph: Heschel 1934, "David Koigen," 4–5.

20. From an audiotape of a memorial evening in honor of Koigen; courtesy of Mala Brand, Jerusalem.

21. Koigen preserved the group's minutes, which survived his widow and son's emigration to Palestine before the Second World War. The texts were typed by each reporter, with some written emendations. Each report begins with the day, the date, the hour, and a list of the participants. The group remained relatively stable. Starting in January 1930, the following are listed, by last name only: Prof. Koigen, Frau Prof. Koigen, and [Haim] Borodianski, Heschel, Peysack, [Hirsch] Poppers, [Fritz] Salomonski, [Jehuda or Judah] Rosenthal, Weinberg. Somewhat later Birnbaum, Plass (or Pless), and Ley arrived. In 1931 were added Lifshitz, Himmelweit (or Himelveit), [Moses]

Schulwas (or Szulvass), Brandenburg, and [Ernst] Hoffmann. In 1932, Aaron Brand and Dr. Moldenau arrived. Also Wolf Rabinowicz, author of a book on Lithuanian Hasidism. Minutes preserved at the Central Archives for the History of the Jewish People, Hebrew University, Givat Ram campus, P196, cited with permission. Among the known participants: Haim Borodianski (1894–1978, Bar-Dayyan after his emigration to Palestine), a scholar of Semitic philology who co-edited, with Ismar Elbogen, Julius Guttmann, Fritz Bamberger, Simon Rawidowicz, Bruno Strauss, and Leo Strauss, Mendelssohn's *Gesammelte Schriften;* Borodianski wrote an introduction to vol. 16 (1929) on Hebrew vocabulary in Mendelssohn.

Hirsch Leib Poppers, born in Brody, Galicia (in 1905), to a prominent rabbinical family, moved to Vienna in 1914; he studied at a gymnasium and entered the Berlin Hochschule in 1927, joining the Koigen Circle in 1930. In 1931 he undertook research in London, applying Koigen's "universalistic vision" for a doctoral dissertation for the University of Berlin in history on "the fundamentals of biblical thought that shaped the world view in seventeenth-century England" and its revolutions. Document from American Jewish Archives, Cincinnati.

Fritz Salomonski was probably the son of Rabbi Martin Salomonski, chaplain during World War I; Pless was perhaps Willi Pless, co-editor with Leo Breindler of *Jüdische Nachrichtenblatt* (Berlin, 1938–42). Jehuda (or Judah) Rosenthal was later on the faculty of the College of Jewish Studies, Chicago (like Shulvass). See *List of Displaced German Scholars* (volume marked, strictly confidential), London, Autumn 1936; at Leo Baeck Institute, New York.

22. Meeting of 2 February 1933; 11:20 A.M.–2:00 P.M.; present: Prof. Koigen, Mrs. Koigen, Borodianski, Heschel, Peysack, Rosenthal, Salomonski, Weinberg. Protokollführer: Salomonski.

23. Meeting of 23 February 1930; 11:30 A.M.–2:00 P.M. Present: Prof. Koigen, Mrs. Koigen, Borodianski, Heschel, Peysack, Peper [Poppers], Rosenthal, Salomonski, Weinberg.

24. Meeting of 2 March 1930; 11:30 A.M.–2:00 P.M. Present: Mr. and Mrs. Koigen, Salomonski, Borodianski, Heschel, Peysack, Rosenthal, Poppers. Protokollführer: Poppers.

25. See Heschel 1949, "The Mystical Element in Judaism" (reprinted in *Moral Grandeur and Spiritual Audacity*, 164–84); Heschel 1950, *The Earth Is the Lord's;* Heschel 1966, *Insecurity of Freedom.*

26. First published in 1902. Trans. Georg Wobbermin, *Die religöse Erfahrung in ihrer Mannigfaltigkeit: Materialien und Studien zu einer Psychologie und Pathologie des religiösen Lebens* (Leipzig: J. C. Hinrichs, 1907; 1914; reprinted in 1917).

27. Meeting of 16 March 1930; 12:45–2:00 P.M. Present: Prof. Koigen, Mrs. Koigen, Borodianski, Heschel, Peysack, Poppers, Salomonski. Protokollführer: Salomonski.

28. Meeting of 18 March 1930; 9:20 P.M.–12:45 A.M. Present: Mr. and Mrs. Koigen, Borodianski, Heschel, Peysack, Poppers, and Salomonski. Protokollführer: Borodianski.

29. Around this time an important paper on "reverence" by Julius Goldstein, "Ehrfurcht,

eine Grundforderung des Judentums," *Der Morgen* vol. 5 (1929): 399–409, was widely read: cited by Alexander Altmann, in "Metaphysik und Religion" (Metaphysics and religion) in *Jeschurun* 17, 9–12 (1930): 321–47. Altmann 1991, 11–12n35, 159.

30. On 23 March, Heschel analyzed the chapter "The Melancholy Soul," and on 31 March he continued with "The Religious Conversion."

31. Present: Prof. Koigen, Frau Prof. Koigen, Heschel, Peysack, Pless, Rosenthal, Salomonski, Weinberg. Protokollführer: Salomonski.

32. Story recounted by Dr. Aaron Brand at a memorial evening devoted to David Koigen at the Brand home in Jerusalem; tape courtesy of his widow, Mala Brand. Confirmed by their son-in-law, Dr. Samuel Shafler, interview 1991.

33. Reisen 1967, *Leksikon fun der naye yidishe literatur,* Kressel, 2, 889–90; interviews with Shulvass.

34. Published with papers and program of *Second Conference of the World Union for Progressive Judaism* (19–22 July 1930): 58; the entire paper (58–72) is relevant to Heschel's later writings. Koigen's correspondence with Lily Montagu, summaries, press releases, and *Jüdische Rundschau* article are preserved with Koigen's papers at the Center for History of the Jewish People, Hebrew University, Givat Ram campus, Jerusalem.

35. *Second Conference* (1930): 59. Heschel himself, at the 1953 conference of Reform rabbis, placed equal emphasis on authentic prayer—but in the context of halakhah, traditional Jewish law.

36. Heschel 1953, "Toward an Understanding of Halacha," 386–409. Heschel 1953, "The Spirit of Prayer," 151–215. These important essays are reprinted in Heschel 1996, *Moral Grandeur and Spiritual Audacity,* 100–126. In slightly revised form, in Heschel 1954, *Man's Quest for God.*

37. Heschel to Abraham Liessen, 24 February 1930.

38. The following anecdote appeared in *The Jewish Spectator* (Fall 1994): 67–68, as reported to the editor, Robert Bleiweiss; it was originally told in confidence by Rabbi Sonderling to a "prominent Reform rabbi" who chose to remain anonymous—but who decided to report it after Sonderling's death. As published, the story purportedly explains "Schneerson's vendetta against non-Orthodox converts." Although its authenticity has been categorically denied by Sylvia Heschel and Susannah Heschel, this incident deserves serious consideration. Samuel Dresner has verified the story with the Reform rabbi under the condition of remaining anonymous, and our retelling has been modified to retain the objective elements. Shimon Deutsch, author of a multivolume biography of the Lubavitcher rebbe, considers the incident to be plausible.

39. Menahem Mendel Schneerson married Chaya Mushka Schneerson in November 1928; they remained in Berlin until 1934, when they went to Paris. See Deutsch 1997, *Larger Than Life,* vol. 2, chap. 4, "The Rebbe Enters the University of Berlin."

40. Heschel 1969, "Teaching Jewish Theology," 26n39; reprinted partially in *Moral Grandeur and Spiritual Audacity*, 154–63 (discussion in 1969, 18–33 is missing); also Heschel 1966, *Insecurity of Freedom*, "Religion and Race," 88.

Chapter 8. Poetic Vision and Prophetic Sympathy

Note to epigraph: Heschel 1950, *The Earth Is the Lord's*, 28.

1. Interview with Ludwig Kahn.

2. *Zukunft* was founded in 1892 as an organ of the Socialist Labor Party, acquired in 1912 by the Forward Association. It was not necessary to be a Bundist or even to express leftist sympathies in order to have writings appear in its pages. Its editorial offices were located at 175 East Broadway, New York City. See Liptzin 1985, 97–98.

3. Liessen correspondence at YIVO in New York, Liessen papers, folder 382.

4. Letter to Liessen dated 4 November 1929 from Berlin, signature illegible.

5. The poems appeared in this order in *Zukunft*, vol. 34 (December 1929: 825): "God pursues me everywhere . . ."; "Millions of eyes choke on one teardrop . . ."; "Evening on the streets"; "I and Thou." Translations based on Zalman Schachter-Shalomi but often significantly revised to remain closer to the original.

6. The return address was 56a Kant Strasse, c/o Pasemann. Ravitch Archive of the National Library, Hebrew University, Jerusalem.

7. Reprinted in *Unzer Zeit* (1973), 46; the text is the same as the original, also consulted.

8. In Heschel's 1933 collection *Der Shem Hameforash: Mentsh*, the poem was dated "Winter 1928–29," 19–20. See translation and commentary by Shandler 1993, 256–57.

9. In theory, these two dimensions of his creative personality are not one and the same. But his use of a singular verb ("hot Got dehert likhten veynen in a nigun") identifies their missions as one. When the "weeping luminous God" is silent, as is usually the case, the poet speaks for God to the world. Heschel's own "songs," modestly named, are really *nigunim*, sacred Hasidic melodies striving to become wordless prayers.

10. Liptzin 1985, 370–71. In 1936 Abraham Nochem Stencl (as Shtenzl spelled his name in English) fled to England, where he continued writing in Yiddish. Only three issues of *Berliner Bleter* appeared: November 1931, December 1931, and January–February 1932.

11. The *Berliner Bleter* sequence is "I and Thou"; "Dusk"; "Transformations"; "Need"; "The Pauper"; "God pursues me everywhere . . ." (untitled in *BB*).

12. Heschel's Yiddish poem "Ikh un Du" was first published in *Zukunft* in December 1929. It was reprinted in *Berliner Bleter* in November 1931, and it opens the 1933 collection (I, i, 9). It was also translated into German by Leo Hirsch, *Der Morgen*, June 1935. See below, chap. 14, p. 213.

13. Republished in his 1933 collection under the title "Between Me and the World" (IV, 1, 55), dated Winter 1929, and dedicated to Yehiel Hofer, his childhood companion.

14. Renamed "God's Tears" (I, 7, 15) in the 1933 collection.

15. In the 1933 collection (II, 1, 23), he dedicated the poem "To My Teacher David Koigen, of Blessed Memory."

Chapter 9. Paradigm Shift

Note to epigraph: Heschel 1953, "Toward an Understanding of Halacha," 386–87.

1. Heschel 1953, "Toward an Understanding of Halacha," 386–87; compare with 1954, *Man's Quest for God,* 94–95, where these passages about Kant are omitted. The original text is more useful; reprinted in *Moral Grandeur and Spiritual Audacity,* 127–45. The following quotations are from this 1953 speech to the annual meeting of Reform rabbis in the United States.

2. Cassirer 1944, *Essay on Man,* 21.

3. Schilpp, ed. 1949, *The Philosophy of Ernst Cassirer;* and article on Cassirer by S. Korner, in Edwards 1969, 44–46.

4. See catalogue of Hochschule.

5. The original editions: *Philosophie der symbolischen Formen,* three volumes (1923, 1925, 1929). See Charles W. Hendel's introductions to Ralph Manheim's translation of *The Philosophy of Symbolic Forms* (New Haven and London: Yale University Press, 1953; 1955; 1957; with additional bibliographical indications). Interview with Yochanan Muffs.

6. Cassirer 1944, *Essay on Man,* 228, final paragraph; this book summarizes Cassirer's findings in pellucid English. See article by Fritz Kaufmann, also Heschel's friend, in Schilpp 1949 on the limits of Cassirer's study of religion.

7. "Metaphysics and Religion," originally published as "Metaphysik und Religion," in *Jeschurun: Monatsschrift für Lehre und Leben im Judentum,* vol. 17, 9–12 (Berlin, 1930), 321–47, and republished as a brochure in 1931. See Altmann 1991, 1 sqq. and note p. 166.

8. Heschel 1953, "Toward an Understanding of Halacha," 387–88.

9. Just as Kant had effected a Copernican revolution in philosophy by displacing human evaluation of thinking from external reality to the mind, so Heschel, as a philosopher of religion, taught biblical thinking which examines human life from God's perspective.

10. Heschel 1953, "Toward an Understanding of Halacha," 389–90; repr. in *Man's Quest for God,* 96–98, which translates the Hebrew prayers quoted in Heschel's 1953 speech and adds brief explanations of terms.

11. Heschel 1953, "Toward an Understanding of Halacha," 391–93; the version included in Heschel 1954, *Man's Quest for God* (98) explains the reference: "How would I dare miss an evening prayer? Out of *eymah,* out of fear of God, do we read the *Shema. (Me-eyma-tai,* the first word of the tractate *Berachoth,* Rabbi Levi Yizhak.)"

12. Ibid.

13. Alexander Altmann cites Cassirer to introduce his discussion of halakhah: "Thus, unlike [Hermann] Cohen, we do not locate religion after the mythical stage; rather, it precedes myth phenomenally and in its real development. It is not, after all, morality suffused with myth but, according to its primal meaning, the unfolding of the tendency toward participation. Cassirer explains that the authentic objectivization of basic religious emotion takes place not in the image of the divine, but in the cult. 'Doing is primary, whereas the mythical explanation, the *hieros logos,* only follows later.' [Cassirer vol. 2., 271; also 270, 271 ff., also Dilthey . . .]." Altmann 1991, 15.

Chapter 10. God's Active Presence

Note to epigraph: Heschel 1936, *Die Prophetie,* 171.

1. Heschel letter to Liessen, 5 December 1932, return address: Mommsen Strasse, c/o Koigen. New York YIVO archives, Liessen Papers, Folder 382.

2. Return address: the Wiggert residence, 10 Holtzendorff Strasse, in Charlottenburg, not far from the Koigens. Humboldt University Archives.

3. Heschel's correspondence with university officials is preserved at the Humboldt University Archives, Promotionsverfahren no. 800.

4. We quote from Heschel's published revision of his dissertation; the Humboldt University Archives does not possess the original typescript. Heschel 1936, *Die Prophetie,* 127–83, Section 1, "Knowing God and Comprehending God" (*Gotteserkenntnis und Gottesverständnis*) further specifies his phenomenological method, inspired, in large part, from Dilthey's hermeneutics and especially from Max Scheler's study of sympathy: "The point of departure of the comprehension [*Verstehens*] is every event as it is experienced as 'expression' [*Ausdruck*] of God; its realization consists in becoming conscious of the meaning of that expression—its result is a *comprehension by God* [*Verständnis für Gott*] (not an impersonal knowledge). The highest degree of prophetic intercourse with God is the agreement of understanding (not unifying fusion)."

5. Heschel 1936, *Die Prophetie:* Parts I and II (7–126) analyzes the pre-exilic prophets: Amos, Hosea, Isaiah, and Jeremiah. Heschel takes particular care to refute psychological explanations of prophetic insight as forms of temporary psychosis, ecstasy, or poetic inspiration. The final Part III (127–83), consisting of two chapters, sets out the author's real agenda.

6. Heschel 1969, "Teaching Jewish Theology," 7; Heschel 1996, *Moral Grandeur and Spiritual Audacity,* 156.

7. Present were Prof. and Mrs. Koigen, Weinberg, Salomonski, Borodianski, Brandenburg, Schulwas, Poppers, and Heschel. The following week, 21 December 1931, Heschel's previous assertion was rebutted. "Koigen now states that in ethical relations there is no subject-object relationship, but the ethical process elevates the object and turns it into a corresponding subject; this transformation constitutes the eth-

ical act." Present: Prof. and Mrs. Koigen. Borodianski, Brandenburg, Heschel, Hoffmann, Poppers, Salomonski, Schulwas, Weinberg. Protokollführer: Salomonski.

8. Max Scheler, *The Nature of Sympathy*, trans. Peter Heath (London: Routledge & Kegan Paul, 1954). See Heschel 1962, *The Prophets*, 319n22: "There is no fusion of being, *unio mystica*, but an intimate harmony in will and feeling, a state that may be called *unio sympathetica*," referring to Scheler's work on sympathy; see ibid., 313n10. Heschel also cites Koigen's *Construction of the Social World* to differentiate the human "private I-side" of the prophetic event from the divine side. See above, n4.

9. Heschel 1936, *Die Prophetie*, 128–29, 129n2.

10. Ibid., part I, 28.

11. Ibid., 53.

12. Ibid., 53–55.

13. Ibid., 53–55.

14. Ibid., 131. Two chapters of part II (56–126) elaborate the principle of pathos.

15. Again at a crucial point in his demonstration, Heschel cites David Koigen, this time an article published in *Ethos*. See "Historische Gegenstandslehre," *Die Prophetie*, 104n1. The important subsection "Anthropotropism and Theotropism" names God's need to direct His concern toward humanity (115–19). Revelation is what God does with His "anthropotropism."

16. Ibid., 137.

17. Ibid., 143–45. The text continues: "It is not a prediction, the foreknowledge of a future event, which forms the prophet's spiritual possession, but the knowledge [*Wissen*] of present pathos." The next quotation, ibid., 166.

18. Ibid., 170n2. Heschel published another book citing the Talmudic sources of his theology of pathos, *Torah min ha-shamayim* (1962, 1965).

19. Ibid., 171. Nine additional sections develop further technical distinctions, including "Prophetic Nationalism," "Prophetic Morality," "The Meaning of Prophetic Exhortation," "Pathos, Passion, and Sympathy," "Imitation of God and Sympathy," and "The Form of Prophetic Sympathy."

20. "Im Erlebnis wird die transzendente Aufmerksamkeit erfahren, die Gottbesinnung ist Selbstbesinnung." Cf. Heschel 1962, *The Prophets*, 488—the final sentence of the book.

21. Humboldt University Archives.

Chapter 11. A Year of Grief and Rage

Note to epigraph: Heschel 1955, *God in Search of Man*, 377.

1. *Judisze Togblatt* (Warsaw), 6 January [8 Tevet] 1933. Front page.

2. The Novominsker rebbe's *yikhus* (which Heschel shared) was also recalled: he was the son of Reb Yankele (Jacob Perlow) and descendant of the Trisker Maggid (Avraham Twersky, 1860–1889) and the Kedushas Levi (Levi Yitzhak of Berditchev).

3. Quoted from the Warsaw *Judisze Togblatt*.

4. Heschel 1950, *The Earth Is the Lord's*, 16, in the chapter entitled "The Sigh."

5. Each professor's concise, handwritten report was appended to the form submitted to Dean Hartung and initialed by him. Materials from Humboldt University Archives: Doktoranden-Buch no. 68, Dean's Year 1932–33.

6. See Dawidowicz 1976, 63–68 and sqq. The menace was known to people who paid attention. In New York City, the American Jewish Committee (AJC) was meticulously collecting information about European events. In 1933 the AJC published a factual handbook, *The Jews in Nazi Germany*, which detailed Hitler's anti-Jewish legislation and its effect on the population. The revised edition of April 1935, with the added chapter on "The Results of Two Years' Oppression," was not revised further; abbreviated as AJC 1935.

7. As early as 3 January 1933, Koigen wrote to Martin Buber, asking for financial help: "My old friends have died off and I am suffocating under the burdens of three major projects on which I have been reflecting for years." Martin Buber Archive, Ms. Var. 350/379:22.

8. Dawidowicz 1976, 67.

9. AJC 1935, 75.

10. Interview with Fritz Rothschild. See below, chap. 15.

11. See esp. AJC 1935, 38–46.

12. Heschel first republished this piece in a Yiddish brochure printed by YIVO commemorating the twenty-fifth anniversary of Yung Vilne (12 March 1955), with this explanation: "Berlin, 1 April 1933; written when the Nazis in the Berlin Opern-Platz burned the works of Jewish philosophers. Printed under the pseudonym of 'Itzik' in the Warsaw *Haynt*, 10 May 1933." See the excellent translation by Shandler 1993, 260–63, which the translation below generally follows after the first two stanzas.

13. Elbogen 1944, 642–43.

14. See Heschel's letter to Liessen, 30 July 1933, YIVO Archives, New York. Heschel's first letter to the Polish Academy of Arts and Sciences was dated 8 March 1934; see minutes of the Polish Academy, University of Kraków Archives. Heschel then began a long correspondence, in Polish, with Professor Dr. Tadeusz Kowalski, who supervised the acceptance, correction, and printing of Heschel's thesis, which appeared two years later. See Halkowski 1992, 226.

15. Heschel letter to Liessen, 30 July 1933.

16. At the Nobel residence, 36 Kessel Strasse, near Sports Square, in North Berlin.

Chapter 12. A Poet's Self-Portrait

Note to epigraph: Heschel, "Symbolism and Jewish Faith," in Johnson, ed., 1954; repr. Heschel 1954, *Quest*, 124; repr. *Moral Grandeur and Spiritual Audacity*, 80–99. For an elaboration of this sacred humanism see also Heschel 1966, "Sacred Image of Man," *Insecurity of Freedom*, 150–67.

1. His brother, Jacob, around the same time composed poems in Hebrew (without distributing them), perhaps anticipating emigration to Palestine. Copies preserved by Jacob's daughter, Thena Heshel Kendall.

2. The book was a complete Warsaw production. Printed in Yiddish is the following information: published by Farlag "Indzl" (Indzl Publishing House), set in type by Hutner Publishing Company, printed by "Grafia" on Nowolipki, no. 7. It cost two guilden and could be ordered from Al. Welczer, at 39 Mila, apartment 6, in Warsaw. Printed in English: "Copyright by Abraham Heszel Warsaw." Our quotations based on the "free renderings" of Zalman Schachter-Shalomi (1973) and translations of Jeffrey Shandler (1991) occasionally modified. It is strange that not one of Heschel's Yiddish poems appeared in an anthology after World War II.

3. Conversation with Heschel, 6 February 1971. See Heschel 1955, *God in Search of Man*, 63–64n9, 70–71. According to the Bible (Gen. 1:26–27), humankind is God's only visible image; see Heschel 1966, *Insecurity of Freedom*, 151–52. Also Dresner, ed., 1985, introduction to Heschel, *Circle of the Baal Shem Tov*, x, n2 on the kabbalistic gematria of God's name being equivalent to humankind.

4. "Millions of Eyes Choking," also previously published, repeats the poet's threat to broadcast God's moral indifference; and "Suicides," previously entitled "Dusk," asks why God did not respond to a person's despair before it was too late. "God's Tears" (published in 1931 as "The Pauper") leads to the bold suggestion in the poem "God and Mankind" that alleviating suffering takes precedence over doctrinal faith: "No blasphemy pains You more/ Than human despair." Section 1 concludes with "Call Through the Night" as the poet takes upon himself the anguish of prostitutes, alcoholics, and abandoned corpses.

5. The brief "Palaces of Time" (*Palasn in der tsayt*) flows into "City Evenings" (*Oventn in shtot*), which also celebrates the sacred feelings aroused at day's end. Heschel located the poem rather cryptically "in Berlin." The modern city must become his new Jerusalem.

6. Heschel 1951, *The Sabbath*, chap. 1, "A Palace in Time," 13–24.

7. Of these ten pieces, only one had been published previously. "The Longing of My Early Youth," published in *Zukunft*, now emphasizes the positive energy of his immature wishes.

8. In the United States, Heschel fell in love with Sylvia Straus, a concert pianist; they were married in December 1946.

9. Poems 33–37 of the collection: "Between Me and the World," "Youth," "Secrets of My Longing," "In the Park," "Lonely."

10. It first appeared as "Transformations" in *Berliner Bleter* (1931); renamed "Between Me and the World," he dedicated it to Yehiel Hofer, his dearest childhood friend.

11. Years later, he used the same image to highlight the positive aspect of God's presence: "To the religious man nothing is ever deserted or unclaimed; it is as if God stood between him and the world. The most familiar retires from his sight, and he discerns the original beneath the palimpsests of things." Heschel 1951, *Man Is Not Alone*, 37.

12. Heschel 1950, *The Earth Is the Lord's*, 19; Heschel originally referred to Mendele Moykher Sforim's story, "Fishke the Cripple," in his speech in Yiddish: "The Eastern European Era in Jewish History," published in translation in *YIVO Annual* (1946), 91n3. See Shandler 1993, 272.

13. Zalman Schachter-Shalomi's introduction to the mimeographed copy of his translation.

14. See Dresner 1974, *Levi Yitzhak of Berditchev*, 77–90.

15. Bialik 1939, *Igrot* (Letters, in Hebrew), volume 5.

Chapter 13. Spiritual and Intellectual Biographies

Note to epigraph: Heschel 1982, *Maimonides*, 244.

1. Ernst Hoffmann 1934, "Koigens Kampf um die Geschichte" (Koigen's battle with history), sketches the life of "this lonely Jewish thinker" who probed the different modalities of Jewish collective existence. Later that year, Schocken published an anthology of Koigen's Jewish writings, *Das Haus Israel* (The house of Israel), in their pocket-sized Bücherei series.

2. Diary. Interview with Moses Shulvass.

3. Heschel 1934, "David Koigen."

4. "Situational thinking is necessary when we are engaged in an effort to understand issues on which we stake our very existence," Heschel 1955, *God in Search of Man*, 5, section entitled "Situational Thinking"; also Heschel 1965, *Who Is Man?*

5. The phrase is from Jacob Neusner, "Faith in the Crucible of the Mind," *America Magazine;* repr. in Neusner and Neusner 1990.

6. *Jüdische Rundschau,* 6 July 1934, front page.

7. Interview with Fritz Rothschild.

8. This and the next quotation from a letter from W. Gunther Plaut, 18 March 1988. See Plaut's autobiography, *Unfinished Business* (1981).

9. Guttmann states that he ordained Heschel in 1935. See Alexander Guttmann 1972, "Hochschule Retrospective," 78.

10. The list of five unpublished papers appended to Heschel's CV includes "Die Apokryphen, Pseudoepigraphen und die Halachach." We found no other confirmation and assume Heschel's CV to be accurate.

11. Sent to Dr. Künstlinger and former professor Archutowski. Following documents from the Archives of the Polish Academy of Arts and Sciences, Jagiellonian University, Kraków. To our knowledge, Heschel's letters to Kowalski are his only writings in Polish. See Halkowski 1992.

12. Heschel had moved to 4 August Strasse, close to the Hochschule and the Rabbiner-Seminar, c/o Scherz. The second address was 77/78 August Strasse, c/o Schauer.

13. Dean's letter from Humboldt University Archives. See Hartshorne 1937; Baumgardt 1965.

14. American Jewish Committee 1935, esp. 75–90, chap. 4, "Anti-Jewish Legislation."

15. Between 1908 and 1936, Reiss's company published 418 titles by 222 authors (54 of whom were foreign), and 49 translations.

16. Sylvia Heschel, foreword to the English trans. Heschel 1982, *Maimonides,* ix. We date the meeting slightly earlier than 1935, which is given there.

17. Minutes of 21 February 1935. Polish Academy Archives, Jagiellonian University.

18. The General Secretary, Kutrzeba, was historian of Polish law and professor at the Jagiellonian University.

19. Letter from Heschel to Kowalski, 26 March 1935, Polish Academy Archives, Jagiellonian University.

20. The Polish Academy acknowledged receipt of his deposit a few days later. The minutes of 25 May 1935 recorded that Heschel still owed them 8,000 zloty.

21. Brenner 1996.

22. See Simon 1956.

23. Halbey 1980–81, 1128–1256.

24. Heschel to Max Grünewald, 26 November 1934; return address: 4 August Strasse, Berlin IV, 24. Hebrew University Jerusalem, 4o 1182, box 2–4. Citing an article Grünewald published in 1913, Heschel asked him to verify if "Maimonides boarded a ship at the port of Tanger," and if, "in Palestine, Maimonides failed to find any *means of subsistence* and for this reason left Palestine."

25. Heschel 1982, *Maimonides,* 21. Citations from *Maimonides* are first from the 1982 English translation, followed by a slash and the page reference to the 1935 German edition. The English translation has sometimes been modified.

26. *Maimonides,* 24/ 27, and 25–26/ 28–29.

27. Heschel 1945, 1950, "Prophetic Inspiration in the Middle Ages." See E. Kaplan 1996, chap. 9, "Metaphor and Miracle: Modern Judaism and the Holy Spirit."

28. *Maimonides,* 65–66/ 73.

29. Ibid., 19/ 21, and 127/ 141. See chap. 13, "The Transformation."

30. Ibid., 129/ 142–43.

31. Ibid., 135/ 151. Here is Heschel's summary: "His victory over the passions, the transformation of his image of the world, the elimination of the feeling of self-importance, the change of language, the modification of his existence by practicing medicine, all these show how deep was the crisis he endured" (138/ 155).

32. Ibid., 180/ 180.

33. The editorial comment at the head of chap. 15, "Meditation on God," states Heschel's preference for the study of consciousness, over abstract thought, as a means of penetrating the essence of a philosophy—and a person. Ibid., 258/ 286, notes.

34. Ibid., 180/180.

35. Ibid., 212/237–38.

36. Ibid., 196/220.

37. Ibid., 214–15/240–41.

38. Ibid., 215–16/242. See Goldberg 1989, 133–36, esp. notes, 208–10. It is not true that one cannot find sexuality or eros in Heschel's work; in addition to his poetry see Heschel 1951, *Man Is Not Alone*, 263: "Judaism does not despise the carnal. It does not urge us to desert the flesh but to control and to counsel it; to please the natural needs of the flesh so that the spirit should not be molested by unnatural frustrations." Also Heschel 1973, *Passion for Truth*, 216–22, *Kotsk*, vol. 2, 235–43; Dresner 1981, 161–62n69.

39. Translated in Heschel 1966, *Insecurity of Freedom*, 289–90.

40. *Maimonides*, 243/274. See Heschel 1966, *Insecurity of Freedom*, 290.

41. Heschel 1966, *Insecurity of Freedom*, 293.

42. The May–June 1935 publication of the B'nai B'rith.

43. *Diariode* (Madrid), 3 July 1935. A scholarly reviewer in the Catholic *Nouvelle Revue Théologique* from Belgium breathlessly summarized Maimonides's life as an adventure novel, pointing to its ecumenical value: "The section on 'Meditation on God' is an excellent scientific introduction to the study of the Summa." See the review of H. L. (Hans Liebeschütz?) in the *Jüdisches Gemeindeblatt für Frankfurt* 13:12 (August 1935): 462–63.

44. Other contributors included Hanoch Albeck, Judah Bergmann, Ismar Elbogen, Max Grünewald (to whom Heschel wrote about his project), Isaak Heinemann, and Immanuel Löw.

45. Heinemann wrote that rationalistic "expressions such as 'contemplation' or even 'meditation' (pp. 175 ff.) fit better a Bahya [Ibn Pakuda]; the implementation of detail is even less convincing"; *Monatsschrift* 79 (1935): 199–200.

Chapter 14. The German Jewish Renaissance

Note to epigraph: F. A., review of Heschel, *Der Shem Hameforash* in *Der Morgen* 10 (March 1935), 570–71.

1. Glatzer 1956, 122. See Brenner 1996 on the Berlin Volkshochschule.

2. Heschel's CV states that he gave lectures there in 1935; the authors were unable to find catalogues of the Berlin Lehrhaus from January–October 1935, but the Berlin *Gemeindeblatt* does not mention any courses offered by Heschel. He probably gave individual lectures, not a course.

3. During its first eight years, every issue contained at least one article dealing with Nazi ideology. The following analysis is taken from Fraiman 1991.

4. Among contributors to *Der Morgen* were Alexander Altmann, Julius Bab, Leo Baeck, Fritz Bamberger, David Baumgardt, Hugo Bergmann, Martin Buber, Joseph Carlebach (the Orthodox Chief Rabbi of Hamburg), Ernst Cassirer, Max Dienemann,

Paul Eppstein, Ludwig Feuchtwanger, Max Grünewald, Isaak Heinemann, Leo Hirsch, Stefan Kayser, Ignaz Maybaum, Franz Rosenzweig, Hans Joachim Schoeps, Ernst Simon, Max Spanier, Selma Stern (later Stern-Täubler), Margarete Susman, and Max Weiner.

5. *Der Morgen* 9 (January 1934): 391, "Restauration oder Renaissance?"

6. See for example, Paul Schreiber "Unser Weg," *Der Morgen* 9 (August 1933): 217; Michael Graupe, "Stefan George," *Der Morgen* 9 (November 1933): 295; Georg Lubinski, "Aufbruch der Jugend," *Der Morgen* 9 (December 1933): 348.

7. Conversation with Heschel.

8. Interview with Stephen (Stefan) Kayser, later director of New York's Jewish Museum. Subsequent statements attributed to Kayser are from interviews. See Grossman 1991.

9. Among the other, occasional teachers, many appear on previous lists, with some additions: Arnold Berney, Ismar Freund, Hans Friedländer, Walter Gottschalk, Fritz Kaufmann, Hans Liebeschütz, Arnold Metzger, and others. See *Monatsschrift*, vol. 50, Report of the years 1932–35, highly compressed under Nazi censorship, since the previous reports could not be printed for lack of money. See also Fuchs 1967, 11–12.

10. See Mendes-Flohr 1991, "Fin de siècle Orientalism, the *Ostjuden*, and the Aesthetics of Jewish Self-Affirmation," 77–132.

11. Heschel inscribes Leo Hirsch's name with others who helped him in Europe in the dedication to *Kotzk: The Struggle for Integrity*, the two-volume Yiddish book published in 1973 after his death. On Leo Hirsch, see Stern 1970. In addition to poems, essays, and stories in *Der Morgen*, Hirsch published a guide to daily observance, *Praktische Judentumskunde; eine Einführung in die Jüdische Werk* (Berlin: Vortrupp Verlag, 1935), with excerpts from the Torah, Talmud, Siddur (the daily prayerbook), Machsor (Holy Day prayerbook), and the Shulhan Arukh (the standard code of Jewish law). In *Jüdische Mütter* (Berlin: Vortrupp Verlag, 1936), published with Egon Jacobson, Hirsch celebrates Jewish mothers with essays on Glückel von Hameln, Gudula Rothschild, Frumet Mendelssohn, Betty Heine, Amalie Beer, Jeanette Herzl, and Mathilde Rathenau; see review in *Der Morgen* 12 (1936–37): 473.

12. See Hirsch's 1934 essay, "Der Dreitage-Jude: Kritik eines Übergangs" (The three-day Jew: Criticism of a change), which examines the majority of assimilated Jews who attend synagogue but three days a year, during the High Holy Days. *Der Morgen* 10 (1934–35): 295–98.

13. *Der Morgen* 10 (1934–35) [March 1935]: 570.

14. Poem appears in *Der Morgen* 11 (1935–36), June issue: 127.

15. Rachel Wischnitzer, "Vi azoi hot di yiddishe kunst-malerei antvicklt in Rusland un Poiln" (How Jewish Art-Painting Develops in Russia and Poland), in *Berliner Bleter* 3, nos. 3–4 (January–February 1932).

16. Morgenstern 1935, *Der Sohn des verlorenen Sohnes*, was published by Erich Reiss; a translation, *The Son of the Lost Son*, was published by the Jewish Publication Soci-

ety in 1946. Morgenstern presents another version of the meeting in his afterward to his *Pillar of Blood* (*Die Blutsäele*; 1976): 162–67. Interview with Soma Morgenstern.

17. *Der Morgen* reviewed *The Son of the Lost Son* in February 1936. Susi Bing's essay "A Novel of Return" highlights its enthusiastic depiction of "the world of the Podolian, 'caftan Jew,' the content of which forms the most beautiful, artistically rich and ripe pictures of the book." In contrast, she finds less appealing those portions of the novel describing Vienna in the 1920s "with distance and ironic coldness."

18. They met in 1937 after Heschel had left Berlin, according to Morgenstern's recollections; interview with Soma Morgenstern.

19. Interview with Soma Morgenstern.

20. "The capstone was the Law for the Protection of German Blood and Honor. This law forbade marriage and all sexual intercourse between Jews and women of German or related blood, and imposed heavy penalties for transgression." Elbogen 1944, 654.

21. Ibid.

22. He had previously moved back to 150 Kant Strasse, c/o Rüsicke, and now moved down the street, c/o Woisky.

23. On 23 November 1935 the Polish Academy acknowledged receipt of 1,340 zloty and stated that Heschel's book would be twenty-second in their Oriental Studies series.

24. Baumgardt 1965, 261.

Chapter 15. Alliance with Martin Buber

Note to epigraph: Heschel 1953, "Toward an Understanding of Halacha," 388.

1. Interview with Maurice Friedman, December 1994, and his books. See Mendes-Flohr 1989 and Mendes-Flohr 1991, "Martin Buber's Conception of God," in *Divided Passions*, 237–82.

2. Conversation with Heschel. Interview with Fritz Rothschild.

3. Interviews with Fritz Rothschild, Marshall Meyer, and Yochanan Muffs.

4. From Heschel's letter of 18 June 1935, first translated and analyzed in Kaplan 1994, 214–15. Heschel's original letters are preserved in the Martin Buber Archive, Jerusalem, Ms. Var. 290:1–56. Buber's *Briefwechsel* includes only a small number of Heschel's letters. Buber's letters to Heschel may be lost or in the possession of the Heschel family.

5. Interview with Fritz Rothschild.

6. "Sinnbildlische und sakramentale Existenz im Judentum," in *Eranos-Jahrbuch*, vol. 2, 1934 (Zurich: Rhein-Verlag, 1935): 339–67; trans. Maurice Friedman in *The Origin and Meaning of Hasidism* (New York: Harper Torchbooks, 1960): 152–81. Heschel's letter cites pages from the German publication, originally presented in August 1934 in Switzerland.

7. The following quotations are taken from Heschel's letter to Buber, 24 July 1935, published in Buber, *Briefwechsel*, vol. 2, letter no. 510, pp. 568–69; translated and an-

alyzed in Kaplan 1994, 215–16; original in Martin Buber Archive, Jerusalem, Ms. Var. 290:2. Cf. letter of 26 March 1936 from Ernst Michel, the progressive Catholic sociologist, to Buber, thanking him for the same paper: in Buber, *Briefwechsel*, vol. 2, letter no. 510, pp. 568–69.

    Compare the following discussion with Friedman 1983, 230–34. For more details see Kaplan 1996, 82–84. (Since that publication the author has modified his characterization of Buber.) The fuller context of these fundamental issues is studied with great care and ample documentation by Paul Mendes-Flohr 1991, *Divided Passions*. Compare with Maurice Friedman 1960, chap. 19, "Buber's Theory of Knowledge"; chap. 24, "Symbol, Myth, and History."

8. For Heschel's most forthright explanation of his attitude toward Buber, see his 1967 interview with Patrick Granfield: "[Q:] Have you been greatly influenced by Martin Buber? H: I would not say so. I consider the important insights in Buber to be derived from Hasidism, and these I knew before I met him. . . . [Buber] believed [revelation] is a vague encounter. That is untenable. A Jew cannot live by such a conception of revelation. Buber does not do justice to the claims of the prophets. So I have to choose between him and the Bible itself." *Moral Grandeur and Spiritual Audacity*, 384–85.

9. Thanks to Paul Mendes-Flohr for this formulation.

10. We do not possess Buber's answer to Heschel's distressed query, nor do we know whether it was written or oral—or never given.

11. Buber 1949, *The Prophetic Faith*, 96–109: the footnote reads: "Cf. especially Heschel, *Die Prophetie* (1936), 76ff."

12. Heschel 1951, *Man Is Not Alone*, 47.

13. See Stern 1983, "A. J. Heschel, Irenic Polemicist." Heschel's opposition to Buber's exegesis of God's word as symbol advanced an older debate with Buber, when Franz Rosenzweig, in an essay entitled "Atheistic Theology," admonished Buber's early romantic approach to the biblical God. (Heschel recommended Rosenzweig's essay to students as a useful critique of contemporary religion.) See Kaplan 1996, chap. 6, "Sacred versus Symbolic Religion."

14. The essay was translated by Maurice Friedman in Buber 1958, *Hasidism and Modern Man*, 52; original, *Mein Weg zum Chassidismus: Erinnerungen* (Frankfurt: Rütten & Loening, 1918).

15. Buber 1958, 53–54.

16. Ibid., 51.

17. Ibid., 54, 59.

18. Ibid., 59.

19. Heschel: "One of the weaknesses in Buber, who was an exceedingly learned man, was that he was not at home in rabbinic literature. That covers many years. A lot has happened between the Bible and Hasidism that Buber did not pay attention to" (*Moral Grandeur and Spiritual Audacity*, 385).

20. See Diary and told to EK by Heschel.

Chapter 16. Mission Defined

Note to epigraph: Heschel 1936, "Persönlichkeiten der jüdischen Geschichte: Jochanan ben Zakkai," 14.

1. Letter dated 18 December 1935 to Heschel from Gebethner and Wolff Bookstore and Musical Scores; Polish Academy Archives, Kraków, doc. 28.

2. Heschel letter to Kowalski, 9 February 1936; on 3 March 1934 Dessoir officially terminated his association with the university but remained in Berlin to continue other scholarly activities. See Asen 1955.

3. This copy (from Widener Library, Harvard University, received 1 September 1937) contains a *Lebenslauf* printed following the Polish abstract and the page of errata: "Ich bin als Sohn des Rabbiners Moses Heschel am 11. January 1907 in Warschau geboren. Nach Beendigung des Mathematisch-Naturwissenschaftlichen Gymnasiums in Wilna und nach bestandenem Examen am Institut für Ausländer in Berlin studierte ich von 1928 bis 1932 Philosophie, semitische Philologie und Kunstgeschichte an der Berliner Universität. Gleichzeitig gehörte ich der Hochschule für die Wissenschaft des Judentums als ordentlicher Hörer an. In meinen Studien wurde ich hauptsächlich von den Herren Professoren Dessoir, Maier, Wölflin, Koigen und Guttmann gefördert."

4. Two days later, on 10 March, Heschel felt compelled to tell Kowalski that he (Heschel) had written directly to the Polish Academy asking them to send copies of the book to the university. He explained that since the university had, the previous December, made an exception in his case to award him his Promotion, it was all the more imperative to make 150 copies available to them as soon as possible.

5. See information in letter of Polish Academy to Heschel, 12 April 1938, and Heschel's letters to the Chancellery of the Polish Academy of Arts and Sciences, 29 April 1938.

6. See Heschel letter to Kowalski, 24 April 1936.

7. Heschel 1936, *Maïmonide*, trans. Germaine Bernard, preface by Bernard Chapira; first printing June 1936.

8. Heschel to Kowalski, 22 November 1936, from a new address, the Rubens residence at 99 Kurfürsten Strasse (Berlin West 62).

9. Julius Guttmann, Heschel's teacher at the Hochschule, explains how Gabirol made Spain a philosophical center: 1969 *Philosophies of Judaism*, 89–103. The Neoplatonist contributed more to general metaphysics than to Jewish philosophy as such; Gabirol's *Fons Vitae*, despite its evocative title, comprised an abstract system and makes no mention of Jewish sources. The text was even thought to be the work of a Muslim or Christian, and the Latin translation influenced the development of scholasticism, preparing the way for comparative Jewish and Christian theology. See J. Wijnhoven 1965, "The Mysticism of Solomon Ibn Gabirol." At Hebrew Union College, Heschel edited *A Concise Dictionary of Hebrew Philosophical Terms* (mimeographed 1941).

10. Letter in Archives Diplomatiques de Nantes, Berlin fonds C: no. 121, dossier lettre H. Thanks to Mme Stella Corbin for this and other materials in her possession relating to her husband. See also the issue of *Cahiers de L'Herne* 1981.

11. Dated 7 May 1936, copy from the library of Henry Corbin.

12. Letter of Heschel to Corbin, 11 June 1936. Stella Corbin, Paris, personal papers.

13. Among Corbin's acquaintances were Heidegger, Karl Jaspers, Leon Chestov, Jean Baruzi, Vladimir Yankélévitch, Maurice de Gandillac—and literary thinkers, Charles du Bos, Bernard Groethuysen, Henri Michaux.

14. The full title was *Gemeindeblatt der jüdischen Gemeinde zu Berlin*, with offices at 29 Oranienburger Strasse, Berlin N4, the center of the Jewish community. It had a circulation of 52,000. Strauss 1987, 99. The entire section of Strauss (95–120) provides valuable documentation on attitudes expressed through the Jewish press at the time. See references in the present book to Heschel's journalism, most of it previously unknown.

15. See Simon 1956.

16. The Tannaim were rabbinic authorities who established the Oral Law, interpretations of the Bible handed down the generations through master and disciple by memorization. Their opinions were collected in the *Mishnah* around 220 C.E., redacted by Jehuda Ha-Nassi, an ancestor of Maimonides. (The *Mishnah* constitutes the basis of discussions collected in the *Gemara*, clarification of the original legal principles. The *Talmud* is formed of these two compilations of biblical exegesis and legal rulings.)

17. On 17 May Heschel's essay appeared on Rabbi Meir, a pupil and friend of the heretic Elisha ben Abuyah. A disciple of Rabbi Akiba, R. Meir was concerned more with learning than with action.

18. After Heschel moved to Frankfurt in March 1937, he republished these essays in the Frankfurt *Gemeindeblatt*.

19. Rosenzweig 1953, *Life and Thought*, Glatzer's introduction, xvii.

20. "Die Kraft der Buße" (The power of repentance) appeared in the 13 September *Gemeindeblatt;* 16 September 1936, "Die Marranen von Heute" (The Marranos of today); the latter trans. in *Moral Grandeur and Spiritual Audacity* as "The Meaning of Repentance," 68–70, mistakenly dated the eve of Yom Kippur.

21. Rosh Hoshanah, 1 Tishri 1936. Files of Rabbi Meir Wunder, Jerusalem.

Part Four. Frankfurt, the War, and Exile

Note to epigraph: Reprinted in Heschel 1966, *Insecurity of Freedom*, 236.

1. Heuberger 1992.

2. See Rosenzweig 1965, an anthology of Rosenzweig's speeches from the 1920s edited by Nahum Glatzer; also Rosenzweig 1953.

3. Baker 1978, 145.

Chapter 17. Teaching in Times of Crisis

Note to epigraph: Heschel 1986 (orig. 1937), *Don Jizhak Abravanel,* 29; English, 12.

1. These parables continued the rabbinic message he addressed to the community during the High Holy Days: "Die gewaltigen Dinge" (The powerful things) and "Die Verdienste Abrahams" (The merits of Abraham). See References.

2. Friedman 1983, 254–60.

3. We have not found any letters between Heschel and Buber from July 1935 to November 1936. Susannah Heschel describes how Heschel visited Frankfurt in March 1936, where he met with Buber and some of his closest associates: Ludwig Feuchtwanger and Eduard Strauss, "all of whom had read his book on the prophets." Heschel 1996, *Moral Grandeur and Spiritual Audacity,* xv. *Die Prophetie* was available in proof without covers by December 1935, and prepared for sale by March 1936.

4. Kantorowicz took over in March 1938 right after Buber emigrated. Glatzer and Mendes-Flohr 1991, 466n1; also Simon 1958, 80.

5. Heschel letter to Buber, 24 November 1936, 99 Kurfürsten Strasse, Berlin W62, c/o Rubens; Ms. Var. 290:3.

6. S. Heschel 1996, *Moral Grandeur and Spiritual Audacity,* xv.

7. This and the next quotation from Heschel letter to Buber, 24 January 1937, same return address, Ms. Var. 290:4.

8. Heschel letter to Buber, 2 March 1937, Ms. Var. 290:6.

9. Heschel letter to Buber, 3 March 1937, Ms. Var. 290:7.

10. Letter from Heschel, 26 March 1937, receiver not named, cited by S. Heschel 1996, *Moral Grandeur and Spiritual Audacity,* xv–xvi.

11. Heschel's letter of 26 March 1938 continues, *Moral Grandeur and Spiritual Audacity,* xv–xvi, with slight modifications.

12. Quoted in Heschel 1996, *Moral Grandeur and Spiritual Audacity,* xvi. S. Heschel quotes "another letter" (undated) of Heschel's which summarizes their differences in somewhat cryptic language: "In the decisive question I have to say No to him. An apotheosis of the Bible is not permissable. The holiness of the Bible is due to its origins. There is no autarky [self-sufficiency] in it."

13. This was perhaps Heschel's first meaningful encounter with Eduard Strauss, a biochemist by profession who worked with Franz Rosenzweig at the Frankfurt Lehrhaus, teaching well-attended classes in Bible, and who remained one of Buber's closest associates.

14. Heschel letter to Buber, 7 April 1937, Ms. Var. 290:8. The books included: *Ginze Yosef,* a Hasidic classic by Yosef Bloch (Lemberg 1792), *Yismah Yisrael* by Israel Friedman (Vienna, 1933), *Yismah Moshe* by Moshe Teitelbaum on the prophets and writings (Lemberg, 1848–1850), *Nahar Shalom* by Meir Shalom of Porisev (Warsaw, 1908), *Hokhmat ha-Nephesh,* notes of Rabbi J. Dinov and Kabbalistic text by Eleazar of Worms (Lemberg, 1876), and *Ma'amar Mordekai,* by Mordecai Vinograd (Bilgo-

ray, 1932), a collection of Hasidic sayings. Later that month, Heschel consulted with Professor Köster in S. Georgen about books for Buber to buy or to borrow (see letter of 20 April 1937).

15. Friedman 1983, 256. Also Fritz Rothschild and conversation with Heschel.

16. Interview with Mrs. Rose Hertz (née Simon). Letters from Rose Hertz, 19 December 1978, 25 January 1979.

17. At Frankfurt (Main)-Ginnheim, Fuchshohl 67. Some further information from Steven Wertheimer, who knew Heschel in Frankfurt and London.

18. The catalogues of the Frankfurt Lehrhaus and announcements in the Jewish community newspaper of Frankfurt, the *Israelitisches Gemeindeblatt*, give titles of courses Heschel offered. During the October–December 1937 semester, Heschel gave five evening classes on "Moses during the Crisis" at the Westend Synagogue. The following spring semester, May–July 1938, with Ernst Blau he taught a workshop on library research skills. (Rabbi Jakob Horovitz taught a course on Maimonides, as he had for some years.) On 19 October 1938, the Frankfurt *Gemeindeblatt* announced that Heschel would soon lecture on "Jewish religious philosophy."

19. Interview with Fritz Rothschild, 5 October 1989.

20. Rothschild edited the first anthology of Heschel's writings, with his now classic essay on Heschel's philosophy of religion, *Between God and Man* (1959; most recent revision, 1975).

21. Jacob Simon died of a heart attack just before leaving Germany. His two daughters and wife survived. Interviews with Rose Hertz. Samuel Dresner observed the MS of the *Maimonides* translation in Heschel's files after his death. It was retranslated and published in 1982.

22. The quotation continues: "The British journalists were tremendously impressed! By what? They didn't sense the poison in the hearts of these men. Neither did they sense the poison in the words of these men" (Heschel 1969, "Teaching Jewish Theology," 32–33). See also Heschel 1949, *Pikuah Neshama*, in *Moral Grandeur and Spiritual Audacity*, 58–59, which states the year correctly.

23. Heschel 1936, "Die Marranen von Heute," trans. Heschel 1996, *Moral Grandeur and Spiritual Audacity*, 69.

24. English quoted from Heschel 1986, *Abravanel*, 5, 8–12; corrected when necessary. This quotation translated from the German original *Don Jizhak Abravanel*, 1937, 5; passage not included in the William Wolf translation.

25. The full name: Preussischer Landesverband jüdischer Gemeinden (Prussian State Association of Jewish Communities). See the review by Dr. Joseph Heller in *Gemeindeblatt Berlin*.

26. Heschel 1937, *Don Jizhak Abravanel*, 5.

27. Heschel 1986, 5; 1937 German, 6.

28. Heschel 1937, *Don Jizhak Abravanel*, 25–26; omitted in translation.

29. Ibid., English, 10–11; German 1937, 27.

30. Ibid., English, 12; German, 29.

31. Ibid., English, 8; German, 11.

32. Ibid., English, 12; German, 30, final paragraph. Cited also from Heschel 1969, *Israel*, 114.

33. Fritz Rothschild read Heschel's essay as an eighteen-year-old in Germany and never forgot being impressed by this insightful twist at the end.

34. Translated into Polish by Ozjasz Tilleman, Lwow, 1938; Moses Schorr or Buber may have helped obtain the subvention.

35. Heschel letter of 12 December 1937, Ms. Var. 290:10. See Martin Buber, *Gleichsprüche*, vol. 15 of the Bible translation, Berlin: Schocken Verlag, 1937.

36. On 8 December 1936, the minutes of the Oriental Committee noted with pleasure that "the Committee's publications are being noticed by the Western [i.e., European] critics," in particular works by Heschel, Jablonski, and Kowalski. The minutes of 7 June 1937 acknowledged that *Die Prophetie* had garnered the most reviews. On 15 February 1938, the Oriental Committee noted: "Numerous reviews of the most recent works by the Committee were published, especially the still continuing reviews of Heschel's work on prophecy from Catholic, Protestant, and Jewish theologians." Later that month, Heschel thanked Kowalski for clippings of reviews and requested more, enclosing a list of reviews that appeared without his being able to obtain copies. Heschel to Kowalski, 26 February 1938.

37. Heschel gave this list of reviews with brief excerpts to Henry Corbin in Paris, all dated 1936: *Bne Briss*, 74; *Gemeindeblatt Aachen; Gemeindeblatt Leipzig* 21; *Der Israelit* (Mainz) (10 December): 151; *Jüdische Allgemeine Zeitung* (13 May); *Jüdische Rundschau* (7 October); Ludwig Köhler, *Theologische Rundschau*, 266; Samuel Krauss, *Archiv für oriental* [?] (Prague), 395–96; *Der Orient*, 151; *Protestantische Rundschau*, 249; *Bayrische Israelitische Gemeindezeitung* 8; *Reformierte Kirchenzeitung*, 414; T. H. Robinson, *Expository Times*, 181 ff.; *C. V. Zeitung* 21; H. Junker, *Theologische Revue* 11:439–42; *Theologische Gegenwart*, 112 ff.; *Die Wahrheit* (25 December); *Zeitschrift für Missionskunde und Religionswissenschaft*, 384. Other reviews (selected): *1936:* Dr. H.L., *Frankfurter Israelitisches Gemeindeblatt* 12 (September 1936): 451; Otto Eissfeldt, *Theologische Studien und Kritiken*, 214; Chief Rabbi Carlebach (Hamburg), *Gemeindeblatt Berlin* (23 August 1936). *1937:* H. Wheeler Robinson, *Journal of Theological Studies* (Oxford) 38 (January): 181–82; Leo Hirsch, "Pathos und Sympathie. Ueber Heschels *Prophetie*," *Der Morgen* 12 (February): 514–17; A. Jepsen, *Orientalische Literaturzeitung* (Leipzig), 6 (March): 367–69; C. H., *Nouvelle Revue Théologique* (Louvain) 64, 3 (March): 310; Joseph L. Blau, *Review of Religion* 2, 1 (November): 484–85; Millar Burrows, *Journal of Biblical Literature* (Philadelphia) 56 (December): 398–400; *Ecclesiastical Review* (Philadelphia) 96:649; Max Grünewald, *Monatsschrift für Geschichte und Wissenschaft des Judentums* 81:253–55; Fr. Blome, *Theologie und Glaube* (Paderborn): 575–76. *1938:* L. Ph. Ricard, *Archives de philosophie* 14, *Supplément bibliographique:* 56–57; *Re-*

vue biblique 47. *1939:* H. Bacht, S.J., *Biblica: Commentarii ad Rem Biblicam Scientifice Investigandam* (Pontifical Institute, Rome) 20:202–5. *1940:* Adolphe Lods, *Revue de l'histoire des religions* (Paris) 121:89–92.

Chapter 18. A Prophetic Witness

Note to epigraph: Heschel 1951, *Man Is Not Alone,* 153.

1. Heschel wrote Tadeusz Kowalski on 10 April, informing him of his move, asking for clippings of reviews of *Die Prophetie,* and enclosing a copy of "a short treatise on the philosophy of Gabirol"; Heschel added that a second treatise would soon follow.
2. Letter in French from Else Adler to Henry Corbin, Paris, dated 14 December 1937 from Paris, and another on 24 December from 11 Adelheid Strasse, Frankfurt. Adler had left a copy of the *Revue anglaise* with a review of *Die Prophetie* at Corbin's apartment and wanted him to return it. We have not been able to locate the review. Personal papers of Henry Corbin, Paris.
3. Heschel letter to Corbin, 18 January 1938; courtesy of Mme Stella Corbin, Paris.
4. In his letter to Eduard Strauss, quite exceptionally, Heschel addresses the elder with the familiar *Du.*
5. "Der Begriff des Seins in der Philosophie Gabirols," 68–77. In the same volume, Alexander Altmann, "Olam und Aion," referred favorably to Heschel: "On the structure of prophetic consciousness, cf. the profound descriptions of Abraham Heschel, in his book, *Die Prophetie,* 1936" (13n41).
6. Heschel's book on the prophets was reviewed in the *Monatsschrift,* 1937–38 and also the Freimann Festschrift; in the same issue brief mention was also made of Fishl Schneersohn's Yiddish novel on a Lubavitcher Hasid, *Hayim Gravitzer.*
7. Heschel letter to Henry Corbin, 18 January 1938.
8. Heschel's first article in English, "An Analysis of Piety," was published in 1942. It was an amalgam of two articles from 1939, one in German ("Das Gebet als Äusserung und Einfühlung") and the other in Hebrew ("'Al mahut ha-tefillah").
9. Glatzer and Mendes-Flohr 1991, 467, letter no. 516.
10. From Lachmund, introduction to Heschel 1962; Heschel's original text, "Versuch einer Deutung" (Search for a meaning), 11–13.
11. Heschel published a revised translation of this speech in the United States, first in the *Hebrew Union College Bulletin* (March 1943). A slightly revised version, with specific references to the war, appeared in *Liberal Judaism* (London, 1944). The final chapter of *Man's Quest for God* reproduces the *Liberal Judaism* version, with an incorrect indication of date (March 1938 instead of February). Compare the original speech with Heschel's American translation and revision, published in 1943: "Emblazoned over the gates of the world in which we live is the escutcheon of the demons. The mark of Cain in the face of man has come to overshadow the likeness of God. There have [sic] never been so much guilt and distress, agony and terror. At no time

has the earth been so soaked with blood. Fellow-men turned out to be evil ghosts, monstrous and weird. Ashamed and dismayed to live in such a world, we ask: Who is responsible?" *Hebrew Union College Bulletin* (March 1943): 1. Cf. the third stage of this text in Heschel 1951, *Man Is Not Alone*, chap. 16, "The Hiding God," 151–57.

12. See Heschel 1949, *Pikuah Neshama;* trans. Heschel 1996, *Moral Grandeur and Spiritual Audacity*, 54–67.

13. See Heschel 1966, "Depth Theology," *Insecurity of Freedom*, 115–26.

14. Heschel 1950, *The Earth Is the Lord's*, 72.

15. S. Heschel 1996, *Moral Grandeur and Spiritual Audacity*, xvii.

16. On 13 March the Bubers left for Zurich and Italy, sailing for Palestine on the 19th. They arrived in Haifa on 24 March and soon settled in Talbiyeh, the new, European section of Jerusalem, where most of the recent immigrants were living. After years of unpleasant negotiations and disappointments, Buber became professor of social philosophy at the Hebrew University on Mount Scopus. See Friedman 1983, 257–58; entire chap. 13, and notes (366–67) on Buber's difficulties in getting the job.

17. General Files, Jewish Theological Seminary of America, New York.

18. S. Heschel 1996, *Moral Grandeur and Spiritual Audacity*, xvii.

19. Letters of Heschel to Kowalski, 10 April 1937 from the Simon residence; 22 July 1937 from 11 Adelheid Strasse, Eschersheim; 26 February 1938, from the same address.

20. Interview with Zusya Heschel, son of the Kopitzhinitzer rebbe, in Mintz 1992, 72–73.

21. Rabbi Heschel repeated this loyal sacrifice in the United States when he refused the pleas of many followers who had left Manhattan's Lower East Side for middle-class Borough Park in Brooklyn, preferring to remain so as not to abandon the poorest Jews.

22. Mintz 1992.

23. Interview with Zusya Heschel in Mintz 1992, 72–73.

24. Rosenstein 1990, vol. 2, 937–38.

25. Quoted without date by S. Heschel 1996, *Moral Grandeur and Spiritual Audacity*, xix.

Chapter 19. "Out of the Depths"

Note to epigraph: Heschel 1955, *God in Search of Man*, 245.

1. On 9 April 1938 the Polish Academy responded that they would send 100 copies to his Warsaw address. On 30 March, they sent 100 copies to Warsaw, followed on 12 April by one trunk with 100 more copies. That made 298 copies remaining at the Jagiellonian University printing house. The entire edition comprised 1,500 copies. The General-Secretary of the Academy clarified their records with a letter to Heschel on 12 April.

2. Heschel letter to Buber, 25 April 1938, Ms. Var. 290:12.

3. Buber 1936, *Aus Tiefen rufe ich Dich* (Out of the depths I cry to Thee), Berlin. See Si-

mon 1956, 94–97. The psalms appeared in this sequence: psalms 130, 42, 43, 6, 12, 5, 74, 64, 59, 69, 14, 10, 73, 7, 94, 4, 80, 77, 102, 120, 124, 126, 57.

4. *Die Forderung des Geistes und die geschichtliche Wirklichkeit* (Leipzig: Schocken, 1938), trans. and ed. Friedman 1957, *Pointing Out the Way*, 177–91. See Friedman 1983, 257, 267–71; also M. Kaplan 1967, "Buber's Evaluation of Philosophic Thought and Religious Tradition," 245–57, on the inaugural lecture.

5. Buber 1957, "The Demand of the Spirit and Historical Reality," trans. in *Pointing Out the Way*, 180.

6. Ibid., 188.

7. Heschel letter to Buber, 21 May 1938, Ms. Var. 290:13.

8. Heschel letter to Buber, 21 May 1938, with postscript dated 22 May: Ms. Var. 290:13–14.

9. Cyrus Adler was president of the Jewish Theological Seminary of America, president of Dropsie College in Philadelphia, and editor of the prestigious *Jewish Quarterly Review*, among many other leadership positions. Alexander Marx was a historian and head of the library at the Jewish Theological Seminary. Heschel's investment of sending a copy of *Die Prophetie* to Louis Finkelstein, president after Adler's death of the Conservative rabbinical seminary, took about eight more years to mature.

10. Heschel letter to Buber, 17 June 1938, Ms. Var. 290:16.

11. Heschel letter to Buber, 19 June 1938, 11 Adelheid Strasse, Eschersheim, as return address, Ms. Var. 290:15.

12. Heschel attempted, but without success, to contact the Orthodox Rabbi Isaac Elhanan Seminary in New York, where Joseph Soloveitchik, who emigrated to Boston in 1932, was teaching Talmud. Heschel fulfilled his original goal to teach at the Conservative Jewish Theological Seminary, for he remained on its faculty from 1945 to his death in 1972.

13. Heschel letter to Buber, 27 June 1938, Ms. Var. 290:17.

14. Heschel letter to Tadeusz Kowalski, 18 July 1938, from Frankfurt.

15. Heschel letter to Buber, 12 August 1938, Ms. Var. 290:18.

16. Ibid.

17. S. Heschel writes that Schlosser sent letters of reference to the American consulate, Heschel 1996, *Moral Grandeur and Spiritual Audacity*, xiv. In the 31 July 1938 Berlin *Gemeindeblatt*, Heschel published an article on "Auswanderungsprobleme" (emigration problems).

18. Heschel letter to Buber, 16 August 1938, Ms. Var. 290:19.

19. Heschel letter to Buber, 30 August 1938, Ms. Var. 290:20.

20. In the *Jahrbuch der jüdische-literarische Gesellschaft* (volume 8).

21. Heschel letter to Buber, marked September 1938: Ms. Var. 290:21.

22. See Rothschild ed. 1990, *Jewish Perspectives on Christianity: The Views of Baeck, Buber, Rosenzweig, Herberg, and Heschel*.

23. Heschel letter to Buber, September 1938, Ms. Var. 290:21.

24. This and the following quotations from Heschel 1938, "David Koigens Sinndeutung der jüdischen Geschichte," 4.

25. Heschel letter to Buber, 24 October 1938, Ms. Var. 290:22.

26. The following account appeared in a front-page article in the *New York Times*, on 29 October 1938: "Germany began mass deportations of Polish Jews yesterday because of a new law in Poland barring re-entry after today to Poles living abroad who had not had their passports revalidated. From 4,000 to 18,000 are said to have been arrested. . . . In Berlin the raids began at exactly 5 o'clock this morning, particularly in the eastern Jewish section of the city. Men were hauled out of bed and taken to police stations. Their panic-stricken families followed them, and all day weeping women and children stood around the police stations anxiously questioning everybody leaving them as to the whereabouts of their menfolk. Nobody knew any answer."

27. Interview with Fritz Rothschild. S. Heschel 1996, *Moral Grandeur and Spiritual Audacity*, xvii, adds some details.

28. Among the voluminous literature, see Milton 1984; Maurer 1991; Adler-Rudel 1959, chap. 8, "The End," 152–53; interview with Abraham Wasserstein.

Chapter 20. Struggling to Escape

Note to epigraph: Heschel 1966, "No Religion Is an Island," reprinted in *Moral Grandeur and Spiritual Audacity*, 235.

1. Within three months of the expulsions, in February 1939, Jacob—an ordained and practicing rabbi—found a way to London with his wife and young daughter. Around the same time the Kopitzhinitzer rebbe, Abraham Joshua Heschel, his wife, Sarah, and their family were allowed to leave for the United States.

2. On 1 November 1938 it was reported: "Union of University Graduate Rabbis issues appeal to Jews for participation in celebration of twentieth anniversary of Poland's independence, expressing hope Poland will respect equality of Jews who aided in her creation and development," *Contemporary Jewish Record* 2, 1 (January 1939), 116.

3. Heschel letter to Buber, 9 November 1938, Ms. Var. 290:23. The return address was the home of his mother and sisters, 3 Dzika Street, apt. 103.

4. Heschel's letter continues: "I sent application and curriculum vitae to the Society of the Friends of the Jerusalem University in Meinekes Street. It would be good if the plan could succeed quickly."

5. *Contemporary Jewish Record* 1 (November 1938): 56a–b; see the "Digest of Public Opinion" in the January 1939 issue (41–50).

6. Ibid., 56d.

7. The Erich Reiss Verlag "was never formally given up but confiscated by Goebbels. From 10 November 1938 to 15 December 1938, Reiss was in the concentration camp of Oranienburg, then allowed to emigrate to Sweden where he lived for a year. . . . In 1939 he emigrated to the United States where his brother had been living since 1928.

In 1940 Reiss married the photographer Lotte Jacobi who fled Germany in 1935 and who became director/administrator of her photography studio" (Halbey 1980–81, 1145).

8. *Contemporary Jewish Record* 2, 1 (January 1939), 102–3.

9. Heschel letter to Buber, 19 November 1938; in Buber, *Briefwechsel*, vol. 3: 15–16; Ms. Var. 290:24.

10. Heschel's appointment as Dozent at the Institute was registered with the Polish Ministry of Education (see Heschel letter to Julian Morgenstern from London, 28 July 1939). Tartakover 1944, "The Institute for Jewish Science" (Hebrew, in Ginzberg and Weiss eds. 1944, 171), claims, incorrectly, that Heschel replaced Samuel Atlas, who left for Hebrew Union College; Atlas, in fact, left Warsaw around 1933 to go to London; he came to Cincinnati in 1942. Interview with Celia (Mrs. Samuel) Atlas.

11. Schorr was a founding faculty member of the Institute, rector, and professor of Bible and Hebrew. Born in Przemysl, Galicia, he studied philosophy and history at the University of Vienna and modern Judaic scholarship at the Jüdische-theologische Lehranstalt, where he was ordained a rabbi. See Heschel's letter to Buber of 19 November 1938. Heschel contributed a Hebrew text by Abulafia, "A Cabbalistic Commentary on the Prayerbook," to a volume in memory of Schorr (see Ginzberg and Weiss eds. 1944; biographical sketch of Schorr, 113–26).

12. Tartakover 1944, "The Institute for Jewish Studies in Warsaw" (in Hebrew), in Ginzberg and Weiss eds. 1944, 163–76; Shevach Eden, "The Institute for Jewish Studies and Research in Warsaw" (in Hebrew), in Mirsky ed. 1956, 561–84; Biderman 1976, esp. 75–83, and extensive bibliography.

13. Biderman 1976, 77; esp. Eden in Mirsky 1956. The Institute also published documents from archives, monographs on the history, sociology, economics, literature, etc. of Polish Jewry, and its scholars were associated with several Polish universities.

14. See biographical sketch in *Abraham Weiss Jubilee Volume*, 1964, 1–7, and bibliography. Born in Eastern Galicia, Weiss attended a secular gymnasium in Poland. He was able to leave the Warsaw Ghetto in 1940. In 1952–53 he lectured at the Hebrew University of Jerusalem. Eventually emigrating to New York, he completed a distinguished career at Yeshiva University. Heschel contributed an article, "Studies in Midrashic Literature" (in Hebrew), to the *Abraham Weiss Jubilee Volume*, 349–60.

15. Heschel letter to Buber, 25 November 1938, in Buber, *Briefwechsel*, vol. 3: 31; translated in Glatzer and Mendes-Flohr eds. 1991, 474–75, which we modify slightly; Martin Buber Archive, Jerusalem, Ms. Var. 290:25. On 22 December 1938, Heschel wrote to Eduard Strauss from Warsaw, excusing his delay in writing. Strauss had left for the United States via Havana, Cuba. Letter to Strauss at Leo Baeck Institute, New York.

16. Probably before being expelled from Germany, Heschel was invited to contribute to the volume sponsored by the Warsaw Institute to honor Mayer Balaban's sixtieth birthday—and his accomplishments as scholar, historian, and director of over one

hundred dissertations. The first part of the *Mayer Balaban Jubilee Volume* appeared the next year. Biderman, 78, 83n20, for 1938 volume of the jubilee proceedings. Heschel's essay for the second volume honoring Balaban, "The Essence of Prayer," was written in crisp modern Hebrew. The volume was destroyed by the Nazis before publication.

17. Heschel letter to Buber, 27 December 1938, Ms. Var. 290:27.
18. See Buber, *Der Jude und sein Judentum*, "Das Ende der deutsche-jüdischen Symbiose" (January 1939): 644–46; "Brief an Gandhi" (24 February 1939), 629–31; "Sie und Wir" (November 1939): 648–54; also Buber, *Die Stunde und die Erkenntniss: Reden und Aufsätze, 1933–1935* (Berlin: Schocken Verlag, 1936). See Friedman 1983, 360. Buber and Franz Rosenzweig began their translation of the Bible in 1925, and Rosenzweig died in 1929. See Glatzer and Mendes-Flohr 1991, letter to Gandhi, no. 523, pp. 476–86.
19. As Buber wrote to Eduard Strauss on 8 January 1939: "This amount is utterly impossible to raise, of course, and thus a warrant of arrest for tax evasion will be unavoidable." Glatzer and Mendes-Flohr 1991, no. 522, p. 475. See Friedman 1983, 262–63.
20. Heschel letter to Buber, 1 February 1939, Ms. Var. 290:28.
21. *Geschäftsbericht der Lehranstalt für Wissenschaft des Judentums*, Berlin (Report of 1938, dated Summer 1939), published in the *Monatsschrift* (1939): 631–35.
22. See Meyer 1976. After the Kristallnacht pogrom, Morgenstern asked Ismar Elbogen to draw up a list of scholars who might be brought to the Reform rabbinical institution. Among the many names, Morgenstern chose the following: Alexander Guttmann, Franz Landsberger, Albert Lewkowitz, Isaiah Sonne, Eugen Täubler, Max Weiner, Alfred Gottschalk, Abraham Heschel, and Franz Rosenthal. Official invitations were sent to them on 6 April 1939.
23. Friedman 1983, 263–64.
24. Heschel letter to Eduard Strauss, 3 May 1939, from 3 Dzika Street, Warsaw. Leo Baeck Institute, New York.
25. Heschel letter to Buber, 20 March 1939, Frankfurt poste restante (general delivery), Ms. Var. 290:30.
26. Heschel letter to Buber, 3 April 1939, Ms. Var. 290:31.
27. Heschel letter to Eduard Strauss, 3 May 1939, from 3 Dzika Street. Leo Baeck Institute, New York.
28. This and the following documents from the American Jewish Archives, Cincinnati, Hebrew Union College, file Morgenstern. See Meyer 1976, 363 sqq.
29. Rabbi Shonfeld wrote Ruth's brother in Palestine—as did Heschel. After receiving an application, Heschel answered Ruth on 14 April, alluding to the impossibility of getting money from Palestine.
30. Morgenstern letter to Heschel, 8 June 1938.
31. Heschel received Morgenstern's answer of 8 June to his first letter, and he politely

acknowledged receipt "to assure you of my gratitude for your willingness in helping me" (letter of 26 June 1939 to Morgenstern). Alfred Gottschalk, another refugee who emigrated to the United States, studied at Hebrew Union College, and eventually became its president, remembers that Morgenstern, "together with the late Senator Robert Taft, was able to get extra-maximal visas for Heschel and several others" (letter, 23 February 1995).

32. Heschel letter to Buber, 20 June 1939, return address: 3 Dzika Street, Warsaw; Ms. Var. 290:32.

33. For Buber's open letter to Gandhi of 24 February 1939, see Glatzer and Mendes-Flohr 1991, 476–86.

34. Heschel letter to Buber, 20 June 1939, Ms. Var. 290:32.

Chapter 21. Departure and Deliverance

Note to epigraph: Heschel 1951, *Man Is Not Alone*, 147.

1. Heschel letter to Buber, 13 July 1939; Jacob Heshel's apartment was the return address: 70 Highbury New Park, London N5. Ms. Var. 290:33.

2. Heschel eventually moved to other rooms, but he continued to receive his mail at his brother's apartment; when Heschel emigrated he was living at 8 Lancaster Grove, London NW3. Most of this information from interviews with Thena Heshel Kendall.

3. Interviews with Pearl Twersky and Thena Heshel Kendall.

4. This and the following treated in detail by Hoffmann and Schwartz 1991, 283–96.

5. Letter from Raphael Loewe (son of Herbert Loewe), 2 July 1991.

6. Interview with Steven Wertheimer, 3 January 1994. Rabbi Swift officiated at the synagogue Heschel and Hertz attended; the service was Orthodox.

7. Heschel letter to Buber, 26 July 1939, Ms. Var. 290:34.

8. From Heschel's letter: "Some years ago I have given lectures as assistant of Dr. Albeck on Talmud for advanced students at the Hochschule für die Wissenschaft des Judentums. From 1.3. 1937 till 27.10 1938 (when I have been expelled from Germany) I have been a lecturer and assistant director of the Mittelstelle für jüdische Erwachsenenbildung bei der Reichsvertretung der Juden in Deutschland (Central organization for the education of Jewish adults) at Frankfurt am Main. The director and also lecturer at the Mittelstelle was Prof. Martin Buber. I have given lectures about Jewish philosophy and Bible for students and graduates, especially teachers and rabbis. After my arrival in Warsaw I was appointed by the Institut Nauk Judaistycznych to the vacant chair for Jewish philosophy. Since November 1938 till the end of June, i.e., for a full academic year I have given lectures on Jewish philosophy and (by proxy of Prof. Schorr) Bible." Heschel letter to Morgenstern, 28 July 1939. American Jewish Archives, Cincinnati.

9. Heschel 1966, "No Religion Is an Island," reprinted in *Moral Grandeur and Spiritual Audacity*, 235.

10. Heschel 1951, *Man Is Not Alone*, 147. Years later Heschel wrote: "Dark is the world to me, for all its cities and stars. If not for my faith that God in His silence still listens to my cry, who could stand such agony?" Heschel 1970, "On Prayer," 7; orig. delivered at an interreligious convocation held under the auspices of the U.S. Liturgical Conference in Milwaukee, Wisc., 28 August 1969.

11. Heschel letter to Eduard Strauss, 10 September 1939; return address: 20 Glenwood Road, London NW3. Leo Baeck Institute, New York.

12. Heschel letter to Morgenstern, 13 September 1939, American Jewish Archives, Cincinnati.

13. *Contemporary Jewish Record* (November–December 1939): 77 ff.

14. A. Weiss 1940, "In Nazi Warsaw," *Contemporary Jewish Record* 3, 5 (September–October 1940): 484–97.

15. Heschel 1973, *A Passion for Truth*, 301.

16. The American ambassador to London at the time was Joseph Kennedy.

17. Morgenstern letter to the American Consul, Dublin, Ireland, 25 September 1939.

18. *Contemporary Jewish Record* (November–December 1939): 72–73.

19. Heschel letter to Buber, 22 November 1939: Buber, *Briefwechsel*, vol. 3: letter no. 30, p. 31; Glatzer and Mendes-Flohr eds. 1991, letter no. 529, pp. 490–91; Martin Buber Archive, Jerusalem, Ms. Var. 290:35.

20. Glatzer and Mendes-Flohr eds. 1991, no. 529, p. 490n: "Die Auserwählung Israels," which was duplicated and circulated in Germany. First printed as "Die Erwählung Israels: Eine Befragung der Bibel," in *Almanach des Schocken Verlags aus das Jahr 5699* (1938–1939): 12–31; Buber 1968, "The Election of Israel," *On the Bible*, 80–92.

21. Interview with Thena Heshel Kendall.

22. Heschel letter to Buber, 13 December 1939, Ms. Var. 290:36.

23. Article by Lazar Kahan of Wilno, *The Forward*, 1 December 1939; trans. in *Contemporary Jewish Record* (January–February 1940): 22–25.

24. The Gerer rebbe, Avraham Mordecai Alter, made several pilgrimages to Palestine in the 1930s. In 1940, he and his son Israel managed to escape to Palestine where they reestablished the dynasty.

25. A dispatch of 29 December from Geneva reported, however, that the typhus epidemic had been stamped out. This and the following quotation from *Contemporary Jewish Record* (January–February 1940): 68–69.

26. Ibid.

27. *The Jewish Chronicle* (2 February 1940): 21. Reference thanks to Harry Rabinowicz, London. We should not confuse Heschel's pedagogical activities in London with those of Alexander Altmann, who in September 1938 became the community rabbi of Manchester. In 1941, Altmann founded an Institute for Higher Jewish Education under the auspices of the Manchester Jewish Communal organizations; he attempted to get Heschel involved, but it was established only after the latter's departure. Altmann then founded the scholarly Institute of Jewish Studies in 1953, later transferred to

the University College, London, in Gower Street, where it continues its activities. Sources: Thena Heshel Kendall; letter from Manfred Altman, brother of Alexander, 4 July 1991; letter from Raphael Loewe; also Mendes-Flohr, "Theologian Before the Abyss," introduction to Alexander Altmann 1991, *The Meaning of Jewish Existence;* Glatzer 1956.

28. Other faculty as noted in *The Jewish Chronicle* were Dr. J. Heller, Dr. F. Kobler, Mr. J. Kraemer (the Hon. Secretary), Dr. S. Stein, Dr. I. Maybaum, Mr. M. Perlman, Mr. Berl Lovker, Mr. A. Haendler, Dr. L. Lehrfreund, and Mr. A. P. Michaelis.

29. Interview with Celia (Mrs. Samuel) Atlas.

30. "Die Idee der jüdischen Bildung." The event took place at Maccabi House, 73 Compagne Gardens.

31. Heschel's letter to Morgenstern, 31 January 1940, American Jewish Archives, Cincinnati.

32. Heschel's letter to Buber, 7 February 1940, translated and analyzed in Kaplan 1994, 224–25; Martin Buber Archive, Jerusalem, Ms. Var. 290:37.

33. Heschel refers to Buber's essay "Um die Gerechtigkeit" (On justice), *Neue Wege*, November 1939, 496ff.; trans. "For the Sake of Righteousness," in Buber 1949, *The Prophetic Faith* (first published in Hebrew in 1942), 96–109. See Glatzer and Mendes-Flohr 1991, 489: Buber letter to Leonhard Ragaz, 26 September 1939.

34. Heschel 1936, "Die Marranen von Heute," 2; trans. Heschel 1996, *Moral Grandeur and Spiritual Audacity*, 70.

35. Heschel also inquired after the fate of "Moses Schorr and the other lecturers from Warsaw."

36. Corbin's special issue of *Hermès* included works by two Jewish scholars, an essay by Shlomo Pines on the Qarmat movement, a tenth-century Moslem society for social reform, and extensive excerpts from Heschel's doctoral dissertation. Heschel's chapters appeared in this order: "Prophetic Inspiration"; "Theology of Pathos"; "Religion of Sympathy"; the two concluding sections, "Transcendental Anticipation" and "Reciprocal Intentionality." To selections proposed in Heschel's letter of 18 January 1938, Corbin added the crucial "Theology of Pathos." Published in Brussels and distributed in Paris by José Corti, the avant-garde publisher and bookstore; its editorial committee included Bernard Groethuysen, who was on the Philosophy Faculty at Berlin University during Heschel's time and who was associated with the *Nouvelle Revue française*, and A. Rolland de Renéville, a specialist on poetry and esoteric traditions. Contributors to *Hermès* included many of France's leading literary and religious scholars and writers, under the general editorship of the writer Henri Michaux. According to Corbin, the philosophical method of phenomenology could become a spiritual discipline: "[t]o save the phenomenon by demonstrating its hidden meaning" the Arabic term *kashf al-mahjub:* "'unveiling, uncovering of that which was hidden,'" the term *ta'wîl*, "the hermeneutic practiced by Iranian thinkers, whose technical designation means 'to lead back something to its source'" (xx). Corbin 1971, xix–xxii.

37. "Das Gebet als Äusserung und Einfühlung." Heschel translated this essay and published it in revised form in Heschel 1954, *Quest*, chap. 2, "The Person and the Word," esp. 23–30, 39–40. For the earliest version see Heschel 1945, "Prayer." Laboring under stringent Nazi censorship, Baeck collected the forty-five articles; among the authors (German Jews still residing in Germany were required by law to add "Israel" or "Sarah" to their given or "Aryan" names): Eugen Israel Täubler, Martin Buber, Eugen Israel Mittwoch, Harry Torczyner, Chanoch Albeck, Abraham Marmorstein, Edmund Stein, Alexander Israel Altmann, Julius Guttmann, Max Israel Grünewald, Selma Sarah Täubler-Stern, and Abraham Heschel. See *Monatsschrift für Geschichte und Wissenschaft des Judentums*, reprinted in 1963 by J. C. B. Mohr (Paul Siebeck), Tübingen, with a new preface by Max Grünewald and the original preface dated October 1938 by Baeck.

38. Cf. Heschel 1954, *Quest*, 30.

39. Heschel 1939, "'Al mahut ha-tefillah," prepared for the Mayer Balaban jubilee volume, volume 2, Warsaw; published for the first time in the Hebrew monthly *Bitzaron* (1941). See Biderman 1976, bibliography. See Heschel 1953, "The Moment at Sinai," and Heschel 1954, "A Preface to the Understanding of Revelation." Both essays oppose humanistic or secular presuppositions.

40. Heschel 1955, *God in Search of Man*, 8. Cf. Heschel 1951, *Man Is Not Alone*, 60–61, for a more general statement of Heschel's phenomenological goal.

41. Passenger List no. 7, United States National Archives. The document from the British Home Office notes that the departure was registered on 15 March 1940; although Heschel's file was apparently destroyed, it notes no nationality and that his profession was rabbi. See *New York Times*, 22 March 1940, for an account of the crossing.

42. See Heschel's letter to Morgenstern, 21 March 1940, and letter to Louis Finkelstein, 24 March 1940. General Files, Jewish Theological Seminary of America, New York.

43. Heschel letter to Morgenstern, 8 April 1940, with annotations by Hebrew Union College office.

44. For five years Heschel taught at Hebrew Union College, where Samuel Dresner became his disciple. Heschel began to publish articles and essays in remarkably elegant English, leading to books that established him as an authoritative writer and theologian. In 1945 he moved to New York, joining the faculty of the Jewish Theological Seminary, where he remained for the rest of his life.

Chapter 22. Epilogue

Note to epigraph: Heschel 1962, *The Prophets*, dedication page. See Heschel 1951, *Man Is Not Alone*, chap. 16, "The Hiding God," where Heschel quotes Psalm 44 in its entirety. See Kaplan 1996, chap. 8, "Confronting the Holocaust."

1. *New York Times* (26 July 1940), 1–2. The event was concealed for three months by military censors.

2. Kludas 1976, 124–25.

3. Rabinowicz 1989, 336–37.

4. Stern 1970.

5. Heschel 1962, *Torah min ha-shamayim*, vol. 1.

6. Confirmed by Thena Heshel Kendall. Cf. S. Heschel 1996, *Moral Grandeur and Spiritual Audacity*, xix. The horrible death of Heschel's maternal uncle Rabbi Shlomo Hayim Perlow, the prodigy and rebbe of Bolekhov, was well known. He refused his followers' urgings to join his brother in the United States. His wife and her mother were killed in 1942. The next year he was put in the Ghetto of Satri, having refused to be hidden in the home of a Gentile. In July (11 Tamuz of the Hebrew month), wrapped in his tallit, he was taken with other Jews to the city square to be killed. Refusing orders to remove his clothing, he recited the *Vidui*, the prayer of confession, in a loud voice and was shot. Rabbi Samuel of Tsanz endangered his life to wash and dress the body for proper burial. Wunder 1990, vol. 4, 255.

7. Bezalel Levy was the tutor who instilled in the young Heschel the harsh Hasidism of Kotzk. Yitzhak Meir Levin, also a Kotzker Hasid, helped Heschel to overcome despair by giving him money to pursue his secular studies, and Heschel brought his letters to the United States. The Berlin publisher Erich Reiss gave Heschel a job in 1934 and subsidized his earliest publications. Leo Hirsch introduced Heschel's work to readers of *Der Morgen*. The only person in this list whom Heschel did not meet in Europe was Levi (or Louis) Ginzberg, professor of Talmud at the Jewish Theological Seminary, who threw him another lifeline in 1945—bringing him from Cincinnati to New York.

8. Heschel 1973, *A Passion for Truth*, xiv.

9. Ibid., 283; cf. Dresner 1983, viii.

References

Heschel's articles and reviews published in Berlin from 1936 to 1938 and early Yiddish writings have not appeared in previous bibliographies. However, the most complete listing remains Heschel, *Between God and Man*, ed. Fritz Rothschild (1959; rev. ed. New York: Macmillan, 1975). The best general reference work is the *Encyclopaedia Judaica*, 16 vols. (Jerusalem: Keter, 1972).

Archives Consulted

American Jewish Archives, Hebrew Union College, Cincinnati, Ohio.
Archives of 5e Arrondissement, Paris.
Archives nationales, Paris.
Archives of the Rectorat de Paris.
Leo Baeck Institute, New York.
British Home Office Archives.
Martin Buber Archive, National Jewish Library and Hebrew University, Givat Ram, Jerusalem.

Central Archives for the History of the Jewish People, Hebrew University, Givat Ram, Jerusalem.

Henry Corbin, Paris. Personal papers.

Abraham Joshua Heschel Archive, Jewish Theological Seminary of America, New York.

Humboldt University Archives, Berlin.

Jagiellonian University, Archives of the Polish Academy of Arts and Sciences, Kraków.

Jewish Theological Seminary of America, General Files, New York.

Thena Heshel Kendall, London. Family papers.

Melech Ravitch Archive, National Jewish Library and Hebrew University, Givat Ram, Jerusalem.

United States National Archives, Washington, D.C.

YIVO Archives, New York.

Interviews and Letters to the Authors

Abramowicz, Dina. New York, interview, 28 May 1989 and earlier.

Altman, Manfred. London, interview, and letter, 4 July 1991.

Andernacht, Dietrich. Frankfurt, letter, 19 September 1986.

Aron, Leyzer Yankelovich. Vilna, interview, 1989; letter, 9 February 1990; Paris, interview, 16 June 1992.

Atlas, Celia (Mrs. Samuel). New York, telephone interview.

Beilis, Shlomo. Warsaw, interview by Jack Kugelmass. July 1987.

Brand, Mala (Mrs. Aaron). Jerusalem, May 1992, interviews and letters.

Coffin, William Sloane, Jr. Interview, 9 December 1987.

Cywiak, Rabbi Leib. Brooklyn, N.Y., 14 November 1987.

Derczansky, Alexandre. Paris, interviews, June 1992.

Dobruszkes, Azario. Brussels, telephone interviews, 21 June, 5 July, 1992. Letters.

Dresner, Mrs. Ruth. New York, interviews.

Eichenstein, Mrs. Moses (Sarah Perlow, daughter of the Warsaw Novominsker rebbe). Chicago, interview, June 1992.

Elbogen, Regina (née Klemperer). Memoir on the Hochschule, June 1956. Leo Baeck Institute, New York.

Eydelzon, Mordecai (Motke). Ghent, telephone interview, June 1992.

Feldman, Leon. Telephone interviews, 15 July, November 1995.

Friedman, Israel. New York, several interviews.

Friedman, Maurice. San Diego, interview, 27 December 1994.

Gelbtuch, Joseph. Interview, 21 July 1986.

Graupner, Rainer. Berlin, interview, June 1989.

Green, Arthur. Several interviews.

Grüngard, Mr. Tel Aviv, telephone interview, 8 May 1992.

Hertz, Rose (née Simon). Interviews and letters, 1978–79.

Heschel, Abraham Joshua. New York, conversations with both authors, 1942–1972.

Heschel, Israel. Brooklyn, N.Y., several interviews, and telephone interview, 20 June 1990.

Heschel, Zusya. Brooklyn, N.Y. Interviews.

Hofer, Yehiel. Tel Aviv, interview, c. 1966.

Horovitz, Menahem. Jerusalem, interview and letters.

Horovitz, Ruth. Jerusalem, interview, 5 June 1988, and letters.

Jacobson, Gershon. New York, interview, 21 April 1988.

Kahn, Ludwig. Telephone interview, 26 December 1989.

Kayser, Stephen (Stefan). Los Angeles, interview, 28 April 1988.

Kelman, Wolfe. New York, several interviews, and letter, 4 May 1982.

Kendall, Thena Heshel. London, several interviews, including 1 March, 28 June 1992; 27 June 1994; letters.

Kimelman, Reuven. Several interviews.

Kraus, Pesach. Jerusalem, interviews.

Levinson (Levinsky), N. Peter. Interviews.

Lewin, Abram. Paris, letter, 24 October 1991; interview, 9 June 1992.

Loewe, Raphael. London, letter, 2 July 1991.

Meyer, Marshall. New York, interviews, 3, 10 March 1992.

Minc, Calel. Liège, Belgium, telephone interview, June 1992.

Muffs, Yochanan. New York, interviews, including 13 November 1992.

Nasr, Sayyed Hussein. Washington, D.C., telephone interview, 27 June 1990.

Novak, David. Interviews.

Perlow, Abraham (grandson of the Warsaw Novominsker, son of Aaron Perlow). Brooklyn, N.Y., telephone interview.

Perlow, Bernard (son of Nahum Mordecai, Novominsker rebbe in Brooklyn, and grandson of the Warsaw Novominsker rebbe). Chicago, interview, 17 February 1981.

Perlow, Rabbi Jacob (son of Nahum Mordecai, Novominsker rebbe in Brooklyn, and grandson of the Warsaw Novominsker). Borough Park, Brooklyn, N.Y., interviews, February 1979, 15 November 1987.

Perlow, Jacob (son of the Williamsburg Novominsker, Yehuda Aryeh Lieb, and nephew of the Warsaw Novominsker). New York, interviews.

Perlow, Nehama (Mrs. Joel Teitelbaum), daughter of the Warsaw Novominsker rebbe. Interview.

Plaut, W. Gunther. Montreal, letter 1988; telephone interview.

Pumpiansky, Benjamin. Minsk, letters; Tel Aviv, interview, June 1992.

Rabinowicz, Harry. London, interviews, letters.

Ran, Leyzer. New York, interviews, including 11 December 1987, 24 May 1989, and earlier.

Roskies, David. New York, interviews.

Rothschild, Fritz. New York, several interviews.

Rottenberg, Rabbi F. E. Los Angeles, interview, 21 July 1986; telephone interview, 12, 30 July 1990.

Rozenberg, Szulim. Paris, interviews, June 1992.

Sarabsky, Wolf. Paris, interview, June 1992.

Schaechter, Mordkhe. New York, letter, 27 March 1979.

Schulman, Elias. Letter, 15 March 1979.

Seidman, Hillel. New York, telephone interview, 8 May 1990, and earlier.

Shafler, Samuel. Brookline, Mass., interview, 1991.

Shedletsky, Ephraim. Jerusalem, interview, May 1992.

Shmeruk, Khone. Cambridge, Mass., interview, 29 March 1990.

Shneyderman, Sh. L. New York, telephone interview, December 1992.

Shulvass, Moses. Chicago, interviews, 30 December 1987, 24 September 1988, and earlier.

Soloveitchik, Chaim. Jerusalem, New York, interviews.

Twersky, Isadore. Boston, interviews.

Twersky, Pearl. New York, several interviews.

Twersky, Yitzhak Meir. New York, several interviews.

Wasserstein, Abraham. Telephone interview, 22 December 1988.

Wertheimer, Steven. Telephone interview, 3 January 1994.

Wiesel, Elie. New York. Several interviews, including April 1988.

Wojczyk, Benjamin. Ghent. Telephone interview, 21 June 1992.

Wolf, Arnold Jacob. Chicago, several interviews.

Zajac, Esther Selz. Paris, interviews, June 1992.

Selected Works of Abraham Joshua Heschel
(available reprinted versions noted)

September–November 1922. Hidushei Torah (in Hebrew, notes on points of rabbinic law), in *Sha'arey Torah* (Warsaw), vol. 13, no. 1 (Tishri-Kislev 5683), "Bet Midrash," Part 1, no. 4, Sect. 78 (on Bava Kama 62).

December 1922–February 1923. *Sha'arey Torah*, vol. 13, no. 2 (Tevet-Adar 5683), "Bet Midrash" Part 1, no. 5, sect. 98 (yishuv divrey R. Aharon Halevi on "kinyan de' orayta).

March–April 1923. *Sha'arey Torah*, vol. 13, no. 3 (Nissan-Iyar 5683), "Bet Midrash," Part 1, no. 6, sect. 108 (on Rashi and Bava Kama 28).

21 May 1925. "Der Zaddik fun freyd" (The zaddik of joy), *Illustrirte Vokh* (Warsaw), vol. 3, no. 20 (whole no. 73).

November 1926–1927. Untitled "lid," "Se zilbert zin azoy loyter . . . " ("The womanly skin silvers so purely . . . "), *Varshaver Shriftn*. Warsaw Writers and Journalists Association.

3 June 1927. Untitled poem. "ikh nisht tragn mir mayn harts . . . " (I can no longer carry my heart . . .), *Literarishe Bleter* (Warsaw) 22:417.

December 1929. "Lider" (poems): Got geht mir nokh umetum; in ovent oyf gasn; milionen oygen shtiken zikh; Ikh un Du (God pursues me everywhere . . . , Evening in the streets, Millions of eyes choke . . . , I and Thou), *Zukunft* (New York), vol. 34, 825. Later included in *Der Shem Hameforash: Mentsh,* 1933.

25 April 1930. "I will give you—o world," *Naye Folks-Tsaytung* (Warsaw); reprinted in *Unzer Zeit,* 1973, 46. Later included in *Der Shem Hameforash: Mentsh,* 1933.

August 1930. "Lider" (poems): zumer; ikh volt azoy velen zayn farlibt; aydeler fraynd; ruf durkh di nekht (Summer, O how I want to be in love, Gentle friend, Call through the nights), *Zukunft* (New York), vol. 35, 576. Later included in *Der Shem Hameforash: Mentsh,* 1933.

November 1931. Poems: Ikh un Du; beyn hashmoshos; vanderlungn; noyt; armen; got geht mir nokh umetum (I and Thou, Dusk, Wanderings, Need, The pauper, God pursues me everywhere . . .), *Berliner Bleter far dikhtung un kunst* (Berlin) 1, 1:10–12. Also included in *Der Shem Hameforash: Mentsh,* 1933.

10 May 1933. "In tog fun has" (Day of hate), printed under the pseudonym "Itzik" in *Haynt* (Warsaw). Reprinted for the first time in 1955, *Nusah Vilne* (see below).

1933. *Der Shem Hameforash: Mentsh* (in Yiddish, Mankind: God's Ineffable Name). Warsaw: Farlag Indzl. Freely translated by Zalman Schachter-Shalomi, Winnipeg, Canada, 1973, and distributed privately.

27 February 1934. "David Koigen," *Jüdische Rundschau,* p. 5.

1935. *Maimonides: Eine Biographie.* Berlin: Erich Reiss Verlag. French trans. Germaine Bernard (Paris: Payot, 1936). English trans. Joachim Neugroschel, *Maimonides: A Biography* (New York: Farrar, Straus & Giroux, 1982).

23 February 1936. "Persönlichkeiten der jüdischen Geschichte: Jochanan ben Zakkai" (first of eight essays on Tannaim): in *Gemeindeblatt der jüdischen Gemeinde zu Berlin* 26, 8:14; "Die Religion der Sympathie" (Religion of sympathy, selections from *Die Prophetie*), loc. cit.

8 March 1936. "Rabbi Gamliel II." *Gemeindeblatt der jüdischen Gemeinde zu Berlin,* 26, 10:15.

29 March 1936. "Rabbi Akiba." *Gemeindeblatt der jüdischen Gemeinde zu Berlin,* 26, 13:16.

4 April 1936. Book reviews: "Epochen jüdischer Geschichte: Ein Pessach-Rückblick in Bildern" (Epochs of Jewish history: a Pesach review in pictures), *Gemeindeblatt der jüdischen Gemeinde zu Berlin,* 26, 14:5; "Wie man den Seder hält" (How to perform the Seder), 6; "Eine Festschrift für Samuel Krauss" (A Festschrift for Samuel Krauss), 18.

12 April 1936. "Rabbi Schimon ben Gamliel II." *Gemeindeblatt der jüdischen Gemeinde zu Berlin,* 26, 15:15.

26 April 1936. "Elischa ben Abuja." *Gemeindeblatt der jüdischen Gemeinde zu Berlin,* 26, 17:16.

3 May 1936. Review of "'Der hebräische Lehrer'" (A new publication called "The Hebrew teacher"). *Gemeindeblatt der jüdischen Gemeinde zu Berlin*, 26, 18:22.

10 May 1936. "Eine Fabel Rabbi Meirs" (A story from Rabbi Meir). *Gemeindeblatt der jüdischen Gemeinde zu Berlin*, 26, 19:5; and reviews of: Abraham Danzig and *Chaje Adam* (a compendium of the Shulhan Arukh), loc. cit.

17 May 1936. "Hebräische Lesestücke" (review of essays from the Hebrew supplement to the *Jüdische Rundschau*), and "Pachad Jizchak" (review of the second edition of the Talmud encyclopedia of that name). *Gemeindeblatt der jüdischen Gemeinde zu Berlin*, 26, 20:15; and "Rabbi Meir," 16.

31 May 1936. "Jehuda Ha-Nassi." *Gemeindeblatt der jüdischen Gemeinde zu Berlin* 26, 22:16.

16 August 1936. "Rabbi Chiya." *Gemeindeblatt der jüdischen Gemeinde zu Berlin* 26, 33:15.

[The series "Persönlichkeiten der jüdischen Geschichte" was in part reprinted in the Frankfurt *Gemeindeblatt*, starting in 1938.]

13 September 1936. "Die Kraft der Buße" (The power of repentance), *Gemeindeblatt der jüdischen Gemeinde zu Berlin* 26, 37:4.

16 September 1936. "Die Marranen von Heute" (The Marranos of today), *Gemeindeblatt der jüdischen Gemeinde zu Berlin* 26, 38:2. Translated and reprinted in Heschel 1996, *Moral Grandeur and Spiritual Audacity*, as "The Meaning of Repentance," 68–70.

27 September 1936. Review of J. H. Weiss, *Meine Lebensjahre* (Years of my life), *Gemeindeblatt der jüdischen Gemeinde zu Berlin* 26, 39:9.

30 September 1936. Review of "Chassidische Erzählungen" (Yiddish stories by I. L. Perets, pub. in German by Schocken, Berlin, 1936), and "Hamore Haiwri" (The Jewish Teacher, review of a journal on Hebrew matters pub. by the Zionist Association of Germany), *Gemeindeblatt der jüdischen Gemeinde zu Berlin* 26, 40:10.

25 October 1936. Review of "Ein jüdischer Bibelkommentar" (A Jewish Bible commentary), *Gemeindeblatt der jüdischen Gemeinde zu Berlin* 26, 43:9.

22 November 1936. Announcement of a lecture, "S. R. Hirsch und unsere Zeit" (Samson Raphael Hirsch and our times). *Gemeindeblatt der jüdischen Gemeinde zu Berlin* 26, 47:4; [two parables]: "Die gewaltigen Dinge" (The powerful things), and "Die Verdienste Abrahams" (The merits of Abraham), 17.

29 November 1936. Reviews: "Vom Forschungsinstitut für hebräische Dichtung" (vol. 1, from the research institute for Hebrew poetry, Schocken, Berlin). *Gemeindeblatt der jüdischen Gemeinde zu Berlin* 26, 48:16; "Aus der Wissenschaft des Judentums" (about an issue of the *Monatsschrift* scholarly journal); "Hebräische Redewendungen" (Hebrew idiomatic expressions, book by A. Abraham, Frankfurt, 1936), loc. cit.

20 December 1936. Review of "Jiddische Gedishte" (Yiddish poetry by A. N. Stencl, pub. Funderheim, Berlin, 1936). *Gemeindeblatt der jüdischen Gemeinde zu Berlin* 26, 51:15.

1936. *Die Prophetie*. Kraków: Polish Academy of Arts and Sciences (Mémoires de la

Commission Orientaliste No. 22). Selections published in French in *Hermès. Mystique—Poésie—Philosophie* III (November 1939): 78–110.

3 January 1937. Reviews: Naftali Cohen, *Einleitung zum Talmudstudium* (A guide for studying the Talmud) and *Hebräische Dichtung* (Hebrew poems: Piyyutim by Jannai), *Gemeindeblatt der jüdischen Gemeinde zu Berlin* 27, 1:3.

10 January 1937. Reviews of "Hebräische Dichtung" (Hebrew poetry: *Anthologie der hebräischen Dichtung in Italien*, 317 poems of 129 authors) and "Ein Dichterjubiläum" (A poet's anniversary: tribute to the Yiddish poet David Einhorn on his 50th birthday), *Gemeindeblatt der jüdischen Gemeinde zu Berlin* 27, 2:17.

17 January 1937. Review of "Das Achtzehngebet" (Prayers of the Eighteen Benedictions). *Gemeindeblatt der jüdischen Gemeinde zu Berlin* 27, 3:4.

31 January 1937. Review of "Der Sinn der Lehre" (The meaning of the teaching: review of new edition of Martin Buber, *The Kingdom of God*). *Gemeindeblatt der jüdischen Gemeinde zu Berlin* 27, 5:4.

7 February 1937. "Staatsmann und Theologe" (Statesman and Theologian: biographical sketch of of Don Isaac Abravanel). *Gemeindeblatt der jüdischen Gemeinde zu Berlin* 27, 6:9.

28 February 1937. "Die Wirtschaftswerte der Gemeinden" (The economic values of the communities). *Gemeindeblatt der jüdischen Gemeinde zu Berlin* 27, 9:9.

9 May 1937. Review of "Zur Kunde der biblischen Eigennamen" (On biblical proper names). *Gemeindeblatt der jüdischen Gemeinde zu Berlin* 27, 19:5.

16 May 1937. Review of "Die Tora" (reprint of Netter's Pentateuch edition, Vienna, 1859, by Schocken, Berlin, 1937). *Gemeindeblatt der jüdischen Gemeinde zu Berlin* 27, 20:8.

23 May 1937. Review of "Ein neues Gebetbuch" (Seder Avodat Israel, complete prayerbook with explanatory commentary by S. Baer, Schocken, 1937), *Gemeindeblatt der jüdischen Gemeinde zu Berlin* 27, 21:5.

27 June 1937. Review of "Eine Bibelkonkordanz" (A Bible concordance). *Gemeindeblatt der jüdischen Gemeinde zu Berlin* 27, 26:3.

14 November 1937. Reviews of "Jüdische Lesehefte" (a sourcebook for the festive week and the time of Omer by E. L. Ehrmann) and "Jüdische Erzählungen" (collected stories of Jewish family life entitled, *An Unknown World*, by Judäus, Frankfurt am Main, 1937). *Gemeindeblatt der jüdischen Gemeinde zu Berlin* 27, 46:5.

29 November 1937. "Lichter über dem Meer" (Lights over the sea; a parable). *Gemeindeblatt der jüdischen Gemeinde zu Berlin* 27, 48:4.

1937. *Don Jizhak Abravanel*. Berlin: Erich Reiss Verlag. Polish translation by Ozjasz Tilleman. Lwow: Towa przjacio universytetu hebrajskiego w jerozolimie, 1938. Slightly abridged English translation by William Wolf, *Intermountain Jewish News* (19 December 1986): 5, 8–12.

1937. "Der Begriff des Seins in der Philosophie Gabirols" (The concept of being in

Gabirol's philosophy), *Festschrift Jakob Freimann zum 70. Geburtstag*, Berlin: 68–77; trans. David Wolf Silverman in *Conservative Judaism* 28, 1 (Fall 1973): 89–95.

February 1938. "Persönlichkeiten der jüdischen Geschichte: Rabbi Akiba" (reprint of Berlin series), *Jüdisches Gemeindeblatt für Frankfurt* 16, 5:21–22.

March 1938. "Rabbi Schimon ben Gamliel II" (reprint of Berlin series). *Jüdisches Gemeindeblatt für Frankfurt* 16, 6:5–6.

April 1938. "Zum Eintritt in den Ruhestand" (tribute to the high school teacher Dr. H. Freudenberger upon his retirement). *Jüdisches Gemeindeblatt für Frankfurt* 16, 7:22. Signed: H.

22 May 1938. "Zionismus und Überseewanderung" (Zionism and emigration overseas), *Gemeindeblatt der jüdischen Gemeinde zu Berlin* 28, 21:4; "Kinder in Luft und Sonne" (Children outside in the sun: About an orphan home), 5; "Agnon: Von den höchsten Tagen" (review of Agnon, *The Days of Awe*), 6; reviews: "Ein Mischnatraktat" (A Mishnah tractate), and "Zur Literatur Martin Bubers" (Martin Buber's writings: review of Hans Kohn's biography of Buber, first pub. in 1930), 6.

31 July 1938. "Auswanderungsprobleme" (Emigration problems). *Gemeindeblatt der jüdischen Gemeinde zu Berlin* 28, 31:4–5.

September 1938. "Abschied von der Bockenheimer Synagoge" (Farewell to the Bockenheimer Synagogue), *Jüdisches Gemeindeblatt für Frankfurt* 16, 12:17.

7 October 1938. "David Koigens Sinndeutung der jüdischen Geschichte" (David Koigen's interpretation of Jewish history), *Jüdische Rundschau* 80–81:4.

1938. "Der Begriff der Einheit in der Philosophie Gabirols" (The concept of unity in Gabirol's philosophy), *Monatsschrift für Geschichte und Wissenschaft des Judentums* 82:89–111.

1939. "Das Gebet als Äusserung und Einfühlung" (Prayer as expression and empathy), *Monatsschrift für Geschichte und Wissenschaft des Judentums* 83:562–67.

1939. "Das Wesen der Dinge nach der Lehre Gabirols" (The status of the thing in Gabirol's teaching), in *Hebrew Union College Annual* 14:359–85.

1939. "'Al mahut ha-tefillah" (in Hebrew, The essence of prayer), prepared for the Mayer Balaban jubilee volume (Warsaw), but confiscated by the Nazis; first published in *Bitzaron* 3, 5 (February 1941): 346–53; repr. in Joseph Heinemann, ed., *Ha-Tefillah*. Jerusalem: Amanah, 1960:3–25; also Jakob J. Petuchowski and Ezra Spicehandler, eds., *Essays on Judaism* (in Hebrew). Cincinnati: Hebrew Union College Press, and Jerusalem: M. Newman, 1963, 37–49.

1941. *A Concise Dictionary of Hebrew Philosophical Terms*. Cincinnati: mimeographed.

March 1942. "An Analysis of Piety," *The Review of Religion* 6, 3:293–307; excerpts repr. as "Piety" in *Hamigdal* (New York) 7, 1 (September–October 1946): 12–13; repr. in *Moral Grandeur and Spiritual Audacity*, 305–17.

March 1943. "The Meaning of This War," *Hebrew Union College Bulletin* 2, 3:1–2, 18. See below, "Versuch einer Deutung" (1962). See below, February 1944.

1943. "The Quest for Certainty in Saadia's Philosophy," *Jewish Quarterly Review* 33, 2–3

(1943): 263–313. 1944. "Reason and Revelation in Saadia's Philosophy," *Jewish Quarterly Review* 34, 4 (1944): 391–408.

February 1944. "The Meaning of This War," in *Liberal Judaism,* (London) 11, 10:18–21; repr. in Heschel 1954, *Man's Quest for God;* repr. in *Moral Grandeur and Spiritual Audacity,* 209–215.

1944. *The Quest for Certainty in Saadia's Philosophy* (a broadside of the two previous articles). New York: Philip Feldheim.

1944. "A Cabalistic Commentary to the Prayerbook" (text of Abulafia, in Hebrew), in Ginzberg and Weiss, eds., *Studies in Memory of Moses Schorr, 1874–1941.* New York: The Professor Moses Schorr Memorial Committee, 113–26.

January 1945. "Prayer," *Review of Religion* 9, 2:153–68.

March–April 1945. "Di mizrekh-eyropeishe tkufe in der yidisher geshikte" (in Yiddish, The Eastern European era in Jewish history), *YIVO Bleter* 25, 2:163–83. Translation, see 1946.

1945. "Ha-he'emin ha-rambam shezakhah l'nevuah?" (in Hebrew, Did Maimonides strive for prophetic inspiration?), in *Louis Ginzberg Jubilee Volume.* New York: American Academy for Jewish Research: 159–88. Trans. in Heschel 1996, *Prophetic Inspiration After the Prophets.*

1946. "The Eastern European Era in Jewish History," translated in *YIVO Annual of Jewish Social Science,* vol. 1. New York: Yiddish Scientific Institute–YIVO: 86–106.

1946. *Der mizrakh-eyropeisher yid.* New York: Schocken, 45 pp.

May 1948. "The Two Great Traditions," *Commentary* 5, 5:416–22.

1 October 1948. "After Maidenek: On the Poetry of Aaron Zeitlin" (in Yiddish), *Yidisher Kemfer* 29, 771:28–30.

1949. *Pikuah Neshama* (in Hebrew, To save a soul). New York: Baronial Press. Trans. in *Moral Grandeur and Spiritual Audacity,* 54–67.

1950. *The Earth Is the Lord's: The Inner Life of the Jew in East Europe.* New York: Henry Schuman.

1950. "'Al ruah ha-kodesh bimey ha-beynayim" (Prophetic inspiration in the Middle Ages). *Alexander Marx Jubilee Volume* (Hebrew section). New York: Jewish Theological Seminary of America, 175–208. Trans. Heschel 1996, *Prophetic Inspiration After the Prophets.*

1951. *Man Is Not Alone: A Philosophy of Religion.* New York: Farrar, Straus and Young; Philadelphia: Jewish Publication Society of America.

1951. *The Sabbath: Its Meaning for Modern Man.* New York: Farrar, Straus and Young.

1952. "Umbakante dokumentn tsu der geshikhte fun khasidus" (in Yiddish, Unknown documents in the history of Hasidism). *Yivo Bleter* 36:113–35.

1953. "The Moment at Sinai." *American Zionist* 43, 7 (February): 18–20.

1953. "Toward an Understanding of Halacha," in *Yearbook, The Central Conference of American Rabbis* 63:386–409. Repr. in *Moral Grandeur and Spiritual Audacity,* 127–45.

1953. "The Spirit of Jewish Prayer." *Proceedings of the Rabbinical Assembly of America*

17:151–215. Hebrew trans. by "Alef Lamed" in *Megillot* (New York) 15 (March 1954): 3–24. Repr. in *Moral Grandeur and Spiritual Audacity*, 100–26.

1953. "The Spirit of Jewish Education." *Jewish Education* 24, 2 (Fall): 9–20; repr. in Heschel 1966, *Insecurity of Freedom*, "Jewish Education," 223–41.

1954. "A Preface to the Understanding of Revelation," in *Essays Presented to Leo Baeck on the Occasion of His Eightieth Birthday*. London: East and West Library, 28–35; repr. in *Moral Grandeur and Spiritual Audacity*, 185–205.

1954. *Man's Quest for God: Studies in Prayer and Symbolism*. New York: Charles Scribner's Sons.

1955. *God in Search of Man: A Philosophy of Judaism*. Philadelphia: Jewish Publication Society of America.

March 1955. Reprint of "In tog fun has" (On the day of hate), in *Nusah Vilne* (in Yiddish), a commemorative brochure on the 25th anniversary of Yung Vilne. New York: YIVO 45–46.

1962. *The Prophets*. New York: Harper and Row; Philadelphia: Jewish Publication Society of America.

1962, 1965, 1995. *Torah min ha-shamayim be-aspaklaryah shel ha-dorot* (*Theology of Ancient Judaism*) (in Hebrew, Torah from heaven in the mirror of the generations). London and New York: Soncino Press, vol. 1, 1962; vol. 2, 1965; New York: Jewish Theological Seminary, vol. 3, 1995, containing indices for all three volumes.

1962. "Versuch einer Deutung," in *Begegnung mit dem Judentum: ein Gedenkbuch*. (Stimme der Freunde [Quäker] in Deutschland), Heft 2, ed. Margarethe Lackmund, Bad Pyrmont: 11–13. Contains the first publication of an address in German delivered to a group of Quakers at Frankfurt-am-Main in February 1938. See 1943 for the first version in English.

January–February 1964. "A Visit with Rabbi Heschel," interview with Arthur Herzog. *Think Magazine*, 16–19 [contains excellent photographs]; condensed in *The Jewish Digest* (December 1968): 15–19.

1965. *Who Is Man?* Stanford, Calif.: Stanford University Press. Lectures delivered at Stanford University, 1963.

1966. "No Religion Is an Island," inaugural lecture as Harry Emerson Fosdick Visiting Professor at Union Theological Seminary, New York, November 1965, in *Union Seminary Quarterly Review* 21, 2, Part 1 (January): 117–34. Repr. in Byron Sherwin and Harold Kasimow, eds., *No Religion Is an Island: Abraham Joshua Heschel and Interreligious Dialogue*. New York: Orbis Books, 1991; repr. in *Moral Grandeur and Spiritual Audacity*, 235–50.

1966. *The Insecurity of Freedom: Essays on Human Existence*. New York: Farrar, Straus & Giroux.

1967. "The Moral Outrage of Vietnam," in *Vietnam: Crisis of Conscience*, with Robert McAfee Brown, A. J. Heschel, and Michael Novak. New York: Association Press, Behrman House, Herder & Herder.

1967. "Abraham Joshua Heschel," interview with Patrick Granfield, O.S.B., *Theologians at Work*. New York: Macmillan, 69–85; repr. in *Moral Grandeur and Spiritual Audacity*, "Interview at Notre Dame," 381–94.

1968. "Rabbi Mendel mi-Kotzk" (in Hebrew), *Shedemot* (Tel Aviv) 29 (Spring): 87–94.

1969. "Reflections on Death," in *Genesis of Sudden Death and Reanimation. Clinical and Moral Problems Connected* (Genesi della Morte Improvisa e Rianimazione), Florence, Palazzo Pitti, October 14; *Proceedings of the First International Congress*, ed. Vincenzo Lapiccirella, Florence: Marchi & Bertolli (January): 533–542 (in Italian); English text, 522–533. Abridged version pub. in *Conservative Judaism* 28, 1 (Fall 1973): 3–9; also repr. as "Death as Homecoming," in Jack Reimer, ed., *Jewish Reflections on Death*. New York: Schocken, 1974, 58–73; repr. in *Moral Grandeur and Spiritual Audacity*, 366–78.

1969. "Teaching Jewish Theology at the Solomon Schechter Day School," *The Synagogue School* 28, 1 (Fall): 4–18; partially repr. (without the dialogue) in *Moral Grandeur and Spiritual Audacity*, 154–63.

1969. "Kotzk" (in Hebrew), *Panim el Panim* (Jerusalem) 507 (7 February): 10–11, 18.

1969. "Der Kotzker rebbe" (in Yiddish), *Di Goldene Keyt, Periodical for Literature and Social Problems* 65: 138–56; and 71 (1970): 60–70. Tel Aviv: General Federation of Labour in Israel.

1970. "On Prayer," *Conservative Judaism* 25, 1 (Fall): 1–12; repr. in *Moral Grandeur and Spiritual Audacity*, 257–67.

1971. "In Search of Exaltation," *Jewish Heritage* 13, 3 (Fall); repr. in *Moral Grandeur and Spiritual Audacity*, 227–29.

1972. "Hasidism as a New Approach to Torah," in *Jewish Heritage* 14, 3 (Fall–Winter): 4–21; repr. in *Moral Grandeur and Spiritual Audacity*, 33–39.

1972. Letter to Hofer's widow, published in Hofer, *Lider fun shpisal, Lider fun nacht*. Tel Aviv, 1976.

1973. *A Passion for Truth*. New York: Farrar, Straus & Giroux.

1973. *Kotsk: In gerangl far emesdikeit* (in Yiddish, The struggle for integrity), 2 volumes. Tel Aviv: Hamenora Publishing House.

1973. "A Conversation with Doctor Abraham Joshua Heschel" (recorded December 1972) with Carl Stern, National Broadcasting Company (aired 4 February 1973); repr. in *Moral Grandeur and Spiritual Audacity*, 395–412.

1974. Preface to Leyzer Ran, ed., *Jerusalem of Lithuania*. New York. In Yiddish, English trans. by Shlomo Noble.

1985. Samuel Dresner, ed. *The Circle of the Baal Shem Tov: Studies in Hasidism*. Chicago: University of Chicago Press.

1990. Jacob Neusner with Noam Neusner, eds. *To Grow in Wisdom: An Anthology of Abraham Joshua Heschel*. Lanham, Md.: Madison Books.

1996. Susannah Heschel, ed., *Moral Grandeur and Spiritual Audacity*. New York: Farrar, Straus & Giroux.

1996. *Prophetic Inspiration After the Prophets: Maimonides and Others*. Trans. David Silverman, ed. Morris Faierstein. Hoboken, N.J.: KTAV.

Secondary Sources

Abraham Weiss Jubilee Volume. 1964. New York.

Abramowicz, Dina. 1946. "My School Years in the Real-Gymnasium" (in Yiddish). *Dorem Afrike* (27 May).

Abramowicz, Hirsz. 1958. *Farshvundene geshtaltn* (in Yiddish, Missing or killed: Memories and silhouettes) (originally pub. in *Forverts*, 3 March 1946). Buenos Aires: Tsentral-farband fur Poylishe Yidn in Argentine.

Adler-Rudel, Shalom. 1959. *Ostjuden in Deutschland*. Tübingen: Mohr.

Alfasi, Yitzhak. 1981. *The Rav of Apt: Author of Ohev Yisroel* (in Hebrew). Jerusalem: Institute for the Words of the Righteous. Machon Sifte Hakhamim.

———. 1986. *Entsiklopedyah la-Hasidut* (in Hebrew, Encyclopedia of Hasidut). Jerusalem: Mossad ha-rav Kook.

Alt, Arthur. 1987. "A Survey of Literary Contributions to the Post-World War I Yiddish Journals in Berlin," *Yiddish* 7, 1:42–52.

Altmann, Alexander. 1935. "The Teaching Methods in *Lehrhäuser*," in Altmann 1991, *The Meaning of Jewish Existence*, 88–93.

———. 1956. "Theology in Twentieth-Century Jewry," *Leo Baeck Institute Yearbook* 1:193–216.

———. 1991. Alfred Ivry, ed. *The Meaning of Jewish Existence: Theological Essays, 1930–1939*. Hanover, N.H.: University Press of New England for Brandeis University Press.

American Jewish Committee. 1935. *The Jews in Nazi Germany: A Handbook of Facts Regarding Their Present Situation*. New York: American Jewish Committee.

Aronstein, Fritz [F. A.]. 1935. Review of *Der Schem-Hameforasch—Mensch* in *Der Morgen* 10 (March): 570–71.

Asen, Johannes. 1955. *Gesamtverzeichnis des Lehrkörpers der Universität Berlin*, vol. 1. 1810–1945. Leipzig: Otto Harrassowitz.

Bacon, Gershon C. 1989. "Agudat Israel in Interwar Poland," in Gutman et al., eds., *The Jews of Poland Between Two World Wars*, 20–35.

Baeck, Leo. 1939. Introduction to *Monatsschrift für Geschichte und Wissenschaft des Judentums*. Reprint, Tübingen: J. C. B. Mohr (Paul Siebeck), with a new preface by Max Grünewald and the original preface dated October 1938 by Baeck.

Baedeker Guide: Berlin and Its Environs. 1923. Ed. Karl Baedeker. New York: C. Scribner's Sons.

Baedeker's Russia 1914, with Teheran, Port Arthur, and Peking. Ed. Karl Baedeker. London: George Allen and Unwin; 1971 reprint.

Baker, Leonard. 1978. *Days of Sorrow and Pain: Leo Baeck and the Berlin Jews*. New York: Macmillan.

Bamberger, Fritz. 1960. "Julius Guttmann—Philosopher of Judaism," *Leo Baeck Institute Yearbook* 5:3–31.

Baron, Salo, and Alexander Marx. 1943. Necrology of Ismar Elbogen, *American Jewish Yearbook:* xxiv–xxv.

Baumgardt, David. 1965. "Looking Back on a German University Career," *Leo Baeck Institute Yearbook* 10:239–65.

Bechtel, Delphine. 1991. "Les Revues modernistes yiddish à Berlin et à Varsovie de 1922 à 1924," *Etudes germaniques* (April–June).

Beilis, Shlomo. 1980. "Bei die onheybn fun Yung Vilne" (in Yiddish), *Di Goldene Keyt* (Tel Aviv), vol. 101:11–65. Yung Vilne issue.

Bericht der Hochschule für die Wissenschaft des Judentums in Berlin. 1928–1939.

Bialik, Haim Nahman. 1939. *Igrot* (in Hebrew, Correspondence), vol. 5. Tel Aviv: Dvir.

Biderman, I. M. 1976. *Mayer Balaban: Historian of Polish Jewry*. New York: I. M. Biderman Book Committee.

Bleiweiss, Robert. 1994. Anonymous anecdote in *The Jewish Spectator* (Fall): 67–68.

Brenner, Michael. 1996. *The Renaissance of Jewish Culture in Weimar Germany*. New Haven: Yale University Press.

Bromberg, Abraham. 1963. *Mi-gedolei ha-torah ve-ha-hasidut* (in Hebrew, Masters of Torah and Hasidism), vol. 20. Jerusalem: Ha-techiya Publishers.

Buber, Martin. 1934. "Sinnbildliche und sakramentale Existenz im Judentum," in *Eranos-Jahrbuch*, vol. 2:339–67. Zurich; trans. Maurice Friedman, in Buber, *The Origin and Meaning of Hasidism*. New York: Horizon Press, 1958, 152–81.

———. 1936. *Aus Tiefen rufe ich Dich; dreiundzwanzig Psalmen in der Urschrift mit der Verdeutschung von M. B.* (Out of the depths I cry to Thee). Berlin: Bücherei des Schocken-Verlags, no. 51.

———. 1947. *Tales of the Hasidim: Early Masters*, vol. 1. New York: Schocken Books.

———. 1948. *Tales of the Hasidim: Later Masters*, vol. 2. New York: Schocken Books.

———. 1949. *The Prophetic Faith*. Trans. from the Hebrew by Carlyle Witton-Davies. New York: Macmillan.

———. 1957. *Pointing the Way: Collected Essays*. Trans. and ed. Maurice Friedman. New York: Harper Torchbooks.

———. 1958. *Hasidism and Modern Man*. Trans. Maurice Friedman. New York: Harper Torchbooks.

———. 1968. *On the Bible: Eighteen Studies*. Ed. Nahum Glatzer. New York: Schocken.

———. 1973, 1975. *Briefwechsel aus sieben Jahrzehnten*. Band II: 1918–1938 (1973); Band III: 1938–1965 (1975). Heidelberg: Verlag Lambert Schneider.

———. 1991. *The Letters of Martin Buber: A Life of Dialogue*. Ed. Nahum Glatzer and Paul Mendes-Flohr. New York: Schocken.

Cahiers de l'Herne. 1981. On Henry Corbin. Ed. Christian Jambet. Paris.

Cassirer, Ernst. 1944. *An Essay on Man: An Introduction to a Philosophy of Human Culture*. New Haven: Yale University Press.

Coffin, William Sloane, Jr. 1977. *Once to Every Man*. New York: Atheneum.

Contemporary Jewish Record. A Review of Events and a Digest of Opinion (CJR). New York: American Jewish Committee, 1938, 1939, 1940.

Corbin, Henry. 1939. Translation of Heschel, *Die Prophetie* in *Hermès* (Brussels) 3, 3 (November): 78–110.

————. 1971. *En Islam iranien: Aspects spirituels et philosophiques*, vol. 1. Paris: Gallimard.

Cummings, Philip W. 1969. "Wolfgang Köhler," in *The Encyclopedia of Philosophy*, ed. Paul Edwards, 354–60.

Darton, Lawrence. 1954. *An Account of the Work of the Friends Committee for Refugees and Aliens, first known as the Germany Emergency Committee of the Society of Friends, 1933–1950*. Mimeographed. Friends Committee for Refugees and Aliens.

Davies, Norman. 1982. *God's Playground: A History of Poland*. New York: Columbia University Press.

Dawidowicz, Lucy S. 1976. *The War Against the Jews, 1933–1945*. New York: Holt, Rinehart and Winston.

Degener, Hermann, ed. 1935. *Degeners Wer ist's?* vol. 1, 10th edition. Berlin: Verlag Hermann Degener.

Deutsch, Shaul Shimon. 1995, 1997. *Larger Than Life: The Life and Times of the Lubavitcher Rebbe, Rabbi Menachem Mendel Schneerson*, vol. 1. New York: Chassidic Historical Productions; vol. 2, 1997.

Dobroszycki, Lucjan. 1989. "YIVO in Interwar Poland: Work in the Historical Sciences," in Gutman et al., eds., *The Jews of Poland Between Two World Wars*, 494–518.

Dobruszkes, Azario. 1970. "Four Teachers" (in Yiddish), *Vilner Punkt* 5 (October): 16–18.

————. 1986–87. "Vilna Schools and Teachers" (in Yiddish), *Dorem Afrike* (Johannesburg, South Africa) (July–September): 11–13; (October–December 1986): 26–27; (January–March 1987): 8–9; (April–June 1987): 26–27.

Dresner, Samuel H. 1960. *The Zaddik*. London, New York: Abelard-Schuman; rev. ed., Northvale, N.J.: J. Aronson, 1994.

————. 1974. *Levi Yitzhak of Berditchev: Portrait of a Hasidic Master*. New York, Bridgeport, Conn.: Hartmore House; rev. ed., Northvale, N.J.: J. Aronson, 1994.

————. 1981. "Hasidism and Its Opponents," in Raphael Jospe and Stanley Wagner, eds., *Great Schisms in Jewish History*. New York: KTAV, 119–75.

————. 1983. Introduction to *I Asked for Wonder: A Spiritual Anthology*. New York: Crossroad.

————. 1985. "Introduction: Heschel as a Hasidic Scholar," A. J. Heschel, *The Circle of the Baal Shem Tov*. Chicago: University of Chicago Press.

———. 1985. "Heschel the Man," in John Merkle, ed., *Abraham Joshua Heschel: Exploring His Life and Thought*. New York: Macmillan.

———. 1991. "Heschel and Halakhah," *Conservative Judaism* 43: 18–32.

Eden, Shevach. 1956. "The Institute for Jewish Studies and Research in Warsaw" (in Hebrew), in Mirsky, ed., *Jewish Institutions of Higher Learning in Europe*.

Edwards, Paul, ed. 1969. *The Encyclopedia of Philosophy*. New York: Macmillan.

Eisenstein, Miriam. 1950. *Jewish Schools in Poland, 1919–1939*. New York: King's Crown Press.

Eisler, Rudolf. 1912. *Philosophen-Lexikon*. Berlin: W. de Gruyter.

Eisner, Isi Jacob. 1967. "Reminiscences of the Berlin Rabbinical Seminary," *Leo Baeck Institute Yearbook* 12:32–52.

Elbogen, Ismar. 1944. *A Century of Jewish Life*. Philadelphia: Jewish Publication Society of America.

Elfenbein, Israel. 1958. "Menahem Ziemba of Praga," in Leo Jung, ed., *Guardians of Our Heritage*, 605–16.

Ertel, Rachel. 1982. Introduction to Moyshe Kulbak, *Lundi*. Trans. B. Vaisbrot. Paris: L'Age d'homme.

Ethos: Vierteljahresschrift für Soziologie, Geschichts- und Kulturphilosophie. Ed. David Koigen, Fishl Schneersohn, and Franz Hilker. Berlin. Two volumes, 1925–26, 1928.

Faierstein, Morris. 1983. "The Friday Night Incident in Kotsk: History of a Legend," *Journal of Jewish Studies* 34, 2:179–89.

———. 1989. *The Teachings of Rabbi Mordecai Joseph Leiner of Izbica*. Hoboken, N.J.: KTAV.

Finkelstein, Louis. 1929–30. "Recent Progress in Jewish Theology," *Jewish Quarterly Review* 20:361–66.

———. 1973. "Three Meetings with Abraham Heschel," *Conservative Judaism* 28, 1 (Fall): 19–22.

Fishbane, Michael. 1994. "To Jump for Joy: The Rites of Dance According to R. Nahman of Bratzlav." The Albert T. Bilgray Lecture. University of Arizona.

———. 1994. *The Kiss of God: Spiritual and Mystical Death in Judaism*. Seattle: University of Washington Press.

Fraiman, Sarah. 1991. "The Transformation of Jewish Consciousness in Nazi Germany as Reflected in *Der Morgen*, 1925–1938." Unpublished paper, Brandeis University.

Friedlander, Fritz. 1958. "Trials and Tribulations of Jewish Education in Nazi Germany." *Leo Baeck Institute Yearbook* 3:187–201.

Friedman, Maurice. 1960. *Martin Buber: The Life of Dialogue*. New York: Harper Torchbooks.

———. 1982. *Martin Buber: His Life and Work. The Early Years, 1878–1923*. New York: E. P. Dutton.

———. 1983. *Martin Buber: His Life and Work. The Middle Years, 1923–1945*. New York: E. P. Dutton.

Fuchs, Richard. 1967. "The 'Hochschule für die Wissenschaft des Judentums' in the Period of Nazi Rule," *Leo Baeck Institute Yearbook* 12:3–31.

Fuks, Leo, and Renate Fuks. 1988. "Yiddish Publishing Activities in the Weimar Republic, 1920–1933," *Leo Baeck Institute Yearbook* 33:417–34.

Gay, Peter. 1968. *Weimar Culture: The Outsider as Insider*. New York: Harper and Row.

Giligitsh, Joseph. 1968–69. "The Vilner Real-Gymnasium—the Crown of Yiddish Schools in Poland" (in Yiddish), *Nusah Vilne Bulletin* 10:10–13.

Ginzberg, Louis, and Abraham Weiss, eds. 1944. *Studies in Memory of Moses Schorr, 1874–1941*. New York: The Professor Moses Schorr Memorial Committee.

Glatzer, Nahum. 1956. "The Frankfort Lehrhaus," *Leo Baeck Institute Yearbook* 1:109–18, 122.

Glatzer, Nahum, and Paul Mendes-Flohr, eds. See Buber 1991.

Gold, Ben-Zion. 1989. "Religious Education in Poland: A Personal Perspective," in Gutman et al., eds., *The Jews of Poland Between Two World Wars*, 272–82.

Goldberg, Hillel. 1989. *Between Berlin and Slobodka: Jewish Transition Figures from Eastern Europe*. Hoboken, N.J.: KTAV.

Green, Arthur. 1979. *Tormented Master: A Life of Rabbi Nahman of Bratslav*. New York: Schocken Books.

Greenwood, John Ormerod. 1975. *Quaker Encounters*, vol. 1, "Friends and Relief." York, England.

———. 1978. *Quaker Encounters*, vol. 3, "Whispers of Truth." York, England.

Gressmann, Hugo. 1927. Preface to *Entwicklungstufen der jüdischen Religion*. Berlin: Institutum Judaicum, Giese.

Grossman, Grace Cohen. 1991. "Dr. Stephen S. Kayser: A Personal Testimony." *Three Score and Ten: Essays in Honor of Rabbi Seymour J. Cohen*. Hoboken, N.J.: KTAV, 403–26.

Guide bleu. Poland. (In French). 1939.

Gutman, Yisrael, Ezra Mendelsohn, Jehuda Reinharz, and Chone Shmeruk, eds. 1989. *The Jews of Poland Between Two World Wars*. Hanover, N.H., and London: University Press of New England for Brandeis University Press.

Guttmann, Alexander. 1972. "Hochschule Retrospective," *Central Conference of American Rabbis Journal* (Autumn): 73–79.

Guttmann, Julius. 1959. "Principles of Judaism," trans. David Wolf Silverman. *Conservative Judaism* 14, 1 (Fall): 1–16.

———. 1964. *Philosophies of Judaism: The History of Jewish Philosophy from Biblical Times to Franz Rosenzweig*, trans. David W. Silverman. New York: Holt, Rinehart, and Winston. The original German edition, 1933; chapter on Rosenzweig added for the 1944 Hebrew version.

Halbey, Hans Adolf. 1980–81. *Der Erich Reiss Verlag, 1908–1936: Versuch eines Porträts*. Frankfurt am Main: Buchhändler-Vereinigung: 1127–1255.

Halkowski, Henryk. 1992. "A Brand Plucked from the Fire . . . ," in Andrzej K. Paluck, ed., *The Jews of Poland*, vol. 1. Kraków: Jagiellonian University, 223–34.

Hartshorne, Edward Yarnall, Jr. 1937. *The German Universities and National Socialism*. London: George Allen & Unwin.

Heller, Joseph, ed. 1929. *Jüdische Lexikon*. Berlin.

Hendel, Charles W. 1953–57. Introductions to E. Cassirer, *The Philosophy of Symbolic Forms*. 3 volumes. New Haven: Yale University Press.

Heschel, Susannah, ed. 1996. Preface to Heschel, *Moral Grandeur and Spiritual Audacity: Essays*. New York: Farrar, Straus & Giroux, vii–xxix.

Heschel, Sylvia. 1982. Preface to Heschel, *Maimonides: A Biography*. New York: Farrar, Straus & Giroux.

Heshel, Jacob. 1967. "The History of Hassidism in Austria," in Josef Fraenkel, ed., *The Jews of Austria: Essays on Their Life, History and Destruction*. London: Vallentine, Mitchell, 347–60.

Heuberger, Rachel. 1992. "Orthodoxy Versus Reform: The Case of Rabbi Nehemiah Anton Nobel of Frankfurt a. Main," *Leo Baeck Institute Yearbook* 37:45–58.

Hirsch, Leo. 1934–35. "Der Dreitage-Jude" (The three-day Jew), *Der Morgen* 10:295–98.

———. 1937. "Pathos und Sympathie. Über Heschels *Die Prophetie*," *Der Morgen* 12 (February): 514–17.

Hofer, Yehiel. 1962. *A Hoyf af Muranow* (in Yiddish). 2 vols. Tel Aviv: Farlag Y. L. Perets.

———. 1967. *Milkhome—1914* (in Yiddish), *Zukunft* (October): 381–87.

———. 1976. *Mit yenem un mit zikh* (in Yiddish). Tel Aviv: Hamenorah Publishing House.

Hoffmann, Christhard, and Daniel R. Schwartz. 1991. "Early but Opposed—Supported but Too Late: Two Berlin Seminaries Which Attempted to Move Abroad," *Leo Baeck Institute Yearbook* 36:267–304.

Hoffmann, Ernst. 1934. "Koigens Kampf um die Geschichte" (in German, Koigen's battle with history), *Jüdische Rundschau* (27 February): 5–6.

Holtz, Avraham. 1966. "Hillel Zeitlin: Critic, Mystic, Social Architect," *Conservative Judaism* 20, 3 (Spring): 50–65.

———. 1970–71. "Hillel Zeitlin: Publicist and Martyr," *Jewish Book Annual* 28:141–46.

Howe, Irving, Ruth Wisse, and Khone Shmeruk, eds. 1987. *The Penguin Book of Modern Yiddish Verse*. New York: Penguin.

Hundert, Gershon, ed. 1991. *Essential Papers on Hasidism: Origins to Present*. New York: New York University Press.

Idel, Moshe. 1988. *Kabbalah: New Perspectives*. New Haven: Yale University Press.

Jacobs, Louis. 1993. *Hasidic Prayer*. London and Washington, D.C.: Littman Library of Jewish Civilization. Orig. ed. 1972.

Jahresbericht des Rabbiner-Seminars zu Berlin für 1925, 1926, 1927 (5686–88). Berlin, 1928.

Johnson, F. Ernest, ed. 1954. *Religious Symbolism*. (Religion and Civilization Series.) New York: Institute for Religious and Social Studies, Harper and Brothers, 53–79.

Das Judisze Togblatt (Warsaw). 6 January [8 Tevet] 1933.

Jung, Leo, ed. 1958. *Guardians of Our Heritage*. New York: Bloch.

———. 1964. *Men of the Spirit*. New York: Kymson.

Kaplan, Edward K. 1971. "Form and Content in Abraham J. Heschel's Poetic Style," *Central Conference of American Rabbis Journal* 18, 2 (April): 28–39.

———. 1973. "Language and Reality in Abraham J. Heschel's Philosophy of Religion," *Journal of the American Academy of Religion* 41, 3 (March): 94–113.

———. 1977. Mysticism and Despair in Abraham J. Heschel's Religious Thought," *Journal of Religion* 57 (January): 33–47.

———. 1985. "Heschel's Poetics of Religious Thinking," in John C. Merkle, ed., *Abraham Joshua Heschel: Exploring His Life and Thought*. New York: Macmillan, 103–19.

———. 1993. "Abraham Joshua Heschel," in Steven T. Katz, ed., *Interpreters of Judaism in the Late Twentieth Century*. Washington, D.C.: B'nai B'rith, 131–50.

———. 1994. "Metaphor and Miracle: A. J. Heschel and the Holy Spirit," *Conservative Judaism* 46, 2 (Winter): 3–18.

———. 1994. "Sacred versus Symbolic Religion: Abraham Joshua Heschel and Martin Buber." *Modern Judaism* 14, 3 (October): 213–31.

———. 1994. "God in Exile: Abraham Joshua Heschel, Translator of the Spirit," in Amy Colin and Elisabeth Strenger, eds., *Bridging the Abyss: Essays in Honor of Harry Zohn. Brücken über den Abgrung: Festschrift für Harry Zohn*. Munich: Wilhelm Fink, 239–54.

———. 1995. "The American Mission of Abraham Joshua Heschel," in Robert M. Selzer and Norman J. Cohen, eds., *The Americanization of the Jews*. New York: New York University Press, 355–74.

———. 1996. *Holiness in Words: A. J. Heschel's Poetics of Piety*. Albany: SUNY Press.

Kaplan, Mordecai M. 1967. "Buber's Evaluation of Philosophic Thought," in Schilpp and Friedman, eds., *The Philosophy of Martin Buber*.

Katz, Jacob. 1967. "Jewish Civilization as Reflected in the Yeshivot—Jewish Centers of Higher Learning," *Cahiers d'histoire mondiale. Journal of World History* 10, 4. Neuchâtel: Editions de la Baconnière: 674–704.

Katz, Steven J. 1980. "Abraham Joshua Heschel and Hasidism," *Journal of Jewish Studies* 31 (Spring): 82–104.

Kisch, Guido. 1963. *Das Breslauer Seminar* (The Breslau Seminary memorial volume). Tübingen: J. C. B. Mohr.

Klepfisz, Heszel. 1983. *Culture of Compassion: The Spirit of Polish Jewry from Hasidism to the Holocaust*. Hoboken, N.J.: KTAV.

Kludas, Arnold. 1976. *Great Passenger Ships of the World*. Trans. Charles Hodge, vol. 2:1913–1923. Wellingborough, Eng.: Patrick Stephens.

Koigen, David. 1925. *Apokalyptische Reiter*. Berlin: Erich Reiss Verlag.

———. 1934. *Das Haus Israel: Aus den Schriften von David Koigen.* Ed. Ernst Hoffmann. Berlin: Schocken Verlag.

Kulbak, Moyshe. 1926–27. "Vilne" (Yiddish poem). *Varshaver Shriftn.* Warsaw. Reprinted with translation in Howe, Wisse, and Shmeruk, eds., *The Penguin Book of Modern Yiddish Verse.*

Lehman, Manfred. 1964. "Profile of Great Men of Our Time: J. Soloveitchik," *Algemeiner Journal* (New York), 23 September.

Leksikon fun der nayer yidisher literatur. 8 vols. Various editors, 1956–1981. New York: Altveltlekhn Yiddishn Kultur-Kongres.

Liptzin, Sol. 1985. *A History of Yiddish Literature.* New York: Jonathan David Publishers.

Ludtke, Gerhard, ed. 1930. *Kürschners Deutscher Gelehrten-Kalender 1928/29.* Berlin and Leipzig: Walter de Gruyter. Also 1931 edition.

Mahler, Raphael. 1985. *Hasidism and the Enlightenment: Their Confrontation in Galicia and Poland in the First Half of the Nineteenth Century.* Philadelphia: Jewish Publication Society of America.

Mandelbaum, Jacob Dov. 1976. Introduction to *Index to Sha'arey Torah* (in Hebrew). New York: Institute for the Study of Problems of Orthodox Judaism (Machon le'heker baayot ha-yahadut ha-haredit).

Mander, John. 1959. *Berlin: The Eagle and the Bear.* Westport, Conn.: Greenwood Press.

Marx, Alexander. 1947. *Essays in Jewish Biography.* Philadelphia: Jewish Publication Society of America.

Maurer, Trude. 1991. "The Background of Kristallnacht: The Expulsion of Polish Jews," in Walter H. Pehle, ed., *November 1938: From "Reichskristallnacht" to Genocide,* trans. from the German by William Templer. New York and Oxford: Berg Publishers, 44–72.

Mendelsohn, Ezra. 1983. *The Jews of Poland Between the World Wars.* Bloomington: Indiana University Press.

Mendes-Flohr, Paul. 1989. *Martin Buber: From Mysticism to Dialogue: Martin Buber's Transformation of German Social Thought.* Detroit: Wayne State University Press.

———. 1991. *Divided Passions: Jewish Intellectuals and the Experience of Modernity.* Detroit: Wayne State University Press.

———. 1991. "Theologian before the Abyss," Introduction to Alexander Altmann, *The Meaning of Jewish Existence: Theological Essays, 1930–1939.* Hanover, N.H.: University Press of New England for Brandeis University Press.

Meyer, Michael. 1976. "The Refugee Scholars Project of the Hebrew Union College," in Bertram Korn, ed., *A Bicentennial Festschrift for Jacob Rader Marcus.* New York: KTAV, 359–75.

———. 1988. *Response to Modernity: A History of the Reform Movement in Judaism.* New York: Oxford University Press.

Milton, Sybil. 1984. "The Expulsion of Polish Jews from Germany, October 1938 to July 1939," *Leo Baeck Institute Yearbook* 29:169–99.

Minczeles, Henri. 1993. *Vilna—Wilno—Vilnius. Le Jérusalem de la Lithuanie*. Paris: La Découverte.

Minerva Jahrbuch der gelehrten Welt.

Mintz, Alan. 1989. *Banished from Their Father's Table*. Bloomington: Indiana University Press.

Mintz, Jerome. 1992. *Hasidic People: A Place in the New World*. Cambridge: Harvard University Press.

Mirsky, S., ed. 1956. *Jewish Institutions of Higher Learning in Europe: Their Development and Destruction* (in Hebrew). New York: OGEM.

Monatsschrift für Geschichte und Wissenschaft des Judentums. 1928–1939.

Der Morgen. Berlin, 1925–1938.

Morgenstern, Soma. 1946. *The Son of the Lost Son*. Philadelphia: Jewish Publication Society of America. Original 1935. *Der Sohn des velorenen Sohnes*. Berlin: Erich Reiss Verlag.

Neusner, Jacob. 1981. *Strangers at Home: "The Holocaust," Zionism, and American Judaism*. Chicago: University of Chicago Press.

Neusner, Jacob, ed. 1990. Preface, "A. J. Heschel: The Man," and "Heschel's Intellectual Achievement," in Heschel, *To Grow in Wisdom: An Anthology of Abraham Joshua Heschel*. Lanham, Md.: Madison Books.

Opatoshu, Joseph. 1938. *In Polish Woods*, trans. Isaac Goldberg. Philadelphia: Jewish Publication Society of America.

Perlman, Lawrence. 1989. "Heschel's Critique of Kant," in Jacob Neusner and Ernest Frerichs, eds. *From Ancient Israel to Modern Judaism: Intellect in Quest of Understanding. Essays in Honor of Marvin Fox*, vol. 3. Atlanta: Scholars Press, 213–26.

Perlow, Alter Israel Shimon. 1969. *Tiferet Ish*. Ed. Nahum Mordecai Perlow (Jerusalem) with an appendix on the daily life of his father, *"Minhagei Ham'haber."* Information used by Bromberg 1963.

Perlow, Shlomo Haim of Bolekhov. 1936. *Mikdash Shlomo* (in Hebrew, Commentary to Psalms), 2 vols. (Bilgoray); reprint, Jerusalem, 1976.

Perlow, Towa (Gitla). 1931. *L'Education et l'enseignement chez les juifs à l'époque talmudique*. Paris: Librairie Ernest Leroux.

Piekaz, M. 1990. *Polish Hasidism Between the Wars* (in Hebrew). Jerusalem: Mossad Bialik.

Plaut, W. Gunther. 1981. *Unfinished Business: An Autobiography*. Toronto: Lester and Orpen Dennys.

Pomiane, Edouard de. 1985 (orig. 1920). *The Jews of Poland. Recollections and Recipes*. Garden Grove, Calif.: Pholiota Press.

Prager, Leonard. 1982. *Yiddish Literary and Linguistic Periodicals and Miscellanies*. Darby, Pa.: Association for the Study of Jewish Languages, by Norwood Editions.

Pupko, Haim. 1968–69. "The Vilner Real-Gymnasium" (in Yiddish), *Nusah Vilne Bulletin* 10:5–9.

Rabinowicz, Harry M. 1988. *Hasidism: The Movement and Its Masters*. Northvale, N.J.: Jason Aronson.

Rabinowicz, Tzvi. 1989. *Chassidic Rebbes, From the Baal Shem Tov to Modern Times*. Southfield, Mich.: Targum Press.

Rabinowitsch, Wolf Zeev. 1970. *Lithuanian Hasidism from Its Beginnings to the Present Day*. London: Vallentine, Mitchell.

Ran, Leyzer, ed. 1974. *Jerusalem of Lithuania. Illustrated and Documented*. 3 volumes, with 3,000 illustrations, documents, prints, and tables, and bibliography in English, Yiddish, Russian, and Hebrew. Index of 4,000 persons and 15,000 subjects. New York: privately printed.

Ravitch, Melekh. 1947. *Mayn Leksikon* (in Yiddish), 2 vols. Montreal.

Reisen, Zalman. 1926. *Leksikon fun der yidisher literatur, prese un filologye*. Vilna: Kletskin; see above, *Leksikon fun der nayer yidisher literatur*. Congress for Jewish Culture. New York: Marstin Press.

Die Religion in Geschichte und Gegenwart (1961–1965). Tübingen: J. C. B. Mohr.

Rosenstein, Neil, ed. 1990, revised. *The Unbroken Chain: Biographical Sketches and Genealogy of Illustrious Jewish Families from the 15th-20th Centuries*. 2 volumes. New York, London, and Jerusalem: CIS Publishers.

Rosenthal, Erwin. 1963. "Ismar Elbogen and the New Jewish Learning," *Leo Baeck Institute Yearbook* 8:3–28.

Rosenthal, Yehuda. 1956. "The Hochschule für die Wissenschaft des Judentums in Berlin" (in Hebrew), in Mirsky, ed., *Jewish Institutions of Higher Learning in Europe*, 655–88.

Rosenzweig, Franz. 1953. *F. R. His Life and Thought*. Ed. Nahum Glatzer. New York: Schocken.

———. 1965. *On Jewish Learning*. Ed. Nahum Glatzer. New York: Schocken.

Roskies, Diane, and David Roskies. 1979. *The Shtetl Book*. New York: KTAV.

Rost, Leonhard. 1952. "Alfred Bertholet in memoriam," *Theologische Literaturzeitung* 2:114–18.

Rotenstreich, Nathan. 1974. "On Prophetic Consciousness," *Journal of Religion* 54:185–98.

Rothschild, Fritz A. 1967. "Abraham Joshua Heschel," in Thomas E. Bird, ed., *Modern Theologians*. Notre Dame, Ind.: Notre Dame University Press, 169–82.

———. 1968. "The Religious Thought of A. J. Heschel," *Conservative Judaism* 23, 1 (Fall): 12–24.

———. 1973. "Abraham Joshua Heschel (1907–1972)," *American Jewish Yearbook* 74:533–44.

Rothschild, Fritz A., ed. 1959. Introduction to Heschel, *Between God and Man*. New York: Free Press; most recent revision, 1979.

———. 1990. *Jewish Perspectives on Christianity: The Views of Baeck, Buber, Rosenzweig, Herberg, and Heschel*. New York: Crossroad.

Schachter-Shalomi, Zalman. 1991. *Spiritual Intimacy: A Study of Counseling in Hasidism.* Northvale, N.J.: Jason Aronson.

Schilpp, Paul Arthur, ed. 1949. *The Philosophy of Ernst Cassirer.* New York: Tudor Publishing Company, Library of Living Philosophers.

Schilpp, Paul Arthur, and Maurice Friedman, eds. 1967. *The Philosophy of Martin Buber.* Evanston, Ill.: Open Court Publishing Company, Library of Living Philosophers.

Schnädelbach, Herbert. 1984. *Philosophy in Germany, 1831–1933.* Trans. Eric Matthews. New York: Cambridge University Press.

Schneersohn, Fishl. 1929. *Studies in Psycho-Expedition: Fundamentals of the Psychological Science of Man and a Theory of Nervousness,* "translated from the German [*sic*] by Herman Frank," with prefaces by John Dewey, Columbia University, and Adolf Meyer, Johns Hopkins University. New York: The Science of Man Press. Original Yiddish title: *Der weg tsum mentsh* (The way to humanity). Vilna, 1928.

———. 1936. *Hayim Gravitzer.* 2 vols., Yiddish, Berlin. Translated into Hebrew by Avraham Shlonsky. Tel Aviv: Tzion Press, 1956.

———. 1950. *Sippurei hitgalut hasidiim.* Tel Aviv: Masada.

Schwab, Hermann. 1964. *Chachme Ashkenaz* (in English). London: Mitre Press.

Shandler, Jeffrey. 1993. "Heschel and Yiddish: A Struggle with Signification," *Journal of Jewish Thought and Philosophy* 2:245–99.

Shapiro, Marc. 1995. "Between East and West: The Life and Works of Rabbi Jehiel Jakob Weinberg." Ph.D. diss., Harvard University. Ann Arbor: University Microfilms.

Shedletsky, Ephraim, ed. 1977. *Minsk-Mazowiecki Memorial Book* (in Hebrew and Yiddish). Jerusalem: Organization of Former Inhabitants of Minsk-Mazowiecki.

Shenkman, M. 1960–61. *Nusah Vilne Bulletin* 6–7:12.

Sherwin, Byron, and Harold Kasimow, eds. 1991. *No Religion Is an Island: Abraham Joshua Heschel and Interreligious Dialogue.* Maryknoll, N.Y.: Orbis.

Shirer, William L. 1941. *Berlin Diary.* New York: Alfred A. Knopf.

Shulvass, Moshe. 1956. "The Rabbiner-Seminar in Berlin" (in Hebrew), in Mirsky, ed., *Jewish Institutions of Higher Learning in Europe,* 689–714.

Simon, Ernst. 1956. "Jewish Adult Education in Nazi Germany as Spiritual Resistance," in *Leo Baeck Institute Yearbook* 1:68–104.

———. 1958. "Martin Buber and German Jewry," *Leo Baeck Institute Yearbook* 3:3–39.

Singer, Isaac Bashevis. 1984. *Love and Exile.* Garden City, N.Y.: Doubleday.

Stern, Desider, ed. 1970. *Werke von Autoren jüdischer Herkunft in deutscher Sprache,* 3rd ed. Vienna: B'nai B'rith Book Exhibition.

Stern, Harold. 1983. "A. J. Heschel, Irenic Polemicist," *Proceedings of the Rabbinical Assembly,* 169–77.

Strauss, Herbert A., ed. 1987. *Jewish Immigrants of the Nazi Period,* vol. 6. New York, Munich, London, and Paris: K. G. Saur.

Tartakover, Abraham. 1944. "The Institute for Jewish Studies in Warsaw" (in Hebrew), in Ginzberg and Weiss, eds., *Studies in Memory of Moses Schorr, 1874–1941.*

Verzeichnis der Vorlesungen der Königlichen Friedrich-Wilhelms-Universität zu Berlin. 1927–1933.

Volker, Heinz-Hermann. 1990. "The Hochschule in Berlin, 1900–1942" (in German), in Helmut Walravens, ed., *Bibliographie und Berichte: Festschrift für Werner Schochow.* Munich, London, New York, Paris: K. G. Saur, 196–230.

Waldoks, Moshe. 1984. "Hillel Zeitlin: The Early Years, 1894–1919." Ph.D. diss., Brandeis University. Ann Arbor: University Microfilms.

Walravens, Helmut, ed. 1990. *Bibliographie und Berichte: Festschrift für Werner Schochow.* Munich, New York: K. G. Saur.

Weiss, Abraham. 1940. "In Nazi Warsaw," *Contemporary Jewish Record* (New York) 3, 5 (September–October): 484–97.

Weiss, Joseph. 1985. *Studies in European Jewish Mysticism.* Oxford: Littman Library.

Weltsch, Robert. 1933. "David Koigen," *Jüdische Rundschau* (Berlin) (6 March): 1.

———. 1933. "Tragt ihn mit Stolz, den gelben Fleck!" *Jüdische Rundschau* (4 April).

Wiesel, Elie. 1972. *Souls on Fire: Portraits and Legends of Hasidic Masters.* New York: Random House.

Wijnhoven, Jochanan H. A. 1965. "The Mysticism of Solomon Ibn Gabirol," *Journal of Religion* 45, 2 (April): 137–52.

———. 1976. "Medieval Jewish Mysticism," *Bibliographical Essays in Medieval Jewish Studies,* vol. 2. New York: Anti-Defamation League of B'nai B'rith, 269–330.

Wohlgemuth, Josef. 1931. "Tschuvah. Grundgedanken der Religionsphilosophie Max Schelers im jüdischer Beleuchtung," in Heinrich Eisemann and J. Landau, eds., *Festschrift für Jakob Rosenheim: Anläßlich der vollendung seines 60. Lebenjahres dargebracht von seinen Freunden.* Frankfurt am Main: J. Kaufmann, 19–76.

Wohlgemuth, Juda Ari. 1958. "Joseph Wohlgemuth," in Leo Jung, ed., *Guardians of Our Heritage,* 535–50.

Wunder, Meir. 1981, 1990. *Meorei Galicia* (in Hebrew, Encyclopedia of Galician rabbis and scholars), vol. 2, 1981; vol. 4, 1990, Jerusalem.

Wynot, Edward D. 1983. *Warsaw Between the World Wars: Profile of the Capital City in a Developing Land, 1918–1939.* New York: Columbia University Press, East European Monographs, Boulder.

Zborowski, Mark, and Elizabeth Herzog. 1952. *Life Is with People: The Culture of the Shtetl.* New York: Schocken.

Zeitlin, Aaron. 1964. "Hillel Zeitlin," in Leo Jung, ed., *Men of the Spirit:* 599–621.

Zeitlin, Hillel. 1960. *Bapardes ha-hasidut ve-hakabbalah.* Tel Aviv: Yavneh.

———. 1965. *Al gevul shnei olamot.* Tel Aviv: Yavneh.

Zemba, Abraham. 1956. "The Mesivta in Warsaw" (in Hebrew), in Mirsky, ed., *Jewish Institutions of Higher Learning in Europe.*

———. 1956. "Shtieblakh in Warsaw" (in Hebrew), in Mirsky, ed., *Jewish Institutions of Higher Learning in Europe.*

Permissions and Credits

Reprinted by permission of Farrar, Straus & Giroux, Inc.: Excerpts from *Maimonides* by Abraham Joshua Heschel, translated by Joachim Neugroschel. Translation copyright 1982 by Sylvia Heschel. Excerpts from *The Earth Is the Lord's* by Abraham Joshua Heschel. Copyright 1949 by Abraham Joshua Heschel. Copyright renewed 1977 by Sylvia Heschel. Excerpts from *Man Is Not Alone* by Abraham Joshua Heschel. Copyright 1951 by Abraham Joshua Heschel. Copyright renewed 1979 by Sylvia Heschel. Excerpts from *God in Search of Man* by Abraham Joshua Heschel. Copyright 1955 by Abraham Joshua Heschel. Copyright renewed 1983 by Sylvia Heschel. Excerpts from *A Passion for Truth* by Abraham Joshua Heschel. Copyright 1973 by Sylvia Heschel as Executrix of the Estate of Abraham Joshua Heschel.

Central Archives for the History of the Jewish People, Koigen papers P196; Julian Morgenstern papers, American Jewish Archives, Cincinnati, Ohio; YIVO Institute for Jewish Research, Abraham Liessen Papers; The Jewish National and University Library, Abraham Heschel letters in Martin Buber Archive and in Melech Ravitch Archive; "Toward an Understanding of Halacha," *Yearbook of the Central Conference of America Rabbis*, vol. 63 (1953), Central Conference of American Rabbis; Jeffrey Shandler, translations published in "Heschel and Yiddish: A Struggle with Signification," *Journal of Jewish Thought and Philosophy* 2: 245–99; Zalman Schachter-Shalomi, free translations of Heschel's Yiddish poetry.

Earlier versions of portions of chapters 15 and 18 were previously published in Edward Kaplan, "Sacred Versus Symbolic Religion: Abraham Joshua Heschel and Martin Buber," *Modern Judaism* 14, 3 (October 1994): 213–31, © Johns Hopkins University Press; and in Edward Kaplan, "God in Exile: Abraham Joshua Heschel, Translator of the Spirit," in Amy Colin and Elisabeth Strenger, eds., *Bridging the Abyss: Essays in Honor of Harry Zohn. Brücken über den Abgrung: Festschrift für Harry Zohn* (Munich: Wilhelm Fink, 1984), 239–54.

Photographic Credits

Title page: Abraham Joshua Heschel, Atelier May, 19 Kaiser Strasse, Frankfurt am Main, 1938.

Page 1: Yeshiva students on Nalewki Street. Warsaw, 1928. Photograph by Menakhem Kipnis/Raphael Abramovitch Collection. Courtesy of YIVO Institute for Jewish Research, New York.

Page 73: Vilna street scene. Emil Shaeffer, ed. *Ein Ghetto im Osten (Wilna)*. Zurich: Orell Fussli Verlag, 1929. Courtesy of Leyzer Yankelovich Aron.

Page 97: View of the Brandenburg Gate. Courtesy of the German Information Center, New York.

Page 241: Martin Buber, c. 1939, Jerusalem. Photograph by Dr. Jakob Rosner. Courtesy of Noemi Schwarz.

Acknowledgments

We are grateful for the friendship of Abraham Joshua Heschel's widow, Sylvia Straus Heschel, and their daughter, Susannah Heschel, herself a Judaic scholar and activist. Although Heschel's personal papers and library remain in their private possession, they provided valuable information and encouragement, as did Thena Heshel Kendall, Yitzhak Meir Twersky, Pearl Twersky, and other family members.

Special recognition is due to our friend and colleague Fritz Rothschild, foremost interpreter of Heschel's thought, who gave liberally of his time to this project. His role in Heschel studies cannot be overstated and his advice at various stages was valuable. We also thank Chancellor Ismar Schorsch of the Jewish Theological Seminary and President Jehuda Reinharz of Brandeis University for their encouragement and for providing ample research facilities.

Many friends, relatives, students, and colleagues shared their memories of Heschel and his surroundings during the early period of his life in Europe. The extensive archives collected from these interviews, which made this biography possible, due in large part to the generous support of the National Endowment for the Humanities, and other sources are now housed at the Jewish Theological Seminary. Matching funds were given by the

Nirenberg, Taub, Thaler, Roe, and Blechner Foundations. Particularly helpful was the support provided by Samuel Zell in memory of his father, Bernard Zell, a Polish Jew who already in Europe combined the finest of the old traditions along with modern culture. After fleeing Poland with his wife and small child, they crossed Russia to Japan where they were able to recoup in order to settle in America, bringing an informed and devoted leadership into synagogue and Jewish community life in Chicago.

Later stages of research and composition were supported by the Littauer Foundation and Brandeis University faculty research funds.

In order to gain a concrete sense of Heschel's European life, visits were arranged and guided by the following: the late Leyzer Aron and Arcady Tempelman of Vilna, Ryszard Zielinski of Warsaw, Richard Pincus and Rainer Graupner of Berlin.

Among the many people who helped the authors at various stages gain access to precious documents, in addition to those named as sources, we thank Dina Abramowicz, Fruma Mohrer, and Zachary Baker of the New York YIVO; Winfried Schultze of the Humboldt University Archives; Diane Spielmann of the Leo Baeck Institute in New York; Margot Cohen and Yossel Birstein of the Jewish National and University Library in Jerusalem; Hadassah Assiuline of the Central Archives for the History of the Jewish People in Jerusalem; Abraham Peck and Kevin Proffitt of the American Jewish Archives in Cincinnati; David Peyceré, Rectorat de Paris Archives; Stella Corbin for access to her husband Henry Corbin's library and files. Charles Cutter and James Rosenblum of the Brandeis University Reference Department provided stability, support, and much practical help.

For crucial technical assistance in translations, research, and some detective work, we thank: Jacob Teshima, Marc Gopin, Jonathan Boyarin, Shaul Magid, Stephanie Fine Maroun, Stephanie Wollny, Mordecai Rimor, Susanna Buschmeyer, David Dalin, Bela Shargel, Amy Colin, Beatrice Trum Hunter, Rebecca Potter, Gisela Schwing, Jan Schwing, Israel Francus, Maciej Gadamski, Henryk Halkowski (Kraków), Thena Heshel Kendall and Harry Rabinowicz (London), Yitzhok Niborski and Alexandre Derczansky (Paris), Shaul Shimon Deutsch, biographer of the Lubavitcher rebbe Menahem Mendel Schneerson, and Yitzhak Meir Twersky for family photographs, genealogies, and his generous Heschel spirit. The computer prowess of Adam Kanter spared us unmeasurable frustration.

As the manuscript took shape, the following experts examined chapters and offered valuable criticisms and suggestions: Susannah Heschel, Neil Gillman, Robert Szulkin, Antony Polonsky, Azario Dobruszkes, Arthur Green, Ismar Schorsch, Barbara Hyams, Michael Brenner, Paul Mendes-Flohr, Michael Fishbane, Janna Kaplan. Conversations with Aharon Appelfeld, Bennett Simon, Roberta Apfel, Donald Schön, Maurice Friedman, Jacob Teshima, and especially with Janna Kaplan and Michael Fishbane, were crucial in helping gain and crystalize insights. To Jonathan Brent, our editor at Yale University Press, we express special gratitude for his meticulous critical reading of the manuscript at several stages, and particularly for conversations that were as inspiring as they were challenging. Noreen O'Connor's astute copyediting improved the manuscript in many ways, although for the final book we take full responsibility.

Index

Guttmann, Alexander (1902–94), 119, 198, 209, 212, 338*n*9

Guttmann, Grete (wife of Julius), 116

Guttmann, Julius (1880–1950), 103, *111*, 112–16, 164, 330, 344, 358

Halakhah (Jewish law), 58, 70–71, 104, 119–20, 139, 225, 227–28, 263–64, 320*n*29,30, 334*n*13; and Aggadah, 196, 252

Halpern, Zalman, 88

Hartung (dean of the Philosophical Faculty, Berlin), 163, 178, 198–99, 202

Hasidism, viii–ix, 5–18, 22–30, 54, 99, 113, 120, 151, 158, 168, 196; of Ger, 38–40, 69, 315*n*1; Habad (or Lubavitch), 53–54, 123, 126, 138–39; of Kotzk, 36–40, 69–71, 94, 307; modern or neo-Hasidism, 25, 54–55, 125–27, 205, 213

Haskalah (Jewish enlightenment), ix, 2, 62, 63, 75, 76, 319*n*11

Haynt (Yiddish newspaper, Warsaw), 62, 94, 179

Hebrew language, 53, 58, 60, 62, 99, 112, 118, 193, 247, 306

Hebrew Union College (Cincinnati, Ohio), 269–70, 284, 293–95, 303; *HUC Bulletin*, 349–50*n*11

Heidegger, Martin (1889–1976), 99, 258

Heiler, Friedrich (1892–1967), 223, 227

Heinemann, Isaak (1876–1957), 206

Heller, Haim (1878–1969), 106

Hertz, Joseph Herman (1872–1946), 286, 290

Hertz, Judith, 286

Heschel, Abraham Joshua (1748–1825, of Apt, Heschel's ancestor), 4–6, 17, 26, 139

Heschel, Abraham Joshua (1832–84, of Medzibozh, Heschel's grandfather), 6–8, 159

Heschel, Abraham Joshua (1888–1967, Kopitzhinitzer rebbe, Heschel's first cousin), 22, *32, 33*, 240, 263–64, 302, 320*n*34, 352*n*1

Heschel, Abraham Joshua (1907–72), *59, 78, 249, 251*

—descriptions of: by Beilis (Vilna, 1927), 87–90; by Hertz (Frankfurt, 1938), 246–49; by Kayser (Berlin, 1935), 210–11; by Plaut (Berlin, 1938), 197; by Ravitch (Warsaw, 1925), 64–65

—life: ambitions of, 141, 152, 183, 192–93, 204–05, 235, 302–03; American mission, 188, 300–01, 306–07; ancestry (*yikhus*), xi–xiii, 4–9; arrival in U.S., 301–03; bar mitzvah, 46–47; bereavements, 204; in Berlin, 98–240; betrothal missed, 50–52; and compassion, 288; contradictions of, 40, 42, 64–67, 89–90, 177, 185, 195; death of, 38; dedications, 49, 66, 71, 134, 183, 184–85, 189, 190, 306–07; departure from Europe, 270–71, 290–92, 298, 302; departure from Vilna, 92–93; departure from Warsaw, 71–72, 282–87; doctorate, 57, 142, 162–71, 178, 217; emigration, 251–52, 262–63, 284–87; emotional strength, 204, 211, 266, 269, 277, 293; and English language, 285; escape from danger, 305; examinations, 118, 171, 174; expulsion from Germany, 273–75; and German and Polish languages, 68–69, 141, 254; guilt, 189–90, 282–83, 287, 288; humility, 40, 42,

Yiddish poem), 185; *A Passion for Truth* (1973), 4, 37, 38, 40, 42, 63, 66–67; "Personalities of Jewish History" (1936–37), 236–38; "The Power of Repentance" (1936, Die Kraft der Buße), 239, 300; "Prayer as Expression and Empathy" (1939, Das Gebet als Ausserung und Einfühlung), 287, 300; *Die Prophetie* (1936), 162, 214–17, 225, 233, 236, 254, 257–58, 267, 271, 298, 348nn36,37; *Das prophetische Bewußtsein* (1932–33, dissertation), 163–71, 198, 232, 334n4; *The Prophets* (1962), 169, 303, 306, 309; "Rabbi Akiba" (1936), 237; "Rabbi Chiyah" (1936), 238; Rabbi Elisha ben Abuyah, 238; Rabbi Gamliel II, 237; *The Sabbath* (1951), 26, 185, 197, 337n5; "Search for a Meaning" (1938, Versuch einer Deutung, speech to Quaker leaders), 260–61, 349n11; *Der Shem Hameforash: Mentsh* (1933), 181, 183–93, 212–13, 224, 337n2; "Shimon ben Gamliel II" (1936), 237–38; "The Spirit of Jewish Education" (1953), 242; "Symbolism and Jewish Faith" (1954), 182; Talmudic analyses, 48–50; "Teaching Jewish Theology" (1965), 139, 252, 347n22; *The Theology of Ancient Judaism* (1962, Torah min ha-shamayim), 306; "Toward an Understanding of Halacha" (1953), 100, 108, 153, 218; Yiddish poetry, 42, 50, 57, 67, 71, 89–90, 91–92, 95, 133, 141–52, 164, 178–81, 183–93; "The Zaddik of Joy" (1925, Der zaddik fun freyd), 66

Heschel, Devorah Miriam (Heschel's sister). *See* Dermer, Devorah Miriam Heschel

Heschel, Esther Sima (Heschel's sister), 12, *61*, 183, 189; death of, 296, 302, 306

Heschel, Gittel (Heschel's sister), 12, 33, *61*, 264, 267, 302, 306, 319n9

Heschel, Hannah Susannah (b. 1952, Heschel's daughter), 314n34

Heschel, Israel (1911–94) (Heschel's nephew), 77, 263, 264, 289

Heschel, Israel Sholem Joseph (1852–1911, Heschel's uncle, rebbe of Zinkov), 31, *31*, 310n12

Heschel, Meshullam Zusya (1871–1920, rebbe of Medzibozh, Heschel's uncle), 31, 310n12

Heschel, Meshullam Zusya (b. 1930, son of A. J. Heschel of Kopitzhinitz), 263–64

Heschel, Moshe Mordecai (1873–1916, the Pelzovizna rebbe, Heschel's father), 7, 8, *11*, 12–18, 49, 154, 183; death of, 35–36, 183; divorce of, 11; Hasidic court of, 15, 28–30; tombstone of, *35*

Heschel, Rivka Reizel Perlow (1874–1942, Heschel's mother), 10, *11*, 50–52, 53, 69, 248, 264, 266, 285, 306

Heschel, Sarah Brakha (1891–1964, Heschel's sister), 12, 22, *33*, 263–64, 285, 292, 302, 306

Heschel, Sylvia Straus (Heschel's wife), 318n45, 337n8

Heschel, Yitzhak Meir (1861–1936, Heschel's uncle), 31, *31*, 32, 38, 46, 310n12; death of, 240

Heshel, Jacob (1903–70, Heschel's brother), 12, 13, 33, 47, 58–60, *60*, 264, 277, 285, 289–90, 292,

Kant, Immanuel (1724–1804), 114,
118, 131–32, 155, 157, 167, 174,
234

Kantorowicz, Ernst (1892–1942), 243,
245–46, 266, 277

Kavanah (inner intention), 25, 300–01

Kayser, Stefan (Stephen, 1900–88),
210–11, 341n4

Kelman, Wolfe (1923–90), 93

Kendall, Thena Heshel (b. 1935), 289,
290, 292

Kiev, 54, 98, 125–27

Kishinev, pogrom of, 62

Kletskin, Boris (d. 1938), 85, 322n21

Köhler, Wolfgang (1887–1967), 112,
326n25

Koigen, David (1879–1933), 54, 98,
108, *122,* 122–39, 141, 149, 156,
164, 183, 190, 195–96, 204, 219,
273, 280, 328n4,10, 329n19; *Apocalyptic Horsemen,* 123–27, 200; and
Buber, 54, 124–25, 127, 329n16,
336n7; Circle (personal seminar),
126–27, 129–37, 163, 164–65,
183, 219; death of, 175–77, 273,
307; Heschel's obituary of, 184–85;
"The Idea of God in Light of Modern
Thought" (London paper), 137; *The
Moral God,* 131, 132; and Fishl
Schneersohn, 122, 126–28, 281;
Weltsch's obituary of, 175–77, 328

Koigen, Helene Sulzman (wife of
David), 130, 133

Kowalski, Tadeusz (1889–1948),
200–01, *201,* 215, 217, 230–33,
254, 274

Kraków, Poland, 181, 198, 232

Kristallnacht (Bloody Thursday),
277–79

Kulbak, Moyshe (1896–c.1940), 82,
83, 83–86, 90, 95, 98, 306;

Heschel's visit to, 91–92; teaching
method of, 84–85; "Vilne" (poem),
90, 92

Lancastria (Cunard White Star liner),
302, 305

Levin, Yitzhak Meir, 70–71, 94, 183,
307, 320n31, 359n7

Levi Yitzhak of Berditchev
(1740–1810), 7, 16, 26, 139, 143,
192; tefillin of, 46

Levy, Bezalel, 39–41, 47, 307, 359;
criticism of young Heschel, 40

Lewin, Abram (Abrashke) (b. 1909),
81

Liessen, Abraham (1872–1938),
141–42, 145, 149, 163, 180, 334

Literarishe Bleter (Yiddish periodical,
Berlin), 64, 90–91, 149–52, 322n35

Liturgy, 158–61

Loewe, Herbert Martin James
(1882–1940), 290

London, 137–38, 286–87, 289–92,
297–300, 305

Love: sensual, 185–89

Ma'ariv (evening prayer), 158–61

Maier, Heinrich (1867–1933), 103,
108, 119, 141, 174, 326n19

Maimonides, Moses (1135–1204,
Rabbi Moshe ben Maimon), 48, 57,
194; depression of, 204; Heschel's
biography of, 202–07; and quest for
prophetic inspiration, 204, 205

Marx, Alexander (1878–1958), 351

Mathematics–Natural Science Gymnasium. *See* Real Gymnasium

Medzibozh, Ukraine (in Polish, Miedzyborz), 4, 6, 7, 31, 36, 307

Mendelssohn, Moses (1729–86), 112,
330n21